New Frontiers in Regional Science: Asian Perspectives

Volume 18

New Frontiers in Regional Science: Asian Perspectives

This series is a constellation of works by scholars in the field of regional science and in related disciplines specifically focusing on dynamism in Asia.

Asia is the most dynamic part of the world. Japan, Korea, Taiwan, and Singapore experienced rapid and miracle economic growth in the 1970s. Malaysia, Indonesia, and Thailand followed in the 1980s. China, India, and Vietnam are now rising countries in Asia and are even leading the world economy. Due to their rapid economic development and growth, Asian countries continue to face a variety of urgent issues including regional and institutional unbalanced growth, environmental problems, poverty amidst prosperity, an ageing society, the collapse of the bubble economy, and deflation, among others.

Asian countries are diversified as they have their own cultural, historical, and geographical as well as political conditions. Due to this fact, scholars specializing in regional science as an inter- and multi-discipline have taken leading roles in providing mitigating policy proposals based on robust interdisciplinary analysis of multifaceted regional issues and subjects in Asia. This series not only will present unique research results from Asia that are unfamiliar in other parts of the world because of language barriers, but also will publish advanced research results from those regions that have focused on regional and urban issues in Asia from different perspectives.

The series aims to expand the frontiers of regional science through diffusion of intrinsically developed and advanced modern regional science methodologies in Asia and other areas of the world. Readers will be inspired to realize that regional and urban issues in the world are so vast that their established methodologies still have space for development and refinement, and to understand the importance of the interdisciplinary and multidisciplinary approach that is inherent in regional science for analyzing and resolving urgent regional and urban issues in Asia.

Topics under consideration in this series include the theory of social cost and benefit analysis and criteria of public investments, socio-economic vulnerability against disasters, food security and policy, agro-food systems in China, industrial clustering in Asia, comprehensive management of water environment and resources in a river basin, the international trade bloc and food security, migration and labor market in Asia, land policy and local property tax, Information and Communication Technology planning, consumer "shop-around" movements, and regeneration of downtowns, among others.

More information about this series at http://www.springer.com/series/13039

Tohru Naito • Woohyung Lee • Yasunori Ouchida
Editors

Applied Approaches to Societal Institutions and Economics

Essays in Honor of Moriki Hosoe

Springer

Editors
Tohru Naito
Doshisha University
Kyoto, Japan

Woohyung Lee
Keimyung University
Daegu, Korea (Republic of)

Yasunori Ouchida
Department of Economics
Hiroshima University
Higashi-Hiroshima City
Hiroshima, Japan

ISSN 2199-5974 ISSN 2199-5982 (electronic)
New Frontiers in Regional Science: Asian Perspectives
ISBN 978-981-10-5662-8 ISBN 978-981-10-5663-5 (eBook)
DOI 10.1007/978-981-10-5663-5

Library of Congress Control Number: 2017951197

Printed on acid-free paper

This Springer imprint is published by Springer Nature
The registered company is Springer Nature Singapore Pte Ltd.
The registered company address is: 152 Beach Road, #21-01/04 Gateway East, Singapore 189721, Singapore

To Professor Moriki Hosoe

Preface

This book is written to commemorate the studies, the education, and the 70 years of age of Professor Moriki Hosoe, who is an emeritus professor in Kyushu University and is a designated professor in Kumamoto Gakuen University. Since Professor Hosoe has been always interested in the applicability of economic theory to reality and has proceeded to research many fields of economics and published many books or papers on many kinds of applied economics, which include information economics, law and economics, environmental economics, and regional science. Therefore, his contribution to applied economics is respectfully appreciated.

Professor Hosoe particularly has contributed to the development of applied economics, established the Japan Association for Applied Economics (JAAE) in 2006, and became the first president of JAAE. Although the Western Association of Economics was a local economics association in Kyushu Island, Japan, Professor Hosoe ambitiously constructed a network with many economics researchers both in Japan and abroad and brought up one of famous economics association in Japan. Without the contribution of Professor Hosoe, the current Japan Association for Applied Economics would not exist. Moreover, Professor Hosoe contributed to the Asian Law and Economics Association as president from 2007 to 2008, the Japan Section of RSAI as vice president from 2011 to 2013 and as president from 2017, and the Japan Law and Economics Association as president from 2016 to 2017.

Although there is no doubt that Professor Hosoe is an excellent and powerful researcher in economics, he is also a good educator. Professor Hosoe has worked at some universities, which include Kyushu University, Kumamoto Gakuen University, and so on, for about 40 years, and produced a number of excellent economists. Therefore, this book is also a testimony to Professor Hosoe's contribution to not only research but also education because some contributors of this book are Professor Hosoe's students in the graduate school of economics in Kyushu University and researchers who have research exchanges with Professor Hosoe.

This book focuses on many kinds of applied economics like game theory, information economics, law and economics, environmental economics, public economics, industrial organization, social security, sports economics, regional science, and so on. Thus, this book is very valuable to researchers, scholars, policy makers, and graduate students in applied economics. Essay contributors include his former graduate students and researchers with personal connection to Professor Hosoe in applied economics. Moreover, the other purpose of this book is to celebrate his 70th birthday and acknowledge him for developing applied economics as well as his achievement in education in some universities.

We are grateful that the Japan Section of RSAI and Springer Japan gave us an opportunity to publish this book. Moreover, we have received some financial supports from the Grants-in-Aid for Scientific Research (KAKENHI: 22730201, 26380350, 26285098, 26380466, 15K03453, 15K03749, 16K03719, 16K12374, 16K12998) and the National Research Foundation of Korea (NRF: 2014S1A3A2044643, 2014S1A3A2044032).

Kyoto, Japan — Tohru Naito
Daegu, South Korea — Woohyung Lee
Hiroshima, Japan — Yasunori Ouchida
March 2017

Contents

Contributors

Kiyoshi Arakawa Faculty of Social Information Studies, Otsuma Women's University, Tokyo, Japan

Eunju Chi Korea University, Seoul, South Korea

Toshiyuki Fujita Kyushu University, Fukuoka, Japan

Hirofumi Fukuyama Kagoshima University, Kagoshima, Japan

Takeshi Goto Nanzan University, Nagoya, Japan

Nobuaki Hori Kyushu University, Fukuoka, Japan

Yasuhiro Ikeda Kumamoto University, Kumamoto, Japan

Hiroki Inoue Kyoto University, Kyoto, Japan

Masayuki Kanazaki Kyushu Sangyo University, Fukuoka, Japan

Yasuhiko Kato Kumamoto Gakuen University, Kumamoto, Japan

Akio Kawasaki Oita University, Oita, Japan

Keiki Kumagae Kyushu University, Fukuoka, Japan

Hyeok Yong Kwon Korea University, Seoul, South Korea

Ki-Dong Lee Keimyung University, Daegu, South Korea

Woohyung Lee Keimyung University, Daegu, South Korea

Jun-ichi Maeda Hiroshima Shudo University, Hiroshima, Japan

Isao Miura Kyushu University, Fukuoka, Japan

Yusuke Miyoshi Kagawa University, Takamatsu, Japan

Tohru Naito Doshisha University, Kyoto, Japan

Tatsuhiko Nariu Kyoto University, Kyoto, Japan

Ryutaro Nozaki Kurume University, Kurume, Japan

Yasunori Ouchida Hiroshima University, Higashihiroshima, Japan

Eric Rasmusen Indiana University, Bloomington, IN, USA

Hang Keun Ryu Chung Ang University, Seoul, South Korea

Tomoya Sakagami Kumamoto Gakuen University, Kumamoto, Japan

Kazuhiko Sakai Kurume University, Kurume, Japan

Hideki Sato Fukuoka Women's University, Fukuoka, Japan

Shigeharu Sato Nagasaki Wesleyan University, Isahaya, Japan

Peseth Seng Orkide Villa Co., Ltd, Phnom Penh, Cambodia

Shinya Shimoda Kyushu Sangyo University, Fukuoka, Japan

Shinya Shinozaki Saga University, Saga, Japan

Hajime Sugeta Kansai University, Osaka, Japan

Haruhiko Tsuzuki Saga University, Saga, Japan

Konari Uchida Kyushu University, Fukuoka, Japan

Hiroki Unoki Nakakyushu Junior College, Yatsushiro, Japan

Part I
New Methodology of Game, Contract, and Law

Chapter 1
Intrinsic Motivation and Dynamic Agency Contract

Isao Miura and Keiki Kumagae

1.1 Introduction

In conventional agency theory, the situation in which the principal lets the agents be motivated to choose the desirable action for him by giving a (monetary) reward is mainly considered. Such a motivation given from outside is called extrinsic motivation in psychology. However in reality, a worker in a firm would not necessarily work only for a reward. The worker has incentive produced internally through sense of accomplishment to be acquired from work and a feeling of self-affirmation to feel that work is useful for the firm and for society. We designate such an incentive intrinsic motivation and distinguish such motivations of two types. Actually, when the firm employs workers and manages them, it would be important for the firm to examine how to promote worker motivation for effective management while considering intrinsic motivation. In this model, in addition to an external motivation as a reward, we assume that an agent with intrinsic motivation contributes for the firm by working diligently to let the work succeed. For the firm, which means the principal, we consider how it should design the contract with the worker having intrinsic motivation. Especially, we analyze a dynamic case theoretically in which a short-term contract is updated and agency relations are continued for two periods.

When we examine the dynamic case described above using an adverse selection model by which the agent has private information about his type, two analytical methods are used depending on the commitment by the principal to a contract. One is the case in which the principal commits beforehand to all terms of a contract the beginning of a term. In such a case, we can adapt the "revelation principle."

I. Miura (✉) • K. Kumagae
Kyushu University, Fukuoka, Japan
e-mail: miura@econ.kyushu-u.ac.jp

T. Naito et al. (eds.), *Applied Approaches to Societal Institutions and Economics*, New Frontiers in Regional Science: Asian Perspectives 18,
DOI 10.1007/978-981-10-5663-5_1

The use of the same contract in each period is known to yield an optimal outcome. The other is the case in which a commitment such as that described above is not possible. After the principal observes the action of the agent during the early stage of term of a contract in this case, he confirms the following contract depending on the additional information obtained at that moment.

He might have an incentive by which he takes such an action not to give the principal this information (a so-called Ratchet effect) if the additional information puts the agent at a disadvantage in the contract the following term. To prevent such an incentive, the principal can design a contract giving much information rent in the subsequent term, but the gain of the principal might decrease. Consequently, the principal also might not take the action of gaining the agent's private information positively in the first-term contract. Based upon the foregoing, when a commitment is not possible, then it is generally impossible to adapt the revelation principle in designing a contract. We were able to characterize each term contract in noncommitment situation using a Perfect Bayesian Equilibrium. Specifically considering that the belief to the type of the agent which the principal has in the first term might be updated by Bayes' rule depending on the additional information, the contract is derived from a second period (the final period) using the backward method.

Laffont and Tirole (1993) and Ito (2003) considered details of such a noncommitment case. In particular, Laffont and Tirole's model regarded a regulated firm as an agent and the government as the principal. The purpose of the government is to maximize social welfare. In contrast, for these analyses, we regard a worker as an agent and the firm as the principal to analyze the internal structure of the firm. Therefore, we consider the situation in which the firm entrusts a worker with reduction duties of the practice expense that it costs for a project to maximize his own profit. In addition, there are two types of workers from the viewpoint of efficiency of the production: efficient and inefficient. The worker chooses an effort level for cost reduction on the project. The realization level of the practice expense is observable and verifiable, but these types and effort level are private information of the worker. Recently, studies that took up intrinsic motivation in agency theory have been increasingly conducted.

Delfgaauw and Dur (2008) obtain an interesting result related to the employment strategy of workers varying in the degree of intrinsic motivation.[1] Makris (2009) analyzes a benevolent agent taking the gain of the principal as intrinsic utility. Murdock (2002) assumes that the contents of the project affect the intrinsic utility of the agent and analyzes the property of an optimal contract. In addition, Benabou and Trole (2003) consider the case in which the signal which the principal with private

[1]When agents are classified as a devoted type, a standard type, or a sluggard type depending on the degree of intrinsic motivation, it is desirable for the firm that she does not employ a standard type and employs a devoted type and a sluggard type. Because a sluggard type becomes higher in cost than a standard type, the firm uses a contract that lets a sluggard type choose low effort for a low reward when principals employ a sluggard type in substitution for a standard type. In that case, as a result of reduction of incentives to pretend that a devoted type is a sluggard type, the employer can save the information rent of a devoted type.

information sends decides the intrinsic motivation of the agent. They show that a contract to give many rewards gives a message that work is not interesting and that it might lower intrinsic motivation.

Including the papers described above, most agency models that took up intrinsic motivation have assumed a static contract structure. However, when we analyze the Japanese management–labor relations, by which long-term employment is mainstream even in the present, while depending on agency theory, sufficient analysis would be impossible in the framework of a static contract. Therefore, we formulate the agency relation using a dynamic model with two terms considering intrinsic motivation and examine how the degree of intrinsic motivation affects each term contract and the firm's profit.

The main results of this paper are two. First, in a static and dynamic contract, as the degree of intrinsic motivation increases, the expectation profit of the principal increases for the amount of equivalence in each term through improvement of the agent's effort level and the reduction of reward to the agent (Propositions 1.3 and 1.5). This result holds in the complete information case (Proposition 1.1) and the commitment case. Therefore, we infer that these outcomes are robust in a meaning to be operated in a widespread framework without depending on the model structure. Therefore, it becomes important that the principal thinks about a strategy to raise the intrinsic motivation of the agent, even in terms of the external environment. Secondly, when the principal uses a mixed strategy in a dynamic contract, the mixed strategic use raises the principal's profit locally if a discount factor is small and the probability that the agent is an efficient type is high (Proposition 1.4). Moreover, we show that intrinsic motivation is neutral for the influence that a mixed strategy gives to the principal's profit (Proposition 1.4).

The structure of this paper is the following. The following section formulates a basic model and derives the optimal static contract under complete information and investigates its features. Section 1.3 expands the previous static model in a dynamic model of two terms and characterizes it using Perfect Bayesian Equilibrium and examines its properties. The final section mentions a summary of this paper and a future problem.

1.2 Static Model: Short-Term Contract

1.2.1 The Model

Our model is based on Laffont and Tirole (1993). We study a principal–agent model with two risk-neutral players: an agent (worker) and his principal (firm). The principal has a project with a payoff $S > 0$. The principal hires the worker to reduce the observable project's cost: $C = \theta - a$. θ, an efficiency parameter of the worker, can be either of two types ($\theta \in \{\underline{\theta}, \overline{\theta}\}$, where $\overline{\theta} > \underline{\theta}$). Let $\Delta\theta \equiv \overline{\theta} - \underline{\theta} > 0$. ν $(1 - \nu)$ denote the probability with which the parameter is $\underline{\theta}$ $(\overline{\theta})$. a denotes the worker's cost-reduction effort. The workers' disutility of effort, $\phi(a)$, is a convex function. For simplicity, we consider $\phi(a) = \frac{c}{2}a^2 (c > 0)$. The principal cannot observe the worker's type, θ, or effort supply, a. Therefore, these parameters are private information.

In our model, the worker is motivated intrinsically because of the enjoyment of the worker's contribution to the firm. We denote the intrinsic motivation as $\gamma \in [0, 1)$ and the intrinsic utility as $\psi(a) = \gamma a$ in the manner described by Delfgaauw and Dur (2008). Assuming that γ is common knowledge, then the worker's utility U takes the form of

$$U = w - \frac{c}{2}a^2 + \gamma a. \tag{1.1}$$

We consider $d(a) = \frac{c}{2}a^2 - \gamma a$ the worker's disutility of effort with intrinsic motivation. Therefore, we assume that $d'(a)$ is strictly positive ($a > \frac{\gamma}{c}$). We normalize the worker's reservation utility to zero.

Let $W = S - C - w$ denote the principal's expected net return from the project. Therein, W stands for the difference between the project's payoff S and the project's cost C and her payment to the worker, w. Using the definition of the project's cost to eliminate C, we find that the principal's net return is

$$W = S - \theta + a - w. \tag{1.2}$$

Before we study the optimal contract with asymmetric information, we examine the contract with symmetric information as benchmark case. These allocations are denoted with superscript *fb*. The principal maximizes her net return W with respect to a and w, subject to the participation constraint for the workers of a different type. Consequently, the principal solves the problem

$$\max_{a,w} \; S - \theta + a - w \quad \text{subject to} \quad U \geq 0.$$

Let a^{fb} and w^{fb} denote solutions of the problem above and $W^{fb}(\theta)$ denote the principal's payoff at the first-best case. Then we have

$$a^{fb} = \frac{1+\gamma}{c}, \; w^{fb} = \frac{1-\gamma^2}{2c}, \; W^{fb}(\theta) = S - \theta + \frac{(1+\gamma)^2}{2c}.$$

a^{fb} is decreasing in the cost of a delivery effort c and increasing in motivation γ. Lower cost and higher motivation reduce the worker's disutility of effort. This enables the worker to provide higher effort, which constrains the worker's participation binding. As a result, the principal's net return is particularly increasing in γ ($\frac{\partial W^{fb}}{\partial \gamma} = a^{fb} > 0$). Therefore, we obtain the following proposition.

Proposition 1.1 *Under complete information, every 1-unit increase of motivation increases the principal's net return by* a^{fb}.

1.2.2 Optimal Short-Term Contract

We next examine the optimal short-term contract under asymmetric information. The contract must satisfy two participation constraints:

$$\underline{U} = \underline{w} - \frac{c}{2}(\underline{\theta} - \underline{C})^2 + \gamma(\underline{\theta} - \underline{C}) \geq 0$$

and

$$\overline{U} = \overline{w} - \frac{c}{2}(\overline{\theta} - \overline{C})^2 + \gamma(\overline{\theta} - \overline{C}) \geq 0,$$

requiring that each worker be offered at least his reservation utility. These constraints can be expressed as

$$\underline{U} = \underline{w} - \frac{c}{2}\underline{a}^2 + \gamma\underline{a} \geq 0, \qquad (\underline{PCS})$$

and

$$\overline{U} = \overline{w} - \frac{c}{2}\overline{a}^2 + \gamma\overline{a} \geq 0. \qquad (\overline{PCS})$$

The worker must also be motivated to report his type accurately. That is,

$$\underline{U} = \underline{w} - \frac{c}{2}(\underline{\theta} - \underline{C})^2 + \gamma(\underline{\theta} - \underline{C}) \geq \overline{w} - \frac{c}{2}(\underline{\theta} - \overline{C})^2 + \gamma(\underline{\theta} - \overline{C}),$$

and

$$\overline{U} = \overline{w} - \frac{c}{2}(\overline{\theta} - \overline{C})^2 + \gamma(\overline{\theta} - \overline{C}) \geq \underline{w} - \frac{c}{2}(\overline{\theta} - \underline{C})^2 + \gamma(\overline{\theta} - \underline{C}).$$

Such incentive constraints require that type $\underline{\theta}$ ($\overline{\theta}$) prefers his own contract to the one designed for type $\overline{\theta}$ ($\underline{\theta}$). These constraints can be written as

$$\underline{U} = \underline{w} - \frac{c}{2}\underline{a}^2 + \gamma\underline{a} \geq \overline{w} - \frac{c}{2}(\overline{a} - \Delta\theta)^2 + \gamma(\overline{a} - \Delta\theta), \qquad (\underline{ICS})$$

and

$$\overline{U} = \overline{w} - \frac{c}{2}\overline{a}^2 + \gamma\overline{a} \geq \underline{w} - \frac{c}{2}(\underline{a} + \Delta\theta)^2 + \gamma(\underline{a} + \Delta\theta). \qquad (\overline{ICS})$$

We define the principal's problem in a static model [P] as described below.

Problem [P] $\max_{\underline{a},\overline{a},\underline{w},\overline{w}} \; \nu[S-\underline{\theta}+\underline{a}-\underline{w}]+(1-\nu)[S-\overline{\theta}+\overline{a}-\overline{w}]$

subject to,

$$\underline{U}=\underline{w}-\frac{c}{2}\underline{a}^2+\gamma\underline{a}\geq 0, \qquad (\underline{\text{PCS}})$$

$$\overline{U}=\overline{w}-\frac{c}{2}\overline{a}^2+\gamma\overline{a}\geq 0, \qquad (\overline{\text{PCS}})$$

$$\underline{U}=\underline{w}-\frac{c}{2}\underline{a}^2+\gamma\underline{a}\geq \overline{w}-\frac{c}{2}(\overline{a}-\Delta\theta)^2+\gamma(\overline{a}-\Delta\theta), \qquad (\underline{\text{ICS}})$$

$$\overline{U}=\overline{w}-\frac{c}{2}\overline{a}^2+\gamma\overline{a}\geq \underline{w}-\frac{c}{2}(\underline{a}+\Delta\theta)^2+\gamma(\underline{a}+\Delta\theta). \qquad (\overline{\text{ICS}})$$

Respectively, $\{\underline{a}_s, \overline{a}_s\}$, $\{\underline{U}(\nu), \overline{U}(\nu)\}$, and $W_S(\nu)$ represent the optimal effort levels, the worker's information rent, and the principal's expected net return in the static model.

Lemma 1.1 *Under asymmetric information, the optimal effort level, the worker's information rent, and the principal's expected net return are as follows:*

$$\underline{a}_s=a^{fb}=\frac{1+\gamma}{c},\ \overline{a}_s=\frac{1+\gamma}{c}-\frac{\nu}{1-\nu}\Delta\theta,$$

$$\underline{U}(\nu)=\left(1-\frac{c}{2}\frac{1+\nu}{1-\nu}\Delta\theta\right)\Delta\theta,\ \overline{U}(\nu)=0,$$

$$W_S(\nu)=S-\nu\left[\underline{\theta}-a^{fb}+\frac{c}{2}(a^{fb})^2+\frac{c}{2}(\overline{a}_s)^2-\frac{c}{2}(\overline{a}_s-\Delta\theta)^2-\gamma(a^{fb}+\Delta\theta)\right]$$
$$-(1-\nu)\left[\overline{\theta}-\overline{a}_s+\frac{c}{2}(\overline{a}_s)^2-\gamma\overline{a}_s\right].$$

This lemma is proved in Appendix A. We assume that $\underline{U}(\nu)=1-\frac{c}{2}\frac{1+\nu}{1-\nu}\Delta\theta>0$ to ensure that $\overline{a}_s>0$. First, we examine the interplay between motivation, γ, and information rent to the efficient type, $\underline{U}(\nu)$. Let $\underline{w}_s$ denote the optimal wage for type $\underline{\theta}$. Then, the rent is $\underline{U}(\nu)=\underline{w}_s-\frac{c}{2}(a^{fb})^2+\gamma a^{fb}$. We can write $\underline{w}_s$ as $\underline{w}_s=\frac{c}{2}(a^{fb})^2+\frac{c}{2}\overline{a}_s^2-\frac{c}{2}(\overline{a}_s-\Delta\theta)^2-\gamma(a^{fb}+\Delta\theta)$ when $\overline{\text{PCS}}$ and $\underline{\text{ICS}}$ are binding. The optimal wage for type $\underline{\theta}$ decreases as motivation increases. That is,

$$\frac{d\underline{w}_s}{d\gamma}=\frac{\partial\underline{w}_s}{\partial\gamma}+\frac{\partial\underline{w}_s}{\partial a^{fb}}\frac{\partial a^{fb}}{\partial\gamma}+\frac{\partial\underline{w}_s}{\partial\overline{a}_s}\frac{\partial\overline{a}_s}{\partial\gamma}=-\frac{\gamma}{c}(<0).$$

Although motivation increases the first-best effort level, the worker's disutility of effort, $\phi(a)$, is decreasing in motivation:

$$\frac{d}{d\gamma}\left[-\frac{c}{2}(a^{fb})^2+\gamma a^{fb}\right]=-ca^{fb}\frac{\partial a^{fb}}{\partial\gamma}+a^{fb}+\gamma\frac{\partial a^{fb}}{\partial\gamma}=\frac{\gamma}{c}(>0).$$

Therefore, these effects by the increase of motivation are mutually offsetting. These are summarized in Proposition 1.2.

Proposition 1.2 *In the static model, the information rent to the efficient type remains unaffected by the increase of worker's motivation.*

Next, we examine the interplay among motivation, γ, and the principal's expected net return: $W_S(\nu)$. For simplicity of notation, redefine $W_S(\nu) \equiv W_S$. Differentiating with respect to γ, we obtain

$$\frac{dW_S}{d\gamma} = \frac{\partial W_S}{\partial \gamma} + \frac{\partial W_S}{\partial a^{fb}}\frac{\partial a^{fb}}{\partial \gamma} + \frac{\partial W_S}{\partial \overline{a}_s}\frac{\partial \overline{a}_s}{\partial \gamma}.$$

Therefore, the envelope theorem implies that

$$\frac{dW_S}{d\gamma} = \frac{\partial W_S}{\partial \gamma} = \nu(a^{fb} + \Delta\theta) + (1-\nu)\overline{a}_s > 0.$$

Because the optimal wage of the efficient type is $\underline{w}_s = \frac{c}{2}(a^{fb})^2 + \frac{c}{2}\overline{a}_s^2 - \frac{c}{2}(\overline{a}_s - \Delta\theta)^2 - \gamma(a^{fb} + \Delta\theta)$, every 1-unit increase of motivation decreases the worker's wage by $a^{fb} + \Delta\theta$. a^{fb} denotes an increase of the worker's intrinsic utility with γ, and $\Delta\theta$ means a decrease of the worker's utility with γ when the worker of type $\underline{\theta}$ does not report truthfully (because of the final term on the RHS of $\underline{\text{ICS}}$). Consequently, the principal can save the wage by $a^{fb} + \Delta\theta$. Because the optimal wage of inefficient type is $\overline{w}_s = \frac{c}{2}\overline{a}_s^2 - \gamma\overline{a}_s$, every 1-unit increase of motivation decreases the wage by $\overline{a}_s$. Similarly to the explanation presented above, the principal can save the wage by $\overline{a}_s$. We can rewrite $dW_S/d\gamma$ as

$$\frac{dW_S}{d\gamma} = \nu(a^{fb} + \Delta\theta) + (1-\nu)\left(a^{fb} - \frac{\nu}{1-\nu}\Delta\theta\right) = a^{fb}. \tag{1.3}$$

The discussion presented above establishes the following result:

Proposition 1.3 *In the static model, as motivation increases 1 unit, the principal's net return increases by a^{fb}.*

Finally, we consider the interplay between the probability with which the worker is an efficient type and the principal's expected net return. Differentiating $W_S(\nu)$ with respect to ν and using the envelope theorem, we have

$$\begin{aligned}\frac{dW_S(\nu)}{d\nu} &= \frac{\partial W_S(\nu)}{\partial \nu} + \frac{\partial W_S(\nu)}{\partial \overline{a}_s}\frac{\partial \overline{a}_s}{\partial \nu}\\ &= \left[-\frac{c}{2}(a^{fb})^2 + (1+\gamma)a^{fb}\right] - \left[-\frac{c}{2}(\overline{a}_s - \Delta\theta)^2 + (1+\gamma)(\overline{a}_s - \Delta\theta)\right].\end{aligned}$$

Because $a^{fb} = \frac{1+\gamma}{c}$ maximizes $-\frac{c}{2}a^2 + (1+\gamma)a$, $dW_S(\nu)/d\nu$ is strictly positive. Consequently, the principal's net return increases in the probability of type $\underline{\theta}$. We can infer that this occurs because the rent to the efficient type decreases in ν.

For the discussion presented in the next section, we redefine the information rent to the efficient type:

$$\underline{U}(\nu) = \begin{cases} \left(1 - \frac{c}{2}\frac{1+\nu}{1-\nu}\Delta\theta\right)\Delta\theta & \text{if } \nu < 1, \\ 0 & \text{if } \nu = 1. \end{cases}$$

1.3 Dynamic Model: Long-Term Contract

In this section, the static model in the previous section will be extended to a dynamic model for two periods. We examine a series of short-term contracts in the two-period repetition of the static model and characterize the contracts using Perfect Bayesian Equilibrium.

We first consider the contract in the second period. Because the worker's action in the first period affects the probability of the worker's type, the principal designs the contracts under the updated beliefs. Let $\underline{\nu}$ ($\overline{\nu}$) be the probability of type $\underline{\theta}$ that the principal evaluates in the second period when the worker reports $\underline{\theta}$ ($\overline{\theta}$) in the first period. We can solve the problem in the second period as in the one-period model, except for updating of the principal's beliefs.

Next, we model the problem in the first period considering of the effect on the second-period contract. Let $(\underline{w}_1, \overline{w}_1, \underline{a}_1, \overline{a}_1)$ denote the first-period contract that the principal offers to the worker. Then, this contract must satisfy the following participation constraints to ensure that the worker prefers to accept her offer:

$$\underline{w}_1 - \frac{c}{2}(\underline{a}_1)^2 + \gamma\underline{a}_1 + \delta\underline{U}(\underline{\nu}) \geq 0, \qquad (\underline{\text{PCD}})$$

$$\overline{w}_1 - \frac{c}{2}(\overline{a}_1)^2 + \gamma\overline{a}_1 \geq 0, \qquad (\overline{\text{PCD}})$$

where $\delta > 0$ is the discount factor and $\delta\underline{U}(\underline{\nu})$ is the discounted information rent to the efficient worker. The rent to the inefficient worker in the second period is zero.

The contract must also hold the following incentive constraints to compel the worker to tell the truth:

$$\underline{w}_1 - \frac{c}{2}(\underline{a}_1)^2 + \gamma\underline{a}_1 + \delta\underline{U}(\underline{\nu}) \geq \overline{w}_1 - \frac{c}{2}(\overline{a}_1 - \Delta\theta)^2 + \gamma(\overline{a}_1 - \Delta\theta) + \delta\underline{U}(\overline{\nu}), \qquad (\underline{\text{ICD}})$$

$$\overline{w}_1 - \frac{c}{2}(\overline{a}_1)^2 + \gamma\overline{a}_1 \geq \underline{w}_1 - \frac{c}{2}(\underline{a}_1 + \Delta\theta)^2 + \gamma(\underline{a}_1 + \Delta\theta). \qquad (\overline{\text{ICD}})$$

The principal maximizes her expected net return for two periods under the four constraints above. We can summarize their constraints in the next constraint (see Appendix B for the proof).

$$(\underline{a}_1 - \overline{a}_1 + \Delta\theta)c\Delta\theta \geq \delta[\underline{U}(\overline{\nu}) - \underline{U}(\underline{\nu})]. \tag{$\overline{\text{ICD}'}$}$$

Therefore at the optimum, we have two cases of equilibrium. In a Case A equilibrium, ($\underline{\text{ICD}}$) alone is binding. In a Case B equilibrium, both ($\underline{\text{ICD}}$) and ($\overline{\text{ICD}}$) are binding.

Case A: Incentive Constraint of Only the Efficient Type Binding

In this case, because the inefficient type strictly prefers to tell the truth (($\overline{\text{ICD}}$) is not binding), he reports his own type $\overline{\theta}$ with probability 1. Because the efficient type is indifferent between $(\underline{w}_1, \underline{a}_1)$ and $(\overline{w}_1, \overline{a}_1)$, he uses a mixed strategy and chooses $(\overline{w}_1, \overline{a}_1)$ with probability $\underline{x}^A$.[2] Using Bayes' rule, we have the following updated probability:

$$\underline{\nu}^A = 1, \tag{1.4}$$

$$\overline{\nu}^A = \frac{\nu\underline{x}^A}{\nu\underline{x}^A + (1-\nu)}. \tag{1.5}$$

Let W_D^A denote the principal's expected net return of the dynamic model for two periods in Case A. Using both binding ($\overline{\text{PCD}}$) and ($\underline{\text{ICD}}$), W_D^A is

$$\begin{aligned}
W_D^A &= \nu(1-\underline{x}^A)[S - \underline{\theta} + \underline{a}_1 - \underline{w}_1 + \delta W_S(1)] \\
&\quad + (\nu\underline{x}^A + 1 - \nu)[S - \overline{\theta} + \overline{a}_1 - \overline{w}_1 + \delta W_S(\overline{\nu}^A)] \\
&= \nu(1-\underline{x}^A)\Big[S - \underline{\theta} + \underline{a}_1 - \frac{c}{2}(\underline{a}_1)^2 - \frac{c}{2}(\overline{a}_1)^2 + \frac{c}{2}(\overline{a}_1 - \Delta\theta)^2 + \gamma(\underline{a}_1 + \Delta\theta) \\
&\quad - \delta[\underline{U}(\overline{\nu}^A) - \underline{U}(\underline{\nu}^A)] + \delta W_S(1)\Big] \\
&\quad + (\nu\underline{x}^A + 1 - \nu)\Big[S - \overline{\theta} + \overline{a}_1 - \frac{c}{2}(\overline{a}_1)^2 + \gamma\overline{a}_1 + \delta W_S(\overline{\nu}^A)\Big].
\end{aligned}$$

Let $\underline{a}_1^A$, $\overline{a}_1^A$ be the optimal effort level in Case A. We get them with the first-order conditions[3]:

$$\underline{a}_1^A = a^{fb} = \frac{1+\gamma}{c}, \tag{1.6}$$

$$\overline{a}_1^A = \frac{1+\gamma}{c} - \frac{\nu(1-\underline{x}^A)}{\nu\underline{x}^A + 1 - \nu}\Delta\theta. \tag{1.7}$$

---

[2]Because ($\underline{\text{ICD}}$) is binding and the efficient type is a second mover, the contract is decided before he uses the mixed strategy. Consequently, his payoff does not change by any mixed strategy. Therefore, it is noteworthy that not the worker but the principal uses a mixed strategy in terms of maximizing her expected net return.

[3]The Perfect Bayesian Equilibrium in Case A is equivalent to a renegotiation-proof contract (see, for more details, Miura 2003, chapter 4).

$\overline{a}_1^A$ is strictly increasing in $\underline{x}^A(\partial\overline{a}_1^A/\partial\underline{x}^A > 0)$. One can infer that, as $\underline{x}^A$ is increasing, the effort level of the inefficient type is implemented frequently. The effort level of the inefficient type maximizes and corresponds to the first-best effort level a^{fb} if both types report inefficient type ($\underline{x}^A = 1$). The effort level of the inefficient type minimizes and corresponds to the inefficient type's effort level in the static model, $\overline{a}^S$ if the worker's types are fully separated ($\underline{x}^A = 0$). We therefore have the following result about the optimal effort level:

$$\underline{a}_1^A = a^{fb} \geq \overline{a}_1^A \geq \overline{a}_S.$$

We now study the condition under which the equilibrium exists in Case A. Substituting $\underline{a}_1^A, \overline{a}_1^A$ into $(\overline{\text{ICD}'})$ and using $\underline{U}(1) = 0$ in the previous section, we can obtain the condition as

$$\frac{c\Delta\theta^2}{\nu\underline{x}^A + 1 - \nu}\frac{1}{\underline{U}(\overline{v}^A)} \geq \delta. \tag{1.8}$$

Therefore, for δ sufficiently small, the equilibrium in Case A exists.

In fact, is it optimal for the principal to make the worker use a mixed strategy? To answer this question, we should consider the effects that a mixed strategy, $\underline{x}^A$, have on the principal's expected net return in the equilibrium, W_D^A. However, because $dW_D^A/d\underline{x}^A$ is so complicated, it is difficult to check the sign with straightforward calculations. Therefore, we examine the sign of $dW_D^A/d\underline{x}^A$ in the neighborhood of $\underline{x}^A = 0$:

$$\left.\frac{dW_D^A}{d\underline{x}^A}\right|_{\underline{x}^A=0} = -\frac{\nu c(\Delta)^2}{2(1-\nu)}\left(\frac{1}{1-\nu} + \delta\right) + \frac{\nu(1+\nu)\delta c(\Delta)^2}{2(1-\nu)^3}. \tag{1.9}$$

The proof is Appendix C. Equation (1.9) can be written as

$$\left.\frac{dW_D^A}{d\underline{x}^A}\right|_{\underline{x}^A=0} = \frac{\nu c(\Delta)^2}{2(1-\nu)^2}\left[-\delta\nu^2 + (3\delta + 1)\nu - 1\right].$$

We can consider the square bracket quadratic function of ν for all δ which holds (1.8):

$$0 < \nu^* = \frac{3\delta + 1 - \sqrt{(3\delta + 1)^2 - 4\delta}}{2\delta} < 1.$$

When $\nu > \nu^*$ holds, we have $\left.\frac{dW_D^A}{d\underline{x}^A}\right|_{\underline{x}^A=0} > 0$. Moreover from (1.9), we conclude that in the neighborhood of $\underline{x}^A = 0$, the parameter γ expressing degree of intrinsic motivation plays a neutral role for the influence that the increase of $\underline{x}^A$ gives to the firm's expected profit in two terms because it is not reflected on the right side. We summarize the discussion presented above in the next proposition.

Proposition 1.4 *In Case A, using the mixed strategy raises the principal's profit locally if a discount factor is small and the probability with which the agent is an efficient type is high. Moreover, intrinsic motivation is neutral for the influence that the mixed strategy gives to a principal's profit.*

In Case A, when the efficient type tells the truth in the first period, the principal finds the worker to be the efficient type ($\underline{\nu}^A = 1$). Then, the efficient type cannot obtain the information rent in the second period ($\underline{U}(1) = 0$). When the efficient type mimics the inefficient one, he can obtain the rent in the second period ($\underline{U}(\overline{\nu}^A) > 0$). As δ increases, the efficient worker evaluates the second period's rent as higher and has stronger incentive to tell a lie. Consequently, because the optimal wage for the efficient type is

$$\underline{w}_1^A = \frac{c}{2}(\underline{a}_1^A)^2 + \frac{c}{2}(\overline{a}_1^A)^2 - \frac{c}{2}(\overline{a}_1^A - \Delta\theta)^2 - \gamma(\underline{a}_1^A + \Delta\theta) + \delta\underline{U}(\overline{\nu}^A),$$

the principal needs to give a higher wage. That gives inefficient type incentives to mimic the efficient type. As a result, when δ is large, not only $(\underline{\text{ICD}})$ but also $(\overline{\text{ICD}})$ might be binding (Case B).

Case B: Both Incentive Constraints Binding

In Case B, because $(\overline{\text{ICD}})$ is binding, the principal can make not only the efficient type, but the inefficient one chooses a mixed strategy. The efficient type chooses $(\overline{w}_1, \overline{a}_1)$ with probability $\underline{x}^B$, whereas the inefficient one chooses $(\underline{w}_1, \underline{a}_1)$ with probability $\overline{x}^B$. Using Bayes' rule,

$$\underline{\nu}^B = \frac{\nu(1-\underline{x}^B)}{\nu(1-\underline{x}^B) + (1-\nu)\overline{x}^B}, \tag{1.10}$$

$$\overline{\nu}^B = \frac{\nu\underline{x}^B}{\nu\underline{x}^B + (1-\nu)(1-\overline{x}^B)}. \tag{1.11}$$

Because $(\overline{\text{ICD}})$ is binding, we have $\underline{a}_1 = \overline{a}_1 - \Delta\theta + \frac{\delta[\underline{U}(\overline{\nu}) - \underline{U}(\underline{\nu})]}{c\Delta\theta}$. Substituting this equality into $(\underline{\text{ICD}})$, $(\underline{\text{ICD}})$ can be expressed as

$$\begin{aligned}\underline{w}_1 = {} & \frac{c}{2}\left(\overline{a}_1 - \Delta\theta + \frac{\delta[\underline{U}(\overline{\nu}) - \underline{U}(\underline{\nu})]}{c\Delta\theta}\right)^2 + \frac{c}{2}(\overline{a}_1)^2 - \frac{c}{2}(\overline{a}_1 - \Delta\theta)^2 \\ & - \gamma\left(\overline{a}_1 + \frac{\delta[\underline{U}(\overline{\nu}) - \underline{U}(\underline{\nu})]}{c\Delta\theta}\right) + \delta[\underline{U}(\overline{\nu}) - \underline{U}(\underline{\nu})].\end{aligned} \tag{$\underline{\text{ICD}}$}$$

Let W_D^B denote the principal's expected net return of the dynamic model for two periods in Case B. Using $(\overline{\text{PCD}})$,$(\overline{\text{ICD}})$, and $(\underline{\text{ICD}})$, W_D^B is

$$\begin{aligned}W_D^B = {} & [\nu(1-\underline{x}^B) + (1-\nu)\overline{x}^B][S - \underline{\theta} + \underline{a}_1 - \underline{w}_1 + \delta W_S(\underline{\nu}^B)] \\ & + [\nu\underline{x}^B + (1-\nu)(1-\overline{x}^B)][S - \overline{\theta} + \overline{a}_1 - \overline{w}_1 + \delta W_S(\overline{\nu}^B)] \\ = {} & [\nu(1-\underline{x}^B) + (1-\nu)\overline{x}^B]\left[S - \underline{\theta} + \overline{a}_1 - \Delta\theta + \frac{\delta[\underline{U}(\overline{\nu}) - \underline{U}(\underline{\nu})]}{c\Delta\theta}\right.\end{aligned}$$

$$- \frac{c}{2}\left(\overline{a}_1 - \Delta\theta + \frac{\delta[U(\overline{\nu}) - \underline{U}(\underline{\nu})]}{c\Delta\theta}\right)^2 - \frac{c}{2}(\overline{a}_1)^2 + \frac{c}{2}(\overline{a}_1 - \Delta\theta)^2$$
$$+ \gamma\left(\overline{a}_1 + \frac{\delta[\underline{U}(\overline{\nu}) - \underline{U}(\underline{\nu})]}{c\Delta\theta}\right) - \delta[\underline{U}(\overline{\nu}) - \underline{U}(\underline{\nu})] + \delta W_S(\underline{\nu}^B)\Bigg]$$
$$+ [\nu\underline{x}^B + (1-\nu)(1-\overline{x}^B)]\left[S - \overline{\theta} + \overline{a}_1 - \frac{c}{2}(\overline{a}_1)^2 + \gamma\overline{a}_1 + \delta W_S(\overline{\nu}^B)\right].$$

Let $\underline{a}_1^B, \overline{a}_1^B$ be the optimal effort level in Case B. The solution is solved using the first-order conditions and $(\overline{\text{ICD}})$ as

$$\underline{a}_1^B = \frac{1+\gamma}{c} + \frac{\delta[\underline{U}(\overline{\nu}) - \underline{U}(\underline{\nu})]}{c\Delta\theta}[\nu\underline{x}^B + (1-\nu)(1-\overline{x}^B)] - \Delta\theta, \tag{1.12}$$

$$\overline{a}_1^B = \frac{1+\gamma}{c} - \frac{\delta[\underline{U}(\overline{\nu}) - \underline{U}(\underline{\nu})]}{c\Delta\theta}[\nu(1-\underline{x}^B) + (1-\nu)\overline{x}^B]. \tag{1.13}$$

Because $\underline{a}_1^B - \overline{a}_1^B = \frac{\delta[\underline{U}(\overline{\nu}^B) - \underline{U}(\underline{\nu}^B)]}{c\Delta\theta} - \Delta\theta$ must hold under the optimal contract from $(\overline{\text{ICD}})$, there exists no monotonicity of the optimal effort level that is apparent in conventional agency theory.

We next examine the effect that motivation gives to the principal's expected net return for two periods in the dynamic model. First, in Case A, substituting (1.6) and (1.7) into W_D^A, we differentiate W_D^A with respect to γ (see Appendix D for the proof):

$$\frac{dW_D^A}{d\gamma} = a^{fb} + \delta\left[\nu(1-\underline{x}^A)a^{fb} + (\nu\underline{x}^A + 1 - \nu)a^{fb}\right] = a^{fb} + \delta a^{fb}.$$

The first term is the effect of increasing γ in the first period (see Proposition 1.3 for details). The second term is the effect of increasing γ in the second period. $\nu(1-\underline{x}^A)a^{fb}$ is the increment of the principal's profit when the worker reports $\underline{\theta}$ with probability $\nu(1-\underline{x}^A)$. Then because information is symmetric, 1-unit increase of motivation increases the principal's net return by a^{fb} from Proposition 1.1. $(\nu\underline{x}^A + 1 - \nu)a^{fb}$ is the increment of the principal's profit when the worker reports $\overline{\theta}$ with probability $\nu\underline{x}^A + 1 - \nu$. Then as motivation increases 1 unit, the principal's net return increases by a^{fb} from Proposition 1.3.

Next, in Case B, differentiating W_D^B with respect to γ, we can have

$$\frac{dW_D^B}{d\gamma} = a^{fb} + \delta a^{fb}.$$

The proof is Appendix D. There necessarily exists uncertainty about the type in the second period unlike Case A. Then, whichever type is reported, 1-unit increase of motivation increases the principal's net return by a^{fb} from Proposition 1.3. These outcomes are summarized in Proposition 1.5.

Proposition 1.5 *In the dynamic model, as motivation increases 1 unit, the principal's net return increases by* a^{fb} *in each period.*

1.4 Concluding Remarks

Our paper considered the principal as a firm and considered the agent as a worker and presumed that the worker had intrinsic motivation for work other than a reward paid by a firm depending on a model presented by Laffont and Tirole (1993). In other words, we introduced a viewpoint by which the worker obtained utility from that effort. The volume of the utility was changed by the degree of intrinsic motivation. We used a dynamic model consisting of two periods to analyze long-term management–labor relations and to examine how intrinsic motivation affected each period's contract and firm profit.

Results show that if the degree of intrinsic motivation rises 1 unit, then the expected firm's profit in each period raises the first-best effort level of the worker, as we posited in Propositions 1.1, 1.3, and 1.5. That is, the increase of the degree of intrinsic motivation raises the worker utility. The firm can reduce the reward amount and increase its expected profit. Secondly, when the principal uses a mixed strategy in a dynamic contract, we showed that the mixed strategic use raised the principal's profit locally if a discount factor was small and the probability that the agent was an efficient type was high (Proposition 1.4). Moreover, we showed that intrinsic motivation was neutral for the influence that a mixed strategy gives to the principal's profit (Proposition 1.4).

The results for the dynamic model above depend on the assumption that a parameter of the intrinsic motivation for two periods does not change. According to a discussion of a feeling of self-effect that Bandura (1977) proposed, the person has conviction toward the person's own ability by experiencing success. The person comes to make an effort more positively the next time.[4] The incentive to the effort of the worker in the first would change and influence the result if we introduce the way that the second motivation is decided based on the first outcome from this viewpoint. Furthermore, in this paper we presumed that the parameter of the intrinsic motivation was constant irrespective of the efficiency of the worker and that the firm can completely grasp it. A problem to be addressed in future studies is to revise the handling of the parameter of this intrinsic motivation while adding a realistic viewpoint and analyzing the issue of dynamic agency again.

[4]Bandura (1977) systematized an action necessary to bring about a certain result and proposed the concept of feeling of self-effect as faith about the ability in pursuance of a series of actions. He performs it without regretting an effort for accomplishment if a feeling of this self-effect is high. In addition, a feeling of self-effect is revised depending on four sources of information: success experience, substitute experience, persuasion from the society, and physiological emotional state.

A Proof of Lemma 1.1

First, we show that the contract satisfying ($\underline{\text{ICS}}$) and ($\overline{\text{PCS}}$) satisfies participation constraint ($\underline{\text{PCS}}$) ($\underline{\text{PCS}}$) with strict inequality. By ($\underline{\text{ICS}}$) and ($\overline{\text{PCS}}$)

$$\begin{aligned}\underline{U} &\geq \overline{w} - \frac{c}{2}(\overline{a} - \Delta\theta)^2 + \gamma(\overline{a} - \Delta\theta)\\ &\geq \left\{\frac{c}{2}\overline{a}^2 - \gamma\overline{a}\right\} - \left\{\frac{c}{2}(\overline{a} - \Delta\theta)^2 - \gamma(\overline{a} - \Delta\theta)\right\} > 0.\end{aligned}$$

As $d[\frac{c}{2}a^2 - \gamma a]/da > 0$ by the assumption, the last inequality described above holds unbinding. Therefore, these constraints are arranged as ($\underline{\text{ICS}}$), ($\overline{\text{PCS}}$), and ($\overline{\text{ICS}}$). Hereinafter, we verify that the optimal contract satisfying ($\underline{\text{ICS}}$) and ($\overline{\text{PCS}}$) satisfies ($\overline{\text{ICS}}$).

Assuming that ($\overline{\text{PCS}}$) holds unbinding under the optimal contract, then we can design new contracts that satisfy the other constraint ($\underline{\text{ICS}}$) and improve the value of the firm's purpose function merely by decreasing $\overline{w}$. This contradicts an original presumption. Consequently, under the optimal contract ($\overline{\text{PCS}}$) holds binding, that is, $\overline{w} = \frac{c}{2}\overline{a}^2 - \gamma\overline{a}$. Substituting ($\overline{\text{PCS}}$) into ($\underline{\text{ICS}}$) and arranging it, we have

$$\underline{w} \geq \frac{c}{2}\underline{a}^2 + \frac{c}{2}\overline{a}^2 - \frac{c}{2}(\overline{a} - \Delta\theta)^2 - \gamma(\underline{a} + \Delta\theta). \qquad (\underline{\text{ICS}})$$

($\underline{\text{ICS}}$) also holds binding under the optimal contract by reduction to absurdity as described above. Therefore, substituting ($\overline{\text{PCS}}$) and ($\underline{\text{ICS}}$) into the firm's purpose function, we have

$$\begin{aligned}\max_{\underline{a},\overline{a}}\ &\nu[S - \underline{\theta} + \underline{a} - \frac{c}{2}\underline{a}^2 - \frac{c}{2}\overline{a}^2 + \frac{c}{2}(\overline{a} - \Delta\theta)^2 + \gamma(\underline{a} + \Delta\theta)]\\ &+ (1-\nu)[S - \overline{\theta} + \overline{a} - \frac{c}{2}\overline{a}^2 + \gamma\overline{a}].\end{aligned}$$

Calculating the first-order condition with respect to $\underline{a}$, $\overline{a}$ and arranging it, we obtain that $\underline{a}_s = a^{fb} = \frac{1+\gamma}{c}$, $\overline{a}_s = \frac{1+\gamma}{c} - \frac{\nu}{1-\nu}\Delta\theta$.

Finally, we show that these optimal solutions satisfy ($\overline{\text{ICS}}$).

$$\begin{aligned}&\overline{U} - \left\{\underline{w}_S - \frac{c}{2}(\underline{a}_S + \Delta\theta)^2 + \gamma(\underline{a}_S + \Delta\theta)\right\}\\ =&0 - \left\{\frac{c}{2}\underline{a}_S^2 + \frac{c}{2}\overline{a}_S^2 - \frac{c}{2}(\overline{a}_S - \Delta\theta)^2 - \gamma(\underline{a}_S + \Delta\theta)\right\} + \frac{c}{2}(\underline{a}_S + \Delta\theta)^2 - \gamma(\underline{a}_S + \Delta\theta)\\ =&[\underline{a}_S - \overline{a}_S + \Delta\theta]c\Delta\theta > 0.\end{aligned}$$

Here the last inequality holds using $\underline{a}_S > \overline{a}_S$.

B Derivation of $(\overline{\text{ICD}'})$

First, we demonstrate that the contract satisfying $(\underline{\text{ICD}})$ and $(\overline{\text{PCD}})$ satisfies the participation constraint $(\underline{\text{PCD}})$ with strict inequality. By $(\underline{\text{ICD}})$, $(\overline{\text{PCD}})$, and $\delta \underline{U}(\overline{\nu}) \geq 0$, we have

$$
\begin{aligned}
\underline{w}_1 - \frac{c}{2}(\underline{a}_1)^2 + \gamma \underline{a}_1 + \delta \underline{U}(\underline{\nu}) &\geq \overline{w}_1 - \frac{c}{2}(\overline{a}_1 - \Delta\theta)^2 + \gamma(\overline{a}_1 - \Delta\theta) + \delta \underline{U}(\overline{\nu}) \\
&\geq \overline{w}_1 - \frac{c}{2}(\overline{a}_1 - \Delta\theta)^2 + \gamma(\overline{a}_1 - \Delta\theta) \\
&\geq \left\{\frac{c}{2}(\overline{a}_1)^2 - \gamma\overline{a}_1\right\} - \left\{\frac{c}{2}(\overline{a}_1 - \Delta\theta)^2 - \gamma(\overline{a}_1 - \Delta\theta)\right\} \\
&> 0.
\end{aligned}
$$

Because $d[\frac{c}{2}a^2 - \gamma a]/da > 0$ by assumption, the last inequality described above holds unbinding.

Next we show that $(\overline{\text{PCD}})$ holds binding. Assuming that $(\overline{\text{PCD}})$ holds unbinding under the optimal contract, then we define a new wage contract as reducing $\underline{w}_1$, $\overline{w}_1$ slightly each and satisfying $(\underline{\text{ICD}})$ and $(\overline{\text{ICD}})$. This contract improves the firm's purpose function. Therefore, it contradicts the assumption that $(\overline{\text{PCD}})$ holds unbinding under the optimal contract. The optimal contract makes $(\overline{\text{PCD}})$ hold binding, that is, $\overline{w}_1 = \frac{c}{2}(\overline{a}_1)^2 - \gamma\overline{a}_1$.

Substituting $(\overline{\text{PCD}})$ into $(\underline{\text{ICD}})$ and $(\overline{\text{ICD}})$ and arranging it, we obtain

$$
\underline{w}_1 \geq \frac{c}{2}(\underline{a}_1)^2 + \frac{c}{2}(\overline{a}_1)^2 - \frac{c}{2}(\overline{a}_1 - \Delta\theta)^2 - \gamma(\underline{a}_1 + \Delta\theta) + \delta[\underline{U}(\overline{\nu}) - \underline{U}(\underline{\nu})] \quad (\underline{\text{ICD}})
$$

$$
0 \geq \underline{w}_1 - \frac{c}{2}(\underline{a}_1 + \Delta\theta)^2 + \gamma(\underline{a}_1 + \Delta\theta). \quad (\overline{\text{ICD}})
$$

Here we assume that $(\underline{\text{ICD}})$ holds unbinding. We can design a new contract that reduces $\underline{w}$ slightly and which satisfies another constraint $(\overline{\text{ICD}})$. This contract improves the firm's purpose function. It contradicts the assumption presented above. Therefore, under the optimal contract $(\underline{\text{ICD}})$ holds binding, i.e., $\underline{w}_1 = \frac{c}{2}(\underline{a}_1)^2 + \frac{c}{2}(\overline{a}_1)^2 - \frac{c}{2}(\overline{a}_1 - \Delta\theta)^2 - \gamma(\underline{a}_1 + \Delta\theta) + \delta[\underline{U}(\overline{\nu}) - \underline{U}(\underline{\nu})]$. Substituting $(\underline{\text{ICD}})$ into $(\overline{\text{ICD}})$ and arranging it, we have

$$
\left\{\frac{c}{2}(\underline{a}_1 + \Delta\theta)^2 - \frac{c}{2}(\underline{a}_1)^2\right\} - \left\{\frac{c}{2}(\overline{a}_1)^2 - \frac{c}{2}(\overline{a}_1 - \Delta\theta)^2\right\} \geq \delta[\underline{U}(\overline{\nu}) - \underline{U}(\underline{\nu})]
$$

$$
\longleftrightarrow \quad (\underline{a}_1 - \overline{a}_1 + \Delta\theta)c\Delta\theta \geq \delta[\underline{U}(\overline{\nu}) - \underline{U}(\underline{\nu})]. \quad (\overline{\text{ICD}'})
$$

C Derivation of Eq. (1.9)

Differentiating expected profit W_D^A with respect to $\underline{x}^A$, we obtain the following equation:

$$\frac{dW_D^A}{d\underline{x}^A} = \frac{\partial W_D^A}{\partial \underline{x}^A} + \frac{\partial W_D^A}{\partial \underline{a}_1^A}\frac{\partial \underline{a}_1^A}{\partial \underline{x}^A} + \frac{\partial W_D^A}{\partial \overline{a}_1^A}\frac{\partial \overline{a}_1^A}{\partial \underline{x}^A} + \frac{\partial W_D^A}{\partial \underline{U}(\overline{\nu}^A)}\frac{\partial \underline{U}(\overline{\nu}^A)}{\partial \overline{\nu}^A}\frac{\partial \overline{\nu}^A}{\partial \underline{x}^A}$$
$$+ \frac{\partial W_D^A}{\partial W_s(\overline{\nu}^A)}\frac{\partial W_s(\overline{\nu}^A)}{\partial \overline{\nu}^A}\frac{\partial \overline{\nu}^A}{\partial \underline{x}^A}.$$

By the envelope theorem, the above equation can be simplified as shown below:

$$\frac{dW_D^A}{d\underline{x}^A} = \frac{\partial W_D^A}{\partial \underline{x}^A} + \left(\frac{\partial W_D^A}{\partial \underline{U}(\overline{\nu}^A)}\frac{\partial \underline{U}(\overline{\nu}^A)}{\partial \overline{\nu}^A} + \frac{\partial W_D^A}{\partial W_s(\overline{\nu}^A)}\frac{\partial W_s(\overline{\nu}^A)}{\partial \overline{\nu}^A}\right)\frac{\partial \overline{\nu}^A}{\partial \underline{x}^A}.$$

Therefore, we have

$$\left.\frac{dW_D^A}{d\underline{x}^A}\right|_{\underline{x}^A=0} = \left[\frac{\partial W_D^A}{\partial \underline{x}^A} + \left(\frac{\partial W_D^A}{\partial \underline{U}(\overline{\nu}^A)}\frac{\partial \underline{U}(\overline{\nu}^A)}{\partial \overline{\nu}^A} + \frac{\partial W_D^A}{\partial W_s(\overline{\nu}^A)}\frac{\partial W_s(\overline{\nu}^A)}{\partial \overline{\nu}^A}\right)\frac{\partial \overline{\nu}^A}{\partial \underline{x}^A}\right]_{\underline{x}^A=0}.$$

We calculate each term of the right-hand side in the above equation. The first term is the following:

$$\left.\frac{\partial W_D^A}{\partial \underline{x}^A}\right|_{\underline{x}^A=0} = -\nu\left[S - \underline{\theta} + a^{fb} - \frac{c}{2}(a^{fb})^2 - \frac{c}{2}(\overline{a}^s)^2 + \frac{c}{2}(\overline{a}^s - \Delta\theta)^2 + \gamma(a^{fb} + \Delta\theta)\right.$$
$$\left. - \delta\underline{U}(\nu) + \delta W_s(1)\right] + \nu\left[S - \overline{\theta} + \overline{a}^s - \frac{c}{2}(\overline{a}^s)^2 + \gamma\overline{a}^s + \delta W_s(\nu)\right].$$

Here $W_s(1)$, $W_s(\nu)$, $\underline{U}(\nu)$ can be written respectively as shown below:

$$W_s(1) = S - \underline{\theta} + a^{fb} - \frac{c}{2}(a^{fb})^2,$$
$$W_s(\nu) = S - \nu\left[\underline{\theta} + a^{fb} - \frac{c}{2}(a^{fb})^2 - \frac{c}{2}(\overline{a}^s)^2 + \frac{c}{2}(\overline{a}^s - \Delta\theta)^2 + \gamma(a^{fb} + \Delta\theta)\right]$$
$$- (1-\nu)\left[\overline{\theta} - \overline{a}^s + \frac{c}{2}(\overline{a}^s)^2 - \gamma\overline{a}^s\right],$$
$$\underline{U}(\nu) = \left(1 - \frac{c}{2}\frac{1+\nu}{1-\nu}\Delta\theta\right)\Delta\theta.$$

Arranging these equations, we have

$$\left.\frac{\partial W_D^A}{\partial \underline{x}^A}\right|_{\underline{x}^A=0} = -\frac{\nu c(\Delta)^2}{2(1-\nu)}\left(\frac{1}{1-\nu} + \delta\right).$$

The sign of the above equation becomes negative. We can interpret the sign in the first term as follows: The possibility exists that efficient type reports non-efficiency type falsely in the first. Therefore, when the contract for the non-efficiency type is implemented in the first, the firm designs the second contract under incomplete information because it updates the probability of the efficient type to positive in the second beginning. Consequently, this situation reduces the firm's expected profit in two terms. Next we calculate the second term and have

$$\left[\left(\frac{\partial W_D^A}{\partial \underline{U}(\overline{\nu}^A)}\frac{\partial \underline{U}(\overline{\nu}^A)}{\partial \overline{\nu}^A}+\frac{\partial W_D^A}{\partial W_s(\overline{\nu}^A)}\frac{\partial W_s(\overline{\nu}^A)}{\partial \overline{\nu}^A}\right)\frac{\partial \overline{\nu}^A}{\partial \underline{x}^A}\right]_{\underline{x}^A=0}=\frac{\nu(1-\nu)\delta c(\Delta)^2}{2(1-\nu)^3}.$$

The sign of the expression above becomes positive because the second term operates the effects by which the second information rent decreases and the second firm's profit increases with the former independently. Therefore we have

$$\left.\frac{dW_D^A}{d\underline{x}^A}\right|_{\underline{x}^A=0}=-\frac{\nu c(\Delta)^2}{2(1-\nu)}\left(\frac{1}{1-\nu}+\delta\right)+\frac{\nu(1+\nu)\delta c(\Delta)^2}{2(1-\nu)^3}.$$

D Proof of Proposition 1.5

In Case A, differentiating expected profit W_D^A with respect to γ, we obtain the following equation:

$$\frac{dW_D^A}{d\gamma}=\frac{\partial W_D^A}{\partial\gamma}+\frac{\partial W_D^A}{\partial a^{fb}}\frac{\partial a^{fb}}{\partial\gamma}+\frac{\partial W_D^A}{\partial \overline{a}_1^A}\frac{\partial \overline{a}_1^A}{\partial\gamma}+\frac{\partial W_D^A}{\partial W_s(1)}\frac{\partial W_s(1)}{\partial\gamma}+\frac{\partial W_D^A}{\partial W_s(\overline{\nu}^A)}\frac{\partial W_s(\overline{\nu}^A)}{\partial\gamma}.$$

By the envelope theorem, the equation above can be simplified as shown below:

$$\begin{aligned}\frac{dW_D^A}{d\gamma}&=\frac{\partial W_D^A}{\partial\gamma}+\frac{\partial W_D^A}{\partial W_s(1)}\frac{\partial W_s(1)}{\partial\gamma}+\frac{\partial W_D^A}{\partial W_s(\overline{\nu}^A)}\frac{\partial W_s(\overline{\nu}^A)}{\partial\gamma}\\&=\{\nu(1-\underline{x}^A)(a^{fb}+\Delta\theta)+(\nu\underline{x}^A+1-\nu)\overline{a}_1^A\}+\delta\nu(1-\underline{x}^A)a^{fb}\\&\quad+\delta(\nu\underline{x}^A+1-\nu)\left[\overline{\nu}^A(a^{fb}+\Delta\theta)+(1-\overline{\nu}^A)\overline{a}^s(\overline{\nu}^A)\right]\\&=\left\{\nu(1-\underline{x}^A)(a^{fb}+\Delta\theta)+(\nu\underline{x}^A+1-\nu)\left(a^{fb}-\frac{\nu(1-\underline{x}^A)}{\nu\underline{x}^A+1-\nu}\Delta\theta\right)\right\}\\&\quad+\delta\nu(1-\underline{x}^A)a^{fb}+\delta(\nu\underline{x}^A+1-\nu)\left[\overline{\nu}^A(a^{fb}+\Delta\theta)+(1-\overline{\nu}^A)\left(a^{fb}-\frac{\overline{\nu}^A}{1-\overline{\nu}^A}\Delta\theta\right)\right]\\&=a^{fb}+\delta\nu(1-\underline{x}^A)a^{fb}+\delta(\nu\underline{x}^A+1-\nu)a^{fb}=a^{fb}+\delta a^{fb}.\end{aligned}$$

Next in Case B, differentiating expected profit W_D^B with respect to γ, we obtain the following equation:

$$\frac{dW_D^B}{d\gamma} = \frac{\partial W_D^B}{\partial \gamma} + \frac{\partial W_D^B}{\partial \underline{a}_1^B}\frac{\partial \underline{a}_1^B}{\partial \gamma} + \frac{\partial W_D^B}{\partial \overline{a}_1^B}\frac{\partial \overline{a}_1^B}{\partial \gamma} + \frac{\partial W_D^B}{\partial W_s(\underline{\nu}^B)}\frac{\partial W_s(\underline{\nu}^B)}{\partial \gamma} + \frac{\partial W_D^B}{\partial W_s(\overline{\nu}^B)}\frac{\partial W_s(\overline{\nu}^B)}{\partial \gamma}.$$

Using the envelope theorem again, the equation above can be simplified as shown below:

$$\begin{aligned}
\frac{dW_D^B}{d\gamma} &= \frac{\partial W_D^B}{\partial \gamma} + \frac{\partial W_D^B}{\partial W_s(\underline{\nu}^B)}\frac{\partial W_s(\underline{\nu}^B)}{\partial \gamma} + \frac{\partial W_D^B}{\partial W_s(\overline{\nu}^B)}\frac{\partial W_s(\overline{\nu}^B)}{\partial \gamma} \\
&= [\nu(1-\underline{x}^B) + (1-\nu)\overline{x}^B]\left(\overline{a}_1^B + \frac{\delta[\underline{U}(\overline{\nu}) - \underline{U}(\underline{\nu})]}{c\Delta\theta}\right) \\
&\quad + [\nu\underline{x}^B + (1-\nu)(1-\overline{x}^B)]\overline{a}_1^B \\
&\quad + \delta[\nu(1-\underline{x}^B) + (1-\nu)\overline{x}^B][\underline{\nu}^B(a^{fb} + \Delta\theta) + (1-\underline{\nu}^B)\overline{a}_s(\underline{\nu}^B)] \\
&\quad + \delta[\nu\underline{x}^B + (1-\nu)(1-\overline{x}^B)][\overline{\nu}^B(a^{fb} + \Delta\theta) + (1-\overline{\nu}^B)\overline{a}_s(\overline{\nu}^B)] \\
&= \overline{a}_1^B + \frac{\delta[\underline{U}(\overline{\nu}) - \underline{U}(\underline{\nu})]}{c\Delta\theta}[\nu(1-\underline{x}^B) + (1-\nu)\overline{x}^B] \\
&\quad + \delta[\nu(1-\underline{x}^B) + (1-\nu)\overline{x}^B]\left[\underline{\nu}^B(a^{fb} + \Delta\theta) + (1-\underline{\nu}^B)\left(a^{fb} - \frac{\underline{\nu}^B}{1-\underline{\nu}^B}\Delta\theta\right)\right] \\
&\quad + \delta[\nu\underline{x}^B + (1-\nu)(1-\overline{x}^B)]\left[\overline{\nu}^B(a^{fb} + \Delta\theta) + (1-\overline{\nu}^B)\left(a^{fb} - \frac{\overline{\nu}^B}{1-\overline{\nu}^B}\Delta\theta\right)\right] \\
&= a^{fb} - \frac{\delta[\underline{U}(\overline{\nu}) - \underline{U}(\underline{\nu})]}{c\Delta\theta}[\nu(1-\underline{x}^B) + (1-\nu)\overline{x}^B] \\
&\quad + \frac{\delta[\underline{U}(\overline{\nu}) - \underline{U}(\underline{\nu})]}{c\Delta\theta}[\nu(1-\underline{x}^B) + (1-\nu)\overline{x}^B] \\
&\quad + \delta[\nu(1-\underline{x}^B) + (1-\nu)\overline{x}^B]a^{fb} + \delta[\nu\underline{x}^B + (1-\nu)(1-\overline{x}^B)]a^{fb} \\
&= a^{fb} + \delta a^{fb}.
\end{aligned}$$

References

Bandura, A. 1977. Self efficacy: Toward a unifying theory of behavioral change. *Psychological Review* 84: 191–215.

Benabou, R., and J. Trole. 2003. Intrinsic and extrinsic motivation. *Review of Economic Studies* 70: 489–520.

Delfgaauw, J., and R. Dur. 2008. Incentives and workers' motivation in the public sector. *Economic Journal* 118(525): 171–191

Ito, H. 2003. *Keiyaku no Kezai Riron*. Yuhikaku (in Japanese).

Laffont, J.-J., and J. Tirole. 1993. *A theory of incentives in procurement and regulation*. Cambridge: The MIT Press.

Makris, M. 2009. Incentives for motivated agents under an administrative constraint. *Journal of Economic Behavior and Organization* 71: 428–440.

Miura, I. 2003. *Koukyou Keiyaku no Keizai Riron*. Kyushu University Press (in Japanese).

Murdock, K. 2002. Intrinsic motivation and optimal incentive contracts. *RAND Journal of Economics* 33(4): 650–671.

Chapter 2
Impact of Lower Interest Rate Ceilings on the Lending Market

Haruhiko Tsuzuki and Yusuke Miyoshi

2.1 Introduction

2.1.1 Interest Rate Ceilings and Lending Market

In Japan, financial institutions are prohibited from lending money at an interest rate higher than the specified limit. In 2000, the Financial Services Agency amended the Investment Law to modify the interest rate ceiling. But the contractual loan interest rates maintained at the level of the ceiling interest rate.

From the perspective of economics and law, however, nonbanks lending at high interest rates cannot be regarded collectively as vicious moneylending in violation of the Moneylenders Act and disturbing the economic order. When the lending market is examined in economic terms, however, the argument is often developed without considering the details or characteristics of specific loan rate regulations.

Particularly, lending businesses subject to the regulations tend to be analyzed while being viewed identically to the general market for trading goods. Accordingly, reconsideration of the potential viewpoints if the necessity of such regulation is to be justified and whether the current loan market conforms to the demand–supply model generally used, while considering the characteristics of the regulation rules (the interest rate levels and types of moneylending practices that are subject to

H. Tsuzuki (✉)
Saga University, Saga, Japan
e-mail: tsuzukih@cc.saga-u.ac.jp

Y. Miyoshi
Kagawa University, Takamatsu, Japan
e-mail: miyoshiy@gsm.kagawa-u.ac.jp

T. Naito et al. (eds.), *Applied Approaches to Societal Institutions and Economics*, New Frontiers in Regional Science: Asian Perspectives 18,
DOI 10.1007/978-981-10-5663-5_2

regulation), might be useful. Furthermore, a proper empirical analysis of the reality of the lending market in economics to identify the impact of the outcomes of the loan interest reduction policy on the lending market is necessary.

This study aims to present the theoretical model that is most appropriate for describing the current lending market in Japan, to identify the characteristics that differ from other goods markets, and subsequently, to explain the propriety of the model through an empirical analysis. One characteristic of the analysis in this study is its specific examination of the effect of changes in the interest rate ceilings made in the past to analyze their effects on lending.

Taking such characteristics of lenders into consideration, the following introduces the major preceding studies of the loan market. First, studies of the lending market that incorporate such asymmetric information include Stiglitz and Weiss (1981), Freixas and Rochet (2008), and others. They have demonstrated that the problems of adverse selection and credit rationing arise when asymmetric information exists between a bank, the lender, and a risk-neutral company, the borrower, in the case of collateralized loans under a limited liability system. To overcome the asymmetry of information, the lender not only sufficiently examines the borrower's solvency and risk but incurs the cost of collecting repayment associated with lending. Such a cost is called the agency cost. These results of the studies cannot be applied to the case of lenders such as consumer finance companies, in which the borrower is generally an individual assumed to be risk averse or, more specifically, to have a risk-averse utility function, and lending without collateral requires a high agency cost in preparation for the risk of nonpayment.

Finally, the latest study has been presented by Tsutsui et al. (2007). This study analyzes seemingly irrational behaviors of borrowers, such as multiple debts in the loan market, in consideration of the hyperbolic discounting of borrowers. In an ordinary model in economics, the discount rate for an individual's time is constant, and the discount rate for multiple periods is expressed as an exponent, which is therefore called exponential discounting. In contrast, hyperbolic discounting is when the discount rate for time is degressive.

This article assumes that the borrower prioritizes the current consumption by adopting hyperbolic discounting, resulting in the problem of multiple debts of the borrower. Results show that the interest rate ceiling might not be effective when credit rationing does not exist. When credit rationing exists, it might be effective when the percentage of people with high-rate hyperbolic discounting is high. The empirical analysis did not produce results showing that the lenders were oligopolistic. The study also indicated that asymmetric information existed between the borrowers and lenders. In any event, this constituted an analysis of a particular case in which the borrowers had hyperbolic discounting. There is room for additional examination of the borrowers' model, and the conclusion cannot be accepted universally as a general model of borrowers.

In this study, the lender facing risk maximizes its profit to derive a supply curve. This study first demonstrates that the supply curve takes a backward-bending shape and that the current level of interest rate ceiling is the downward sloping part of the supply curve accompanied by excess demand. The study also reveals that lenders tend to reduce lending as the interest rate increases. In addition, the amount of internal funds of lenders does not become a constraint on lending. These results suggest that, in a situation in which the lending market has a downward supply curve and excess demand, the ceiling on the interest rate is necessary and that further reduction of the interest rate is desirable in view of social welfare. The next section will develop theoretical models of the lender and borrower.

2.2 Theoretical Models of the Lending Market

2.2.1 *The Borrower's Model*

We consider the following two-period model. A borrower borrows funds from a moneylender in the first period (current period), in addition to the initial amount available for consumption, and carries out consumption activities. In the second period (next period), the borrower pays the principal borrowed from the moneylender along with interest based on the contractual loan interest rate while continuing to carry out consumption activities. We assume that the borrower's income during the i-th period is Y_i, that debt is D_i, and that the real amount available for consumption, i.e., net income, is $y_i = Y_i - D_i$. The borrower is assumed to be aware of the borrower's own net income in the first and second periods. In other words, the borrower holds perfect information about its own net income in the first and second periods. The consumption amount below which a consumer could no longer survive in each period is $c > 0$ (minimum consumption). The minimum consumption is an amount guaranteed by the social security system. Even a bankrupt consumer would be exempt from repayment obligations that would reduce consumption for the period to a level below that of the minimum consumption.

The borrower borrows funds from the moneylender in the first period but must repay the borrowed amount added with interest in the second period. The borrower goes bankrupt if the amount remaining after paying the borrowed principal and interest from the net income in the second period is less than the amount of c. If the borrower is bankrupt, then the lender collects the amount remaining after subtracting c from the borrower's net income. Alternatively, if the borrower's net income is less than c, then the lender is unable to collect any of the amount loaned. Although the bankrupt borrower can consume at the minimum level through a social security system and other programs, it suffers substantial damage because of a loss of social trust. We assume that, in the first period, the consumer does not have savings even if it spends less than its income.

Under such conditions, the borrower's utility function is determined as follows: When C_1 and C_2, respectively, represent the amounts consumed in the first period and second period, L is the amount borrowed in the first period, and R is the interest rate on the borrowing.

We assume that $u(C_1, C_2) = u(y_1 + L, y_2 - (1 + R)L)$ when $C_1,\ C_2 > c$, $u(C_1,\ C_2) > 0$,

when $C_1, C_2 > c$, $\frac{\partial u}{\partial C_1}, \frac{\partial u}{\partial C_2} > 0$.

when $C_1, C_2 < c$, $u(C_1, c) = u(c, C_2) = 0$,

when $C_1 < c$ or $C_2 < c$, $u(C_1,C_2) < 0$,

and the marginal rate of substitution of $u(C_1, C_2)$ degresses and $L \geq 0$.

The borrower determines the utility-maximizing amount of borrowing, L, and borrows the amount in the first period.

In this model, because the borrower knows its net income in the first and second periods, when it borrows funds from the moneylender in the first period, it is aware of whether the amount borrowed can be repaid in the second period.

A rational borrower would try to avoid excessive borrowing beyond its repayment capability to the greatest extent possible in the first period because the utility becomes 0 if it goes bankrupt in the second period. This, however, does not apply if the net income y1 in the first period is below the minimum consumption amount c. If the budget line for consumption expenditure of the borrower's consumption C_1 in the first period and consumption C_2 in the second period is $C_2 - y_2 = -(1 + R)(C_1 - y_1)$, the borrower's behavior varies depending on the conditions of its net income y_1 in the first period, net income y_2 in the second period, minimum consumption c, and this consumption expenditure budget line. The borrower's utility-maximizing behavior is solved as an application of analysis of a two-period model of intertemporal consumption. The possibility of the borrower's bankruptcy, however, must be examined. The following conditions are given:

(1) If $y_1 > c$, then the borrower does not borrow funds in the first period ($L^* = 0$).
(2) If $y_1 < c$, then the borrower borrows funds in the first period ($L^* > 0$).

This includes the following cases:

(2–1) $y_2 \geq c + (1 + R)L^*$: The borrower repays $(1 + R)L^*$ in the second period.
(2–2) $c + RL^* \leq y_2 < c(1 + R)L^*$: The borrower borrows anew to return L from another lender and repays $(1 + R)L^*$ in the second period.
(2–3) $c < y_2 < c + RL^*$: The borrower goes bankrupt in the second period and repays $0 \leq y_2 - c < RL^*$.
(2–4) $y_2 \leq c$: The borrower goes bankrupt in the second period and makes no repayment at all.

In the case of (2–2), if the borrower goes bankrupt, borrower's utility is zero. To avoid bankrupt, the borrower borrows anew to return $(1 + R)L^*$. In the case of (2–3) and (2–4), such behavior of the borrower is not sustainable. So, in these cases the borrower goes bankrupt.

When all the above cases are considered, the borrower's demand function is a decreasing function of the contractual interest rate on loans. In other words, the market demand curve in the loan market is a decreasing function of the contractual loan interest rate.

2.2.2 The Lender's Model

The lender's models in the loan market have been examined by Stiglitz and Weiss (1981) and Freixas and Rochet (2008) among others. They specifically examined the profit-maximizing behavior of the lender when information asymmetry exists between the lender, such as a bank, and a business operator, being the borrower. These cannot be used as a model of lender's profit maximization and supply curve derivation considered in this study.

In the model of Stiglitz and Weiss (1981), the borrower's profit function is the increasing convex function of project income. The lender provides collateralized loans. Its profit function is assumed to be a concave function of the income. The conclusion of the occurrence of credit rationing because of adverse selection derived from the model of Stiglitz and Weiss (1981) fundamentally relies on these assumptions. This model of Stiglitz and Weiss (1981) cannot be used as an assumption for the model of this study because it assumes that the borrower's utility function is a quasi-concave function, that funds are loaned without collateral, and that the lender's profit function will not be a concave function of the borrower's income because of limited liability, which guarantees the borrower's minimum consumption.

Furthermore, Freixas and Rochet (2008) also examined lender behavior when information asymmetry prevails between the lender and borrower. In this case of modeling, the lender is monopolistic and is able to determine the interest rate independently, the model is not one that determines the amount of loans (the loan amount 1 is given), and like Stiglitz and Weiss (1981), there is no minimum consumption guaranteed by the social security system that will not need to be repaid even if the borrower goes bankrupt. This, therefore, cannot be used as the model of loan market that we are developing, which assumes that the loan interest rate is determined by a competitive market and that the borrower is under limited liability that minimum consumption is guaranteed.

For the reasons described above, this study develops its original profit maximization model, considering the characteristics of loan market related particularly to moneylenders in Japan and their borrowers.

As in the case of borrowers, the following two-period model is assumed. The lender (moneylender) lends $L \geq 0$ to its borrower in the first period (current period) at the contractual loan interest rate of $R(R > 0)$. Whereas the contractual loan interest rate R is determined in the loan market and the lender can only accept it, R will never be an infinitely large value because of the interest rate ceiling set by the government. We assume, in this case, that $0 < R < 1$. The lender is uncertain about the net income of the borrower in the second period and is exposed to the risk of bad debts caused by the borrower's bankruptcy. If the net income of the borrower in the second period is less than the minimum consumption c, then the borrower goes bankrupt, and none of the loan principal or interest will be repaid. If the net income of the borrower in the second period is less than the sum total of the minimum consumption, loan principal, and interest, only the amount remaining after subtracting the minimum consumption from the net income will be repaid. The borrower, however, is aware of its own net income in the second period. Therefore, remarkable asymmetry prevails between the information held by the borrower and that held by the lender. Taking such default risk fully into consideration, the lender determines the amount of loan after estimating the probability distribution of the borrower's income in the second period. We assume that the lender estimates the probability distribution of the borrower's net income in the second period based on a normal distribution with mean μ, variance σ^2, and density function $f(y_2)$. The lender does not hold individual pieces of information related to the net income of the borrower in the second period. Therefore, it will estimate such net income using the net income distribution of general people. For the cost of lending to the borrower, we assume that the interest rate on financing in the external capital market is r. Borrowing sources based on debts include corporate bonds issued and bank borrowing. The agency cost and other costs aside from the cost of financing when the loan amount is L are $C(L)$. $C'(L)$ and $C''(L)$ are fully small positive values and are assumed to be $0 < C'(L),\ C''(L) < 1$.

The profit Π of the lender (moneylender) in this case is expressed as follows:

$$\begin{aligned}\Pi &= \int_{-\infty}^{c} 0 \cdot f(y_2)dy_2 + \int_{c}^{c+RL} (y_2 - c)f(y_2)dy_2 \\ &\quad + \int_{c+RL}^{\infty} (1+R)Lf(y_2)dy_2 - (1+r)L - C(L) \\ &= \int_{c}^{c+RL} (y_2 - c)f(y_2)dy_2 + \int_{c+RL}^{\infty} (1+R)Lf(y_2)dy_2 - (1+r)L - C(L) \quad (2.1)\end{aligned}$$

The lender maximizes its profit based on the contractual loan interest rate R determined in the market and decides the loan amount L. The optimum lending amount L satisfies the following (2.2):

$$-RLf(c+RL) + (1+R)\int_{c+RL}^{\infty} f(y_2)dy_2 - (1+r) - C'(L) = 0 \quad (2.2)$$

Let R^* be the contractual loan interest rate that satisfies (2.2) and the following (2.3):

$$-(2+R)Lf(c+RL) - RL^2 f'(c+RL) + \int_{c+RL}^{\infty} f(y_2)dy_2 = 0 \quad (2.3)$$

The amount loaned by the lender increases if $R < R^*$, reverses if $R = R^*$, and decreases if $R > R^*$. Consequently, the lender's supply curve slopes upward when the contractual loan interest rate is low, subsequently reverses, and slopes downward when the contractual loan interest rate is at a high level. In other words, a backward-bending curve is drawn (Fig. 2.1). At this point, we will examine the profit after profit maximization, i.e., the relation between the profit function Π^* and the contractual loan interest rate R. The profit function Π^* is expressed by the

Fig. 2.1 Loan supply curve

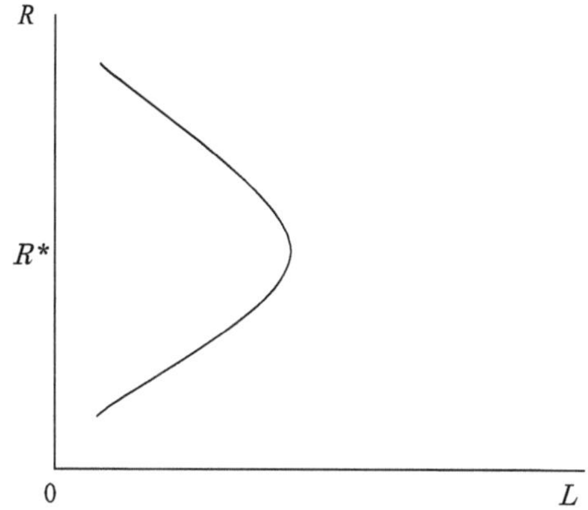

following equation. If L that satisfies the conditions for profit maximization (2.2) is $L^*(R)$ $(L = L^*(R))$.

$$\Pi^* = \int_{c}^{c+RL^*(R)} (y_2 - c) f(y_2) dy_2 + \int_{c+RL^*(R)}^{\infty} (1+R) L^*(R) f(y_2) dy_2 - (1+r) L^*(R) - C(L^*(R)) \quad (2.4)$$

The definite integral of the derivative with respect to R of Π^* from R_2 to R_1 is indicated below.

$$\int_{R_2}^{R_1} L^*(R)\{-L^*(R) f(c+RL^*(R)) + \int_{c+RL^*(R)}^{\infty} f(y_2) dy_2\} = \int_{R_2}^{R_1} L^* dR - \int_{R_2}^{R_1} L^*(R)^2 f(c+RL^*(R)) dR - \int_{R_2}^{R_1} L^*(R) F(c+RL^*(R)) dR \quad (2.5)$$

This value is positive if the lender is lending.

2.2.3 *Simulation of the Loan Supply Curve*

This section verifies that the actual loan supply function of lenders slopes upward when the contractual loan interest rate is at a low level and subsequently reverses to slope downward when the contractual loan interest rate is at a high level, thereby forming a backward-bending curve, using data (in 2006) from questionnaires completed by people who have used the services of lenders, as obtained through the cooperation of lawyers in Kumamoto and Oita Prefectures. The number of valid responses collected were 73 in Kumamoto Prefecture and 47 in Oita Prefecture.

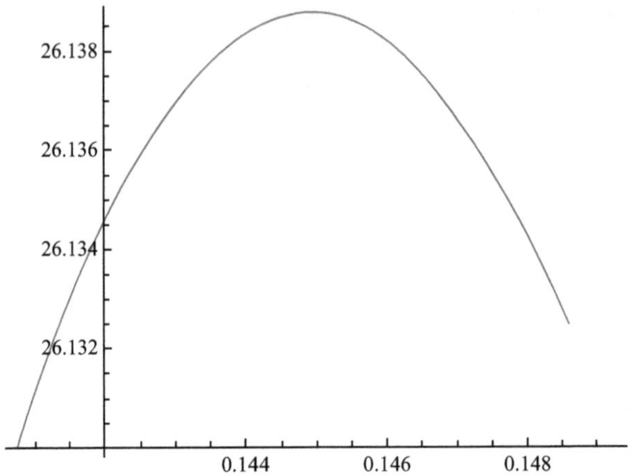

Fig. 2.2 Loan supply curve of Kumamoto

The result of the questionnaire conducted in Kumamoto indicated that the variance (σ^2) of the income of the borrowers was 106.7 and the mean (μ) was 26.9 (in 10,000 yen). In Oita, the variance (σ^2) of the income of the borrowers was 121.2, and the mean (μ) was 26.7 (in 10,000 yen). Therefore, we assume that lenders in Kumamoto estimate a normal distribution with the variance of borrowers' income of 106.7 and the mean of 26.9, and lenders in Oita estimate a normal distribution with the variance of borrowers' income of 121.2 and the mean of 26.7. We also assume that the borrowers' minimum consumption c is 80,000 yen. The interest rate on borrowing (r) and the marginal cost of lending $C'(L)$ are sufficiently small in comparison to the loan amount and contractual loan interest rate, which are assumed to be $(1 + r) + C'(L) = 1.01 + \frac{L}{10{,}000}$ (assuming $C(L) = \frac{1}{2}\left(\frac{L}{100}\right)^2$). When the horizontal axis represents the contractual loan interest rate (percentage) and the horizontal axis the loan amount (in 10,000 yen), then the supply curve as a result of simulation is as shown below.

For example, Figs. 2.2 and 2.3 reveals that lenders in Kumamoto and Oita tend to increase the loan amounts until the contractual loan interest rate is at the level of 14.5% and 18.5%, respectively. When the interest rate is above this level, they gradually reduce the loan amounts in fear of the risk of bad debts. In other words, the conventional assumption of a supply curve that slopes upward only (reflecting higher loan interest rates causing increased loan amounts) does not apply to the actual loan market. The theoretical model described earlier demonstrated that the supply curve was backward-bending, which is evidently supported also by the actual data in the result presented above.

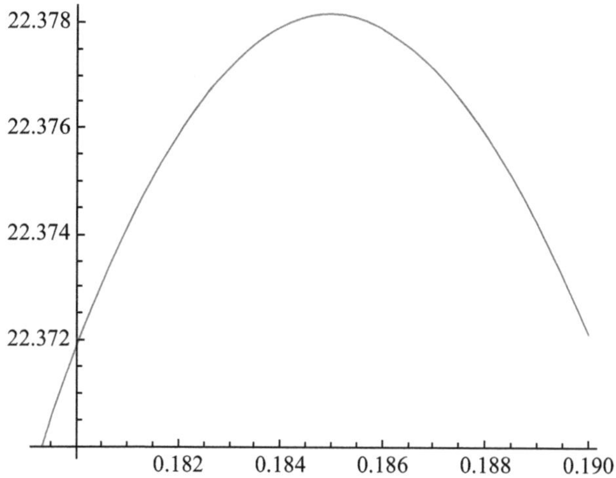

Fig. 2.3 Loan supply curve of Oita

2.2.4 Loan Market Equilibria and Hypothesis

Now that the market demand curve of the borrower and the market supply curve of the lender are known, we will consider the loan market equilibria. The loan market is presumably as shown in the following diagrams. D represents the market demand curve of the loan market, and S expresses the market supply curve. The possibility exists that the market equilibria form two types in this case. When the market equilibrium with a high interest rate is A and that with a low interest rate is B, Market Equilibrium A is in the state of Walrasian instability. Therefore, the neighborhood of A will not be adjusted toward A because of interest rate fluctuations but rather, diverged from A, going away from the equilibrium interest rate. Assuming that the demand curve and supply curve of the loan market form such shapes, the situation varies depending on the level of interest rate ceiling ($\underline{R}$) established by the government. (1) If the level of interest rate ceiling ($\underline{R}$) exceeds the interest rate level of Equilibrium A, then the interest rate level realized in the market is consistent with the interest rate ceiling, resulting in excess demand with the amount demanded greater than the amount supplied. The supply curve is in the state of a decreasing function of the interest rate. A reduced interest rate ceiling increases social surplus. (2) If the interest rate ceiling level ($\underline{R}$) is in between the interest rate level of Equilibrium A and that of Equilibrium B, Equilibrium B is achieved through Walrasian adjustment, which converges to market equilibrium, which equalizes the amount demanded and amount supplied and invalidates the significance of the interest rate ceiling. (3) If the level of the interest rate ceiling ($\underline{R}$) falls below the interest rate level of Equilibrium B, then the interest rate level realized in the market is consistent with the interest rate ceiling, resulting in excess demand with the amount demanded

Fig. 2.4 Loan market equilibria

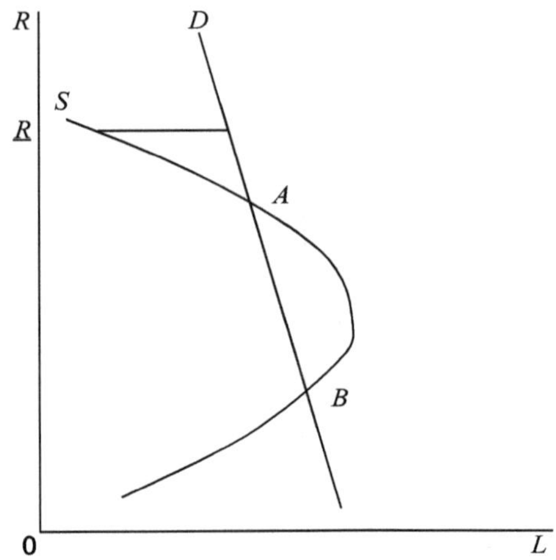

greater than the amount supplied. The supply curve is in a state of an increasing function of the interest rate. A lower interest rate ceiling reduces the social surplus.

As noted earlier, in the current lending market, the contractual loan interest rates of consumer lenders remain at the interest rate ceiling level, the contractual loan interest rates show a declining trend, the amounts of loans have not been reduced, and excess demand is likely to occur in such conditions. The current situation realized in the loan market is not in equilibrium, in which supply increases because of lower interest rates (i.e., the supply curve is a decreasing function) and the interest rates remain at the level of the interest rate ceiling. This situation is conceivably best described by case (1), among the cases described earlier, in which the interest rate ceiling exceeds the interest rate of Equilibrium *A*. In this case, if the current interest rate is at the ceiling level, then the Walrasian adjustment mechanism in the market does not function, and the interest rate will stay at the ceiling level. Because the supply curve in this condition slopes downward, any reduction of contractual loan interest rates in alternative nonbank industries such as credit card businesses in which interest rate ceiling is not imposed would increase the amount of lending in the entire nonbank industry. Excess demand also occurs when the interest rate ceiling is enforced.

As suggested in Fig. 2.4, when the supply curve is sloping downward and the demand is excessive, the interest rate ceiling is lowered, and the social surplus increases as the ceiling approaches the equilibrium interest rate. To verify this, we assume that the interest rate ceiling is lowered from R_1 to $R_2 (R_1 > R_2)$. In this case, the lenders' surplus in the lending market decreases for the addition of the decrease in the lenders' surplus of individual companies indicated in (2.5) for the number of companies in the market.

Meanwhile, lowering the level of the interest rate ceiling increases the consumer's surplus, as shown with the shaded area in Fig. 2.5. This increase includes

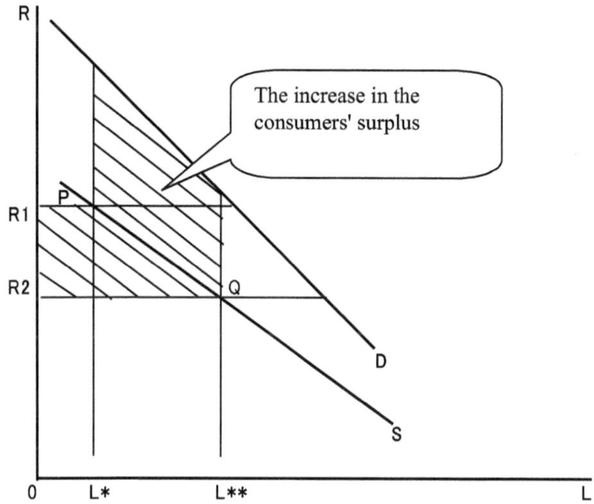

Fig. 2.5 The increase in the consumer's surplus after lowering the level of interest rate ceilings

the area of R_1PQR_2 expressed as an addition of $\int_{R_2}^{R_1} L^*(R)dR$ for the number of companies. The increase in the consumers' surplus therefore exceeds the decrease in the lenders' surplus, resulting in an increase in the social surplus. Based on the explanation above, the conclusion is drawn that a policy to lower the interest rate ceiling would be desirable when the ceiling exceeds the equilibrium interest rate. Such a model above helps to explain the loan market of lenders adequately by providing uncollateralized loans that have not been explained clearly in the past. The following hypotheses can be presented based on the theoretical model presented above.

Hypothesis 1 Substantial asymmetry of information represents an extremely high risk to the lender, causing the loan supply curve to slope downward at the current interest rate level (i.e., the adjustment mechanism that approaches the equilibrium interest rate does not function because there is a negative relation between the loan amount and contractual loan interest rate and the lending market is in the Walrasian unstable state).

Hypothesis 2 All loan interest rates are set at the level attributable to the interest rate ceiling in the current lending market, causing excess demand (i.e., the demand curve is steeper than the loan supply curve, and a lower interest rate ceiling contributes to a decreasing trend of excess demand).

The social surplus is not maximized in this situation in which the interest rate remains at the ceiling level higher than the market equilibrium interest rate. A reduction of the interest rate ceiling is likely to help increase the social surplus, which is the sum of consumer's surplus and lenders' surplus. In this state, therefore, the desirable policy would be to lower the interest rate ceiling further from the current level.

The loan supply curve derived from the model described above relies largely on the type of belief held by the lender, who is the lender about the borrower's income in the second period. If the lender is extremely pessimistic about the borrower's income in the second period and believes that debt is likely to be irrecoverable, then the supply to the market might be inadequate, and the intersection of the supply and demand curves might not exist. In such a case, the conclusion made earlier is unchanged if the supply curve slopes downward at the current interest rate level.

The next and subsequent sections analyze the lending environment of lenders based on the above theoretical background in this study. Estimation in this study also incorporates variation according to whether loans are provided for positive lending opportunities and whether there is an effect of capital structure through analysis added with the effect of variables that express Tobin's q and agency cost of lending. Given asymmetric information, the financing structure is known to affect corporate value and the cost of financing. It is thought to affect loan amounts to a considerable degree. The financing structure can therefore be incorporated as a proxy variable that expresses the degree of the asymmetry of information. Major variables that express the financing structure include internal funds (cash flow) and the debt-to-equity ratio. The effect of these variables on loans is also examined.

The next and subsequent sections first analyze, as specific procedures, whether the market is out of equilibrium and explicitly express the concept of demand and supply of loans. This will be followed by a discussion of whether lending is affected by the interest rate ceiling. The results of the estimation will be described one by one after presenting the hypothesis and objectives, estimation model, and dataset.

2.3 Empirical Analysis

2.3.1 Sampling

Nonbanks are financial businesses other than securities and insurance companies that engage in credit business without accepting deposits. More specifically, this industry is represented by consumer finance, commercial and industrial loan providers, credit sales companies, credit companies, leasing companies, and venture capital companies. The source of the data is "Zaimu (finance) CD" published by Toyo Keizai Inc. Consolidated financial results were used for the financial data.

Table 2.1 presents each of the descriptive statistics of nonbanks as a whole, lenders subject to interest rate ceiling reduction and lenders for consumers. The vif test of the correlations among these variables indicates a very low probability of multicollinearity with major explanatory variables, except for some variables. Consequently, these annual data will be used as unbalanced panel data for analyses.

Table 2.1 The descriptive statistics of nonbanks as a whole

	Obs	Mean	Std. Dev	Min	Max	Vif
Amount of loans[a]	210	12,479	1.306	9.236	14.385	
Loan interest rate[b]	210	0.209	0.061	0.075	0.304	1.75
ROA(%)[c]	210	1.379	3.616	−26.534	7.219	8.87
Cash flow[d]	210	0.080	0.352	−3.320	0.526	6.84
Tobin's q[e]	142	1.157	0.308	0.617	2.274	1.76
Debt-to-equity ratio[f]	208	51.886	16.506	18144	90.157	1.8
Nonperforming loan ratio[g]	200	0.039	0.037	0.002	0.394	1.52
Yield on short-term debts[h]	210	0.011	0.012	0	0.053	
Yield on debts within a year	210	0.014	0.014	0	0.054	
Yield on long-term debts	210	0.013	0.012	0	0.054	2.64
Corporate bond yield at issue	207	0.010	0.012	0	0.04665	2.27
Commercial paper yield at issue	206	0.003	0.007	0	0.0463	1.55
Interest rate ceiling reduction[i]	210	0.567	0.497	0	1	6.55
GDP[j]	210	13142	0.036	13.100	13.215	2.29

[a]Amount of loans: the logarithm of amount of loans
[b]Interest rate on lending: interest on operating loans ÷ balance of operating loans
[c]ROA(%): net income ÷ total assets
[d]Cash flow(net income + depredation expenses) ÷ sales
[e]Tobin's q: (total debts + market capitalization) ÷ total assets
[f]Debt-to-equity ratio(%): (short-term debts + long-term debts) ÷ total assets
[g]Nonperforming loan ratio: (amount of loss on bad debts + transfer amount of claims provable in bankruptcy) ÷ amount of lending
[h]The interest rate and yield are the average interest rate (final yield) presented in bond statements and debt statements, respectively
[i]Regulation of interest rates: a dummy variable that is 0 until year 2000 and 1 thereafter
[j]GDP: the logarithm of GDP

2.3.2 Estimation Formula and Test Method to Be Used

Disequilibrium analysis is characterized by the quantitative understanding of the disequilibrium state through the estimation of loan demand and supply functions and derivation of the equilibrium interest rate on loans. This section first describes formulation of the demand and supply functions in a disequilibrium market sequentially and the estimation method by following Fair and Jaffee (1972) and Maddala and Nelson (1974).

To estimate the coefficients of the structural formula, we first describe the demand and supply functions using only observable variables with the equilibrium interest rate and the interest adjustment equation. This study accordingly used a technique called dynamic GMM for the problems arising from the own-lag term and individual effect and performed estimation using Arellano–Bond GMM estimation, which is a dynamic GMM technique (see Chap. 3 of Hayashi 2000). In doing this, predetermination was assumed also for a part of the variables (ROA and debt-to-equity ratio) of $R_{i,t}$ and $X_{i,t}$ in the previous period, which were used as instrumental variables together with some variables (nonperforming loan ratio and GDP) in the demand function of equation. The purpose is to identify which causes changes in the amount of loans, the supply side or demand side.

2.4 Parallel Rate in Response to the Interest Rate Ceiling

The view exists that the loan interest rate in the lending market is linked in some ways to interest rate regulation. Such a case might assume a situation in which the loan interest rate directly reacts not only to excess demand but changes in the interest rate ceiling. Accordingly, the following breaks down the loan interest rate into a portion that is linked to the regulation and the portion affected by the mechanism of partial adjustment to equilibrium and reestimates the system.

In this way, we consider an estimation method incorporating the consistency of a model containing the partial adjustment formula of the loan interest rate added with the linking part of the interest rate ceiling. Then, estimation of the supply function of the structural form will be possible as in the past by estimating the sign of the adjusted part of the demand and supply after subtracting the parallel rate following the ceiling interest rate among the changes in the interest rate. The results of the structural form estimation are presented in Table 2.2.

As in the previous section, the GMM estimation of Arellano–Bond is applied. The results of the structural form estimation are presented in Table 2.2, which suggests that the estimated values of both functions do not vary greatly even when the direct effect of the interest rate ceiling is considered. In particular, the value of μ_i expressing the speed of interest rate adjustment still does not support the equilibrium hypothesis. This analysis confirms the minor direct effect of the interest rate ceiling on the loan interest rate and the very slow reaction to the supply–demand factors of the interest rate.

Reconfirmation of the estimation results for the interest rate reveals the slope of $R_{i,t} - R_{i,t-1}$ as 0.786, a positive value at the 10% significance level. The fact that a lower interest rate ceiling increases lending to a level greater than the desired amount demanded has also been observed (the estimation result at the left end indicates that a 1% lower interest rate increases the amount supplied by approximately 80%).

When the amount that is lent is on the horizontal axis and the interest rate is on the vertical axis, the slopes of the demand and supply curves are mutually reciprocal, indicating that the slope of the supply curve is gentler than that of the demand curve. Based on this, this analytical result represents the case, in which the interest rate ceiling exceeds the level of the interest rate of Equilibrium A. In such a case, an interest rate ceiling higher than the equilibrium level means that excess demand is occurring. Reduction of the ceiling therefore causes the interest rate to approach the market equilibrium level and causes the social surplus to increase, thereby constituting a desirable policy.

Table 2.2 Each estimation formula for the supply function of the structural form – the GMM estimation of Arellano–Bond and the instrumental variables (IV) estimation–

(1)				(2)			(3)		
Dependent variable: the amount lent	Coef	Std Err.	P> |t|	Coef.	Std Err.	P> |t|	Coef	Std Err.	P> |t|
Amount of loans in the previous period	0.897	0.075	0	0.849	0.091	0	0.947	0.064	0
Loan interest rate	−2.245	0.667	0.001	−2.087	0.672	0.002	−1.097	0.658	0.095
Changes in loan interest rates	0.786	0.424	0.064	0.581	0.414	0.161	0.189	0.524	0.718
ROA	0.018	0.008	0.024	0.006	0.008	0.482	0.020	0.010	0.053
Cash flow	−0.128	0.085	0.135	−0.035	0.084	0.681	−0.164	0.103	0.113
Tobins q	0.051	0.066	0.442	0.121	0.068	0.074	0.104	0.060	0.084
Debt-to-equity ratio	−0.004	0.009	0.67	0.000	0.009	0.995	0.019	0.009	0.042
Debt-to-equity ratio squared				0.000	0.000	0.506			
Nonperforming loan ratio	0.103	0.436	0.813	0.156	0.475	0.742	−0.404	0.345	0.242
Yield on long-term debts				0.052	0.021	0.011			
Corporate bond yield at issue				−0.005	0.022	0.801			
Commercial paper yield at issue				0.009	0.021	0.655			

(continued)

Table 2.2 (continued)

(1)				(2)			(3)		
Dependent variable: the amount lent	Coef	Std Err.	P> |t|	Coef.	Std Err.	P> |t|	Coef	Std Err.	P> |t|
Interest rate ceiling reduction	0.033	0.039	0.397	0.008	0.041	0.852	−0.009	0.031	0.771
Constant	−0.013	0.009	0.147	−0.000	0.010	0.37	0.230	0.859	0.789
Observations	79			79			123		
Sargan's overidentification restriction test	60.15 [0.11]			27.48 [0.44]					
The first autocorrelation test	2.32 [0.02]			−1.68 [0.10]					
The secondary autocorrelation test	0.12 [0.91]			0.35 [0.73]					
The Durbin–Wu–Hausman test							3.48 [0.06]		
Adjusted R2							0.772		

p–values in parentheses
The regressions also include dummy variables for the different time periods that are not reported
Results in column 1 and column2 are from regression using the Arellano–Bond GMM estimator
Results in column 3 are from regression using the instrumental variables (IV) estimation of proposed by Anderson and Hsiao (1981)
Loan ratio and further lags, RCA, and debt-to-equity ratio in the previous period are used as instruments for the loan interest rate together
Sargan is a test of the overidentifying restrictions for the GMM estimator; the null hypothesis is that the instruments used are not correlated with the residuals of the secondary autocorrelation test of Arellano–Bond GMM; the null hypothesis is that the errors in the first-difference regression exhibit no second-order serial correlation

2.5 Conclusion

This study has produced the following three findings through the analysis described above. First, because the lending market has significant asymmetry of information about the borrowers and presents a high risk of bad debts, the lenders operate their businesses that reflect such a background. The higher the interest rate, the more the lenders tend to reduce lending. When the information is substantially asymmetric, first, an increase in the loan interest rate reduces lending opportunities. In other words, the loan supply curve is sloping downward, and the lending market is in the Walrasian unstable state.

Consequently, the reduction of the ceiling interest rate enforced in June 2000 is apparently not influential on the lending market. When the supply curve is sloping downward and the demand is excessive, however, the interest rate ceiling is lowered, and the social surplus increases as the ceiling approaches the market equilibrium interest rate. Reduction of the interest rate ceiling as a policy can therefore be considered socially desirable.

Moreover, by analyzing the lending market, which includes not only consumer finance companies that are subject to the reduction of the ceiling interest rate but also other lenders that are not, this study has revealed what effects the tighter regulation of the loan interest rate by the government have on the entire consumer finance market and how the effects penetrate into the market.

Acknowledgements In preparing this paper, we received a research grant from a Grants-in-Aid for Scientific Research (KAKENHI:26380466) and the Murata Science Foundation. Thank you very much for taking this opportunity.

References

Arellano, M., and S.R. Bond. 1991. Some tests of specification for panel data: Monte Carlo evidence and an application to employment equations. *Review of Economic Studies* 58: 277–297.

Freixas, X., and J. Rochet. 2008. *Microeconomics of banking*. Cambridge: MIT Press.

Hayashi, F. 2000. *Econometrics*. 1st ed. Princeton: Princeton University Press.

Maddala, G., and F. Nelson. 1974. Maximum likelihood methods for models for markets in disequilibrium. *Econometrica* 42: 1013–1030.

Stiglitz, J.E., and A. Weiss. 1981. Credit rationing in markets with imperfect information. *The American Economic Review* 71(3): 393–410.

Tsutsui, Y., F. Hiruma, F. Ohtake, and S. Ikeda. 2007. Are interest rate ceilings in Japanese consumer loan market justified?: A behavioral economic approach. *Modern Finance* 22: 25–73.

Chapter 3
Ownership Structure, Tax Regime, and Dividend Smoothing

Shinya Shinozaki and Konari Uchida

3.1 Introduction

Since the novel study of Lintner (1956), it has become a widespread idea that US firms only gradually adjust dividend levels toward long-term targets (Fama and Babiak 1968; Mueller 1967; Brav et al. 2005; Leary and Michaely 2011). Dividend smoothing helps firms mitigate problems that arise from information asymmetry (e.g., signaling and reduction of agency costs). Gugler (2003) and Michaely and Roberts (2012) show evidence supporting this idea by using data from the UK and Austria, respectively. However, single country analyses do not provide conclusive answers to the question of why firms smooth dividends. There are significant variations in agency relationships across countries which generate substantial differences in dividend smoothing behaviors. Shleifer and Vishny (1997) point out that in continental Europe and East Asian countries, corporate ownership structures are highly concentrated and there are less severe conflicts between controlling shareholders and management. This fact naturally leads to the idea that international data provides us with an appropriate research setting in which to address the question.

This chapter investigates dividend smoothing behaviors for approximately 6,000 companies from 28 countries. We predict that dividend smoothing is evident in firms with dispersed ownership structures, while dividend smoothing is less evident in firms with concentrated ownership structures. Since controlling shareholders have access to various informal channels to intervene in management, managers

S. Shinozaki
Saga University, Saga, Japan

K. Uchida (✉)
Kyushu University, Fukuoka, Japan
e-mail: kuchida@econ.kyushu-u.ac.jp

T. Naito et al. (eds.), *Applied Approaches to Societal Institutions and Economics*, New Frontiers in Regional Science: Asian Perspectives 18,
DOI 10.1007/978-981-10-5663-5_3

with strong controlling shareholders have less need to adopt dividend smoothing to mitigate problems attributable to information asymmetry. Using a rich dataset, we compute speed of adjustment (SOA) at the firm level and relate them to corporate ownership structure.

We present robust evidence that the percentage ownership held by the largest shareholder is positively (negatively) associated with SOA (dividend smoothing). This tendency is evident when the target dividend level is lower than dividends of previous years. Managers of companies with concentrated ownership structures can quickly decrease dividends because severe agency conflicts do not exist. This result also suggests that controlling shareholders care about their firms' survival and will allow managers to cut dividends during years in which the firms perform poorly.

Previous studies suggest that tax treatments on dividends significantly affect corporate payout policy (Lasfer 1996; Lee et al. 2006; Brown et al. 2007; Chetty and Saez 2005; Pattenden and Twite 2008; Henry 2011; Alzahrani and Lasfer 2012). Pattenden and Twite (2008) show evidence that the volatility of gross dividend payments in Australian firms became more volatile after the introduction of the imputation system in 1987. In our research, firms located in countries with classical tax regimes smooth dividends the most, followed by those under a partial imputation tax system, and then by those under a full imputation regime. Overall, we argue that corporate ownership structure and tax regime have a significant impact on dividend smoothing behaviors.

The research presented contributes significantly to the literature. Our results support the notion that dividend smoothing is associated with corporate ownership structures. Recent studies have suggested that non-US companies smooth dividends less than US ones do by comparisons between a few countries (e.g., Khan 2006; Andres et al. 2009; Chemmanur et al. 2010). We confirm this result by using a larger set of international data and providing a convincing explanation of why US firms smooth dividends; it is attributable to the ownership structure (less concentrated and high institutional ownership) and the classical tax system. Recent papers intensively use international data to examine corporate dividend policy (La Porta et al. 2000; Denis and Osobov 2008; Brockman and Unlu 2009; Ferris et al. 2009; Alzahrani and Lasfer 2012; Fatemi and Bildik 2012; Kuo et al. 2013; Breuer et al. 2014). We extend this research trend to dividend smoothing as proposed by Lintner (1956).

The rest of the chapter is organized as follows. Section 3.2 presents a literature review and then describes our hypotheses and dividend smoothing measures. Section 3.3 presents the sample selection procedure and data. Section 3.4 shows the empirical results. Finally, Sect. 3.5 presents a brief summary of this research.

3.2 Literature Review, Hypothesis, and Dividend Smoothing Measures

3.2.1 Previous Studies and Hypothesis

Many US corporations pay dividends that are relatively stable over time. Accordingly, Lintner (1956) finds that SOA of dividend payments in US firms is only 30 percent. Early US studies (e.g., Mueller 1967; Fama and Babiak 1968) confirm the dividend smoothing policy, and a recent survey by Brav et al. (2005) suggests that US managers view stable dividend payments as an important financial policy. Leary and Michaely (2011) show evidence that US firm SOA declines over time and that the median SOA reached 0.09 during the period 1998–2007.

Previous studies focus on information asymmetry between shareholders and managers as the main explanation for dividend smoothing. Easterbrook (1984) and Jensen (1986) suggest that high and stable dividend payments demonstrate a firm's commitment to not undertake value-destroying projects, and to mitigate agency conflicts between shareholders and managers.[1] Bhattacharya (1979), John and Williams (1985), and Miller and Rock (1985) formally demonstrated that dividends serve as a signal of a firm's future cash flow. For instance, firms whose stocks are undervalued have an incentive to send a signal of their profitability through dividend increases. Some previous studies suggest that firms whose future cash flow become volatile are more likely to smooth a dividend under information asymmetry (Kumar 1988; Kumar and Lee 2001; Guttman et al. 2010). Information asymmetry in the capital markets increases the cost of external capital and thereby provides firms with incentives for accumulating large cash holdings. Cash requirements cause firms to hesitate about increasing dividends for years in which the firms perform well.

Agency conflicts and signaling needs are likely to differ considerably depending on the firm's ownership structure. Controlling shareholders who have substantial equity stakes can closely monitor management in various ways, including informal channels, and managers of those firms are less likely to rely on dividend payments to mitigate agency problems (Dewenter and Warther 1998; Chemmanur et al. 2010). Put differently, dividend smoothing behaviors for signaling or agency cost prevention should be pronounced for firms that are owned mainly by arms-length shareholders.[2] Controlling shareholders also care less about short-term undervaluation of their stocks due to long-term equity holdings and therefore reduce the importance of dividend signaling. Controlling shareholders are also likely to care about their firms' survival and allow managers to cut dividends for years in which the firms perform poorly. Gugler (2003) provides evidence that in Austria, family-

[1]Using data from Norwegian savings banks and commercial banks, Bohren et al. (2012) document evidence that dividend payments mitigate conflicts between owners and non-owner stakeholders.

[2]Low et al. (2001) document evidence that the negative stock price reaction to dividend omissions weakens when the firm has bank debt. This result suggests that the effect of dividend signaling declines when the firm has alternative monitoring device.

controlled firms which are not subject to information asymmetry and conflicts of interest engage less in dividend smoothing than state-controlled firms which are viewed as manager-controlled firms. Michaely and Roberts (2012) find that in the UK, public firms smooth dividends more than private companies, suggesting that diffused ownership structures are an important cause of dividend smoothing. These discussions lead to the following hypothesis.

Hypothesis 1 *Ownership concentration is negatively related to dividend smoothing.*

Previous studies have suggested that tax treatments on dividend income affect corporate dividend policy (Lasfer 1996; Chetty and Saez 2005; Lee et al. 2006; Brown et al. 2007; Pattenden and Twite 2008; Henry 2011; Alzahrani and Lasfer 2012). These findings naturally raise the question of whether or not tax treatments affect dividend smoothing (Chemmanur et al. 2010). Among the issues surrounding tax treatments (e.g., tax clientele effects and impacts of tax rate change), we place emphasis on the degree of double taxation on dividend income. Pattenden and Twite (2008) show evidence that gross dividend payments in Australian firms became more volatile after the introduction of the imputation system, in which shareholders could receive tax credits for taxes the corporation paid on distributed income. US firm dividend smoothing behaviors are potentially attributable to the fact that the US adopts a classical tax system, in which shareholders are subject to double taxation. We raise the following hypothesis to examine these ideas.

Hypothesis 2 *Firms located in countries with a classical tax system smooth dividends more than firms in countries that provide tax benefits on dividend income.*

International data show wide variations in ownership structures and tax regimes and therefore serve as good research material to examine our hypotheses. La Porta et al. (1999) suggest that the degree of ownership concentration differs considerably across countries. We adopt percentage ownership by the largest shareholder as a measure of ownership concentration. As mentioned, the classical tax system is adopted in the USA, while several countries (e.g., France and Spain) adopt a partial imputation system in which shareholders receive tax credits for part of the taxes the company pays, and other countries (e.g., Australia) provide tax credits for all the tax the company pays (full imputation system). Following previous studies, we adopt two dummy variables indicating the country tax regime: D_PI (one for countries with partial imputation systems and zero for others) and D_FI (one for countries with full imputation systems and zero for others) (La Porta et al. 2000; von Eije and Megginson 2008; Alzahrani and Lasfer 2012). See Table 3.1 for the definition of variables. Countries' tax regime information is available from the OECD tax database (www.oecd.org/ctp/taxdatabase) as well as from Endres et al. (2010).

There are several non-US studies on dividend smoothing behaviors. Andres et al. (2009) find German firms have a SOA for target dividends ranging from 0.21 to 0.49. Chemmanur et al. (2010) investigate Hong Kong companies that operate under no tax disadvantage and have more concentrated ownership structures. They show

Table 3.1 Definition of variables

Variable	Definition
$SOA_{Lintner}$	The firm's speed of adjustment for the target dividend level, which is obtained by OLS estimation of Eq. (3.2). At maximum, 11-year data during the period 2001–2011 are used for the estimation
SOA_{LM}	The firm's speed of adjustment for the target dividend level, which is obtained by OLS estimation of Eq. (3.3). At maximum, 11-year data during the period 2001–2011 are used for the estimation
LOWN	Percentage ownership by the largest shareholder. We use the total percentage ownership when it is available, which includes indirect ownership as well as direct ownership. When the total percentage ownership is unavailable, direct ownership is used
D_PI	Dummy variable that takes a value of one for companies located in a country with the partial imputation system. We treat the partial inclusion system as a partial imputation system. We classified Italy that adopts both classical and partial imputation systems as a classical system country
D_FI	Dummy variable that takes a value of one for companies located in a country with the full imputation system. We classify Greece (no shareholder taxation) as a full imputation country
Revised-ADRI	Revised anti-director right index proposed by Djankov et al. (2008)
LnAsset	Natural logarithm of the firm's average total assets during 2001–2011
LEVER	The firm's average leverage during the period 2001–2011. Leverage is computed by total liabilities over total assets
CASH	The firm's average cash holdings during the period 2001–2011. Cash holdings are computed as cash and marketable securities divided by total assets
AvROA	The firm's average ROA during the period 2001–2011. We compute ROA as EBIT divided by total assets
SALESGROW	The firm's average annual sales growth rate during the period 2001–2011
ROARISK	The firm's standard deviation of ROA during the period 2001–2011
TANGIBLE	The firm's average of net PPE (plants, property, and equipment) divided by total assets during the period 2001–2011

evidence that Hong Kong companies have a higher SOA than US firms. However, applying statistical analyses to investigate the relation between agency conflicts, tax treatments, and dividend smoothing in a single country or across a few countries is difficult as the variations in ownership structure and tax system are limited.

3.2.2 *Dividend Smoothing Measures*

Lintner (1956) originally presented the following partial adjustment model of dividend payments:

$$D_{it} - D_{it-1} = \alpha + \beta(D_{it}^{*} - D_{it-1}) + u_{it},$$

where D is the actual dividend payment and D^* is the target dividend level computed by the net income times the target payout ratio. β represents the SOA. Since the target payout ratio is unknown to researchers, many previous studies including Lintner (1956) estimate β by using the following equations:

$$\Delta D_{it} = a + bE_{it} + cD_{it-1} + v_{it} \tag{3.1}$$

$$D_{it} = d + eE_{it} + fD_{it-1} + w_{it} \tag{3.2}$$

where E is net income. Under the Eq. (3.1), the SOA is estimated as $-\hat{c}$, while it is $1 - \hat{f}$ under Eq. (3.2). Under the Eq. (3.1), the target payout ratio is calculated as $-\mathrm{b}/\hat{c}$, while it is $-\mathrm{b}/(1-\hat{f})$ under Eq. (3.2). Although models (1) and (2) have been commonly used in previous studies, Leary and Michaely (2011) point out that these models suffer from the small sample bias in AR(1) models. Alternatively, they propose the following model to estimate the SOA:

$$\Delta D_{it} = g + h(\hat{D}^*_{it} - D_{it-1}) + x_{it}, \tag{3.3}$$

where $\hat{D}^*_{it}$ is computed as the median payout ratio of the during the period multiplied by net income. Although estimations of Eq. (3.3) successfully avoid the bias associated with AR(1) models, it depends highly on the assumption that the median payout ratio represents the firm's target payout ratio. However, Lintner (1956) suggests that firms only gradually adjust dividend payments toward the target ratio. This means that the median payout ratio can be far from the true target payout ratio. This fact suggests that Eq. (3.3) is also subject to estimation biases. To present robust evidence, we estimate SOA by using model (2) as well as model (3). The estimated SOAs are denoted by $\mathrm{SOA}_{\mathrm{Lintner}}$ and $\mathrm{SOA}_{\mathrm{LM}}$, respectively.

3.3 Sample Selection and Data

We construct our initial sample from the Osiris database provided by Bureau van Dijk Electronic Publishing. This database includes financial data of listed companies around the world as well as ownership structure data. We limit our attention to nonfinancial companies in countries for which the dividend tax regime is available from the OECD database and Endres et al. (2010). We also delete countries from our analyses for which a revised anti-director right index (ADRI) is unavailable from Djankov et al. (2008). Financial data for those companies during the period 2000–2011 are obtained from the Osiris database. Our initial sample companies are also required to satisfy the following conditions: (a) data on dividends (both during current and previous years) and net income are available for at least 5 years during the period 2001–2011; (b) pay dividends for at least 3 years during the sample period; and (c) report positive net income for at least 3 years during the period.

Besides, we delete companies located in countries in which less than ten companies meet the aforementioned criteria. We estimate SOA_{Lintner} and SOA_{LM} for each of the initial sample companies by OLS estimations of models (2) and (3) (a maximum 11-year data for the period 2001–2011 are used for the estimation). These procedures leave 8,062 companies from 28 countries as our initial sample.

The Osiris database provides us with shareholder information for individual companies including direct and total ownership levels. Direct ownership simply indicates the level of direct shareholdings of each shareholder, whereas total ownership is the sum of the direct and indirect shareholdings. It is well known that controlling shareholders can keep substantial control rights of a firm (e.g., firm X) through indirect shareholdings in which the shareholder holds substantial shares of another company that directly holds shares of firm X. In this research, we identify each shareholder's percentage ownership by the total ownership, while we use the direct ownership when the total ownership is unavailable. Our access was limited to shareholder information for 2009 and subsequent years. The following analyses use year 2009 data for the firm's ownership structure. We delete 883 companies due to lack of ownership variables; 7,179 firms from 28 countries are left in our sample.

We estimate SOA for each of those companies and construct a SOA database that includes one figure per company. Since the distribution of estimated SOA is highly skewed, we treat SOA variables higher (lower) than the 99th percentile (1st percentile) as missing values. This procedure eliminates 231 companies (6,948 firms remain in the sample). To test Hypothesis 1, we define the maximum value of the firm's shareholders' percentage ownership as largest shareholder ownership (LOWN). We predict LOWN to be positively associated with SOA.

We also include several control variables that potentially affect corporate dividend policy. Firm size is represented by the natural logarithm of the firm's average assets during the period 2001–2011 (LnASSET) (Grullon and Michaely 2002; Fenn and Liang 2001; Cuny et al. 2009; Leary and Michaely 2011). Several previous studies suggest that leverage influences corporate dividend policy and we compute it as the firm's average of total liabilities over assets (LEVER) (Fenn and Liang 2001; Cuny et al. 2009). Cash-rich firms are subject to free cash flow problems and therefore need to pay high, stable dividends. Alternatively, cash-rich firms will be able to increase dividends more frequently than cash-poor companies. To test these ideas, we use cash and marketable securities divided by assets (CASH) (DeAngelo et al. 2006; Brockman and Unlu 2009). Firms' profitability and risk, which are measured by the average ROA (AvROA) and the standard deviation of ROA (ROARISK) during the period (we compute ROA as EBIT divided by assets), also affect dividend policy (Jagannathan et al. 2000; Fenn and Liang 2001; Grullon and Michaely 2002; DeAngelo et al. 2006; Denis and Osobov 2008; Chay and Suh 2009). We also adopt beta as a risk measure instead of ROARISK and obtain qualitatively the same results. To control for firms' growth opportunities, we adopt the firm's mean of annual percentage sales growth during the period (SALESGROW) (La Porta et al. 2000; DeAngelo et al. 2006; Cuny et al. 2009). Our main results are materially unchanged when we replace SALESGROW by the market-to-book ratio. Finally, asset tangibility (net PPE divided by assets; denoted by TANGIBLE) is included to represent the degree of information asymmetry (Leary and Michaely 2011).

We find that some control variables have highly skewed distributions (LEVER; Av_ROA; ROARISK; SALESGROW). We treat the top and bottom one percent values of these variables as missing values. We also delete companies for which those control variables are not obtained. As a result of these procedures, 6,311 companies from 28 countries are selected as our entire sample.

3.4 Empirical Results

3.4.1 Firm-Level Analyses

To test our hypotheses, we implement firm-level regression analyses of SOA. The key independent variables are LOWN, D_PI, and D_FI. Given that La Porta et al. (1998) suggest ownership concentration is associated with legal investor protection, we include the revised anti-director right index (ADRI) proposed by Djankov et al. (2008). This variable is important because La Porta et al. (2000) and others show evidence that legal investor protection affects payout levels (Brockman and Unlu 2009; Alzahrani and Lasfer 2012; Ferris et al. 2009). We also include variables presented in Sect. 3.3 to control for various firm characteristics.

Table 3.2 presents firm-level descriptive statistics. The mean SOA ranges from 0.39 to 0.53, suggesting that the worldwide average firm engages in dividend smoothing, but the adjustment speed is higher than that of US companies reported in previous studies. Untablulated results show that US companies are the slowest to adjust dividends in the world regardless of the SOA measure. Twenty or more countries have SOA that is double or more of SOA in the US. Those figures suggest that the well-documented dividend smoothing is not a universal phenomenon.

Our regression results are presented in Table 3.3. Since SOA is likely correlated among firms within a single country, we compute standard errors by using country-clustering robust standard errors in OLS estimations. To address potential biases from the correlations within a country, we also employ country-fixed effects model estimations (although the model does not generate coefficients on country-level variables like the tax regime dummies). Regardless of the choice of dependent variable and estimation method, Table 3.3 carries a positive and significant coefficient on LOWN, which supports Hypothesis 1. Controlling shareholders require less to smooth dividends for the purpose of mitigating agency costs and sending signals because they are well informed and have various ways to monitor management. The result is consistent with the information asymmetry-based explanation of dividend smoothing.

This table presents descriptive statistics of the variables. See Table 3.1 for definition of the variables.

Table 3.2 Descriptive statistics

Variable	Mean	Standard deviation	Minimum	Median	Maximum	*N*
$SOA_{Lintner}$	0.536	0.422	−0.549	0.490	1.870	6,311
SOA_{LM}	0.393	0.350	−0.270	0.306	1.492	6,311
Target payout ratio (Eq. 3.2)	0.245	0.520	−3.104	0.172	3.524	6,311
Median payout ratio	0.328	0.230		0.291	1.274	6,311
LOWN	0.207	0.223		0.097	1.000	6,311
Total assets (million US dollars)	3,800	16,600	2.614	439.916	676,000	6,311
LEVER	0.142	0.121		0.116	0.569	6,311
CASH	0.136	0.116	0.000	0.105	0.829	6,311
AvROA	0.073	0.058	−0.079	0.063	0.352	6,311
SALESGROW	0.131	0.150	−0.080	0.093	1.346	6,311
ROARISK	0.056	0.050	0.008	0.041	0.470	6,311
TANGIBLE	0.299	0.200	−0.012	0.267	0.993	6,311

OLS estimations in Table 3.3 engender a positive and significant coefficient on D_PI and D_FI. Consistent with Hypothesis 2, D_FI has larger coefficients than D_PI, which suggests that companies located in the classical tax system smooth dividends the most, followed by those in the partial imputation system, and then by those under the full imputation system. The estimated coefficient suggests that firms located in the full (partial) imputation tax system have 20–28% (8–13%) higher SOA than those with the same characteristics located in the classical tax system; the tax effect on dividend smoothing is economically large. Overall, we argue that ownership concentration and tax regimes are strongly associated with dividend smoothing policy. Previous studies have suggested that US firms smooth dividends but that this payout policy is not necessarily universal. Our evidence suggests that this fact is attributable to low ownership concentration and the classical tax system.

This table indicates regression results of SOA measures ($SOA_{Lintner}$; SOA_{LM}). In the OLS estimation, *t*-statistics are computed by using country-clustering robust standard errors. See Table 3.1 for definition of the variables.

With respect to control variables, Table 3.3 suggests that well-performing (high AvROA) companies have high SOA_{LM}. It is likely that profitable companies tend to pay high dividends and therefore need less to provide stable dividends. Large companies tend to smooth dividends, a result that is consistent with Leary and Michaely's (2011) US findings but inconsistent with the idea that firms suffering information asymmetry tend to smooth dividends. A plausible interpretation is that large companies tend to view a certain amount of dividend payments as a strong commitment to shareholders. SALESGROW has a positive and significant coefficient, suggesting that growing companies adjust dividends quickly to the long-term target.

Table 3.3 Regression results

Dependent variable	$SOA_{Lintner}$				SOA_{LM}			
	(1)		(2)		(3)		(13.1)	
	OLS		Country-fixed effects		OLS		Country-fixed effects	
	Coefficient	t-value	Coefficient	t-value	Coefficient	t-value	Coefficient	t-value
LOWN	0.215[a]	2.94	0.079[b]	2.23	0.176[a]	3.27	0.081[c]	2.73
D_PI	0.131[b]	2.58			0.083[b]	2.18		
D_FI	0.278[a]	3.58			0.201[a]	3.42		
Revised-ADRI	−0.035	−0.87			−0.028	−0.98		
LnASSET	−0.039[a]	−6.05	−0.025[a]	−8.9	−0.025[a]	−3.78	−0.014[a]	−3.93
LEVER	0.077	0.62	0.060	0.68	0.035	0.33	0.023	0.24
CASH	0.111	1.00	0.150[b]	2.11	0.021	0.22	0.059	0.95
SALESGROW	0.110[b]	2.25	0.030	0.67	0.179[a]	3.95	0.105[a]	3.24
AvROA	0.343	1.36	0.268	1.44	1.253[a]	4.66	1.159[a]	6.07
ROARISK	−0.610[b]	−2.47	−0.271	−1.45	−0.578[a]	−2.90	−0.356[c]	−1.74
TANGIBLE	0.067	1.28	0.049	1.67	0.052	1.21	0.033	1.01
Constant	1.108[a]	4.78	0.920[a]	18.93	0.668[a]	4.01	0.512[a]	6.75
Industry dummy	Yes		Yes		Yes		Yes	
Adj.R2	0.15		0.03		0.182		0.06	
N	6,311		6,311		6,311		6,311	

[a]Significant at the 1% level [b]Significant at the 5% level [c]Significant at the 10% level

1. *Asymmetry of SOA*

Leary and Michaely (2011) show that US firms adjust dividends more quickly when they should increase dividends than when they can decrease. We estimate SOA separately for firm-years in which the previous year's dividends are higher than the target dividend level and those in the opposite situation to further examine the effects of ownership concentration and tax regime on dividend smoothing. Specifically, we estimate the following model for all sample companies (Leary and Michaely 2011):

$$\Delta D_{\mathrm{it}} = g + h_{\mathrm{Inc}}(\hat{D}^*_{\mathrm{it}} - D_{\mathrm{it-1}}) \times I_{\mathrm{Inc}} + h_{\mathrm{Dec}}(\hat{D}^*_{\mathrm{it}} - D_{\mathrm{it-1}}) \times I_{\mathrm{Dec}} + x_{\mathrm{it}}, \quad (3.4)$$

where I_{Inc} is a binary variable that takes a value of one when the firm should increase dividends ($\hat{D}^*_{it} > D_{it-1}$) and zero otherwise ($\hat{D}^*_{\mathrm{it}} < D_{\mathrm{it-1}}$). I_{Dec} is a similar indicator variable that takes a value of one when the firm can decrease dividends ($\hat{D}^*_{\mathrm{it}} > D_{\mathrm{it-1}}$). As with the Eq. (3.3) estimation, we employ the firm's median payout ratio to compute $\hat{D}^*_{\mathrm{it}}$. Firms whose median payout ratio is zero are excluded from the estimation of Eq. (13.1). We also delete firm-years in which $\hat{D}^*_{\mathrm{it}}$ equals $D_{\mathrm{it-1}}$.

Panel A of Table 3.4 presents summary statistics of $\mathrm{SOA_{Inc}}$ ($\hat{h}_{\mathrm{Inc}}$) and $\mathrm{SOA_{Dec}}$($\hat{h}_{\mathrm{Dec}}$). As with Leary and Michaely (2011), we find that the SOA is higher when the firm should increase dividends (the mean is 0.42) than for firm-years when it can decrease them (the mean is 0.36).

Panel B of Table 3.4 presents regression results of $\mathrm{SOA_{Inc}}$ and $\mathrm{SOA_{Dec}}$. It shows that LOWN has a positive and significant coefficient in the regression of $\mathrm{SOA_{Dec}}$ (models (3) and (4)), while it has an insignificant coefficient in the regression of $\mathrm{SOA_{Inc}}$ (models (1) and (2)). Although firms with controlling shareholders do not quickly increase dividends for years in which they perform well, those firms decrease dividends quickly when the target dividends are lower than the previous year's dividends. This result suggests that controlling shareholders care less about dividend cuts, because they have mechanisms in place to monitor management, and managers do not need to pay dividends to mitigate agency problems (there is no strong commitment regarding dividend payments). Another explanation is that controlling shareholders care about the firm's survival and thus allow management to decrease dividends.

With respect to other variables, AvROA has a significantly positive impact on SOA only when the firm can decrease dividends, suggesting that poorly performing companies tend to cut dividends quickly. Growing companies tend to rapidly increase dividends, especially when the target dividends are higher than the previous year. We do not find clear evidence that firm size affects dividend smoothing in an asymmetric manner.

Panel A indicates summary statistics for $\mathrm{SOA_{Inc}}$ and $\mathrm{SOA_{Dec}}$. $\mathrm{SOA_{Inc}}$ ($\mathrm{SOA_{Dec}}$) is the speed of dividend adjustment when the target dividend level is higher (lower) than previous year dividends. Panel B indicates regression results of $\mathrm{SOA_{Inc}}$ and $\mathrm{SOA_{Dec}}$, respectively. t-statistics are computed by using country-clustering robust standard errors. See Table 3.1 for definition of the variables.

Table 3.4 Asymmetric SOA

Panel A: summary statistics

	Mean	Standard deviation	Minimum	Median	Maximum	N
SOA_{Inc}	0.422	0.884	−5.012	0.321	5.288	5,844
SOA_{Dec}	0.358	0.580	−1.990	0.231	2.900	5,844

Panel B: regression of SOA

	SOA_{Inc}				SOA_{Dec}			
	(1)		(2)		(3)		(13.1)	
	OLS		Country-fixed effects		OLS		Country-fixed effects	
	Coefficient	t-value	Coefficient	t-value	Coefficient	t-value	Coefficient	t-value
LOWN	0.141	1.58	−0.010	−0.14	0.227[a]	3.82	0.131[a]	3.74
D_PI	0.051	0.83			0.111[b]	2.21		
D_FI	0.263[b]	2.38			0.243[a]	3.60		
Revised-ADRI	−0.064	−1.17			−0.001	−0.03		
LnASSET	−0.028[b]	−2.30	−0.014	−1.55	−0.027[a]	−3.73	−0.015[a]	−3.23
LEVER	−0.077	−0.52	0.003	0.02	0.049	0.41	0.004	0.04
CASH	−0.106	−0.56	−0.171	−1.12	−0.007	−0.05	0.053	0.48
SALESGROW	0.427[a]	3.36	0.307[b]	2.35	−0.003	−0.04	−0.084	−1.48
AvROA	0.011	0.03	0.073	0.25	1.542[a]	4.78	1.422[a]	6.51
ROARISK	0.121	0.39	0.664[b]	2.58	−0.502	−1.49	−0.312	−0.9
TANGIBLE	0.033	0.40	−0.020	−0.24	0.070	1.03	0.042	0.73
Constant	1.086[a]	2.91	0.810[a]	4.86	0.351[c]	1.75	0.294[a]	2.91
Industry dummy	Yes		Yes		Yes		Yes	
Adj.R2	0.04		0.01		0.08		0.17	
N	5,844		5,844		5,844		5,844	

[a]Significant at the 1% level
[b]Significant at the 5% level
[c]Significant at the 10% level

3.5 Conclusion

Previous studies have argued that US firms slowly adjust dividend levels to the long-term target. However, it is still unclear whether dividend smoothing is a universal phenomenon and what factors are associated with this behavior. To address this issue, we investigate the relationship between SOA, corporate ownership structure, and tax regime by using approximately 6,000 companies from 28 countries.

Our data present evidence that the percentage ownership held by the largest shareholder is positively (negatively) associated with SOA (dividend smoothing). Especially, firms with controlling shareholders adjust dividends quickly when the target dividend level is below the previous year's dividend. The results support the agency theory of dividend smoothing as well as the idea that controlling shareholders care about the survival of their companies. We also find that companies located in a classical tax system smooth dividends more than companies in a partial or full imputation system. Overall, we argue that ownership structure and tax regime have a significant impact on dividend smoothing behaviors.

Previous studies have suggested that non-US companies smooth dividends less than US companies (e.g., Andres et al. 2009; Chemmanur et al. 2010), and we confirm this result by using broader international data and presenting a convincing argument for why US firms smooth dividends; it is attributable to less concentrated ownership structures and the classical tax system. Recent papers intensively use international data to examine corporate dividend policy (La Porta et al. 2000; Brockman and Unlu 2009; Ferris et al. 2009; Alzahrani and Lasfer 2012; Fatemi and Bildik 2012; Kuo et al. 2013; Breuer et al. 2014), and we extend this trend to research on dividend smoothing as proposed by Lintner (1956).

Acknowledgements An earlier version of this paper was presented to the Asian Finance Association's annual meeting, Midwest Finance Association annual meeting, and Japan Finance Association annual meeting. We thank Jeffrey Coles, Wolfgang Drobetz, Toshinori Sasaki, and Jin Yu for their helpful comments and suggestions. This research is financially supported by JSPS KAKENHI Grant Number 15H03367.

References

Alzahrani, M., and M. Lasfer. 2012. Investor protection, taxation, and dividends. *Journal of Corporate Finance* 18:745–762.

Andres, C., A. Betzer, M. Goergen, and L. Renneboog. 2009. Dividend policy of German firms: A panel data analysis of partial adjustment models. *Journal of Empirical Finance* 16:175–187.

Bhattacharya, S. 1979. "The bird in the hand" fallacy. *Bell Journal of Economics* 10:259–270.

Bohren, O., Josefsen, M.G., and P.E. Steen. 2012. Stakeholder conflicts and dividend policy. *Journal of Banking and Finance* 36:2852–2864.

Brav, A., J.R. Graham, C.R. Harvey, and R. Michaely. 2005. Payout policy in the 21st century. *Journal of Financial Economics* 77:483–527.

Breuer, W., M.O. Rieger, and K.C. Soypak. 2014. The behavioral foundations of corporate dividend policy a cross-country analysis. *Journal of Banking and Finance* 42:247–265.

Brockman, P., and E. Unlu. 2009. Dividend policy, creditor rights, and the agency costs of debt. *Journal of Financial Economics* 92:276–299.
Brown, J.R., N. Liang, and S. Weisbenner. 2007. Executive financial incentives and payout policy: Firms responses to the 2003 dividend tax cut. *Journal of Finance* 62:1935–1965.
Chay, J.B., and J. Suh. 2009. Payout policy and cash-flow uncertainty. *Journal of Financial Economics* 93:88–107.
Chemmanur, T.J., J. He, G. Hu, and H. Liu. 2010. Is dividend universal? New insights from a comparative study of dividend policies in Hong Kong and the US. *Journal of Corporate Finance* 16:413–430.
Chetty, R., and E. Saez. 2005. Dividend taxes and corporate behavior: Evidence from the 2003 dividend tax cut. *Quarterly Journal of Economics* 120:791–833.
Cuny, C.J., G.S. Martin, and J.J. Puthenpurackal. 2009. Stock options and total payout. *Journal of Financial and Quantitative Analysis* 44:391–410.
DeAngelo, H., L. DeAngelo, and R. Stulz. 2006. Dividend policy and the earned/contributed capital mix: A test of the life-cycle theory. *Journal of Financial Economics* 81:227–254.
Denis, D.J., and I. Osobov. 2008. Why do firms pay dividends? International evidence on the determinants of dividend policy. *Journal of Financial Economics* 89:62–82.
Dewenter, K.L., and V.A. Warther. 1998. Dividends, asymmetric information, and agency conflicts: Evidence from a comparison of the dividend policies of Japanese and U.S. firms. *Journal of Finance* 53:879–904.
Djankov, S., R. La Porta, F. Lopez-de-Silanes, and A. Shleifer. 2008. The law and economics of self-dealing. *Journal of Financial Economics* 88:430–465.
Easterbrook, F.H. 1984. Two agency-cost explanations of dividends. *American Economic Review* 74:650–659.
Endres, D., C. Fuest, and C. Spengel. 2010. *Company taxation in the Asia-Pacific region, India, and Russia*. Berlin/Heidelberg: Springer.
Fama, E.F., and H. Babiak. 1968. Dividend policy: An empirical analysis. *Journal of the American Statistical Association* 63:1132–1161.
Fatemi, A., and R. Bildik. 2012. Yes, dividends are disappearing: Worldwide evidence. *Journal of Banking and Finance* 36:662–677.
Fenn, G.W., and N. Liang. 2001. Corporate payout policy and managerial stock incentives. *Journal of Financial Economics* 60:45–72.
Ferris, S.P., N. Jayaraman, and S. Sabherwal. 2009. Catering effects in corporate dividend policy: The international evidence. *Journal of Banking and Finance* 33:1730–1738.
Grullon, G., and R. Michaely. 2002. Dividends, share repurchases, and the substitution hypothesis. *Journal of Finance* 57:1649–1684.
Gugler, T. 2003. Corporate governance, dividend payout policy, and the interrelation between dividends, R&D, and capital investment. *Journal of Banking and Finance* 27:1297–1321.
Guttman, I., O. Kadan, and E. Kandel. 2010. Dividend stickiness and strategic pooling. *Review of Financial Studies* 23:4455–4495.
Henry, D. 2011. Ownership structure and tax-friendly dividends. *Journal of Banking and Finance* 35:2747–2760.
Jagannathan, M., C.P. Stephens, and M.S. Weisbach. 2000. Financial flexibility and the choice between dividends and stock repurchases. *Journal of Financial Economics* 57:355–384.
Jensen, M.C. 1986. Agency costs of free cash flow, corporate finance, and takeovers. *American Economic Review* 76:323–329.
John, K., and J. Williams. 1985. Dividends, dilution, and taxes: A signaling Equilibrium. *Journal of Finance* 40:1053–1070.
Khan, T. 2006. Company dividends and ownership structure: Evidence from UK panel data. *Economic Journal* 116: C172–C189.
Kumar, P. 1988. Shareholder-manager conflict and the information content of dividends. *Review of Financial Studies* 1:111–136.
Kumar, P., and B. Lee. 2001. Discrete dividend policy with permanent earnings. *Financial Management* 30:55–76.

Kuo, J.-M., D. Philip, and Q. Zhang. 2013. What drives disappearing dividend phenomenon? *Journal of Banking and Finance* 37:3499–3514.

La Porta, R., F. Lopez-de-Silanes, A. Shleifer, and R.W. Vishny. 1998. Law and finance. *Journal of Political Economy* 106:1113–1155.

La Porta, R., F. Lopez-de-Silanes, and A. Shleifer. 1999. Corporate ownership around the world. *Journal of Finance* 54:471–518.

La Porta, R., F. Lopez-De-Silanes, A. Shleifer, and R.W. Vishny. 2000. Agency problems and dividend policies around the World. *Journal of Finance* 55:1–33.

Lasfer, M.A. 1996. Taxes and dividends: The UK evidence. *Journal of Banking and Finance* 20:455–472.

Leary, M.T., and R. Michaely. 2011. Determinants of dividend smoothing: Empirical evidence. *Review of Financial Studies* 24:3198–3249.

Lee, Y.T., Y.J. Liu, R. Roll, and A. Subrahmanyam. 2006. Taxes and dividend clientele: Evidence from trading and ownership structure. *Journal of Banking and Finance* 30:229–246.

Lintner, J. 1956. Distribution of incomes of corporations among dividends, retained earnings, and taxes. *American Economic Review* 46:97–113.

Low, S.-W., L. Glorfeld, D. Hearth, and J.N. Rimbey. 2001. The link between bank monitoring and corporate dividend policy: The case of dividend omissions. *Journal of Banking and Finance* 25:2069–2087.

Michaely, R., and M.R. Roberts. 2012. Corporate dividend policies: Lessons from private firms. *Review of Financial Studies* 25:712–746.

Miller, M.H., and K. Rock. 1985. Dividend policy under asymmetric information. *Journal of Finance* 40:1031–1051.

Mueller, D.C. 1967. The firm decision process: An econometric investigation. *Quarterly Journal of Economics* 81:58–87.

Pattenden, K., and G. Twite. 2008. Taxes and dividend policy under alternative tax regimes. *Journal of Corporate Finance* 14:1–16.

Shleifer, A., and R.W. Vishny. 1997. A survey of corporate governance. *Journal of Finance* 52:737–783.

von Eije, H., and W.L. Megginson. 2008. Dividends and share repurchases in the European union. *Journal of Financial Economics* 89:347–374.

Chapter 4
Economic Evaluation of Japanese Attorney Fees

Yasuhiro Ikeda

4.1 Introduction

The Japanese judicial system does not differ greatly from those of most other civil law countries (Ota 2001). Especially in terms of allocating litigation costs between plaintiffs and defendants, Japanese rules of cost allocation in litigation resemble the American rules. The American rules hold that each party is responsible for paying their own attorney fees. In contrast, there is an allocation rule of costs between a client and one's own attorney can be used. That is mainly a contingent fee contractual arrangement, which is very common in the United States, especially for tort litigation. Under a contingent fee, a client is charged for an attorney's services only if the lawsuit is successful. That is, a client pays a percentage (usually one-third) of the recovery to the attorney.[1] However, as for allocating costs between a defendant and an attorney, the Japanese legal system differs from the American system. It is a reverse contingent fee. The reverse contingent fee is one by which a defense attorney's compensation depends in part on how much money his attorney saves the defendant: the lower the judgment given, the higher the attorney's fee (Garner 2009). Actually, reverse contingent fees are prohibited or substantially restricted in many other common law and civil law legal systems (Rubinfeld and Scotchmer 1998). In Japan, however, deregulation of attorney's fees began in 2004

[1]See Miceli (2004) and Kakalik and Pace (1986) reported a US survey showing that 96% of individual plaintiff attorneys in tort litigation paid their attorneys on a contingency basis, but almost all the defendants' attorneys were paid according to an hourly rate.

Y. Ikeda (✉)
Kumamoto University, Kumamoto, Japan
e-mail: ikeyasu@kumamoto-u.ac.jp

T. Naito et al. (eds.), *Applied Approaches to Societal Institutions and Economics*,
New Frontiers in Regional Science: Asian Perspectives 18,
DOI 10.1007/978-981-10-5663-5_4

by the Judicial Reform of Japan. Therefore, reverse contingent fees are not banned under the Japanese legal system (Japan Federation of Bar Association 2008).

Earlier reports of the literature describe no study of models in which both clients hire their own attorneys on a contingent fee basis, except for one report by Baik (2008). Baik (2008) models a situation in which each litigant (a plaintiff and defendant) hires an attorney under fixed and contingent fees. In his article, all players are risk neutral and attorney abilities are equal. The model includes two legal systems with a nonnegative fixed fee constraint and with the contingent fee cap. Results show that the system with the nonnegative fixed fee gives rent to the attorneys, but the system with the contingent fee cap leaves the rent to the client (plaintiff and defendant).

This article attempts to analyze actual Japanese attorney's fee system theoretically. We model each client (plaintiff and defendant) as offering compensation to its own attorney (agent) on a contingent fee basis. In this article, different from Baik (2008), we model each litigant as hiring its own attorney without those constraints. In addition, attorney abilities are not equal.

We organize this article as follows. Section 4.2 presents the civil litigation model. Section 4.3 shows the determination of attorney fees. Section 4.4 presents a model of fixed and contingent fees with risk attitude. Finally, we present concluding remarks.

4.2 The Model

Our model has one plaintiff with her attorney (p-attorney) and one defendant with his attorney (d-attorney). Attorneys make effort for the respective litigants in context in civil litigation, under the fee rule by which each party is responsible for paying its own attorney's fees.

The plaintiff hires the p-attorney to receive compensation for her own damages, filing a suit against the defendant. The defendant hires the d-attorney to defend against the plaintiff's lawsuit. Damages from the plaintiff claims are denoted by V (> 0) and are observable to all players. The effort level of the p-attorney is represented as x_p (≥ 0) and is observable only to the p-attorney herself; that of the d-attorney is x_d (≥ 0) observable only to the d-attorney himself. The marginal cost of the efforts are, respectively, c_p (≥ 0) for the p-attorney and c_d (≥ 0) for the d-attorney. Each marginal cost stands for each attorney's ability.

We assume that civil litigation under the adversarial system is adopted at the trial.[2] The adversarial system is a procedural system where the process is party controlled. Then, the probability of prevailing for the plaintiff (of losing for the defendant) is defined as follows:

[2]See Tullock (1975, 1980), Parisi (2002), and Baik (2008).

$$p(x_p, x_d) = \begin{cases} \dfrac{x_p}{x_p + x_d} & \text{if } x_p + x_d > 0 \\ \\ \dfrac{1}{2} & \text{if } x_p + x_d = 0 \end{cases} \tag{4.1}$$

When each effort level is zero, the default degree is a half. Regarding the plaintiff side, we can describe the contingent fees by which a portion of the expected judgments pV is received by the p-attorney. On the part of the defendant side, we explain it as a portion to the d-attorney of the difference between damages claimed by the plaintiff and the expected judgments (values correspond to the degree of contribution to the d-attorney's defense). The portion of the contingent fees assigned to the p-attorney is denoted as $\beta_p \in [0, 1]$. The portion of the contingent fees assigned to the d-attorney is denoted as $\beta_d \in [0, 1]$.

We show the timing of the model. In period 0, the plaintiff and the defendant, respectively, hire attorneys simultaneously. By this timing, each attorney's ability is determined as the marginal cost of effort by each attorney. We assume the switching cost of changing the hired attorney as very high. Then, both litigants continue to hire attorneys. In period 1, the plaintiff makes a take-it-or-leave-it offer of an arrangement of a contingent fee (β_p) to the p-attorney. The defendant also makes a take-it-or-leave-it offer of (β_d) to the d-attorney simultaneously. If the offer is accepted, then the game proceeds to the next stage. Otherwise, the litigant must make an effort by itself, causing inefficiency. We assume the reservation payoff of each attorney as zero. In period 2, each attorney chooses the effort level simultaneously. Each effort level is observable only to each own attorney. Then, the court passes judgment that is observable to all players. Each attorney accepts fees according to the attorney's fee arrangement. Expected payoffs for the plaintiff and the p-attorney are denoted, respectively, as Π_p and π_p. Because the contingent fee to the p-attorney is the portion of the expected gains, we describe the expected payoff for the plaintiff as follows:

$$\Pi_p = p(1 - \beta_p)V. \tag{4.2}$$

The expected payoff for the p-attorney is

$$\pi_p = p\beta_p V - c_p x_p. \tag{4.3}$$

We also, respectively, describe expected payoffs for the defendant and the d-attorney as Π_d and π_d. The defendant's expected stake is the difference between pV, the saved values produced by the d-attorney, and the payments V in no defense.[3] Then, because the defendant's expected stake is $V - pV$ and the defendant attorney's share is $(1 - p)\beta_d V$, the defendant's expected payoff is the following:

$$\Pi_d = (1 - p)(1 - \beta_d)V\,. \tag{4.4}$$

[3]We assume that the defendant pays V because he has no defense if defendant does not hire an attorney and assume payment pV if he hires an attorney.

The expected payoff for the d-attorney is:

$$\pi_d = (1-p)\beta_d V - c_d x_d \,. \tag{4.5}$$

Following the setting above, we use backward induction to solve the game. In period 2, each attorney expends some effort simultaneously, given that each contract of attorney's fees $(\beta_p, \ \beta_d)$ is determined. First, anticipating the level of the d-attorney's effort, the maximization problem of the p-attorney's expected payoff is the following:

$$\max_{x_p} \ \pi_p = \left(\frac{x_p}{x_p + x_d}\right)\beta_p V - c_p x_p. \tag{4.6}$$

We obtain the reaction function of the p-attorney by the first-order condition as follows:

$$x_p = -\, x_d + \sqrt{\frac{\beta_p V x_d}{c_p}}. \tag{4.7}$$

This reaction function includes the strategic complemental part and the strategic substitutive part. Next, the maximization problem of the d-attorney's expected payoff, anticipating the level of the p-attorney's effort, is the following:

$$\max_{x_d} \ \pi_d = \left(\frac{x_d}{x_p + x_d}\right)\beta_d V - c_d x_d. \tag{4.8}$$

Then, the reaction function of the d-attorney is obtained by first-order conditions as follows:

$$x_d = -\, x_p + \sqrt{\frac{\beta_d V x_p}{c_d}}. \tag{4.9}$$

Therefore, we find the following Nash equilibrium (x_p^*, x_d^*) by solving simultaneous Eqs. (4.7) and (4.9):

$$(x_p^*, \ x_d^*) = \left(\frac{\beta_p^2 \, \beta_d \, c_d V}{(\beta_p c_d + \beta_d c_p)^2}, \ \frac{\beta_p \, \beta_d^2 \, c_p V}{(\beta_p c_d + \beta_d c_p)^2}\right). \tag{4.10}$$

We examine the comparative statics of this equilibrium (4.10):

$$\frac{\partial x_p^*}{\partial V} > 0 \,, \ \frac{\partial x_d^*}{\partial V} > 0 \,, \ \frac{\partial x_p^*}{\partial \beta_p} > 0 \,, \ \frac{\partial x_d^*}{\partial \beta_d} > 0 \tag{4.11}$$

We denote the expression (4.11) as Lemma 4.1:

Lemma 4.1 *Greater damages mean that each attorney makes a greater effort. Furthermore, the higher the fraction of a contingent fee for an attorney becomes, the greater the effort expended by him.*

4.3 Determination of Attorney Fees

By anticipating the equilibrium effort level of each attorney in the second stage, each of the plaintiff and the defendant solves the expected payoff maximizing problem simultaneously in the first stage. We examine the probability of prevailing for the plaintiff and the expected payoff for the respective attorneys at the equilibrium of the second stage. Beforehand, we present a comparison of the p-attorney's and the d-attorney's marginal cost by the ratios $c_p/c_d = h$ and $c_d/c_p = k$. These ratios reflect the relative abilities of the respective attorneys. Now, substituting each equilibrium effort (4.10) in the second stage for the expression (4.1), we obtain the plaintiff's probability of prevailing in the case in equilibrium as:

$$p^*(x_p^*, x_d^*) = \frac{\beta_p}{\beta_p + h\,\beta_d}. \tag{4.12}$$

We check the comparative statics of this equilibrium as:

$$\frac{\partial p^*}{\partial \beta_p} \geq 0\ ,\ \frac{\partial p^*}{\partial \beta_d} \leq 0\ ,\ \frac{\partial p^*}{\partial h} \leq 0. \tag{4.13}$$

Therefore, in equilibrium, the higher the d-attorney's fee becomes, the more the plaintiffs' probability of prevailing falls. In contrast, the higher the p-attorney's fee becomes, the more the plaintiffs' probability of prevailing increases. Lower p-attorney ability reduces the plaintiff's probability of prevailing.

Next we examine each attorney's expected payoff. First, substituting expression (4.10) for the p-attorney's payoff (4.3), we can obtain the following form:

$$\pi_p^* = \frac{V\beta_p^3}{(\beta_p + h\beta_d)^2}\ . \tag{4.14}$$

Therefore, we obtain the following for comparative statics:

$$\frac{\partial \pi_p^*}{\partial \beta_p} > 0\ ,\ \frac{\partial \pi_p^*}{\partial \beta_d} < 0\ ,\ \frac{\partial \pi_p^*}{\partial V} > 0\ ,\ \frac{\partial \pi_p^*}{\partial h} < 0 \tag{4.15}$$

Secondly, in similar manner to that shown above, we obtain the d-attorney's expected payoff in equilibrium:

$$\pi_d^* = \frac{V\beta_d^3}{(k\beta_p + \beta_d)^2} \, . \tag{4.16}$$

The comparative statics is then derived as:

$$\frac{\partial \pi_d^*}{\partial \beta_d} > 0 \, , \; \frac{\partial \pi_d^*}{\partial \beta_p} < 0 \, , \; \frac{\partial \pi_d^*}{\partial V} > 0 \, , \; \frac{\partial \pi_d^*}{\partial k} < 0 \, . \tag{4.17}$$

We summarize this interpretation as the following lemma:

Lemma 4.2 *In equilibrium, the greater the damages, the greater the expected payoff for each attorney becomes. The higher own attorney's fees become, the greater the expected payoff for each attorney becomes. The higher the opponent attorney's fees become, the lower the expected payoff for each attorney becomes. Furthermore, in equilibrium, the higher an attorney's ability is, the greater the payoff from the attorney becomes.*

We show the first-stage solution. We consider that the contracts of the plaintiff and the defendant are satisfied with each attorney's participating constraint. First, we examine the contract of the plaintiff side. Substituting the expression (4.10) for the plaintiff's expected payoff (4.2), and assuming the reservation payoff as zero for simplicity, we obtain the maximizing problem for the plaintiff using Eq. (4.12) as shown below:

$$\max_{\beta_p} \; \Pi_p = \left(\frac{\beta_p}{\beta_p + h\beta_d} \right) (1 - \beta_p)V, \tag{4.18}$$

$$s.t. \;\; \pi_p^* = \frac{V\beta_p^3}{(\beta_p + h\beta_d)^2} \geq 0 \tag{4.19}$$

The constraint condition (4.19) is satisfied. Therefore, we can calculate the first-order condition of Eq. (4.18), throwing the condition (4.19) away. We obtain the first-order condition[4] as $\beta_p^2 + 2\beta_p\beta_d - h\beta_d = 0$. Therefore, we obtain the plaintiff's reaction function as:

$$\beta_p = -h\beta_d + \sqrt{h^2\beta_d^2 + h\beta_d}. \tag{4.20}$$

Next we examine the plaintiff's reaction function shape. Then differentiating β_p with β_d of the Eq. (4.20), we obtain the following form without difficulty: $\partial\beta_p/\partial\beta_d > 0$, $\partial^2\beta_p/\partial^2\beta_d^2 < 0$.

[4]The second-order condition can be confirmed easily.

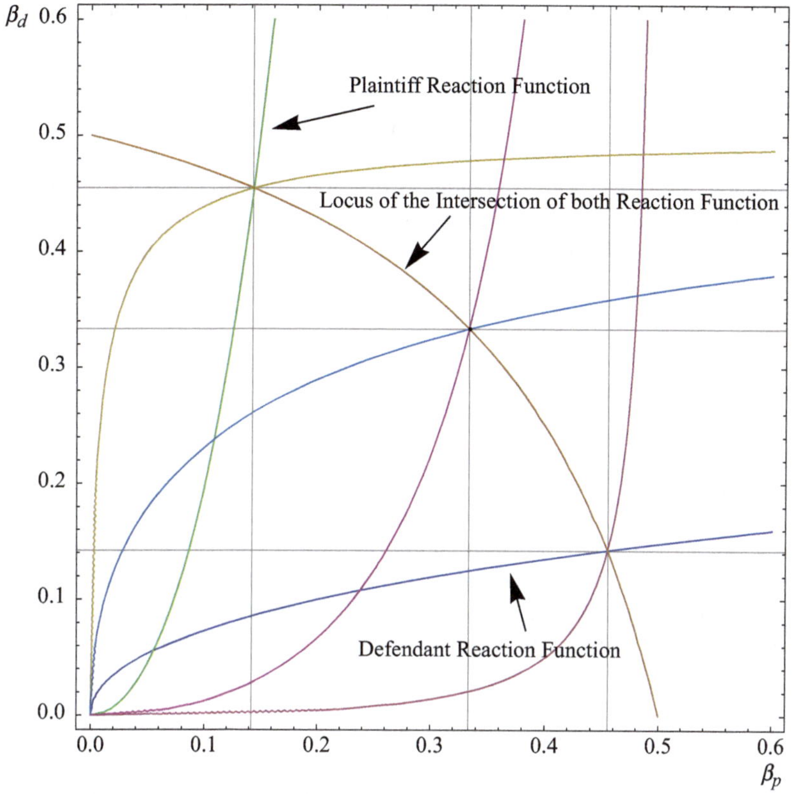

Fig. 4.1 Locus of the equilibrium

We examine the effect of parameter h on the plaintiff's reaction function:

$$\frac{\partial \beta_p}{\partial h} = \frac{2\beta_d^2 + \beta_d - 2\beta_d\sqrt{h^2\beta_d^2 + h\beta_d}}{2\sqrt{h^2\beta_d^2 + h\beta_d}} > 0 \tag{4.21}$$

The positive sign of the numerator can be confirmed without difficulty. These graphs of the plaintiff's reaction functions are presented in Fig. 4.1.

Secondly, we specifically examine the fee contract of the defendant side. We formalize the defendant's maximization problem as shown below:

$$\max_{\beta_d} \ \Pi_d = \left(\frac{\beta_d}{k\beta_p + \beta_d}\right)(1 - \beta_d)V, \tag{4.22}$$

$$s.t. \ \pi_d^* = \frac{V\beta_d^3}{(k\beta_p + \beta_d)^2} \geq 0 \tag{4.23}$$

Similarly to the method used for the plaintiff side, we obtain the defendant's reaction function in the following form:

$$\beta_d = -k\beta_p + \sqrt{k^2\beta_p^2 + k\beta_p}\ . \tag{4.24}$$

We examine the shape of the defendant's reaction function using a similar method to that presented above: β_d increases as β_p rises; marginal β_d with respect to β_p decreases because $\partial\beta_d/\partial\beta_p > 0$, $\partial^2\beta_d/\partial^2\beta_p^2 < 0$. The effect of parameter k to the defendant's reaction function is derived as follows in a similar way as that for the plaintiff's side:

$$\frac{\partial\beta_d}{\partial k} = \frac{2\beta_p^2 + \beta_p - 2\beta_p\sqrt{k^2\beta_p^2 + k\beta_p}}{2\sqrt{k^2\beta_p^2 + h\beta_p}} > 0 \tag{4.25}$$

We present these graphs of the defendant's reaction function in Fig. 4.1.

Now we should solve the Nash equilibrium for respective attorney's fees in all games. We derive the intersection of the plaintiff reaction function and the defendant reaction function. Consequently, we can obtain the locus of the intersection of both reaction functions, solving the Eqs. (4.20) and (4.24) with respect to h as follows:

$$\beta_d = \frac{2\beta_p - 1}{2\beta_p - 2} \tag{4.26}$$

This locus is presented in Fig. 4.1. We can specify the parameters now. If $h = k = 1$, i.e., $c_p = c_d$, then this case means that the p-attorney's ability is equal to that of the d-attorney. In this case, we represent $((\beta_p{}^*,\ \beta_d{}^*) = (1/3,\ 1/3))$ as the equilibrium. The locus in northwest implies that the p-attorney is superior to the d-attorney in ability. The locus in the southeast signifies the opposite. Therefore, we can understand the following properties by the comparative parameters.

$$\frac{\partial\beta_p{}^*}{\partial h} > 0,\ \frac{\partial\beta_d{}^*}{\partial h} < 0,\ \frac{\partial\beta_d{}^*}{\partial k} > 0,\ \frac{\partial\beta_p{}^*}{\partial k} < 0 \tag{4.27}$$

We summarize these results as the following proposition:

Proposition 4.1 *In equilibrium, the greater the superiority of the opponent attorney, the more likely a client is to make a fee contract with his attorney to raise attorney fees. In contrast, the more inferior the opponent attorney, the more likely a client is to make a fee contract to decrease attorney fees.*

4.4 Fixed and Contingent Fee with Risk Attitude

In this section, we introduce fixed fees (t_p for the plaintiff's side and t_d for the defendant's side) and the degree of attorney attitude with risk aversion. Then we use parameter $\theta_p \in (0, 1]$ for the p-attorney and $\theta_d \in (0, 1]$ for the d-attorney as the degree of it. These parameters being close to zero signify that the attorney is moderately risk averse. In contrast, we assume that the plaintiff and the defendant are risk neutral. Then, we solve this problem using backward induction.

We formulate the expected p-attorney payoff with risk-averse (π_p^r) as shown below:

$$\pi_p^r = \left(\frac{x_p}{x_p + x_d}\right)(\beta_p V)^{\theta_p} - c_p x_p + t_p \tag{4.28}$$

We can obtain the first-order condition as the following equation:

$$x_p = -x_d + \sqrt{\frac{x_d(\beta_p V)^{\theta_p}}{c_p}} \tag{4.29}$$

Next, the expected payoff of d-attorney with risk-averse (π_d^r) is:

$$\pi_d^r = \left(\frac{x_d}{x_p + x_d}\right)(\beta_d V)^{\theta_d} - c_d x_d + t_d. \tag{4.30}$$

The first-order condition is obtained as the following equation:

$$x_d = -x_p + \sqrt{\frac{x_p(\beta_d V)^{\theta_d}}{c_d}} \tag{4.31}$$

These reaction functions have almost identical shape to those of the previous section. We solve the Nash equilibrium in the second stage simultaneously. Then we can obtain the equilibrium effort of each attorney as $\{x_p^r, x_d^r\}$:

$$\{x_p^r, x_d^r\} = \left\{\frac{c_d(\beta_p V)^{2\theta_p}(\beta_d V)^{\theta_d}}{(c_d(\beta_p V)^{\theta_p} + c_p(\beta_d V)^{\theta_d})^2}, \frac{c_p(\beta_p V)^{\theta_p}(\beta_d V)^{2\theta_d}}{(c_d(\beta_p V)^{\theta_p} + c_p(\beta_d V)^{\theta_d})^2}\right\} \tag{4.32}$$

We can ascertain the plaintiff's winning probability (p^r), the p-attorney's expected payoff (π_p^r), and the d-attorney's expected payoff (π_d^r) by anticipating the second-stage solution as shown below:

$$p^r = \frac{x_p^r}{x_p^r + x_d^r} = \frac{(\beta_p V)^{\theta_p}}{(\beta_p V)^{\theta_p} + h(\beta_d V)^{\theta_d}} \tag{4.33}$$

$$\pi_p^r = p^r(\beta_p V)^{\theta_p} - c_p x_p^r + t_p = \frac{(\beta_p V)^{3\theta_p}}{((\beta_p V)^{\theta_p} + h(\beta_d V)^{\theta_d})^2} + t_p \tag{4.34}$$

$$\pi_d^r = (1 - p^r)(\beta_d V)^{\theta_d} - c_d x_d^r + t_d = \frac{(\beta_d V)^{3\theta_d}}{((\frac{1}{h})(\beta_p V)^{\theta_p} + (\beta_d V)^{\theta_d})^2} + t_d \tag{4.35}$$

Therefore, we can formulate the plaintiff payoff maximization problem as follows, where $\hat{\pi}_p^r$ (constant) is the reservation payoff for the p-attorney:

$$\max_{\beta_p} \Pi_p = \left(\frac{(\beta_p V)^{\theta_p}}{(\beta_p V)^{\theta_p} + h(\beta_d V)^{\theta_d}} \right) (1 - \beta_p)V - t_p \tag{4.36}$$

$$s.t. \ \pi_p^r = \frac{(\beta_p V)^{3\theta_p}}{((\beta_p V)^{\theta_p} + h(\beta_d V)^{\theta_d})^2} + t_p \geq \hat{\pi}_p^r \tag{4.37}$$

Then, binding the constraint condition to equality, we obtain the fixed fee as shown below:

$$t_p = \hat{\pi}_p^r - \frac{(\beta_p V)^{3\theta_p}}{((\beta_p V)^{\theta_p} + h(\beta_d V)^{\theta_d})^2} \tag{4.38}$$

We substitute Eq. (4.38) into the plaintiff's payoff function (4.36). Therefore, the plaintiff's payoff maximization problem is the following:

$$\max_{\beta_p} \Pi_p = \frac{(\beta_p V)^{\theta_p}}{(\beta_p V)^{\theta_p} + h(\beta_d V)^{\theta_d}} (1 - \beta_p)V - \hat{\pi}_p^r + \frac{(\beta_p V)^{3\theta_p}}{((\beta_p V)^{\theta_p} + h(\beta_d V)^{\theta_d})^2} \tag{4.39}$$

Next, we can obtain the defendant's payoff maximization problem similarly to the process used for the plaintiff, where $\hat{\pi}_d^r$ (constant) is the reservation payoff for the d-attorney:

$$\max_{\beta_d} \Pi_d = \left(\frac{(\beta_d V)^{\theta_d}}{k(\beta_p V)^{\theta_p} + (\beta_d V)^{\theta_d}} \right) (1 - \beta_d)V - t_d \tag{4.40}$$

$$s.t. \ \pi_d^r = \frac{(\beta_d V)^{3\theta_d}}{\left(k(\beta_p V)^{\theta_p} + (\beta_d V)^{\theta_d}\right)^2} + t_d \geq \hat{\pi}_d^r \tag{4.41}$$

Similarly to the plaintiff case, we bind the constraint condition to equality. Thereby, we obtain the fixed fee for the defendant in the following form:

$$t_d = \hat{\pi}_d^r - \frac{(\beta_d V)^{3\theta_d}}{\left(k(\beta_p V)^{\theta_p} + (\beta_d V)^{\theta_d}\right)^2} \tag{4.42}$$

We substitute Eq. (4.42) into the defendant's payoff function (4.40). Therefore, the defendant's payoff maximization problem is the following:

$$\max_{\beta_d} \Pi_d = \frac{(\beta_d V)^{\theta_d}}{k(\beta_p V)^{\theta_p} + (\beta_d V)^{\theta_d}}(1-\beta_d)V - \hat{\pi}_d^r + \frac{(\beta_d V)^{3\theta_d}}{\left(k(\beta_p V)^{\theta_p} + (\beta_d V)^{\theta_d}\right)^2} \quad (4.43)$$

It is necessary to derive the equilibrium in the first stage. However, in general, it would be difficult to seek them analytically unless some parameters were specified. Let us choose some specific parameters in advance as $h = 1$ $(k = 1)$, $\theta_p = \theta_d = \theta$ $(\theta \in (0, 1])$, which set each attorney's ability as equal and each attorney's risk attitude as equivalent. We then compare moderate risk aversion with slight risk aversion.

We can examine an example of two cases for attorney risk attitude: $\theta = \{\underline{\theta}, \bar{\theta}\}$ $(\underline{\theta} < \bar{\theta})$. Specifically, $\underline{\theta} = 0.5$, $\bar{\theta} = 0.75$. Taking numerical examples, one can obtain equilibrium points $(\beta_p^r, \beta_d^r) \doteqdot (0.2057,\ 0.2057)$ if $\underline{\theta} = 0.5$ and $(\beta_p^r, \beta_d^r) \doteqdot (0.3133,\ 0.3133)$ if $\bar{\theta} = 0.75$. Therefore, we understand that an inner solution is obtainable if the attorney is risk averse. Figure 4.2 shows reaction functions of the plaintiff and the defendant and two intersections of both symmetric reaction functions. The reaction functions of both the plaintiff and the defendant are strategic complements, which means that the greater the opponent's contingent fee, the greater the increase of a contingent fee on one's own side becomes under the best response. To highlight that comparison, it is apparent that the southwest symmetric point is the one by which both attorneys are moderately risk averse. Therefore, we can infer that, as θ decreases, both $(\beta_p^r,\ \beta_d^r)$ decrease, i.e., the greater the risk aversion of both attorneys becomes, the more likely the equilibrium contingent fee is to decrease.

We must address fixed fee situations. Assuming the two cases of θ above, we can compare fixed fees for attorneys' risk attitudes. In the symmetric setting presented above, we shall rewrite the equation of the fixed fee, (4.38) or (4.42) as:

$$t(\underline{\theta}) = \hat{\pi} - \frac{1}{4}\left(\underline{\beta}^r V\right)^{\underline{\theta}} \ \ \textit{if} \ \ \theta = \underline{\theta}\,, \quad t(\bar{\theta}) = \hat{\pi} - \frac{1}{4}\left(\bar{\beta}^r V\right)^{\bar{\theta}} \ \ \textit{if} \ \ \theta = \bar{\theta}. \quad (4.44)$$

where, $\beta = \underline{\beta}$ for $\underline{\theta}$, $\beta = \bar{\beta}$ for $\bar{\theta}$. Because $(\underline{\beta}V)^{\underline{\theta}} < (\bar{\beta}V)^{\bar{\theta}}$ holds if and only if $\beta V > 1$, we understand that $t(\underline{\theta})$ is greater than $t(\bar{\theta})$ if $t(\cdot)$ is positive. Therefore, in a system of the nonnegative fixed fees, the equilibrium contingent fee is lower, and the equilibrium fixed fee is higher when the attorney is moderately risk averse.

We summarize these results as the following proposition:

Proposition 4.2 *In equilibrium, when the attorney is moderately risk averse, the contingent fee is lower, and the fixed fee is higher under the condition of moderately highly reservation payoff of the attorney.*

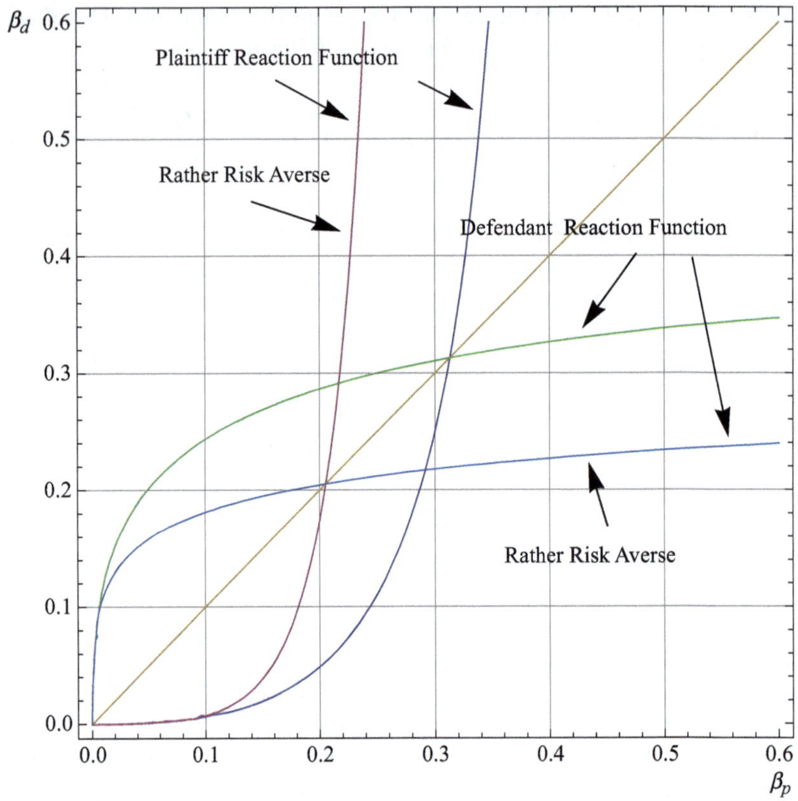

Fig. 4.2 Reaction functions with various risk attitudes

4.5 Concluding Remarks

As described herein, we have presented some examination of the Japanese attorney's fee system since deregulation of attorney's fees began in Japan in 2004. Under the Japanese attorney fee system, a plaintiff is able to use a contingent fee. A defendant is free to use a reverse contingent fee. These are features that are unique to Japan. We have produced a model in which each plaintiff and defendant offers a combination of a fixed fee and a contingent fee to an attorney without a cap and nonnegative constraint. We also have explicitly introduced attorney capabilities into the model. Results show that if the opponent attorney is superior to one's own, the client is likely to make a fee contract to raise his own attorney's fees. When the attorney is moderately risk averse, the contingent fee is likely to be lower, and the fixed fee is likely to be higher under conditions of a moderately high reservation payoff of the attorney. Further extension of the model to address settlement issues and asymmetric player situations is expected to be crucially important for our future research.

References

Baik, K.H. 2008. Attorneys' compensation in litigation with bilateral delegation. *Review of Law and Economics* 4(1):259–289.
Garner, B. (ed.). 2009. *Black's law dictionary*. 9th ed. St. Paul: West Group.
Japan Federation of Bar Association. (2008) *Rules concerning Attorney's fees*, JFBA Official Web Page (In English).
Kakalik, J.S., and N. Pace. 1986. *Costs and compensation paid in tort litigation*. Santa Monica: Rand Institute for Civil Justice.
Miceli, J.T. 2004. *The economic approach to law*. Stanford: Stanford University Press.
Ota, S. 2001. Reform of civil procedure in Japan. *The American Journal of Comparative Law* 49:561–583.
Parisi, F. 2002. Rent-seeking through litigation: Adversarial and inquisitorial systems compared. *International Review of Law and Economics* 22(2):193–216.
Rubinfeld, D.L., and S. Scotchmer. 1998. Contingent fees. In *The new Palgrave dictionary of economics and the law*, ed. P. Newman, vol. 1, 415–420. New York: Stockton Press.
Tullock, G. 1975. On the efficient organization of trials. *Kyklas* 28:745–762.
Tullock, G. 1980. *Trials on trials*. New York: Columbia University Press.

Chapter 5
Fixed Payments in Production Contracts for Private Labels: An Economic Analysis of the Japanese Subcontract Act

Takeshi Goto and Tatsuhiko Nariu

5.1 Introduction

In recent years, sales of private label goods have been increasing worldwide.[1] Private label goods are produced mostly by suppliers under production contracts signed with retailers. In many cases, terms of such production contracts include a uniform unit price of products (purchase price) to be paid by the retailer as well as fixed and predetermined (or upfront) payments from a supplier. In Japan, some private label goods are produced by small suppliers: subcontractors.[2] Such fixed payments from subcontractors, known as contribution fees or a monetary contribution, have been an important issue in Japanese competition policy because certain types of retailers' procuring money from subcontractors is strictly regulated by the Subcontract Act (Act against Delay in Payment of Subcontract Proceeds, etc. to Subcontractors).

The Subcontract Act is a special law based on the Japanese competition law: the Antimonopoly Act (Act on Prohibition of Private Monopolization and Maintenance of Fair Trade, hereinafter AMA). Article 2(9)5 of the AMA allows the Japanese competition agency the Japan Fair Trade Commission (JFTC) to regulate the

[1]For instance, the market size of the Japanese private labels was JPY 3 trillion in 2012.

[2]Although almost no subcontractor has its own national products, some suppliers that have their own national products also produce some retailers' private labels.

T. Goto (✉)
Nanzan University, Nagoya, Japan
e-mail: tgoto@nanzan-u.ac.jp

T. Nariu
Kyoto University, Kyoto, Japan

T. Naito et al. (eds.), *Applied Approaches to Societal Institutions and Economics*, New Frontiers in Regional Science: Asian Perspectives 18,
DOI 10.1007/978-981-10-5663-5_5

"abuse of superior bargaining position (hereinafter ASBP)." The Subcontract Act is designed to allow JFTC to regulate the ASBP effectively.[3]

The ASBP should be distinguished from the "abuse of dominant power" (or monopolization): the JFTC can apply the ASBP to an offender who has no market power. Indeed, in some cases, the offender has no market power.[4] In addition, the ASBP requires no somewhat anti-competitive effects of the conduct. In fact, market definition and market power assessments were absent in some cases to which the ASBP was applied. The ASBP requires only a "superior bargaining position" of the offender and its "unjust" use.[5]

Although the ASBP is applicable to any relation, including a subcontract relation between retailers and suppliers, it often takes a long time to assess whether these were requirements of the ASBP or not. Therefore, the JFTC has been applying the Subcontract Act to supply chains between retailers and their small suppliers. The Subcontract Act requires only a difference between the retailer and the supplier in terms of their capital, irrespective of whether the retailer has a superior bargaining position or not. The requirement for capital size is the following: (i) the retailer's capital exceeds JPY 300 million, and the supplier's capital does not exceed JPY 300 million, or (ii) the retailer's capital is between JPY 10 million and JPY 300 million, and the supplier's capital does not exceed JPY 10 million. When their subcontract relation meets this size requirement, the retailers are restricted from doing the practices listed in Articles 4(1) and (2) of the Subcontract Act.[6] This list of course includes retailers' procuring fixed payments (a contribution fee).

The ASBP of the AMA and the Subcontract Act have been controversial areas of Japanese competition policy. Nevertheless, the AMA amendment in 2009 allows the JFTC to impose surcharges on the offender of the ASBP. Accordingly, the JFTC has been more proactive in applying the Subcontract Act to subcontract relations

[3]Wakui and Cheng (2015) present a very useful and insightful survey of the ASBP of the AMA and the Subcontract Act.

[4]JFTC (2010) said that "In order for one party to a transaction (Party A) to have superior bargaining position over the other party (Party B), it is construed that Party A does not need to have a market-dominant position nor an absolutely dominant bargaining position equivalent thereto, but only needs to have a relatively superior bargaining position as compared to the other transacting party."

[5]As Wakui and Cheng (2015) pointed out, the concepts "superior bargaining position" and "unjustly" are vague and not defined precisely in the AMA. JFTC (2010) considered that the retailer has superior bargaining position to the supplier when the retailer is fundamentally important for the supplier's business. This JFTC consideration is based on their idea such that: "(i) if stopping the transaction with the retailer worsens the supplier's business significantly, then the supplier needs to continue transactions with the retailer; (ii) therefore, the supplier finds it difficult to reject the retailer's request, although it causes substantial disadvantage to the supplier."

[6]This list includes refusal to accept the commissioned products, late payment, retrospective discounts, return of goods, setting the price substantially lower than that of the equivalent product or the market price, forced purchase or usage, and compelling the subcontractor to provide it with economic benefits such as contribution fees and dispatch of employees. Wakui and Cheng (2015, page 14) describe these points.

regarding private label goods. Although the ASBP is still a minority on a global level, it has been gathering more attention from other countries' competition policy.[7]

Although previous studies investigated the economic meanings of payments from manufacturers to retailers, these specifically examined payments from manufacturers producing their national brand goods for retailers, known as "slotting fees" or "slotting contracts." For instance, manufacturers often pay a "slotting allowance" for retailers that are introducing their national brands' new products, a "facing allowance" for their accessing to (sometimes premium) retailers' shelf space (especially, "street money" for aisle displays), and "pay-to-stay fees" for remaining on a retailer's list of purchasing.

Many scholars and most countries' antitrust law authorities have considered that slotting fees might have anti-competitive effects.[8] One idea is that manufacturers can foreclose their rivals by paying slotting fees: it raises rivals' cost. Although this idea explains manufacturers' incentives to pay slotting fees and clarifies the anti-competitive effect, it does not explain retailers' incentives to demand slotting fees. If it might be more profitable for retailers to make their store have plenty of variety, then retailers might be not willing to accept slotting fees from manufacturers.

Chu (1992) and Marx and Shaffer (2007) explain retailers' incentives to accept or demand slotting fees. Chu (1992) shows that transferring slotting fees among manufacturers and retailers can work as a device for screening or signaling manufacturers' private information related to the profitability of their national brand products. This idea implies that the slotting fees enhance economic efficiency. Marx and Shaffer (2007) describe a model with one common manufacturer and two retailers (larger one and smaller one) and show that the larger retailer's demand for slotting fees can exclude a rival (small) retailer from selling a manufacturer's product (or using manufacturer product as his inputs). Based on this idea, slotting fees have an anti-competitive effect again.[9]

We think that we need another model to analyze the economic impact of the Subcontract Act on production contracts of private labels. First, every supplier has no incentive to foreclose anyone from their subcontract relation with a retailer because their vertical relations are originally vertically separated. They are small firms and therefore have no sufficient production facility such that they can act as the common supplier of retailers. Second, each retailer does not need to foreclose rival retailers from distributing their private label goods. Third, almost every retailer

[7]Only Korea, Taiwan, France, and Germany have notions like the ASBP in their (domestic) competition policy. There is no such notion in the competition policies of the United States and the European Union.

[8]On these arguments related to slotting fees, Federal Trade Commission (2003), Klein and Wright (2007), Secrieru (2006), and Rey and Vergé (2008) provide insightful surveys.

[9]However, Klein and Wright (2007) pointed out that some small retailers without any bargaining power use slotting contracts and a large retailer, Wal-Mart, does not use it. This fact is inconsistent with Marx and Shaffer's model. In addition by relaxing Marx and Shaffer's assumptions, Rey and Whinston (2013) demonstrated that exclusion never occurs in Marx and Shaffer's model.

has no market power in the private brand products market. Mostly, private label goods are not differentiated well; severe competition exists in such markets.

We set up a simple model for application to our problem: (i) the supplier's marginal production costs are increasing in quantity (because they are small firms); (ii) the supplier-retailer subcontract relation is vertically separated; (iii) no private label goods are differentiated – its market is perfectly competitive; and (iv) establishing and maintaining a subcontract relation incur some costs. Using this model, we demonstrate that a restriction on contribution fee by the Subcontract Act increases the average cost of supply chains and raises the equilibrium price of private labels market when suppliers have the right to manage their own output level.

The paper continues as follows. Section 5.2 introduces the model and derives the socially optimal outcome in it as a benchmark. In Sect. 5.3 we investigate the suppliers' and retailers' decisions in the case in which retailers are allowed to demand fixed payments. In Sect. 5.4 we assume that such a demand is restricted. The implications of our results, some justifications of the ASBP and the Subcontract Act, and the problem of JFTC's operation on these rules are considered in Sect. 5.5. Concluding remarks follow in Sect. 5.6.

5.2 The Model

We consider a market in which n retailers sell their private label goods in their own stores exclusively.[10] All private label goods are homogeneous. Every retailer faces common consumers' demand $p = P(Q)$, where p denotes the final price or the retail price charged to consumers and $Q(\geq 0)$ denotes the aggregate output. We assume that $P(Q)$ is continuously differentiable and $P'(Q) < 0$ for all Q. This market is perfectly competitive. Consequently, every retailer acts as a price-taker.

Each retailer offers a production contract for a supplier in a take-it-or-leave-it manner.[11] There is no common supplier: all supply chains are strictly exclusive. Retailers and suppliers in each chain, respectively, incur a constant cost $k_D(> 0)$ and $k_U(> 0)$ for establishing and maintaining their relation. We denote $k \equiv k_U + k_D$.

All suppliers have the common cost function $c = C(q)$, where c denotes the cost incurred by each supplier and q denotes the quantity each supplier produced. We assume $C(0) = 0$, $C(q)$ is continuously differentiable, $C'(q) > 0$ and $C''(q) > 0$. Marginal costs are increasing because every supplier is a small firm. Each supplier's outside option is zero.

[10]Although the number of retailers n must be an integer, we assume for simplicity that it can be real number.

[11]This assumption reflects the fact that retailers have strong bargaining power in relation to suppliers.

The timing of our model is the following.[12] First, each retailer offers a production contract $\{w, F\}$ to its supplier, where w is the purchase price per unit (to be paid by the retailer) and F is the amount of fixed payments (to be paid by the supplier).[13] If the supplier accepts this contract, he decides the amount of producing his retailer's private labels. Then retailers' and suppliers' profit are realized. Each retailer's profit is expected to be zero in free-entry equilibrium.

As a benchmark, it is useful to identify the socially optimal outcome of the model. For any aggregate output Q and n, it is socially efficient that every supplier produces the same amount of goods, q, such that $Q = nq$ because $C''(q) > 0$. Consequently, the total surplus (TS) of the market is given as

$$TS(n,q) = \int_0^{nq} P(t)dt - n[C(q) + k].$$

The first-order conditions for maximizing $TS(n, q)$ are given as[14]

$$\frac{\partial TS(n,q)}{\partial n} = P(nq)q - C(q) - k = 0, \tag{5.1}$$

$$\frac{\partial TS(n,q)}{\partial q} = n[P(nq) - C'(q)] = 0. \tag{5.2}$$

The social optimal number of retailers n^* and the quantity produced in each supply chain q^* must satisfy Eqs. (5.1) and (5.2). Using these equations, it is readily apparent that q^* is a function of k determined implicitly by

$$C'(q^*) = \frac{C(q^*) + k}{q^*}. \tag{5.3}$$

Therefore, it is readily apparent that each chain's average cost $AC(q)$, which is given as shown below,

$$AC(q) = \frac{C(q) + k}{q} \tag{5.4}$$

is minimized in the first-best outcome. We define $AC^* \equiv AC(q^*)$. The quantity q^* is irrelevant to n.

---

[12]We need not use subscripts to distinguish each retailer and the supplier: they are identical.

[13]F is predetermined or upfront payments. For the latter case, we should assume that all suppliers have sufficient wealth to pay it.

[14]The second-order conditions $TS_{nn} < 0$ and $TS_{nn}TS_{qq} - (TS_{nq})^2 < 0$ are satisfied with our assumptions.

Using Eqs. (5.2) and (5.3), we can also see that (n^*, q^*) satisfies

$$P(n^*q^*) = C'(q^*).$$

Therefore, marginal cost (and average cost) in each chain must be equal to the market price for social efficiency. The profit of each chain must be zero in the first-best outcome.

Finally, we see that Eqs. (5.3) and (5.4) imply that $\partial n^*/\partial k < 0$ and $\partial q^*/\partial k > 0$ which means that many firms producing small quantities are socially efficient when the cost of establishing and maintaining a relation is small.

5.3 Free-Entry Equilibrium with Fixed Payments

In this section, we examine the case in which retailers are allowed to demand fixed payments in their production contracts. There are no legal rules restricting private agreements on such payments.

We can derive the free-entry equilibrium as follows. First, let us consider suppliers' decision for a given contract $\{w, F\}$. Suppliers choose their output level to maximize $y(q, w) = wq - C(q) - k_U$, where $y(q, w)$ denotes the supplier's profits excluding fixed payments for a given contract.[15] Each supplier's profits depend only on the contract terms and the quantity he produces. In other words, no strategic interactions exist among suppliers. Consequently, it is apparent that each supplier produces $q(w)$, which is given by $w = C'(q)$ for $w > 0$ and $q(0) = 0$. Every supplier earns $y(q(w), w) - F = wq(w) - C(q(w)) - k_U - F$ as their profits for a given contract. We see that $q'(w) = 1/C''(q(w)) > 0$ under the assumption $C''(q) > 0$. Retailers should offer a contract satisfying $y(q(w), w) - F \geq 0$ for their contract to be accepted by suppliers.

Next, let us consider retailer profits given their suppliers' decision. Retailer's profit is given as $z_F(p, w, F) = (p - w)q(w) + F - k_D$. It is rational for retailers to set $F = y(q(w), w)$. Therefore, retailer's profit is also denoted as

$$z_F(p, w) = pq(w) - C(q(w)) - k = q(w)\left\{p - \frac{C(q(w)) + k}{q(w)}\right\}. \tag{5.5}$$

At the free-entry equilibrium, the following two conditions must be satisfied: (i) average cost for retailers is minimized, and (ii) retailer profits are zero. If condition (i) does not hold, then retailers that have lower average cost can enter the market. Such a situation cannot realize the free-entry equilibrium. Condition (ii) is straightforward.

[15]The amount of fixed payments does not affect the supplier's decision.

Retailers' average cost in this case is given as $[C(q(w))+k]/q(w)$ (see Eq. (5.5)). Therefore, the output level at the free-entry equilibrium q^F must be equal to q^*. The market price at the free-entry equilibrium p^F must be equal to $[C(q^*)+k]/q^*$ for condition (ii), meaning that $p^F = P(n^*, q^*)$. Therefore, the equilibrium number of retailers in the free-entry equilibrium n^F is equal to n^*.

These facts immediately imply that the free-entry equilibrium in this case achieves the first-best outcome. Finally, we characterize the contracts offered at the free-entry equilibrium. The purchase price at the free-entry equilibrium, w^F, induces suppliers to produce the amount of q^* of their private labels: $w^F = C'(q^*)$. Therefore, the purchase price w^F is equal to the market price at the free-entry equilibrium: $w^F = p^F = P(n^*, q^*)$. The amounts of fixed payments in the free-entry equilibrium are given as $F^F = y(q^F, w^F)$. It is apparent that

$$F^F = y(q^F, w^F) = P(n^*, q^*)q^* - C(q^*) - k_U = k - k_U = k_D.$$

Therefore, the amount of fixed payments is equal to retailer's expenditure to supply chain in the free-entry equilibrium.

Proposition 5.1 *If retailers are allowed to demand fixed payments in their production contracts, then the first-best outcome is achieved in the free-entry equilibrium.*

Intuitively, this proposition can be stated as follows. By demanding the fixed payments, each retailer can obtain all profits (or surplus) of their supply chain (so-called full-extraction). This means that the retailers' average cost is equal to the channel's average cost. At the free-entry equilibrium, the retailers' average cost should be minimized. Therefore, the output level is equal to the first-best level. In addition, each retailer's profit must be zero in the free-entry equilibrium. Therefore, the market price must be equal to the average cost.

5.4 Free-Entry Equilibrium Without Fixed Payments

In this section, we examine the case in which retailers' demand for fixed payments in their production contracts is strictly restricted by some legal rules such as the Subcontract Act. In this case, any contract that a retailer can offer includes only the purchasing price: $\{w\}$.

Even if so, suppliers in each relation also produce $q(w)$ in this case. As described in the previous section, the amount of fixed payments does not affect the supplier's decision. Therefore, the restriction on fixed payments is irrelevant for supplier decisions. Each supplier earns $y(q(w), w)$ instead of $y(q(w), w) - F$ as their profits in this case. Each retailer should offer a contract satisfying $y(q(w), w) \geq 0$. We denote w that satisfies $y(q(w), w) = w \cdot q(w) - C(q(w)) - k_U = 0$ as $\bar{w}$. We see that $\bar{w} > 0$ unless $k_U = 0$, because $q(0) = 0$, $y(q(0), 0) = -C(0) = 0$, and $dy(q(w), w)/dw = q(w) > 0$. The condition $y(q(w), w) \geq 0$ is equivalent to $w \geq \bar{w}$ because $dy(q(w), w)/dw = q(w) > 0$. Retailer's profit is given as $z_N(p, w) = (p - w)q(w) - k_D$ in this case.

At the free-entry equilibrium, retailers' average cost should be minimized. In this case, retailers' average cost is given as $w+k/q(w)$. We assume here that the problem

$$\min_{w \geq 0} \quad w + \frac{k}{q(w)} \tag{5.6}$$

has an interior solution. We denote it hereinafter as $\hat{w}$.

When $\hat{w} < \bar{w}$, the purchase price at the free-entry equilibrium is given as $w_N = \bar{w}$. Let us first characterize this equilibrium. By the definition of $\bar{w}$, it is straightforward that each supplier's output level $\bar{q} = q(\bar{w})$ satisfies $\bar{w}\cdot\bar{q} - C(\bar{q}) - k_U = 0$. The fact that $\bar{q} < q^*$ can be shown as follows. Let us introduce a function $f(q) \equiv C'(q)q - C(q)$. By the assumption on $C(q)$, $f(0) = 0$ and $f'(q) = C''(q)q > 0$ hold. Additionally, we assume hereinafter that $f''(q) = C'''(q)q + C''(q) > 0$. The first-best output level q^* minimizes $(C(q) + k)/q$. Therefore, $f(q^*) = k$ holds. On the other hand, the output level in this case satisfies $C'(\bar{q})\bar{q} - C(\bar{q}) - k_U = 0$, which means that $f(\bar{q}) = k_U$. The fact that $f(q)$ is increasing and $k > k_U$ implies $\bar{q} < q^*$.

Regarding the market price in free entry equilibrium of this case $\bar{p}$, we can obtain $\bar{p} > p^*$. Because $\bar{p}$ is given as $(\bar{p} - \bar{w})\bar{q} - k_D = 0$ and $\bar{w}\bar{q} - C(\bar{q}) - k_U = 0$, $\bar{p}\bar{q} = C(\bar{q}) + k_U + k_D$ hold. Therefore, we obtain the following:

$$\bar{p} = \frac{C(\bar{q}) + k}{\bar{q}} > \frac{C(q^*) + k}{q^*} = p^*.$$

The purchase price at the free-entry equilibrium is given as $w_N = \hat{w}$ when $\hat{w} \geq \bar{w}$. Let us next characterize this equilibrium. Since $\hat{w}$ is the solution of (5.6), it satisfies $1 - q'(\hat{w})k_D/\{q(\hat{w})\}^2$. We denote $\hat{q} = q(\hat{w})$ hereinafter.

We can show $\hat{q} < q^*$ as follows. First, we see that $f'(\hat{q})\hat{q} = k_D$ and $f(q^*) < f'(q^*)q^*$ hold. The former follows from the fact that $\hat{q}$ satisfies $1 - q'(w)k_D/\{q(w)\}^2$. To see that the latter holds, let us introduce the function $h(q) \equiv f(q)q - f(q)$. By our assumptions, $h(0) = 0$ and $h'(q) > 0$. Therefore, $h(q) \equiv f(q)q - f(q) > 0$ for any given $q > 0$. Next, suppose that $\hat{q} \geq q^*$. Then $k_D = f'(\hat{q})\hat{q} \geq f'(q^*)q^*$ holds because $f'(q) > 0$. However, $f'(q^*)q^* > f(q^*) = k$ must hold by definitions. This is a contradiction because $k > k_D$.

Finally, we consider the market price in free-entry equilibrium of this case, $\hat{p}$. It is apparent that $\hat{p} > p^*$ as follows. Because $\hat{p}$ satisfies $(\hat{p} - \hat{w})\hat{q} - k_D = 0$ in the free-entry equilibrium and because $\hat{w}\hat{q} - C(\hat{q}) - k_U > 0$ holds by the definition of $\hat{w}$, we obtain $\hat{p} \cdot \hat{q} > C(\hat{q}) + k_U + k_D$, which implies that

$$\hat{p} > \frac{C(\hat{q}) + k}{\hat{q}} > \frac{C(q^*) + k}{q^*} = p^*.$$

In addition, the number of chains in free-entry equilibrium can be higher or lower than the number of firms in the first-best outcome. The output level of each relation is less than the first-best level, whereas the equilibrium price is higher than the first-best level. We summarize the analysis above as the following.

Proposition 5.2 *If retailers are restricted to demand fixed payments in their production contracts, then the first-best outcome cannot be achieved in free-entry equilibrium. Each supply chain produces less than the socially efficient quantity; thereby average cost of each relation is not minimized. Additionally, the equilibrium price of this market is raised. This eventuality worsens consumer welfare, whereas each supplier can earn positive profits despite their outside option being zero.*

An intuition of this proposition can be stated as follows. When retailers are restricted to demand any fixed payment from a supplier, they cannot obtain all profits of their chain unless they set a purchase price at a certain level. Therefore, they lose incentive to minimize their chain's average cost. They only minimize their own average cost. This brings allocative inefficiency.

This proposition is related closely to the result shown by Ghosh and Morita (2007): allocative inefficiency is likely brought if retailers have sufficiently low bargaining power. We demonstrated that allocative inefficiency occurs when suppliers have the right to manage their output level and retailers' procurement of money from a supplier is restricted even if retailers have full bargaining power.

5.5 Discussion

5.5.1 Policy Implications of Our Result

Propositions 5.1 and 5.2 state that the restriction of retailers' procuring fixed payments from their supplier worsens economic welfare in the private label goods market when suppliers have the right to manage their output level. This restriction prevents retailers from using fixed payments to coordinate the supplier's incentives to produce and therefore adversely affects economic efficiency. Especially, this restriction decreases consumer welfare, an important factor in the JFTC's policy making because it raises the equilibrium price of the private labels market. One might regard this result as readily apparent: any restriction on voluntary contracts worsens economic welfare to the extent that there are no third-party effects, imperfect competition, or information asymmetry.[16] However, we regard this as an important first step for considering the ASBP of the AMA and the Subcontract Act from the viewpoint of economics. In fact, some legal scholars and the JFTC still

[16]However, we think that introducing imperfect competition into our model does not change our conclusion. Even if a retailer is a monopolist, it might still have incentive to minimize the average costs of relations with their subcontractor. When a market is a duopoly, both retailers require fixed payments in Nash equilibrium in a Cournot quantity setting game because such requirements are strategic substitutes.

equate the contribution fee with a reduction of the purchase price. As explained in this article, these might have different effects on economic efficiency.

In our model, if retailers' demands for fixed payments in their subcontract contracts are restricted, then suppliers can enjoy positive profits in the interior solution case. The JFTC might think this is justice because this is brought by a prevention of retailers' exploitation from subcontractors. However, this is merely transferring wealth from consumers to subcontractors with economic inefficiency, as described in this article. In addition, even if retailers are prohibited from procuring any fixed payment from their supplier, they can set their supplier's profits as zero by reducing their purchasing price. When setting such a purchase price is optimal for retailers, it brings only economic inefficiency and does not help any subcontractor.

The Subcontract Act has other side effects for the Japanese economy. If suppliers increase their capital, then the Subcontract Act no longer protects them. Therefore, each supplier might not have sufficient incentive to be a big firm. In fact, a ratio occupied by small firms of the total number of firms is 99.7%. Small firms employ 69.7% of all workers in Japan. This fact also means that any policy against "protecting subcontractors" will have difficulty being accepted. In other words, the Subcontract Act might itself retain their *raison d'être*: small firms.

Additionally, the ASBP of AMA and the Subcontract Act are not applied extraterritorially: conduct by Japanese firms to foreign firms or by foreign firms to Japanese firms is free from restriction.[17] The former will allow Japanese retailers to make subcontract contracts with foreign firms. This will bring "hollowing out" in production of private labels. The latter will give some benefits to foreign retailers for producing and selling their private products in Japan.

There is a possibility that the ASBP of the AMA and the Subcontract Act has no impact to the economy. When those retailers in our model can make a contract on the quantity q as well as the purchasing price, each retailer can minimize average cost of their relation by simply offering a contract such that $\{w, q\} = \{(C(q^*) + k_U)/q^*, q^*\}$, without using contribution fees. In this case, the restriction has no effect on economic welfare, excepting the government expenditure related to its enforcement. This result is analogous to the well-known results related to the double-marginalization problem in manufacturer–retailer relations: Manufacturers can solve the double marginalization problem by quantity fixing even if procuring a franchise fee from retailers.[18]

[17]This is only a conventional application. The AMA and the Subcontract Act have no article related to extraterritorial application.

[18]Shaffer (1991) analyzed slotting allowances and RPM in a model where producers compete to obtain retailer shelf space for their national brands.

5.5.2 Some Justifications for Restricting Contribution Fees

In Sect. 5.5.1, we insisted that the restriction of retailers' procuring of money from suppliers has negative or zero effects on economic welfare. However, several justifications exist for restricting contribution fees.

First, there are arguments such that restriction of contribution fees prevents retailers' overinvestment for promoting products. In some cases to which the Subcontract Act is applied, retailers demanded contribution fees for promoting their private labels. Then retailers can enjoy the benefits of investments without bearing the full costs of promotion. This might bring retailers' overinvestment in promotion.

Another justification is presented by Itoh and Kagami (1998): a restriction on contribution fees prevents occurrence of the so-called hold-up problem. When the supplier makes noncontractible relation-specific investments for the retailer's private label before the transaction takes place, then the retailer might use opportunistic behavior because the supplier is held up: retailers can change the contract terms retroactively (e.g., reducing the purchase price), require some money as contribution fees which was not included in the original contract, and so on. Such retailer behavior discourages suppliers from making relation-specific investments. Every practice listed in Articles 4(1) and (2) of the Subcontract Act and JFTC's ASBP guideline can be interpreted as retailers' opportunistic behavior.

We think these justifications are not persuasive for several reasons. The contract party, retailer and supplier, will use appropriate contract terms or commitment devices to coordinate their incentives or to prevent themselves from taking opportunistic behavior. Regarding private labels, there might be several important investments simultaneously: one by a retailer and another by a supplier. Fixed payments are useful to coordinate these incentives simultaneously: sometimes a fixed payment from retailers to supplier is privately efficient for them; sometimes so it is from supplier to retailer.[19] There is no reason to restrict the latter only.

If there are possibilities of the "hold-up" problem occurring because of retailers' opportunistic behavior, then retailers will commit themselves not to do so using appropriate practices or devices, e.g., repeated transaction, to the extent that such a commitment increases their profits. Of course, the restriction might be useful: retailers sometimes fail to commit themselves not to behave opportunistically. Even if so, it is not necessary that such a restriction be a compulsory provision, as Matsumura (2006) pointed out. Furthermore, this justification gives no explanation of the fact that the ASBP of the AMA and the Subcontract Act devote attention only to retailers' opportunistic behavior, although there might be a "hold-up problem" caused by suppliers' opportunistic behavior.

---

[19]Lee and Png (1990), Edlin (1996), Farrell (2001), and Foros et al. (2009) all describe fixed payments.

5.5.3 Cases

Based on our results, fixed payments from suppliers to retailers in production contracts enhance allocative efficiency to the extent that it covers the cost of establishing and maintaining their supply chain (and it is determined ex ante). In spite of that, JFTC has been applying the Subcontract Act on such cases.

For instance, in September 2012, JFTC issued a recommendation to the Japanese Consumers' Co-operative Union (J-COOP) for its violation of Articles 4(1) and (2) of the Subcontract Act.[20] J-COOP, a retailer in Japan, supplies food and other daily necessities (including many private label products) to its members through home delivery services. It also has many stores in which nonmember consumers can also enjoy purchasing. Because of this recommendation, J-COOP refunded and compensated about JPY 2.6 billion to its 449 suppliers.

The list of conduct regarded as violation included J-COOP's requirement of "compensation for the costs of test marketing" to their suppliers. This can be regarded as fees covering the cost of establishing and maintaining their supply chain. Furthermore, J-COOP and its supplier agreed with it, as it answered to the media interview.[21] If they agreed with it after suppliers made some relation-specific investments, this JFTC decision can be interpreted and justified as a device for preventing hold-up problem. However, JFTC did not specify timing of this agreement in the recommendation.

A recommendation to the CGC Japan in September 2016 is another example of the costs of test marketing.[22] CGC Japan develops many private label goods and consigns production to its subcontractors. It requires the costs of designing packages of private labels and test marketing. JFTC regarded these conducts as a violation of the Subcontract Act, although these can be regarded as the cost of establishing and maintaining their supply chain.

Recommendations to Sunlive–Marushoku Group (a supermarket chain in Kyushu district, Japan) in June and August 2014 are examples of the cost of information systems for the supply chain.[23] JFTC regarded their requirements of "EOS information fee (fee for using their information system)" to suppliers as a violation of the Subcontract Act. We think this also covers the cost of establishing and maintaining their supply chain.

As noted in Sect. 5.1, the JFTC tends to apply the Subcontract Act to subcontract relation regarding private labels formally, although they stated themselves that it is important whether procuring money between contractual parties enhances economic efficiency or not. We infer that more careful application is needed.

[20] 'Recommendations to the Japanese Consumers' Co-operative Union' (JFTC Press Release, 25 September 2012).

[21] For instance, The Nikkei (Nikkei Shimbun) 25 September 2012 (in Japanese).

[22] "Recommendations to CGC JAPAN" (JFTC Press Release, 27 September 2016).

[23] "Recommendations to Sunlive" (JFTC Press Release, 30 June 2014) and "Recommendations to Marushoku" (JFTC Press Release, 28 August 2014).

5.6 Conclusion

In this paper, we analyzed economic effects of applying the ASBP of the AMA and the Subcontract Act to production contracts for private labels, in a model that reflects features of the actual situation related to private label production in Japan. Additionally, we pointed out problems of justifications for the restriction on retailers' procuring money from their suppliers and of the JFTC's actual enforcement of the ASBP and the Subcontract Act.

Because it might depend on the simplicity of our model, we do not regard our result as robust. Reality might be more complex. Suppliers often produce and sell their national brand products in addition to retailer's private labels. Should the Subcontract Act be applied to such a situation? Does retailers' abuse of their superior bargaining position have some anti-competitive effects in the long run or not? Retailers can avoid sanctions by the Subcontract Act by making production contracts with large manufacturers: why do they choose small firms as their partners? Such issues remain as subjects for future research.

Acknowledgements The authors thank the participants of the annual meeting of the Japanese Association for Applied Economics (Autumn 2013), 33rd symposium in Economics at Daito Bunka University (Autumn 2013), and seminar at the Department of Economics and Finance of the University of Canterbury, New Zealand (Autumn 2016), for helpful comments and suggestions. The final version of this article was written when one of the authors, Goto, visited the University of Canterbury in 2016–2017 as a visiting fellow. The hospitality of the University of Canterbury is gratefully acknowledged. Nariu was supported by JSPS KAKENHI grants 26285098 and 15K03749 for this work.

References

Chu, Wujin. 1992. Demand signaling and screening in channels of distribution. *Marketing Science* 11(4): 327–347.

Edlin, Aaron S. 1996. Cadillac contracts and up-front payments. *Journal of Law, Economics, & Organization* 12(1): 98–118.

Farrell, Joseph. 2001. Some thoughts on slotting allowances and exclusive dealing. U.S. Department of Justice.

Federal Trade Commission. 2003. Slotting allowances in the retail grocery industry: Selected case studies in five product categories. U.S. Government Printing Office.

Foros, Øystein, Hans Jarle Kind, and Jan Yngve Sand. 2009. Slotting allowances and suppliers' retail sales effort. *Southern Economic Journal* 76(1): 266–282.

Ghosh, Arghya, and Hodaka Morita. 2007. Social desirability of free entry: A bilateral oligopoly analysis. *International Journal of Industrial Organization* 25(5): 925–934.

Itoh, Motoshige, and Kazuaki Kagami. 1998. Kigyou-kan torihiki to Yuuetsuteki-chii no Ranyou (Transaction among Firms and the Abuse of Superior Bargaining Position). In *Kaisha-Hou no Keizaigaku (Economics of corporate law)*, ed. Yoshiro Miwa, Hideki Kanda and Noriyuki Yanagawa. University of Tokyo Press [In Japanese].

Japan Fair Trade Commission (JFTC). 2010. Guidelines concerning abuse of superior bargaining position under the antimonopoly act.

Klein, Benjamin, and Joshua D. Wright. 2007. The economics of slotting contracts. *Journal of Law and Economics* 50(3): 421–454.

Lee, Tom K., and I.P.L. Png. 1990. The role of installment payments in contracts for services. *RAND Journal of Economics* 21(1): 83–99.

Marx, Leslie M., and Greg Shaffer. 2007. Upfront payments and exclusion in downstream markets. *RAND Journal of Economics* 38(3): 823–843.

Matsumura, Toshihiro. 2006. Yuetsuteki-chii no Ranyo no Keizai Bunseki (Economic Analysis of Abuse of Superior Bargaining Position). *Nihon Keizai Hou Gakkai Nenpo (Annual of Japan Association of Economic Law)* 27: 90–102 [In Japanese].

Rey, Patrick, and Thibaud Vergé. 2008. The economics of vertical restraints. In *Handbook of antitrust economics*, ed. Paolo Buccirossi. Cambridge: MIT Press.

Rey, Patrick, and Michael D. Whinston. 2013. Does retailer power lead exclusion? *RAND Journal of Economics* 44(1): 75–81.

Secrieru, Oana. 2006. The economic theory of vertical restraints. *Journal of Economic Surveys* 20(5): 797–822.

Shaffer, Greg. 1991. Slotting allowances and resale price maintenance: A comparison of facilitating practices. *RAND Journal of Economics* 22(1): 120–135.

Wakui, Masako, and Thomas K. Cheng. 2015. Regulating abuse of superior bargaining position under the Japanese competition law: An anomaly or a necessity? *Journal of Antitrust Enforcement* 3(2): 302–333.

Chapter 6
Managers' Window Dressing and Liability for Damages to a Stock Sales in Management Buyouts

Ryutaro Nozaki

6.1 Introduction

This paper analyzes the inverse window dressing of managers in their management buyouts (MBOs) and the claims of damages for compensation filed by the small shareholders against the manager.[1]

In Japan, a part of Financial Instruments and Exchange Act (FIEA)[2] was amended in May 2014, namely, FIEA (2014). In recent years in Japan, the situation that managers planning an MBO have deliberately lowered the stock price of their firm and purchase the shares cheaply from shareholders occurred. Before the FIEA (2014), only the shareholders who bought shares approved the claim for damages under the FIEA. But because shareholders who sold their shares had to file a claim for damages under the civil law and bear the burden of proof, it was difficult for them to conduct lawsuit of damages against a manager. Therefore, the Financial Services Agency (FSA) amended the FIEA to address this issue in 2014. In Financial Services Agency (2014), the main aim of the FIEA (2014) is to protect the profit of the shareholders who had already sold the stock from the inverse window dressing by the manager.

[1]In the aspect of corporate accounting point of view, "dressing" refers to the value embroidery reported by managers, more than the real, and "inverse dressing" is in contrary sense.

[2]The origin of FIEA had been enacted in 2007.

R. Nozaki (✉)
Kurume University, Kurume, Japan
e-mail: nozaki_ryuutarou@kurume-u.ac.jp

T. Naito et al. (eds.), *Applied Approaches to Societal Institutions and Economics*, New Frontiers in Regional Science: Asian Perspectives 18,
DOI 10.1007/978-981-10-5663-5_6

It seems important for us to investigate that managers prevent the inverse window dressing. So we analyze the effect of the amendment of the FIEA on preventing the inverse window dressing by the managers.

Cuny and Talmor (2007) analyze the substitution of incumbent manager with new one under asymmetric information. However, they have not analyzed shareholders protection.

Stein (1988) deals with the determination of stock prices. While he analyzes the timing at which the corporate information disclosure is to be addressed to the threat of hostile takeover by tender offer buyout (TOB), the behavior of the manager is not shown explicitly.

Hanamura (2011) is similar to Stein (1988), and he extends Stein (1988)'s model by employing a signaling game in the analysis. The result shows that in the case of low TOB cost and high threat of TOB, the manager is more likely to disclose firms' information.

Elitzur et al. (1998) investigated whether incumbent managers would implement MBO and show that the incumbent managers implement MBO when the gains from MBO are higher. In addition, they analyze the level of efforts of managers in implementing MBO and show that this increases when going private by incumbent managers than at the time of stock launch. However, they deal only with the case of asymmetric information.

Kato (2011) shows the role of the court in the acquisition of shares in MBO from the legal perspective in Japan. In this paper, the rationality of the issuer company making a misrepresentation disclosure in the share market to be liable for damages against investors is examined from the perspective of the amount of damages that the investor should incur and the damage suffered by the investor.

Tamayama (2010) analyzed the liability of damages to investors and the court's ex post function by using numerical examples in MBO. We assume that asymmetric information exists between the manager who intends to execute MBO and the shareholders. It is possible that socially undesirable MBO would be implemented when managers disrupt the firm value before MBO.

Based on the mentioned above, we investigate information disclosure on the firm value of manager in MBO by using a signaling game. In the analysis, we consider two strategies: pooling strategy and separating strategy, and then we analyze the small shareholders' legal action for damages and investigate the effect of transferring the burden of proof to the injurer through FIEA (2014).

The main results of this paper are as follows. Transferring the burden of proof is effective in deterring the inverse window dressing by managers. However, depending on the degree of damages, even if the burden of proof is passed on, it is not necessarily effective to deter false disclosure.

The rest of the paper is structured as follows. The next section explains the model. In Sect. 6.3, we analyze some cases where the small shareholder has the burden of proof as a benchmark, and then, we analyze the extent of suppression of the inverse window dressing of managers by request of compensation by civil law by small shareholders. In Sect. 6.4, we analyze the effect of suppressing the inverse window dressing by managers, where we transfer the burden of proof to managers and then compare the results with those of Sect. 6.3. In the final section, we describe the conclusion.

6.2 Model

There exist a manager, many small shareholders, and the court. Further, assume that all agents are risk neutral.

In the beginning, the manager owns $\alpha\%$ of the firm's shares, and the many small shareholders own the remaining $1 - \alpha\%$. The manager wants to acquire all the shares owned by small shareholders in order to acquire a firm. In other words, he is planning an MBO. If he succeeds in the MBO, the firm value would be either V_h with probability p or $V_l(< V_h)$ with probability $1 - p$. At t = 1, small shareholders and the court know only the distribution of the firm value. Hereafter, V_h type is the manager who realized V_h, and V_l type is the manager who realized V_l.

Manager At t = 2, the manager knows the realized firm value when MBO succeeds and sends the firm value as a signal to small shareholders and the court. The manager does not always send correct signals. However, assume that the signals are a verifiable value of the firm. For example, as a signal, we consider the company publishes a settlement of accounts, interim settlements, or performance adjustment reports. As this paper focuses on the inverse window dressing problem of the manager, when V_h is realized, it is possible for the manager to send an incorrect signal (that is, reporting V_l). However, assuming that V_l is realized, the manager only report it correctly. Sending an incorrect signal when V_h is realized implies that part of the firm value is verified. However, it will seem that making a false report is costly for the manager. So we assume that the firm value decreases at the rate of $\phi(0 < \phi \leq 1)$, when the manager makes a false report.[3] Simultaneously, the manager offers a share purchase price to small shareholders. For simplicity of analysis, we suppose the share purchase price which manager offers to the small shareholders, corresponding to the reported firm value. In other words, regardless of the type, we assume that the manager offers the same price when reporting V_l. Further, denote the share purchase price to b_i when he/she reports $V_i(i = h, l)$.

Next, we explain the burden of proof of manager. Assuming that when the small shareholders have burden of proof, the manager will not act. Either, when the manager has burden of proof, he/she will make a defensive effort to influence the judgment of the court if small shareholders sue. Further, the court judges based on

[3]For example, see Burkart and Panunzi (2006)

evidence submitted by small shareholders or the manager. In this paper, we assume that when the management has a burden of proof and if he does not defend, the court would accept the shareholder's assertion. Meanwhile, the manager may oppose the small shareholders' damage claims. Here, denote e to the level of defense efforts that the manager would make and assume the defense success probability itself. Further, assuming that the cost increases with the defense effort, the cost function of effort is defined as follows. Also, d denotes as a cost parameter.

$$C(e) = \frac{de^2}{2} \tag{6.1}$$

Small shareholders Small shareholders are assumed to be homogeneous. And the number of shares owned per small shareholder is very small. At t = 2, they receive, sent a signal related to the firm value, and are offered a share purchase price. Then, these shareholders expect that when V_h is realized, the manager sends an incorrect signal to them with the probability $q(0 \leq q \leq 1)$ and the correct signal at probability $1 - q$. Therefore, when a small shareholder receives a signal V_l, he/she updates the belief as follows.

$$Prob(V_h|V_l) = \frac{pq}{pq + 1 - p}, \quad Prob(V_l|V_l) = \frac{1 - p}{pq + 1 - p}$$

In this paper, the small shareholders are assumed to sell the stock once at the price offered by the manager.[4] Also, the small shareholders may have monitoring ability. In case of filing a lawsuit against damages, when the small shareholders are responsible for proof, they will investigate the information of the firm and try to find evidence.[5]

The level of monitoring by small shareholders is defined as m. Further, let m be the probability of monitoring success. Therefore, the monitoring level itself is assumed to be the discovery probability $(0 < m \leq 1)$. The cost function of monitoring is defined as follows. Also, a denotes as a cost parameter.

$$C(m) = \frac{am^2}{2} \tag{6.2}$$

Court and Damages Before FIEA (2014), small shareholders who sold shares had to file a lawsuit of damage claim under the civil law. Moreover, they had to bear burden of proof. On the other hand, after FIEA (2014), the manager has to prove that he/she is not causing damage.

[4]While it is important to consider the type that the stock price would be, in this paper, we focus on damage claim action after sale.

[5]If there is only a few small shareholder, the cost of litigation would be very high, and there is a possibility of abandoning the lawsuit. However, here, we are considering a class action lawsuit by small shareholders.

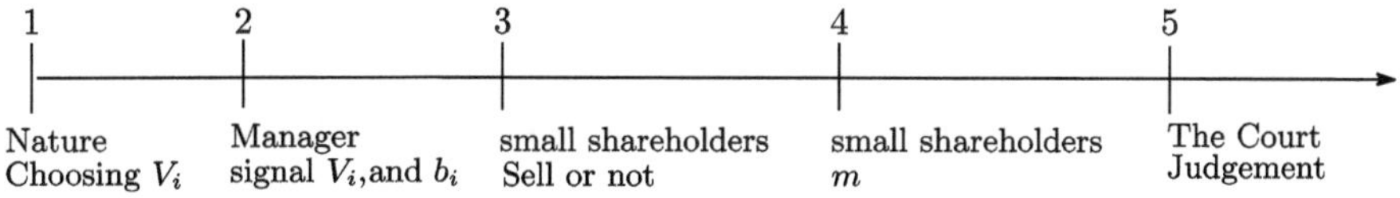

Fig. 6.1 Timelines for small shareholders with burden of proof

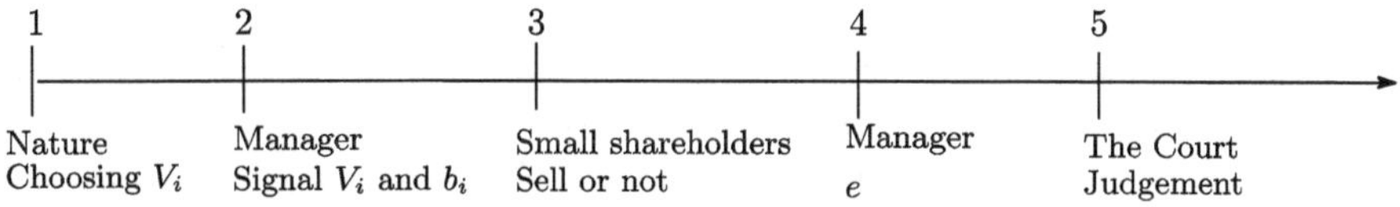

Fig. 6.2 Timelines for the manager with burden of proof

Based on the above, the judgment of the court is assumed as follows. When the burden of proof is on the small shareholders, the court makes a judgment based on the evidence of the small shareholders. If small shareholders fail to find evidence, the court would not accept their damage claims. On the contrary, when the manager has the burden of proof, the court makes a judgment based on the evidence or assertion of the manager. If the manager makes efforts to the level of e, the court may admit his argument and decide not to accept the small shareholders' damage claim at probability e.

Now, we explain the amount of damages decided by the court. When there is a burden of proof on the small shareholders, the amount of damages that the court considers as payment to the small shareholders is up to the amount of damages the small shareholders have suffered due to management false reports, that is $(V_h - b_l)$. On the other hand, when the manager has a burden of proof, the court may judge the punitive damages. Therefore, the court may judge the amount of damages greater than the amount of actual damages suffered by the small shareholders. We define $\beta(V_h - b_l)$ $(\beta \in [0, \bar{\beta}])$ for damages to be paid to small shareholders from the manager. Also, we assume that $\bar{\beta} > 1$, which means punitive damages. Finally, the actions of all agents are shown by the next timelines (Figs. 6.1 and 6.2).

6.3 When Small Shareholders Have Burden of Proof

In this section, we analyze the cases where small shareholders are responsible for the proof.

6.3.1 When Small Shareholders Can Not Monitor

6.3.1.1 Conditions for the Sale of Shares by Small Shareholders

After receiving the signal V_i and offering the share purchase price b_i, the small shareholders decide whether to sell the shares.

While the small shareholders update their beliefs with the received signals, because they cannot monitor, they decide whether to sell at the offering price based on the signal reported by the manager at t = 2. Therefore, the condition of the sale of the stock of the small shareholders will be as follows according to the received signal,

$$b_i \geq V_i. \tag{6.3}$$

That is, the small shareholders sell their stocks if the manager has offered a share price higher than the firm value reported by the manager.

6.3.1.2 The Manager's Decision of Reporting Strategy and Offering Share Purchase Price

The manager offers a share price to small shareholders on the basis of his reporting strategy. We consider each case of the reporting.

Case of Correct Reporting

Consider that the manager sends a correct signal on firm value. Denote Π_I^{ij} as the manager's profit (subscript I represents the manager superscript, i represents true type of the manager(in actually realizing firm value), and superscript j means signal $V_j(j = h, l)$ sent to the small shareholders and the court). When type i manager sends the correct signal, his profit is

$$\Pi_I^{ij} = V_i - (1 - \alpha)b_i. \tag{6.4}$$

Therefore, from equation (6.4), manager's participate condition is

$$b_i \leq \frac{V_i}{1 - \alpha}. \tag{6.5}$$

We compare the right-hand side of equation (6.3) and the right-hand side of equation (6.4). Because the value of the latter (equation (6.4)) is greater than the former, the manager could offer the share price that satisfies the participation condition of the small shareholders. In order to increase the manager's profit, he/she offers the share price bound to equation (6.3), that is, $b_i = V_i$. Therefore, the profit of each type of manager is as follows:

$$\Pi_I^{ij} = V_i - (1-\alpha)V_i = \alpha V_i \tag{6.6}$$

When the Manager Sends Wrong Signal

Next, we consider the case of a wrong signal sent by the manager. Then, small shareholders are obliged to decide to sell shares at the price according to the firm value V_l that the manager has reported. Thus, the condition of selling the shares for small shareholders is $b_l \geq V_l$. On the other hand, because the V_h-type manager sends a wrong signal, he/she obtains $\Pi_I^{hl} = (1-\phi)V_h - (1-\alpha)b_l$. Therefore, the range of share purchase price that he can offer is

$$b_l < \frac{(1-\phi)V_h}{1-\alpha}. \tag{6.7}$$

A V_h-type manager can offer a stock price that fulfills the participation condition $b_l \geq V_l$ of the small shareholders, if it satisfies

$$\phi \leq \frac{\Delta V + \alpha V_l}{1-\alpha}(\Delta V \equiv V_h - V_l). \tag{6.8}$$

Now, assume the ϕ satisfied equation (6.8).

However, because the V_l-type manager sends the correct signal, the share price that he offers is similar to equation (6.5). Further, as well as sending the correct report, each type of manager sets $b_l = V_l$ since the gain would rise. Then, the profit of the V_l-type manager is (6.6). Otherwise, profit of V_h type is

$$\Pi_I^{hl} = (1-\phi)V_h - (1-\alpha)V_l. \tag{6.9}$$

The Decision of Reporting Strategies

The manager chooses either the pooling strategy (both types of managers report V_l) or the separating strategy (the managers report different signals corresponding to their respective type). In this paper, we assume that the manager chooses the pooling strategy if he/she gains the same profit regardless of the strategy.

We investigate the characteristics of equilibrium at which the managers choose the pooling strategy. In equilibrium, both types of manager do not have incentive to deviate.

The manager has no incentive to deviate from the pooling strategy when the following conditions are satisfied.

$$(1-\phi)V_h - (1-\alpha)V_l \geq \alpha V_h \tag{6.10}$$

$$\alpha V_l \geq \alpha V_l \tag{6.11}$$

For the V_l type, the choice of strategy is indifferent, and thus, we check the condition for which the equation (6.10) holds. If the following inequality holds, the gain from the false report exceeds the gain from the correct report.

$$\phi \leq \frac{(1-\alpha)\Delta V}{1-\alpha} \tag{6.12}$$

Also, comparing equation (6.8) to equation (6.12), $\frac{\Delta V+\alpha V_l}{V_h} - \frac{(1-\alpha)\Delta V}{V_h} = \alpha > 0$ holds. Therefore, within the range that satisfies the participation condition of V_h type, the pooling strategy becomes the equilibrium strategy that ϕ satisfies (6.12). This implies that the manager would report a false signal if the marginal cost of the false report is less than the marginal profit that manager gains from the false report.

6.3.2 *The Small Shareholders Having the Ability to Monitor*

Here, consider the effect of damage claim lawsuit by small shareholders, when they can monitor after selling the shares and can discover evidence that the report of the management is false.

6.3.2.1 Level of Monitoring by Small Shareholders

After receiving the signal that the manager sent at t = 2, the small shareholders update their belief of the manager's true type. Therefore, they decide the level of monitoring under the ex post belief of it.

When the manager choses the separating strategy, small shareholders recognize the true type of the manager. In the case of the separating strategy, the manager offers the true firm value as the share price, and thus, no damage would occur. Therefore, small shareholders do not monitor. On the other hand, when the manager chooses the pooling strategy in which both types of managers report V_l, small shareholders may monitor the firm.

If small shareholders find the evidence with a probability of m, they win to suit and gain the payment for damages. Thus, their expected profit is as below.

$$(1-\alpha)V_l + m\left\{\frac{pq}{pq+1-p}(1-\alpha)\beta(V_h-b_l) + \frac{1-p}{pq+1-p}0\right\} - \frac{am^2}{2} \tag{6.13}$$

The small shareholders choose the level of monitoring m to maximize the expected profit; therefore, their maximization problem is as follows.

$$\max_m (1-\alpha)V_l + m\left\{\frac{pq}{pq+1-p}(1-\alpha)\beta(V_h-b_l)+\frac{1-p}{pq+1-p}0\right\}-\frac{am^2}{2}$$

From the f.o.c of above, they obtain the optimal level of monitoring m^* as below,

$$m^* = \frac{pq(1-\alpha)\beta(V_h-b_l)}{(pq+1-p)a}. \tag{6.14}$$

Also to ensure interior solution, assume $a > (1-\alpha)\Delta V$. Partial differentiation of optimal solution with q, β, and a, we obtain $\frac{\partial m^*}{\partial q} > 0$, $\frac{\partial m^*}{\partial \beta} > 0$, $\frac{\partial m^*}{\partial a} < 0$. These imply that while if the likelihood of false reporting by the manager increases, or the court accepts more punitive damages, the monitoring level of small shareholders will increase, then the higher the cost structure of monitoring is, the lower the monitoring level becomes.

6.3.2.2 Manager's Decision on the Share Price and Reporting Strategy

The manager decides the share purchase price and reporting strategy by considering the monitoring and legal action by small shareholders.

Decision on the Offering Share Price

Consider manager's offering share price when the manager chooses separating strategy. Because both types of managers report correct signal, then the small shareholders do not monitor the firm. Therefore, the manager chooses $b_i = V_i$ as share price, and so his profit is represented by the value of (6.6).

Next, consider that the manager chooses the share price when he/she selects the pooling strategy. In this case, because the small shareholders would monitor, the expected profit of each type is as follows

$$\Pi_i^{hl} = (1-\phi)V_h - (1-\alpha)b_l - \frac{pq(1-\alpha)^2(V_h-b_l)^2}{(pq+1-p)a}, \tag{6.15}$$

$$\Pi_i^{ll} = V_l - (1-\alpha)b_l. \tag{6.16}$$

Decision on the Share Price Under the Pooling Strategy

Let us derive the conditions under which a pooling strategy is chosen in equilibrium. In order for the pooling strategy to be in equilibrium, the following conditions must be satisfied.

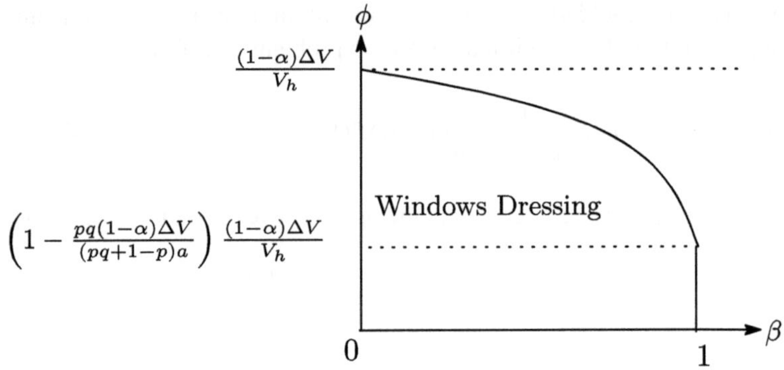

Fig. 6.3 Region of window dressing by the manager under monitoring

$$(1-\phi)V_h - (1-\alpha)b_l - \frac{pq(1-\alpha)^2(V_h-b_l)^2}{(pq+1-p)a} \geq \alpha V_h \quad \text{for } V_h\text{type} \quad (6.17)$$

$$V_l - (1-\alpha)b_l \geq \alpha V_l \quad \text{for } V_h \text{ type.}$$

The second in equation is satisfied if and only if the V_l-type manager offers $b_l = V_l$. Next, under $b_l = V_l$, consider the condition which in equation (6.17) is held. We obtain

$$\phi \leq \left(1 - \frac{pq(1-\alpha)\beta^2(\Delta V)^2}{(pq+1-p)a}\right)\frac{(1-\alpha)\Delta V}{V_h}. \quad (6.18)$$

Proposition 6.1 *Litigation by small shareholders has a decreasing effect on the inverse window dressing of the manager, but when the small shareholders are given the burden of proof, if the manager can easily make false reports, then full compensation cannot deter inverse window dressing.*

Proposition 6.1 is obtained by examining the value on the right side of the (6.18). When in equation $\beta \leq \sqrt{\frac{(pq+1-p)a}{pq(1-\alpha)\Delta V}}$ holds, the value of the right side of the (6.18) is no negative. And the value of the right-hand side of this in equation is more than 1, by interior solution condition of e (Fig. 6.3). Under civil law, the court cannot impose punishment, that is, $\beta \leq 1$. Thus, within $0 \leq \beta \leq 1$, the sign of the right side of (6.18) is positive. Therefore, regardless of the amount of compensation, ϕ exists in which the pooling strategy is supported in equilibrium (Fig. 6.5 is drawn.).

Since the monitoring of small shareholders is costly, the monitoring levels cannot be increased. Moreover, in compensation for damages under the civil law, since the court only accepts up to the amount of damages actually occurred as damages at most, it is not possible to completely suppress the inverse window dressing of the manager.

6.4 Case Where Burden of Proof Is Imposed on the Management

In this section, we would examine the effect of the amendment of the FIEA (2014).

6.4.1 *The Effect of the Transfer of Burden of Proof*

Under the burden of proof to the managers when small shareholders take a legal action, consider the behavior of each agent. Also, when the manager makes the correct report, the small shareholders do not sue the manager as in the past, and thus, the results obtained are the same as before.

6.4.1.1 Manager's Defense Level and Litigation by Small Shareholders

When the small shareholders raise a lawsuit, if the manager does not defend anything, the court will find the true value of the firm. However, if the manager makes efforts to defend, his defense may cause a court's wrong judgment, that is, the court would acknowledge the manager's claim.

Under the firm value V_h being realized, when the manager reports V_l and small shareholders take legal action, the manager chooses level of defense to maximize his expected profit. Therefore, his/her maximization problem is as follows:

$$\max_e (1-\phi)V_h - (1-\alpha)b_l - \{e0 + (1-e)(1-\alpha)\beta(V_h - b_l)\} - \frac{de^2}{2} \tag{6.19}$$

From the f.o.c. of e, we obtain the optimal level of defense,

$$e^* = \frac{(1-\alpha)\beta(V_h - b_l)}{d}. \tag{6.20}$$

The more the damage compensation rate β rises, the more defense effort level rises. And the higher the cost parameter d, the lower the effort level. Here, assume that $d > (1-\alpha)\beta\Delta V$ for the cost parameter d to ensure the interior solution. On the other hand, when V_l is realized, even if a lawsuit is filed, since the manager reports the true firm value, he chooses not to defend.

Next, consider whether the small shareholders take legal action. After selling their shares, if their net profits are increased by going to trial, they take legal action. In this article, the small shareholder's litigation cost is assumed to be zero. Therefore, the small shareholder's expected profit when bringing a lawsuit is

$$(1-\alpha)b_l + \frac{pq}{pq+1-p}\frac{\{d-(1-\alpha)\beta(V_h - b_l)\}(1-\alpha)\beta(V_h - b_l)}{d} > (1-\alpha)b_l$$

The right-hand side of in equation means the gain when not filing a lawsuit, and the gain is higher when the litigation is made, by interior solution conditions. Therefore, small shareholders choose to file a lawsuit.[6]

6.4.1.2 Manager's Offering Share Price and Reporting Signal

Consider that the manager offers the price and reports the signal. The pooling strategy is supported in equilibrium when it satisfies the participation condition of the small shareholders ($b_l \geq V_l$), and the manager has no incentive to report the true value of the firm in both types. V_l type has no incentive to deviate from the pooling strategy while satisfying $(1-\alpha)b_l \geq (1-\alpha)V_l$. Therefore, the condition under which the pooling strategy is in equilibrium is obtained $b_l = V_l$.

When $b_l = V_l$, if the gain when the manager reports a false signal is greater than that when manager reports correct signal V_h, the V_h type of the manager reports a false signal (V_l). That is,

$$\Pi_I^{hl} = (1-\phi)V_h - (1-\alpha)V_l - (1-e^*)(1-\alpha)\beta\Delta V - \frac{de^{*2}}{2} \geq \alpha V_h \quad (6.21)$$

is satisfied. Here, substitute (6.20) with (6.21), and upon its transformation with respect to ϕ, we obtain the following condition,

$$\phi \leq \left(1 - \beta + \frac{(1-\alpha)\beta^2\Delta V}{2d}\right)\frac{(1-\alpha)\Delta V}{V_h}. \quad (6.22)$$

Proposition 6.2 *When the burden of proof is given to the manager and the court is able to impose some punitive damages, the manager always reports the correct signal.*

Proposition 6.2 is obtained by checking the value on the right-hand side of the (6.22). To obtain the condition that the sign of the right-hand side becomes nonnegative, when solving the quadratic inequality $1 - \beta + \frac{(1-\alpha)\beta^2\Delta V}{2d} \geq 0$. Then, we get the next solution

$$0 \leq \beta \leq \frac{d - \sqrt{d(d - 2(1-\alpha)\Delta V)}}{(1-\alpha)\Delta V}, \quad \frac{d + \sqrt{d(d - 2(1-\alpha)\Delta V)}}{(1-\alpha)\Delta V} \leq \beta. \quad (6.23)$$

Substituting $\beta = 0$ into the right-hand side of above in equation, we obtain $\frac{(1-\alpha)\Delta V}{V_h}$, and substituting $\beta = 1$ into the right-hand side of above in equation, we obtain $\frac{(1-\alpha)^2(\Delta V)^2}{V_h} > 0$. Further, we find that $\beta = \frac{d}{(1-\alpha)\Delta V}$ has a local minimum value and

[6]Here, we assume that the cost of litigation is 0 for the simplification of the model. Of course, the magnitude of litigation costs is an important issue, and the results of the analysis can change.

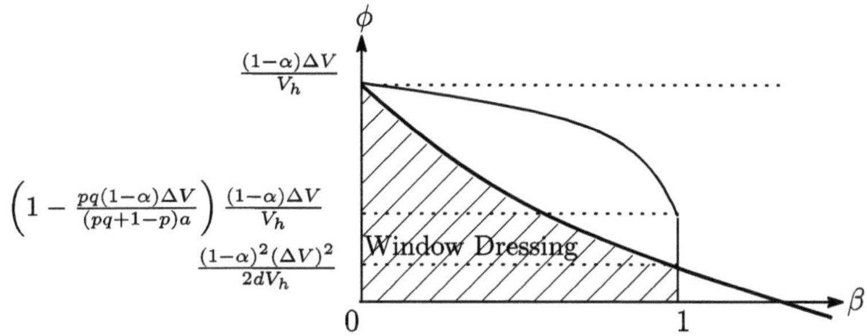

Fig. 6.4 Region of inverse window dressing of the manager when burden of proof is passed on to manager

$\beta = \frac{d}{(1-\alpha)\Delta V} > 1$. So we see that it is at least a β decreasing function within the range of $0 \leq \beta \leq 1$. Therefore, when $\frac{d-\sqrt{d(d-2(1-\alpha)\Delta V)}}{(1-\alpha)\Delta V} \leq \bar{\beta}$, the manager does not make false reports. This figure is shown in Fig. 6.4.

The difference between the previous section and this one is where punitive damages can be made. As mentioned above, if complete reparation merely passes on the burden of proof to the manager, false reports of manager do not necessarily decrease. However, by combining punitive damages, the manager changes his action.

6.4.2 Comparing

We examine the effect of the amendment of the law by comparing the differences between the transfer of the proof of burden and the compensation for damages against the behavior of the manager. We obtain the following proposition.

Proposition 6.3 *Transfer of burden of proof to managers reduces the possibility of inverse window dressing. However, if punitive damages are almost impossible ($\bar{\beta}$ is close to 1), it is better to give shareholders a burden of proof when managers can realize high corporate value with high probability.*

The proof of burden should be given to those who are unlikely to have inverse window dressing by managers. Therefore, we consider whether it is better for managers or small shareholders to have burden of proof to prevent false reports by manager. The possibility of the manager making false reports when small shareholders are given burden of proof is expressed by (6.18). On the other hand, when passing the burden of proof to the manager, it is (6.22). To find out which is desirable, compare the value of ϕ when $\beta = 1$.

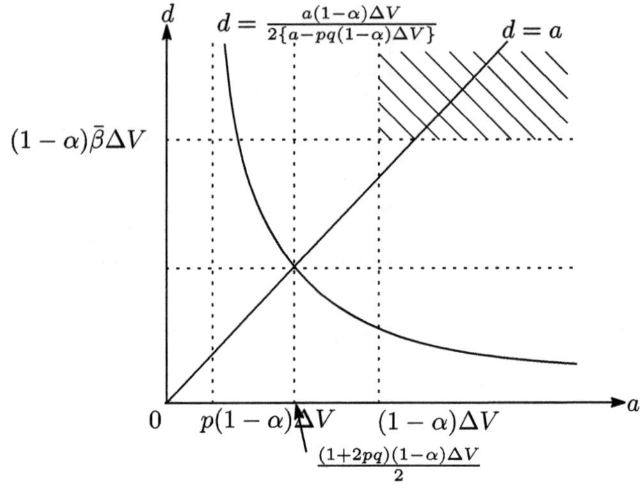

Fig. 6.5 Comparison of the effect of proof burden (case of $pq < \frac{1}{2}$)

In order to compare magnitude relationships, obtain a condition satisfying

$$\left(1 - \frac{pq(1-\alpha)\Delta V}{(pq+1-p)a}\right)\frac{(1-\alpha)\Delta V}{V_h} \geq \frac{(1-\alpha)^2(\Delta V)^2}{2dV_h}. \tag{6.24}$$

The left-hand side is the value obtained by substituting $\beta = 1$ in the (6.22), and the right-hand side is the value obtained by substituting $\beta = 1$ into (6.18). To summarize the above inequalities, we obtain the condition

$$d \geq \frac{a(1-\alpha)\Delta V}{2\{a - pq(1-\alpha)\Delta V\}}. \tag{6.25}$$

When the right-hand side is differentiated with a, the denominator is positive from condition of the interior solution, and we obtain $d' < 0$ and $d'' > 0$. Also, if we obtain the intersection of the straight line $d = a$ and the (6.25), we get

$$d = a = \frac{(1+2pq)(1-\alpha)\Delta V}{2}. \tag{6.26}$$

When examining the magnitude of relationship between the value of (6.26) and $(1-\alpha)\Delta V$ and $(1-\alpha)\bar{\beta}\Delta V$, if $pq < \frac{1}{2}$ hold, $\frac{(1+2pq)(1-\alpha)\Delta V}{2} > (1-\alpha)\Delta V$. Then, in the region satisfying the interior solution condition, $d \geq \frac{a(1-\alpha)\Delta V}{2\{a-pq(1-\alpha)\Delta V\}}$ hold. On the other hand, if $pq > \frac{1}{2}$ holds and $\bar{\beta}$ is close to 1, as shown in the figure, there are areas where it is desirable to have small shareholders account for the burden of proof (Figs. 6.5 and 6.6).

This result is influenced by the incentives for verification efforts. In the situation where the small shareholders have the burden of proof and the compensation is

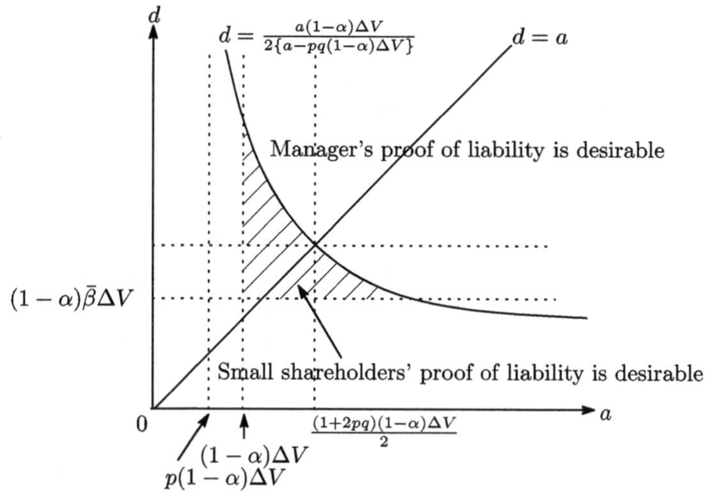

Fig. 6.6 Comparison of the effect of burden of proof (case of $pq > \frac{1}{2}$)

hardly obtained (situation where β is small), there is little incentives to perform effort for proof; thus, the inverse window dressing will be easily performed by the manager. However, as the amount of compensation increases, the effort for proof would increase. Therefore, the possibility of executing inverse window dressing by the manager is low.

On the other hand, even when the manager is charged with proof, the probability of proof is low in a situation where compensation is small (situation where β is small). However, since the manager has to prove himself, the incentive to make a correct report would be strengthened in order to raise his profits. As the amount of compensation increases, the possibility of inverse dressing decreases. Also, unlike cases where the small shareholders have burden of proof, even if the amount of compensation increases, the incentive to stop wrong reporting is gradually small.

In addition, it is thought that managers are more likely to perform inverse window dressing as they gain higher firm value. Therefore, even if decreasing the inverse window dressing, when there is little punitive compensation, the manager may not have the effect of inhibiting inverse window dressing. In that case, it would be more effective to pursue it while leaving the burden of proof to the shareholders seeking to monitor. Therefore, in order to deter inverse window dressing, it will be necessary to recognize punitive compensation to some extent.

6.5 Conclusion

In this paper, the effect of deterring the inverse window dressing of manager is compared based on the civil law and the FIEA (2014).

Naturally, claims for damages by small shareholders have the effect of suppressing the inverse window dressing by the manager. However, it is difficult to deter inverse window dressing perfectly even with full compensation. Meanwhile, under the FIEA (2014), since the burden of proof is passed on to the manager, it is highly effective in deterring the inverse dressing of the manager; furthermore, it can completely deter the inverse window dressing of the manager by punitive damage compensation.

Comparing the two cases, it is possible to show that the pass-through burden of proof to the manager is more deterrent than the burden of proof to the shareholders but even if only passing on the burden of proof is relatively effective to deter. However, if the manager can realize high firm value and cannot almost compensate for punitive damages, it may be desirable for the small shareholders to bear the burden of proof and to pursue. Therefore, it is important as a policy to decide whether to pass the burden of proof burden and punitive damage compensation.

In these analyses, we simplify the model on litigation, assuming that the cost of litigation is zero. In reality, the litigation expenses of shareholders are considered to be very high, so it is necessary to consider it in the model.

References

Burkart, M., and F. Panunzi. 2006. Agency conflicts, ownership concentration, and legal shareholder protection. *Journal of Financial Intermediation* 15: 1–31.

Cuny, C.J., and E. Talmor. 2007. A theory of private equity turnarounds. *Journal of Corporate Finance* 13: 629–646.

Elitzur, R., P. Halpern, R. Kieschnick, and W. Rotenberg. 1998. Managerial incentives and the structure of management buyouts. *Journal of Economic Behavior and Organization*, 36: 347–367.

Financial Services Agency. 2014. *Kinyou Shoushin Torihiki Hou nado no Ichibu wo Kaisei suru Houritu ni kakawaru shiryo*. http://www.fsa.go.jp/common/diet/186/01/setsumei.pdf (In Japanese).

Hanamura, S. 2011. Impact of hostile TOBs on managers and information disclosure. *Syouken Keizai Gakkai Nenpou* 46: 99–108D (In Japanese).

Kato, T. 2011. Ryutsu shijo ni okeru fujistu kaiji to toushika no songai. *Shin Sedai Hou Seisakugaku Kenkyu* 11: 303–346 (In Japanese).

Stein, J. C. 1988. Takeover threats and managerial myopia. *Journal of Political Economy* 96(1): 61–80.

Tamayama, T. 2010. The judicial screening of MBOs. *Nanzan Hougaku* 33(3/4): 313–343 (In Japanese).

Chapter 7
Optimal Default Rule for Breach of Contract

Kazuhiko Sakai

7.1 Introduction

Creditors suffer various types of damage if an obligor violates a contract. For example, in sales contracts for goods between sellers and buyers, it is possible to damage the buyer's property due to defects in the target (goods) and damage to the buyer itself or to cause an economic loss to the creditors. In the event that such damage occurs due to a breach of contract, the creditor can file a suit for damages against the obligor. However, incomplete contracts are common and do not adequately specify the responsibilities of each party related to the damage. To deal with such an incomplete contract, Japan has a default called the Hadley rule (normal-damage rule) as a means of compensation when a contract breach occurs (Civil Code Article 416). In other words, the obligor's liability is limited only to the damage that is likely to occur normally and the damage due to special circumstances that the obligor could foresee at the time of the contract.

By limiting the obligor's liability to foreseeable damage, the creditor has incentives to disclose the magnitude of the damage to the obligor ex ante; thus, Hadley rules are the default rule in a contract violation in many countries such as Japan. On the other hand, the rules in some countries prioritize victims and have a full-damage rule. In the case of a breach of contract, the obligor must compensate creditors for all damages, whatever they are. However, given that victims are compensated for all damages, some argue that victims do not have an incentive to disclose information themselves.

K. Sakai (✉)
Kurume University, Kurume, Japan
e-mail: sakai_kazuhiko@kurume-u.ac.jp

T. Naito et al. (eds.), *Applied Approaches to Societal Institutions and Economics*,
New Frontiers in Regional Science: Asian Perspectives 18,
DOI 10.1007/978-981-10-5663-5_7

Ayres and Gertner (1989), Bebchunk and Shavell (1991), Maskin (2005), and others examined the role of the default rule. However, these studies overlook important issues. The Hadley rule is a compensation rule that the court uses as a standard in a trial when they cannot solve a problem with a party. Therefore, if the problem does not appear in a trial or if the parties resolve the problem themselves, compensation will not be made according to the Hadley rule. However, previous studies do not consider the trial and settlement stages, so it is not clear that the efficiency of the Hadley rule has been analyzed completely.

When considering a trial or settlement, litigation cost is an important problem.[1] Japan, adopted the American rule in which both parties bear the litigation costs. No existing studies analyze the efficiency of the Hadley rule considering the American rule in terms of the stage of suit when proposing optimal liability rule designs for violation of contract.

However, this is not realistic in the real world, so we must consider a model that includes the stage of litigation and settlement. Our analysis focuses on the settlement negotiation when the provision fails, unlike previous studies. Then, by comparing the normal-damage rule and the full-damage rule, our study focuses on the information disclosure effect to verify the efficiency of the normal-damage rule.

With this background, we consider an economy composed of a buyer and a seller in a model based on the well-known case of *Hadleyv.Baxendale*. Then, we introduce the litigation and settlement stages used by Bebchunk (1984) and Nalebuff (1987) into the model. We examine the problem of which default rule for violation of contract is more effective when the American rule dictates the burden of litigation cost.[2]

We proceed as follows. Section 7.2 describes the Hadley model. Section 7.3 examines how the seller determines the level of care and whether the buyer contracts with the seller or not under the normal-damage rule. Section 7.4 analyzes the full-damage rule case, as in Sect. 7.3, then compares the two rules. Section 7.5 provides concluding remarks and discusses areas of future research to test the robustness of our conclusion.

7.2 The Model

Suppose that a risk neutral buyer will sign a sales contract to purchase a service (goods) from a risk neutral seller. B represents the buyer's benefit from the service, which is the buyer's private information. In addition, B expresses the "normal

---

[1]Reinganum and Wilde (1986), Miceli (1997), Wijck and Velthoven (2000), and others analyze the impact of legal costs on litigation and settlements.

[2]Sakai (2016) considered the case where the British rule dictates the burden of litigation cost under the Hadley rule.

benefit," denoted as B_N with probability B_N as q or "supernormal benefit" with probability $1 - q$ expressed as $B_S(> B_N)$.

Even if the seller promises to supply the service and makes a contract with the buyer, there is a risk that the seller will violate the contract. The risk can be reduced, though not completely eliminated, by the seller's taking "care." In addition, as in Ayres and Gertner (1989), we assume seller's chosen level of care is not verifiable (i.e., there is no way to prove the level of care to a third party like a court). With this assumption, the buyer cannot negotiate the level of care in the contract. Thus, to derive an appropriate level of care from the seller, at least in part, the seller must be liable to benefit the buyer in some way provision fails. However, the contract is incomplete and does not clearly state the amount of compensation; compensation for damages will be made depending on the default rules set by the government if it comes to litigation.

If the Hadley rule is adopted as the default rule, the seller is liable for the buyer's "normal" loss B_N if the seller cannot foresee the "supernormal" loss B_S. However, if the seller can foresee the "supernormal" loss B_S, the seller is liable. To model the buyer's ability to foresee the loss, I introduce the cost to reveal the buyer's loss B as $c > 0$. On the other hand, if the full-damage rule is adopted, the seller must always compensate for all damages, regardless of whether the seller could foresee the magnitude of the damage in advance.

However, under either rule, the buyer must bear the cost of litigation to demand compensation for the loss. The buyer (plaintiff) must bring a damage suit against the seller (defendant). Suppose that if the buyer sues, the buyer always wins the suit and is compensated for the loss following the default rule. We denote $c_p(c_d)$ as the buyer's (seller's) litigation cost. Yet, the buyer can negotiate a settlement at a cost of zero for both parties.[3]

The timeline is as follows:

Stage 1: The government sets out a default rule.
Stage 2: The buyer offers the contract.
Stage 3: The seller chooses the level of care.
Stage 4: The buyer chooses between a trial and a settlement in case provision fails.

In Stage 1, the government determines the liability rule, that is, it chooses either the normal-damage or full-damage rule as the default rule for violation of contract. In Stage 2, the buyer offers the contract to the seller. That is, the buyer chooses the price for the service and decides whether or not reveal his loss B. In Stage 3, the seller chooses the level of care e under the default rule for violation of contract and the contract to offer. The seller's level of care e is the seller's private information and represents the cost of care. The probability of successful provision depends on the level of care e with probability $\pi(e)$. Furthermore, we suppose $\pi'(e) > 0$, $\pi''(e) < 0$, $\pi'(0) = \infty$, $\pi'(\infty) = 0$. In Stage 4, the buyer chooses between bringing a

[3]If c=0 and there is no transaction or litigation cost, the Coase theorem holds for this model, as in previous studies like Mas-Colell et al. (1995).

damage suit and negotiating a settlement if provision fails. If the negotiation ends in failure, then the seller brings a trial and compensation follows the default rule or does nothing.

7.2.1 *First Best*

In this subsection, we consider the first best case as a benchmark. The expected gross benefit from a particular choice of e is $\pi(e)B$, and the cost is e. Hence, we define e^{FB} as the first best care level; then e^{FB} should be chosen to maximize

$$SW(e) \equiv \pi(e)B - e. \tag{7.1}$$

Then, we have the first-order condition as

$$\pi'(e^{FB})B - 1 = 0. \tag{7.2}$$

For e^{FB},

$$\frac{de^{FB}}{dB} > 0 \tag{7.3}$$

holds. Since $B_N < B_S$, Eq. (7.3) implies

$$e_N^{FB} < e_S^{FB}. \tag{7.4}$$

That is, the higher the profit, the higher the level of care is.

7.3 The Normal-Damage Rule

Here, we consider the case in which normal-damage rule is adopted for violation of contract at Stage 1. To solve this game by backward induction, we analyze the negotiation for settlement in Stage 4.

7.3.1 *Trial or Settlement (1)*

The buyer's payoff in Stage 4 in case of a trial is

$$D - c_p, \tag{7.5}$$

where D denotes the compensation paid by the seller following the Hadley rule. So, if $D \geq c_p$ holds, then the buyer can bring the suit. Here, we denote as S as the sum of settlement. The buyer then obtains S and has no other cost if choosing a settlement. So, if

$$S \geq D - c_p \equiv \underline{S}^a \tag{7.6}$$

holds, then the buyer chooses the settlement.

Like the buyer, the seller's cost at this stage is

$$D + c_d \quad \textit{if} \quad \textit{trial}, \tag{7.7}$$

$$S \qquad \textit{if} \quad \textit{settlement}. \tag{7.8}$$

So, if

$$S \leq D + c_d \equiv \overline{S}^a \tag{7.9}$$

holds, then the seller chooses a settlement.

Equations (7.6) and (7.9) imply that the constraint of having a settlement is

$$\underline{S}^a \leq S \leq \overline{S}^a. \tag{7.10}$$

Like Ayres and Gertner (1989), I suppose that the buyer has all of the bargaining power. Hence, the buyer chooses the settlement and obtains $\overline{S}^a$ from the seller in this stage. Regarding $\overline{S}^a$,

$$\frac{\partial \overline{S}^a}{\partial D} > 0, \ \frac{\partial \overline{S}^a}{\partial c_p} < 0 \tag{7.11}$$

holds. Since $B_N < B_S$, Eq. (7.11) implies

$$\overline{S}^a_N < \overline{S}^a_S. \tag{7.12}$$

On the other hand, if $D < c_p$ holds, then the buyer does not bring the suit. Hence, the buyer has no compensation, and the seller has no cost in this stage.

7.3.2 Seller's Behavior: Decision on the Care Level

Here, we analyze Stage 3. Because provision fails with probability $1 - \pi(e)$ and the seller must pay $\overline{S}^a$ in Stage 4 if $D \geq c_p$, the seller's expected payoff in Stage 3 under this rule is

$$p - (1 - \pi(e))\overline{S}^a - e, \tag{7.13}$$

if the contract specifies a fixed price p for the service. For convenience, we suppose that the buyer pays the seller this price whether or not provision is successful. Then, we have the first-order condition

$$\pi'(e)\overline{S}^a - 1 = 0. \tag{7.14}$$

Let e^a be the care level satisfying Eq. (7.14). For e^a,

$$\frac{de^a}{d\overline{S}^a} > 0 \tag{7.15}$$

holds. Since $\overline{S}_N^a < \overline{S}_S^a$, Eq. (7.15) implies

$$e_N^a < e_S^a. \tag{7.16}$$

In addition, because $\overline{S}^a > B$ holds, then

$$e^{FB} < e^a. \tag{7.17}$$

holds. Furthermore, the individual rationality constraint of the seller is

$$p \geq (1 - \pi(e^a))\overline{S}^a + e^a \equiv p^a, \tag{7.18}$$

and, for p^a,

$$p_N^a < p_S^a \tag{7.19}$$

holds.

On the other hand, if $D < c_p$ holds, then the seller has no cost if provision fails. Thus, the seller's payoff is

$$p - (1 - \pi(e))0 - e = p - e. \tag{7.20}$$

Hence, the optimal level of care for the seller is zero, and the individual rationality constraint of the seller is

$$p \geq 0. \tag{7.21}$$

7.3.3 Buyer's Behavior: Contract for Sale

Here, we analyze Stage 2. The buyer knows the true B at this stage, so we first analyze the case when $B = B_N$. Like Ayres and Gertner (1989), I consider the case in which the buyer can make a take-it-or-leave-it offer to the seller.

Regardless of whether the buyer reveals the information about the loss B, D equals B_N when $B = B_N$. Thus, if $D \geq c_p$ holds, then the buyer obtains $\overline{S}_N^a$ when the seller breaches the contract. Then, the seller chooses e_N^a in Stage 3, so the buyer's expected payoff when $B_N \geq c_p$ is

$$\pi(e_N^a)B_N + (1 - \pi(e_N^a))\overline{S}_N^a - p. \tag{7.22}$$

It is beneficial for the buyer to reduce p, so the optimal p is p_N^a, and the buyer's expected payoff under p_N^a is

$$\pi(e_N^a)B_N - e_N^a. \tag{7.23}$$

If the buyer reveals the value of B, he must bear the cost c without any benefit of compensation. Hence, if $B = B_N$, the buyer has no incentive to announce damages B to the seller.

On the other hand, if $D < c_p$ holds, then the buyer has no compensation and the seller chooses a zero level of care. Thus, the buyer's expected payoff when $B_N < c_p$ holds is

$$\pi(0)B_N - p. \tag{7.24}$$

Then, the optimal price for the buyer is zero, and the buyer's expected payoff under $p = 0$ is

$$\pi(0)B_N. \tag{7.25}$$

As in the case $B_N \geq c_p$, the buyer has no incentive to reveal the damages if $B = B_N$. Thus, the buyer never announces B if $B = B_N$.

Assume next that $B = B_S$. Then, $D = B_S$ if the buyer announces the true damages, and the buyer receives $\overline{S}_S^a$ when the seller breaches the contract. However, if c_p is larger than D, then the buyer cannot obtain any compensation from the seller. We thus first consider the case in which $c_p \leq B_N$, where the buyer's expected payoff when B is not announced is

$$\pi(e_N^a)B_S + (1 - \pi(e_N^a))\overline{S}_N^a - p. \tag{7.26}$$

Then, the buyer's expected payoff under the optimal price level p_N^a is

$$\pi(e_N^a)B_S - e_N^a. \tag{7.27}$$

On the other hand, the buyer's expected payoff when announcing B is

$$\pi(e_S^a)B_S + (1 - \pi(e_S^a))\overline{S}_S^a - p - c. \tag{7.28}$$

Then, the buyer's expected payoff under the optimal price level p_S^a is

$$\pi(e_S^a)B_S - e_S^a - c. \tag{7.29}$$

Hence, as long as the inequality

$$c \le \{\pi(e_S^a)B_S - e_S^a\} - \{\pi(e_N^a)B_S - e_N^a\} \equiv c_1^a \tag{7.30}$$

holds, the buyer has the incentive to make the announcement and incur cost " c ".[4]

Next, we analyze the case when $B_N < c_p \le B_S$, in which the expected payoff when the buyer does not announce $B = B_S$ is

$$\pi(0)B_S - p. \tag{7.31}$$

Then, the buyer's expected payoff under the optimal price level ($p = 0$) is

$$\pi(0)B_S. \tag{7.32}$$

On the other hand, the buyer's expected payoff when announcing $B = B_S$ is Eq. (7.29). So, when the inequality

$$c \le \{\pi(e_S^a)B_S - e_S^a\} - \{\pi(0)B_S\} \equiv c_2^a \tag{7.33}$$

holds, the buyer announces the true damages and incurs cost " c ".[5]

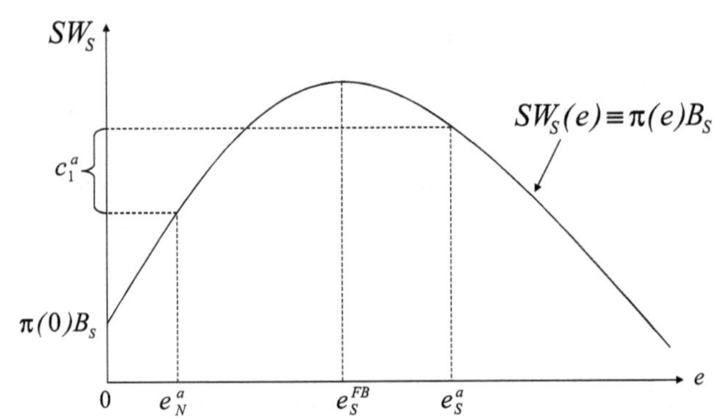

Fig. 7.1 Social welfare under the case of $B_N \ge c_p$

[4]See Fig. 7.1.

[5]See Fig. 7.2.

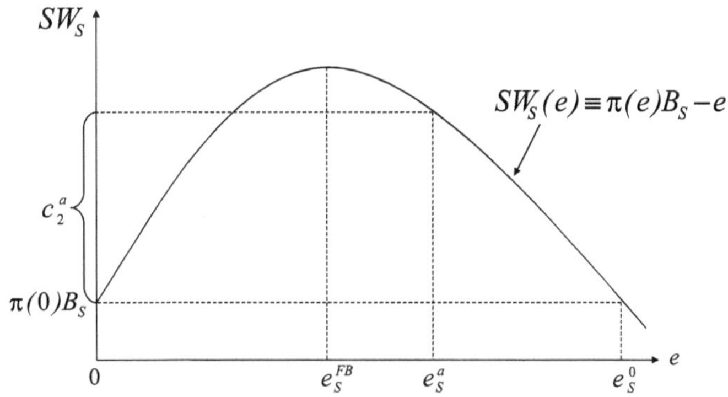

Fig. 7.2 Social welfare under the case of $B_N < c_p \leq B_S$

Finally, we consider the case $c_p \geq B_S$, in which the expected payoff when the buyer does not announce $B = B_S$ is Eq. (7.32). On the other hand, the buyer's expected payoff when announcing $B = B_S$ is

$$\pi(0)B_S - c. \tag{7.34}$$

Hence, in this case, the buyer never announces $B = B_S$.

Comparing c_1^a and c_2^a from Eqs. (7.30) and (7.33), we see that c_2^a is larger than c_1^a. Therefore, summarizing the above discussion, we have the following proposition:

Proposition 7.1 *The information disclosure effect works more strongly as the cost of litigation increases to a certain extent. However, when the cost of litigation is sufficiently large, the information disclosure effect will not work.*

7.4 The Full-Damage Rule

In this section, we consider the case when the government adopts the full-damage rule as the default for breach of contract and verify its effect by comparing it with the results in the previous section. However, rather than analyzing all cases in detail, we focus only on cases that are resolved by settlement and introduce only a few interesting properties. We will examine the case starting with Stage 4 to solve the game backward.

In Stage 4, regardless of the seller's foreseeability, the compensation amount is always $D = B$, and the seller pays $\overline{S}^a$ to the buyer. Let β be the seller's belief that the buyer is low-risk ($B = B_N$) in Stage 3 after seeing the contract presented by the buyer in Stage 2. The seller's expected payoff in Stage 3 is

$$p - \{1 - \pi(e)\}\{\beta\overline{S}_N^a + (1 - \beta)\overline{S}_S^a\} - e. \tag{7.35}$$

Then, we have the first-order condition

$$\pi'(e)\{\beta\overline{S}_N^a + (1-\beta)\overline{S}_S^a\} - 1 = 0. \tag{7.36}$$

Let $\hat{e}^a$ be the level of care satisfying Eq. (7.36). For $\hat{e}^a$,

$$\frac{\partial \hat{e}^a}{\partial \beta} < 0,\ \frac{\partial \hat{e}^a}{\partial \overline{S}_N^a} > 0,\ \frac{\partial \hat{e}^a}{\partial \overline{S}_S^a} > 0 \tag{7.37}$$

holds. Since $\overline{S}_N^a \leq \beta\overline{S}_N^a + (1-\beta)\overline{S}_S^a \leq \overline{S}_S^a$ holds, Eq. (7.35) implies

$$e_N^a \leq \hat{e}^a \leq e_S^a. \tag{7.38}$$

Furthermore, the seller's individual rationality constraint is

$$p \geq \{1-\pi(\hat{e}^a)\}\{\beta\overline{S}_N^a + (1-\beta)\overline{S}_S^a\} + \hat{e}^a \equiv \hat{p}^a, \tag{7.39}$$

and for $\hat{p}^a$,

$$p_N^a \leq \hat{p}^a \leq p_S^a \tag{7.40}$$

holds.

Next, we analyze Stage 2. The equilibrium concept in this stage is a perfect Bayesian equilibrium. However, the buyer does not need to disclose information if it separates the equilibrium and the damages amount becomes complete information. Therefore, we analyze only the pooling equilibrium, in which the seller can judge only the damages amount with the initial belief.

For that reason, we assume the seller's posterior belief when the price deviation from the equilibrium is $1(\beta = 1)$. That is, the seller observing price p outside the equilibrium route determines that the buyer presenting the price is high-risk. By this assumption, $p = p_S^a$ is the pooling equilibrium.[6]

We analyze the case $B = B_S$ first. Under the pooling equilibrium $p = p_S^a$, the buyer's expected payoff is

$$\pi(\hat{e}^a(\beta = q))B_S - \hat{e}^a(\beta = q) + \{1 - \pi(\hat{e}^a(\beta = q))\}q(\overline{S}_S^a - \overline{S}_N^a). \tag{7.41}$$

On the other hand, the expected payoff when information is disclosed is given by Eqs. (7.29), and (7.29) is less than Eq. (7.41). Therefore, high-risk type buyers do not disclose information.

[6]There are many equilibria in addition to $p = p_S^a$. However, $p = p_S^a$ maximizes the gain to low-risk buyers in a pooling equilibrium, and the seller analyzes whether the buyer disclosing the information is low-risk type at that time.

Next, we analyze the case $B = B_N$. Under the pooling equilibrium $p = p_S^a$, the buyer's expected payoff is

$$\pi(\hat{e}^a(\beta = q))B_N - \hat{e}^a(\beta = q) + \{1 - \pi(\hat{e}^a(\beta = q))\}q(\overline{S}_S^a - \overline{S}_N^a). \quad (7.42)$$

On the other hand, the expected payoff when information is disclosed is

$$\pi(e_N^a)B_N - e_N^a - c. \quad (7.43)$$

Thus, when the inequality

$$c \leq \{\pi(e_N^a)B_N - e_N^a\} - \{\pi(\hat{e}^a(\beta = q))B_N - \hat{e}^a(\beta = q) + \{1 - \pi(\hat{e}^a(\beta = q))\}q(\overline{S}_S^a - \overline{S}_N^a)\} \equiv c^F \quad (7.44)$$

holds, the buyer announces the true damages and incurs cost c.

The important point here is that c^F is always positive. On the other hand, the information disclosure condition c_1^a under the Hadley rule may become negative. In that case, the full-damage rule results in a stronger information disclosure effect than under the Hadley rule.

Summarizing the discussion above, we obtain the following proposition:

Proposition 7.2 *Considering the case of trial and settlement at the time of breach of contract under the American rule, the information disclosure effect is stronger than the Hadley rule in some cases under the full-damage rule.*

7.5 Concluding Remarks

The paper examined the normal-damage and full-damage rules as optimal default rules for breach of contract when the American rule determines the allocation of legal fees, as in Japan. The analysis shows that the full-damage rule's disclosure effect is stronger than under the Hadley rule. This means that the full-damage rule may be the socially desirable default rule. Therefore, we conclude that it is necessary to review the default rules in countries that adopt the American rule to determine the burden of litigation cost, as in Japan.

This study leaves a further investigation into the role of the default rule for future research. When considering the trial stage, as Proposition 7.2 shows, we derive a different conclusion from those in previous studies on the information disclosure effect. Therefore, it is not yet clear which is the more efficient default rule. It is also important to consider the "judgment-proof problem" and the role of insurance, which are set aside for future analysis.

References

Ayres, I., and R. Gertner. 1989. Filling gaps in incomplete contracts: An economic theory of default rule. *Yale Law Journal* 99: 87–130.

Bebchunk, L.A. (1984). Litigation and settlement under imperfect information. *Rand Journal of Economics* 3: 404–415.

Bebchunk, L.A., and S. Shavell. 1991. Information and the scope of liability for breach of contract. *Journal of Law, Economics and Organization* 7: 284.

Mas-Colell, A., M. Whinston, and J. Green. 1995. *Microeconomic theory*. Oxford: Oxford University Press.

Maskin, E. 2005. On the rationale for the penalty default rule. *Florida State University Law Review* 33: 557–562.

Miceli, T.J. 1997. *Economics of the law*. Oxford: Oxford University Press.

Nalebuff, B. 1987. Credible pretrial negotiation. *Rand Journal of Economics* 2: 198–210.

Reinganum, J.F., and L.L. Wilde. 1986. Settlement, litigation and the allocation of litigation costs. *Rand Journal of Economics* 17: 557–566.

Sakai, K. 2016. Litigation cost and Hadley rule. *Kyushu Keizai Nenpo* 54: 71–77 (In Japanese).

Wijck, V., and V.B. Velthoven. 2000. An economic analysis of the American and the continental rule for allocating legal costs. *European Journal of Law and Economics* 2: 115–125.

Chapter 8
How to Determine the Lending Level of the Bank to the Firm?

Shinya Shimoda

8.1 Introduction

Financial institutions (banks, insurance firms, securities firms, and so on) are regulated by laws, decrees, or guidance due to their significant economic influence. Therefore, regulators such as the Financial Agency in Japan are always concerned about implementing effective regulations and the means to enforce them on financial institutions. Such regulations include measures to prevent a credit crunch. The Japanese economy experienced several crises in the past 20 years, and banks have implemented screening that makes it very hard for firms to obtain loans. The Financial Agency has frequently announced that the government has requested that banks maintain liquidity by supplying money to firms, especially small firms. We believe that the Financial Agency is able to use its administrative power to extend loans for firms with insufficient liquidity.

However, the regulator's intervention in financial institutions often brings side effects. For example, Aghion et al. (1999) analyze whether to impose responsibility on bankrupt bank managers or not. They point out that when there is a probability of punishment for the bank's manager, the bank's settlement is often window dressing. On the other hand, when the manager is permitted to remain innocent, the bank experiences excess selvage. Cordella and Yeyati (2002) analyze the efficiency of the bank bailout policy and point out that it is more efficient for the government to bail out bankrupt banks when the economy suffers serious damage, even if it enables bank managers' moral hazard. Shimoda and Hosoe (2008) analyze the level of banks' disclosure policy and find that government-mandated, higher level of bank

S. Shimoda (✉)
Kyushu Sangyo University, Fukuoka, Japan
e-mail: shimoda@ip.kyusan-u.ac.jp

T. Naito et al. (eds.), *Applied Approaches to Societal Institutions and Economics*,
New Frontiers in Regional Science: Asian Perspectives 18,
DOI 10.1007/978-981-10-5663-5_8

disclosure is not an efficient policy for depositors when the government considers the marginal cost of disclosures and lawsuits between the bank and the depositor.

On the other hand, Milton and Raviv (2014) analyze the optimal policy when the bank manager prefers high-risk, high-return investments and show that it is efficient for the government to enforce project selection on the bank manager.

In this study, we analyze the policy that determines banks' lending level. We assume an economy in which the firm wants to extend a loan due to the credit crunch and the regulator (government office or central bank) is aware. We also aim to determine whether an "arbitrary" policy or "laissez-faire" policy can meet the firm's request.

The rest of this article proceeds as follows. In Sect. 8.2 we construct the model and analyze the two policies in Sects. 8.3 and 8.4. We compare the models in Sect. 8.5. We obtain the result and offer a discussion in Sect. 8.6.

8.2 Model

There are three players in the economy: a bank regulator (hereafter, regulator), a bank, and a firm. All players are risk neutral. The regulator, who has the authority to regulate the bank, can make decisions about the level of lending under the "arbitrary" and cannot do so directly under the "laissez-faire" policy, in which the bank determines the level of lending.

The bank lends to the firm. The regulator or bank itself determines the level of lending if the regulator allows it. A higher lending level increases not only the possibility of gaining profit but also the bank's lending cost and the possibility of making a loss.

A firm with insufficient funds can execute a new project if it obtains a loan from the bank. When the new project succeeds, the firm can profit; if it fails, the firm does not profit. The firm always pays the cost of effort. We assume that the cost is not monetary, so the firm does not consider the budget constraint.

The timeline of this game is as follows.

Period 1 The regulator selects the policy ("arbitrary" or "laissez-faire" policy), that is, it chooses whether the bank or the regulator determines the lending level.
Period 2 The regulator or the bank determines the lending level, and the bank lends according to the determined level.
Period 3 The firm executes the new project and realizes a profit or loss.

Period 1: The regulatory policy decision

In this period, the regulator chooses between the "arbitrary" and "laissez-faire" policies. In the case of the former, the regulator determines the lending level p to maximize its objective function; otherwise, the bank determines the lending level. The regulator's objective function is the sum of the bank's profit and the firm's profit. However, the regulator notes the proportion of the bank's profit, denoted $\theta(\theta > 0)$.

Period 2: The lending level decision

In this period, the regulator determines the lending level p after choosing the "arbitrary policy," or the bank does so under the "laissez-faire" policy. The lending level p indicates how the regulator intends to extend loans to the firm. A high level of p represents a more positive policy of extending loans to the firm. The bank has to pay the cost $\frac{1}{2}\alpha p^2$ to extend a loan amount p, and α indicates the marginal cost of lending. The bank gains a profit of pB when the firm's project is successful, with probability e, but suffers a loss of p when it fails. B indicates the marginal benefit, and D indicates the marginal loss on the bank loan. Therefore, the bank's utility function (Π_b) is

$$\Pi_b = p\{eB - (1-e)D\} - \frac{1}{2}\alpha p^2. \tag{8.1}$$

We assume that $1 \leq \alpha \leq B$.

Period 3: The decision of the firm's effort

In period 3, the firm determines its effort level $e(0 < e < 1)$, which is the probability that the new project succeeds. The firm has a cost of $\frac{1}{2}\beta e^2$ with effort level e, where β indicates the marginal cost of the firm's effort. The firm gains a profit of pF when the project is successful and pays nothing besides the effort cost otherwise due to limited liability. Therefore, the firm's utility function (Π_f) is

$$\Pi_f = peF - \frac{1}{2}\beta e^2 \tag{8.2}$$

We assume that $1 \leq \beta \leq F$.

8.3 Laissez-Faire Model: The Bank Determines the Lending Level

In this section, we analyze the case when the regulator does not determine the bank's lending level ("laissez-faire" policy). To solve the game in this model, we use a backward analysis of the timeline. Therefore, the bank can determine the lending level to maximize its profit based on predictions of the firm's level of effort.

In period 3, the firm determines its effort level with given p, which is determined by the bank in period 2. From equation (8.2), the firm's optimal effort level e^* is determined by

$$\frac{\partial \Pi_f}{\partial e} = pF - \beta e = 0$$

$$e^* = \frac{pF}{\beta}. \tag{8.3}$$

It is obvious that e^* increases as F increases and decreases with β. That is to say, a larger marginal profit or a smaller marginal cost encourages the firm to put in more effort to gain a higher profit.

In period 2, the bank determines the lending level by predicting the firm's effort level e^*. Considering that $e^* = \frac{pF}{\beta}$, the bank's objective function is

$$\begin{aligned}\Pi_b =& p\{e^* B - (1 - e^*)\} - \frac{1}{2}\alpha p^2 \\ =& p\{\frac{pF}{\beta}B - (1 - \frac{pF}{\beta})\} - \frac{1}{2}\alpha p^2 \\ =& p^2\frac{F(B+1)}{\beta} - p - \frac{1}{2}\alpha p^2,\end{aligned}$$

so the bank determines the optimal level of lending p_b as follows:

$$\begin{aligned}\frac{\partial \Pi_b}{\partial p} =& 2p\frac{F(B+1)}{\beta} - 1 - \alpha p = 0 \\ & p\{\frac{2F(B+1)}{\beta} - \alpha\} = 1 \\ p_b =& \frac{\beta}{2F(B+1) - \alpha\beta}.\end{aligned} \tag{8.4}$$

We easily see that p_b increases with α and β and decreases with F and B.

From the above analysis, we obtain Lemma 8.1.

Lemma 8.1 *In the "laissez-faire" economy, the bank's lending level (p_b) is determined by $p_b = \frac{\beta}{2F(B+1)-\alpha\beta}$. When the marginal cost of the bank's lending (α) and the marginal cost of the firm's project (β) increase, or the marginal profit of the bank (B) and the marginal profit of the firm (F) decrease, the lending level (p_b) increases.*

Proof of Lemma 8.1 From equation (8.4), we obtain $\frac{\partial p_b}{\partial \alpha} = -\frac{-\beta}{\{2F(B+1)-\alpha\beta\}^2} > 0$, $\frac{\partial p_b}{\partial \beta} = \frac{2F(B+1)}{\{2F(B+1)-\alpha\beta\}^2} > 0$. We also obtain $\frac{\partial p_b}{\partial B} = -\frac{2F}{\{2F(B+1)-\alpha\beta\}^2} < 0$, $\frac{\partial p_b}{\partial F} = -\frac{2(B+1)}{\{2F(B+1)-\alpha\beta\}^2} < 0$. □

Lemma 8.1 suggests that a larger α increases the bank's cost. However, increasing the firm's level of effort e increases profit for both the firm and the bank. Therefore, the bank increases the level of lending p to increase profits for both itself and the firm. Additionally, a larger β decreases the firm's effort level e, so the bank increases the level of lending p to encourage the firm to put in more effort.

8.4 Arbitrary Model: The Regulator Determines the Lending Level

In this section, the regulator determines the bank's lending level. The regulator considers both the bank's profit and firm's profit, so the objective function Π_r becomes

$$\begin{aligned}\Pi_r =&\theta \Pi_b + \Pi_f \\ =&\theta[p\{eB - (1-e)\} - \frac{1}{2}\alpha p^2] + peF - \frac{1}{2}\beta e^2. \end{aligned} \tag{8.5}$$

The firm has the same objective function as in Sect. 8.3, so the firm also determines its effort level e as $e^* = \frac{pF}{\beta}$ in period 3.

Predicting the firm's effort level e^*, the regulator determines the lending level p to maximize equation (8.5).

$$\begin{aligned}\Pi_r =&\theta[p\{e^*B - (1-e^*)\} - \frac{1}{2}\alpha p^2] + pe^*F - \frac{1}{2}\beta e^{*2} \\ =&\theta[p\{\frac{pF}{\beta}B - (1 - \frac{pF}{\beta})\} - \frac{1}{2}\alpha p^2] + p\frac{pF}{\beta}F - \frac{1}{2}\beta\frac{p^2F^2}{\beta^2} \\ =&\theta\{p^2\frac{F(B+1)}{\beta} - p - \frac{1}{2}\alpha p^2\} + \frac{1}{2}\frac{p^2F^2}{\beta}\end{aligned}$$

So, the optimal level of p is

$$\begin{aligned}\frac{\partial \Pi_r}{\partial p} &= 2p\theta\frac{F(B+1)}{\beta} - \theta - \alpha p\theta + p\frac{F^2}{\beta} = 0 \\ p\{&\frac{2\theta F(B+1)}{\beta} - \theta\alpha\frac{F^2}{\beta}\} = \theta \\ p_r &= \frac{\theta}{2\theta F(B+1) + F^2 - \theta\alpha\beta}.\end{aligned} \tag{8.6}$$

By comparing equations (8.4) and (8.6), we obtain the following lemma.

Lemma 8.2 *When the regulator determines the lending level directly, the optimal level of lending for the regulator p_r is lower than the optimal lending level for the bank p_b.*

Proof of Lemma 8.2 To compare p_b and p_r, we calculate $p_r - p_b$.

$$p_r - p_b = \frac{\theta}{2\theta F(B+1) + F^2 - \theta\alpha\beta} - \frac{\beta}{2F(B+1) - \alpha\beta}$$

$$= \frac{2\theta\beta F(B+1) - \theta\alpha\beta^2 - 2\theta F(B+1)\beta - \beta F^2 + \theta\alpha\beta^2}{\{2\theta F(B+1) + F^2 - \theta\alpha\beta\}\{2F(B+1) - \alpha\beta\}}$$

$$= \frac{-\beta F^2}{\{2\theta F(B+1) + F^2 - \theta\alpha\beta\}\{2F(B+1) - \alpha\beta\}} \tag{8.7}$$

From assumptions $1 \leq \alpha \leq B$ and $1 \leq \beta \leq F$, the denominator of equation (8.7) is positive, so equation (8.7) is negative. □

8.5 Comparative Statics

In this section, we analyze the comparative statics related to lending levels determined by the regulator p_r, that is to say, how the degree of θ affects p_r.

The regulator that considers only the firm's profit ($\theta = 0$) simply raises the lending level to infinity. However, when the regulator considers the bank's profit, the optimal lending level changes. We can recognize the influence of θ on p_r, as follows:

$$\frac{\partial p_r}{\partial \theta} = \frac{2\theta F(B+1) + F^2 - \theta\alpha\beta - 2\theta F(B+1) + \theta\alpha\beta}{\{2\theta F(B+1) + F^2 - \theta\alpha\beta\}^2}$$

$$= \frac{F^2}{\{2\theta F(B+1) + F^2 - \theta\alpha\beta\}^2} > 0 \tag{8.8}$$

Inequality (8.8) says that a regulator that prioritizes the bank's profit selects the higher level of lending. However, p_r is always smaller than p_b from equation (8.7) (Fig. 8.1).

Fig. 8.1 Relationship between p_r and θ

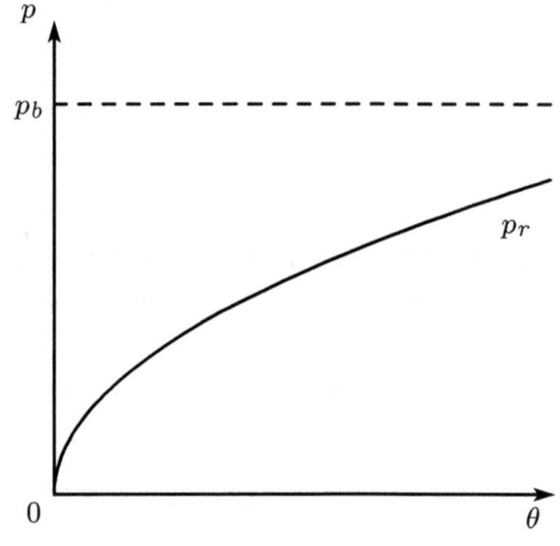

This analysis implies the following result.

A regulator that considers both the bank's profit and the firm's profit always determines a lower level of lending than when the bank itself determines lending levels. Because the firm's cost of effort is irrelevant with p, the regulator considers that decreasing the firm's cost of effort has more merit than the loss of profit of decreasing p.

On the other hand, when the regulator prioritizes the firm's profit (higher θ), increasing p brings the bank more profit because it also encourages the firm to put in more effort (higher e). Thus, the optimal level of lending for the regulator increases.

Now, we obtain the following proposition.

Proposition 8.3 *A regulator that does not select the "laissez-faire" policy results in a lower level of lending than that when the bank determines the level of lending. However, the optimal level of lending determined by the regulator increases with its emphasis on the bank's profit.*

Proof of Proposition 8.3 It is obvious from equation (8.7) and equation (8.8). □

8.6 Conclusion

In this article, we analyzed regulations related to banks' lending levels. We found that the regulator determines a level below that which the bank itself would choose, and the level increases when the regulator considers the bank's profit. This suggests that the regulator's real policy to increase banks' lending considers the banks' profits rather than firms' profit. However, the regulator may be extremely conscious of the firm's profit and thus aim to raise the level of lending as high as the bank would. Nevertheless, it is not feasible to raise the level of lending to infinity, so the model in this study determines that the "laissez-faire" policy is better than the arbitrary policy. Some claim that Japan's financial regulation changed from an enforcement policy to a standard policy. The model in this study may indicate that such a change is an optimal policy objective.

Although this study uses a simple model, it does require an extension.

For example, the regulator pays no cost to execute policy. No organization can enact every policy without a cost, so future studies should analyze the effect of the regulator's cost.

Whether the regulator is benevolent or not is another matter; the regulator may determine policy for its private benefit. In that case, the policy could be affected by bribes from the bank or the firm, as Boot and Thakor (1993) point out. They analyze a model in which the regulator considers its reputation and private benefits and find that such a regulator postpones policy and decreases social welfare.

Moreover, a regulator's ability to enforce policy is yet another consideration. Xu and Pistor (2005) indicate an "incomplete law": there is limit to law enforcement because it is difficult for the regulator to know the actions in the private sector (banks, firms, and so on). Additionally, the regulator has to determine how to enforce the lending levels on the bank in this model.

Furthermore, we plan to continue our analysis in future research to improve the model in this study.

References

Aghion, P., P. Bolton, and S. Fries. 1999. Optimal design of bank bailout: The case of transition economies. *Journal of Institutional and Theoretical Economies* 155: 51–70.

Boot, W.A., and A.V. Thakor. 1993. Self-interested bank regulation. *American Economic Review* 83: 206–212.

Cordella, T., and E.L. Yeyati. 2002. Bank bailouts: moral hazard vs value effect. *Journal of Financial Intermediation* 12: 300–330.

Milton, H., and A. Raviv. 2014. How to get banks to take less risk and disclose bad news. *Journal of Financial Intermediation* 23: 437–470.

Shimoda, S., and M. Hosoe. 2008. Disclosure regulation for financial products and accountability of financial institutions. *Studies in Applied Economics* 2: 44–54 (In Japanese).

Xu, C., and K. Pistor. 2005. Enforcement failure under incomplete law: Theory and Evidence from financial market regulation. Columbia Law and Economics Working Paper No. 222.

Chapter 9
Incomplete Information in Repeated Coordination Games

Eric Rasmussen

9.1 Introduction

It is well known that coordination games have multiple equilibria, depending on player expectations, even if one equilibrium is Pareto superior and players can communicate. This multiplicity is present even in the one-shot game and just gets worse when the game is repeated. Few of the refinements of Nash equilibrium that have been suggested in the context of other kinds of games help with coordination games, and none has gained more than minimal acceptance.

The problem of multiple equilibria in coordination games has attracted attention from various authors. One way to try to predict which equilibrium is played out is to use the behavioral idea of "focal points" from Schelling (1960) that a human's attention is drawn to certain equilibria because they look "different." Thus, if a game's equilibria had payoffs of (1,1), (2,2), and (100,100), the focal point would be (100,100). This is a difficult notion to formalize, though: if the alternatives were (1,1), (99,99), and (100,100), would we predict that the players would end up at (1,1) because it is the most distinctive?

Clearly, the idea of the focal point is important. Philosopher Lewis (1969) divides the idea of the salience of a choice into two parts. The choice has "primary salience" to a player if he believes it is salient to himself; it has "secondary salience" if he believes it has salience to other players. Mehta et al. (1994, p. 661) add "Schelling salience" to primary and secondary salience, as a choice that "seems obvious or natural to people who are looking for ways of solving coordination problems." In their article they report results of experiments trying to distinguish between primary salience—the answers subjects gave to questions when there was no reward for

E. Rasmussen (✉)
Indiana University, Bloomington, IN, USA
e-mail: erasmuse@indiana.edu

T. Naito et al. (eds.), *Applied Approaches to Societal Institutions and Economics*,
New Frontiers in Regional Science: Asian Perspectives 18,
DOI 10.1007/978-981-10-5663-5_9

coordination— and secondary or Schelling salience, the answers when subjects were rewarded for successful coordination. They found that subjects indeed were picking with an eye toward what other subjects would pick; for example, when asked to write down any day of the year, only 6% of the first set of subjects answered December 25, but 44% did when they were rewarded for successful cooperation.

A second approach tries to derive the unique equilibrium from rationality. Gautier (1975, p. 201) defines the "principle of coordination" as "in a situation with one and only one outcome which is both optimal and a best equilibrium, if each person takes every other person to be rational and to share a common conception of the situation, it is rational for each person to perform that action which has the best equilibrium as one of the possible outcomes." Bacharach (1993), Harsanyi and Selten (1988), and Janssen (2001a,b) have pursued this approach, trying to add axioms for rational behavior that require players to avoid dominated equilibria.

Repeating the game does not reduce the number of equilibria, but it does introduce a new angle: finding the optimal way to play a game starting without a convention as to the equilibria. What is the optimal strategy for the two players if they must first grope their ways toward coordination by guessing what the other player will do before they end up at the same action and use it thereafter? That is the project in Crawford and Haller (1990), who find a learning procedure that converges in finite time.

A third approach is to look at evolution in games. Ellison (1993), Kandori et al. (1993), Young (1993), and Binmore and Samuelson (2006) take this approach. Start with a population of pairwise-interacting players with different strategies. They play coordination games and increase or diminish in frequency depending on their payoffs. In such settings, "risk-dominant strategies" emerge as equilibria. In a symmetric two-player setting, this is the strategy a player would choose if he thought there was a 50% probability of the other player choosing each strategy. The risk-dominant strategy is not necessarily the one with the highest payoff; it balances that against the loss if discoordination does occur.

Risk-dominant equilibria also arise in the single-repetition "global games" of Carlsson and van Damme (1994), and Morris and Shin (2003). They ask what happens if players have some small uncertainty over what game they are playing out. It turns out that iterated deletion of interim-dominated strategies can then make the risk-dominant equilibrium the unique equilibrium.

I will show below that adding incomplete information changes the repeated game drastically. Kreps et al. (1982) show that adding a small amount of carefully chosen incomplete information to the model can result in cooperation in the finitely repeated prisoners' dilemma. Fudenberg and Maskin (1986) show more generally that adding incomplete information can generate any of a wide range of average payoffs in finite repeated games by getting around the backward induction of the Chainstore Paradox. Their theorem does not apply to many coordination games, since it depends on a "dimensionality condition" that requires payoffs to vary enough between players to allow equilibria to be supported by punishment phases in which one player is able to punish another without hurting himself. Benoit and Krishna (1985), however, show that if a game has multiple equilibria, as a coordination game does, then a wide range of equilibria can be obtained if the game is repeated enough times by using the threat of punishment phase in an inferior equilibrium to enforce the desired behavior.

I will not be able to reduce the number of equilibria in the one-shot game, but I will show that with a small amount of incomplete information and enough repetitions, any perfect Bayesian equilibrium of even a finitely repeated two-player game will achieve arbitrarily close to the optimal average payoff.

The results will not depend on careful specification of the incomplete information, and it is robust to out-of-equilibrium beliefs. There will be no assumption that "Players are either of type $x = 0$ or type $x = 100$ (with small probability), but never any other value of x." Nor will I specify anything like, "Out of equilibrium, the deviating player is believed to be of type $x \in [0, 34]$." Rather, the intuition is that in coordination games, no player has an incentive to hurt other players, so any attempt to "fool" other players by pretending to be of a particular type will be eagerly accepted by them. This intuition is partly present in the intuition behind the Gang of Four Theorem of Kreps et al. (1982); here, it applies better and so the result is easier to achieve.

9.2 The Coordination Game with Complete Information

Consider a ranked coordination game with $n = 2$ players indexed by i who simultaneously choose actions x_1, x_2 from the interval [0, 100]. The per-period payoff to player i is $\pi(x_i, x_{-i})$ with:

$$(a)\forall x,\ \frac{\partial \pi(x,x)}{\partial x} > 0 \quad (b)\pi(0,0) > \pi(x_i, x_{-i})\ if\ x_i \neq x_{-i} \tag{9.1}$$

Assumption (a) says that a player's payoff rises if he chooses a higher action and the other player chooses the same action as he does. Assumption (b) says that if the players choose different actions, their payoffs are lower than if they coordinated on (0,0).

We will normalize to $\pi(0, 0) = 0$ and $\pi(100, 100) = 100$, which is to say the per-period payoff is 0 when both players choose $x = 0$ and 100 when they both pick $x = 100$. The assumptions then imply that coordination on $x > 0$ yields positive payoffs and discoordination yields negative payoffs.

If the game is unrepeated so $T = 1$, it has a continuum of pure strategy equilibria with x on the continuum from 0 to 100, as well as mixed strategy equilibria. All players prefer the equilibrium in which $x = 100$.

Which equilibrium will be played out depends on player expectations. A reasonable prediction is $x = 100$ because it is Pareto superior to all other equilibria,

Table 9.1 Four types of games

		Time	
		Independent	Dependent
History	Independent	(a) Play 10 in each round	(b) Play 20 in the first round and 25 in the second
	Dependent	(c) Play 30 in each round unless someone deviates, in which case play 30 in the second round	(d) For the first 50 rounds, player 1 picks 2 and the other players pick 14. For the last 10,000 rounds everyone picks 100 unless someone deviates. If someone deviates, all pick 0 for the remainder of the game

a focal point. An equally special equilibrium, however, is $x = 0$. It is easy to imagine how the players could be caught in any equilibrium—if the game was preceded by a malicious outsider's cheap talk announcement that he expected them all to choose $x = 1$, for example, or if the players had a history of playing $x = 5$ for many periods.

Next, let the game be repeated a possibly infinite number T times, with the players observing each other's strategies after each round and no discounting. The equilibrium outcomes and strategies both become more numerous. Let us classify them as follows:

In a **time-dependent equilibrium**, some player's strategy in a round depends on which round number it is. If the strategies are the same in each round, the equilibrium is **time independent**.

In a **history-dependent equilibrium**, some player's strategy in a round depends on the history of play up to that point. If the strategies do not depend on past play, the equilibrium is **history independent**.

Table 9.1 provides examples.

Note that the history-dependent equilibria include equilibria in which the players discoordinate in some periods, receiving flow payoffs of zero. Benoit and Krishna (1985) show that a wide array of outcomes might be observed in equilibrium, supported by punishment strategies similar to strategy (d) in Table 9.1. The players choose any specified pattern of actions in the first S periods because in equilibrium they all play $x = 100$ in the last $(T - S)$ periods, but if anybody deviates earlier, they all play $x = 2$. The observed actions, for example, might be (10, 2), (7, 7), (8, 3), and then (100,100) for the last 200 periods. Thus, mere repetition of the game does not solve the problem of multiple equilibria, and in fact, even more outcomes become possible. The average payoff could even be negative, if the equilibrium has many periods of discoordination, so long as the average payoff is not below the discoordination payoff.

9.3 Incomplete Information: The Single-Action Player

Let us modify the game in the spirit of Kreps et al. (1982), by adding a small amount of incomplete information. Players are of two types. With some arbitrarily small probability $p > 0$, a player i must play $x_i = z_i$ in every round of the game, where z_i is chosen from [0, 100] using an atomless density $f(z_i)$ such that $f(100) > 0$. Such a player is "constrained"; otherwise, the player is "free." Note that the other players do not observe which players are constrained, their exact types, or even how many there are.

What is essential is that there is some possibility a player will choose $x = 100$ and stick with it, which is true of the specification above. All that is needed is a possibility, however small, and it can even have probability zero in the mathematical sense. That is the case in our specification, since any particular value of z has zero probability, despite having positive probability density. What that means is simply that we would predict any particular value of z (e.g., 97.345) with zero probability, even though we would predict a positive probability for any *interval* of types (e.g., $[97, 98.5]$).

How do we interpret the incomplete information? It might be that a constrained player is truly constrained or that he misunderstands the rules of the game or he is irrational and thinks all players will make the same choice as he does (psychology's "magical thinking"; see Daley and Sadowski (2017)). If we use a different specification, such as that there is a .0001% probability that a player is constrained to use $z = 100$, then we could interpret it as that the constrained player wishfully thinks that the equilibrium will be the Pareto-optimal one (perhaps having read some of the references above) or thinks, for whatever reason, that if he starts with $x = 100$, the other players will join him.

In the modified game, some equilibria disappear, as Example 9.1 shows.

Example 9.1 Suppose $T = 20$ and the payoff from discoordination is -500. Is it an equilibrium for a free player to follow the strategy $x = 5$ in every period and for a constrained player of type z to play $x = z$? No.

Consider what happens if player 1 deviates to $x = 100$ in the first round. Is it a best response for player 2 to play $x = 5$ in the second round? That depends on player 2's beliefs, which are generated by Bayes's rule:

$$\begin{aligned} Prob(z_1 &= 100|x_1 = 100) \\ &= \frac{Prob(x_1{=}100|z_1{=}100) * Density(z_1{=}100)}{Prob(x_1{=}100|z_1{=}100) * Density(z_1{=}100) + Prob(x_1{=}100|z_1{=}free) * Prob(z_1{=}free)} \end{aligned} \tag{9.2}$$

The priors tell us that $Prob(player\ 2\ is\ free) = 1 - p$ and $Density(z_1 = 100) = f(100)p$. In the proposed equilibrium, $Prob(x_1 = 100|z_1 = 100) = 1$ and $Prob(x_1 = 100|z_1 = free) = 0$. Thus, equation (9.2) becomes

$$Prob(z_1 = 100|x_1 = 100) = \frac{(1) * f(100)p}{(1) * f(100)p + (0) * (1 - p)} = 1. \tag{9.3}$$

After the first round, player 2 therefore believes that player 1's type is $z_1 = 100$, so he concludes that $x_1 = 100$ for all future rounds. Player 2's best response is not $x = 5$, but to imitate player 1's action, deviating to $x_2 = 100$. If both players then stick with $x = 100$, their payoffs are $(-500 + 19(100), -500 + 19(100))$ compared to the $(20(5), 20(5))$ they would have gotten in the proposed equilibrium. Thus, player 1's deviation has been profitable.

It is not true, however, that the only equilibrium in Example 9.1 is for a player to start with $x = 100$ and to choose in the second and succeeding periods whatever the other player chose in the first period. If $x = 99.9$, it is not worth bearing the initial cost of -500 to deviate. Rather, what we can say is that for large enough w, a time-independent equilibrium strategy must have a player beginning with $x = w$ and then choosing in the second and succeeding periods whatever the other player chose in the first period. In such an equilibrium, the equilibrium payoff is $(20w, 20w)$. The optimal deviation is to $x = 100$, which generates a deviation payoff of $(-500 + 19(100), -500 + 19(100))$. There is no incentive to deviate from equilibrium if and only if $w \geq 92.5$.

Example 9.1 is the essence of this paper. If information is incomplete, then a player can break out of a bad equilibrium at some cost by pretending to be of an unusual type. If the game is repeated long enough, it is worthwhile to bear that cost. Thus, if T is large enough, the game has a much smaller interval of equilibria, and the average payoff becomes arbitrarily close to 100.

Proposition 9.1 *For any ϵ, there exists T large enough that in all pure-strategy equilibria, the average payoff approaches within ϵ of the optimum:*

$$\forall \epsilon > 0, \exists T : \frac{\sum_{t=1}^{T} \pi_{it}}{T} > 100 - \epsilon. \tag{9.4}$$

Proof The probability that a player is constrained is an arbitrarily small p, so the effect that the presence of truly constrained players have on the average equilibrium payoffs will be less than ϵ.

Let the equilibrium with the lowest average payoff call for the players to first choose (a, b) with a or b or both not equal to 100 in round t_1. Without loss of generality, suppose that player 1 chooses $a \neq 100$.

The minimum bound on the payoff is set by player 1 having the deviation option to choose $x = 100$ in that period and convince player 2 that player 1 is constrained of type $z = 100$. Both players would choose $x = 100$ for every succeeding round. This would generate a payoff of $\pi(100, b) + 100(T - 1)$, where $\pi(100, b)$ is the discoordination payoff that arises from that particular deviation, since there would be one period of discoordination, and all other periods will have per-period payoffs of 100. This strategy will have an average payoff of

$$\frac{\pi(100, b)}{T} + \frac{100(T-1)}{T} = 100 + \frac{\pi(100, b)}{T} - \frac{100}{T}. \tag{9.5}$$

If T is large enough, the last two terms, which are both negative, shrink to less than whatever small amount ϵ we might choose. Q.E.D.

The equilibria will be in actions with an average payoff in the interval $[100 - \epsilon, 100]$ for some ϵ that depends on T. This set of equilibria does not depend heavily on the out-of-equilibrium payoffs—just for one period of discoordination loss—and therefore it is not necessarily the same as the set of risk-dominant equilibria. It could be, for example, that for x in [0,50] the discoordination payoff if the other player chooses a different x is -1, but for x in [50, 100] it is $-5,000$, in which case the risk-dominant equilibrium would be (50,50), not (100,100).

9.4 Three or More Players in the Incomplete Information Game

Now let us allow more than two players. Consider a ranked coordination game with $n \geq 2$ players indexed by i who simultaneously choose actions $x_1, \ldots, x_n$ from the interval [0,100]. If $m(x_i)$ players choose the same action x_i, the per-period payoff to player i is $\pi_i(x_i, x_{-i}, m(x_i))$, with:

$$(a')\frac{\partial \pi_i(x_i,x_{-i},m(x_i))}{\partial x_i} \geq 0$$

$$(b')\frac{\Delta \pi_i(x_i,x_{-i},m(x_i))}{\Delta m(x_i)} > 0,$$

$$(c)\frac{\partial^2 \pi_i(x_i,x_{-i},m(x_i))}{\partial x_i \partial x_j} = 0 \tag{9.6}$$

$$(d)\pi_i(0, x_{-i}, n) > \pi_i(100, x_{-i}, n-1),$$

$$(e)\pi_i(w, x_{-i}, l) > \pi_i(w', x_{-i}, l-1) \forall l, w, w' \neq x$$

Assumption (a$'$) says that the payoff to player i rises or stays the same as the magnitude of the group action x_i rises—from 88, say, to 89. Assumption (b$'$) says that the payoff to choosing action x_i rises from being in a bigger group.

Assumption (c) says that the payoff to player i from choices made by players who choose discoordinating actions does not depend on which actions they choose.

Assumption (d) says that group size matters more than action size: the payoff to i from choosing $x_i = 0$ in a group of n is bigger than from choosing $x_i = 100$ in a group of size $n - 1$. Assumption (e) is a more general version of (d), saying that a larger group always gets a bigger payoff, no matter what the size of the action.

My colleagues Michael Rauh and Michael Baye suggested the following as a payoff function that satisfies assumptions (a$'$) through (e):

$$\pi_i(x_i, x_{-i}, m(x_i)) = [m(x_i)(1 + \tfrac{x_i}{1000}) - n](100/1.1n) \tag{9.7}$$

or, without our normalization of $\pi_i(0, x_{-i}, n) = 0$ and $\pi_i(100, x_{-i}, n) = 100$,

$$\pi_i(x_i, x_{-i}, m) = m(x_i)(1 + \frac{x_i}{1000}) \tag{9.8}$$

The complete information game has the usual continuum of equilibria, just as when there are just two players. How about the incomplete information game? Consider Examples 9.2 and 9.3.

Example 9.2 Let there be incomplete information of the following form: with some arbitrarily small probability $p > 0$, player i is "constrained" and must play $x_i = z_i$ in every round of the game, where z_i is chosen from [0, 100] using an atomless density $f(z_i)$ such that $f(100) > 0$. Let there be three players, and consider whether it is an equilibrium outcome to play (5, 5, 5) each of T periods. Suppose player 1 deviates to $x_1 = 100$ in the first period. A unilateral switch by one of the other two players from 5 to 100 would be profitable in the long run in the incomplete information game. Thus, (100,100,100) is the only equilibrium outcome.

Example 9.3 Again, let there be incomplete information of the following form: with some arbitrarily small probability $p > 0$, player i is "constrained" and must play $x_i = z_i$ in every round of the game, where z_i is chosen from [0, 100] using an atomless density $f(z_i)$ such that $f(100) > 0$. Let there be four players, and consider whether it is an equilibrium outcome to play (5, 5, 5, 5) each of T periods. Suppose player 1 deviates to $x_1 = 100$ in the first period. Even if player 1 were truly of type $z = 100$, a unilateral switch by one of the other three players from 5 to 100 would be unprofitable if $\pi_i(x = 5, m = 3) > \pi_i(x = 100, m = 2)$. Thus, (5, 5, 5, 5) would be an equilibrium outcome. Incomplete information does not reduce the number of equilibria.

The situation changes if we change the form of the incomplete information. What is needed now is a more-than-infinitesimal probability of a given constraint value of z. Recall our alternative specification of incomplete information in which player i has probability .01 of being constrained to play $x_i = 100$. In that specification, the probability is not zero; it is strictly positive. That makes a huge difference, as we see in Example 9.4.

Example 9.4 Let there be incomplete information of the following form: with some small probability $p > 0$, player i is "constrained" and must play $x_i = 100$ in every round of the game. Let there be four players, and consider whether it is an equilibrium outcome to play (5, 5, 5, 5) each of T periods. Assume that if the players do not all play the same action, their period payoff is zero. Suppose player 1 deviates to $x_1 = 100$ in the first period. With probability $.99^3$, he is the only player to play 100, and the other players do not imitate him in future periods for the same reason as in Example 9.3. But with probability $1 - .99^3$, at least one of the other players is a true constrained player who also plays 100. If that happens, then in the second and succeeding periods, the remaining two players will play 100. Thus, the expected payoff from deviating (and returning to playing 5 if no other player plays 10 in the first period) will be greater than $.99^3 * (0 + (T-1)(5)) + (1 - .99^3)(0 + (T-1)(100))$

(I say "greater than" because it is slightly higher because of the possibility that not just one but two or even all three of the other players are constrained to play 100). If T is great enough, the deviation payoff is greater than the proposed equilibrium payoff of $5T$. It is worth the high probability of one period with a payoff of 0 in order to have a chance at $(T-1)$ periods with a payoff of 100. If the deviation is profitable, however, then all four of the players will choose 100 in the first and every period, constrained or not.

Thus, with four players or more, incomplete information can still justify a unique efficient equilibrium. The story is a little different, though, because if expectations begin with some action less than 100, the player who deviates puts high probability on his deviation being unprofitable—it is just that if it does work out successfully, he gets a very large payoff increase. For this to work, T must be much larger than when there are only two or three players.

9.5 Mixed Coordination-Conflict Games: The Battle of the Sexes

Incomplete information can actually hurt in mixed coordination-conflict games, by destroying the possibility of pure-strategy equilibria. Consider the Battle of the Sexes in Table 9.2. It has two pure strategy equilibria, (*prizefight, prizefight*) and (*ballet, ballet*), and a mixed strategy equilibrium, in which the man plays *prizefight* with probability $m = A/(A+B)$ and the woman with probability $w = B/(A+B)$.

The total payoffs in the two pure-strategy equilibria are (A, B) and (B, A). The man's one-shot expected payoff is then $AB/(A+B)$, which is less than B since $B < A+B$. The man's expected payoff (and analogously the woman's) in the mixed-strategy equilibrium is lower even than in the pure-strategy equilibrium he likes least.

The T-repeated game has many subgame perfect equilibria, but let us focus on the three time-independent and history-independent equilibria that repeat the single-period equilibria just described.

Now let us add incomplete information, in the form of constrained players. With probability p_1, the man is constrained to play *prizefight*, and with independent probability p_2, the woman is constrained to play *ballet*. This change eliminates (*ballet, ballet*) and (*prizefight, prizefight*) as equilibria. Suppose the woman thought (*ballet, ballet*) was the equilibrium. The man would begin the game by playing

Table 9.2 The Battle of the Sexes

	Woman		
		Prizefight	*Ballet*
Man	*Prizefight*	**A,B**	0,0
	Ballet	0,0	**B,A**

Payoffs to: (man, woman). A > B.

prizefight. The woman would conclude that the man was constrained and would play *prizefight* in all future rounds, so the man would have succeeded in increasing his payoff (if there are enough rounds) to one round of (ballet, prizefight) and $T-1$ rounds of (*prizefight*, *prizefight*). The equilibrium (*prizefight*, *prizefight*) would similarly fail.

The mixed strategy equilibrium survives. If the man deviates to playing *prizefight* as a pure strategy, the woman will interpret this as a realization of the equilibrium strategy. This is ironic, however, because the man's ability to knock out the pure-strategy equilibrium of (*ballet*, *ballet*) ends up hurting him: his payoff is higher in that equilibrium than in the mixed-strategy equilibrium that survives.

9.6 Closing Remarks

Thus, we see that in repeated ranked coordination, the efficient equilibria are robust to incomplete information, but the inefficient equilibria are not, whereas in the Battle of the Sexes, the opposite is true. This model has used a particular specification of incomplete information, to be sure, but if we added other incomplete information without removing the possibility of constraint in this model, the results would often stay the same. The key to the result is that if there is some chance that a deviation beneficial to the deviator will be interpreted as predicting that he will choose the same action in the future, the player will have incentive to deviate.

References

Bacharach, Michael. 1993. Variable universe games. *Frontiers of game theory*, ed. Ken Binmore, Alan Kirman, and Piero Tani, 255–275. Cambridge: MIT Press.

Benoit, Jean-Pierre, and Vijay Krishna. 1985. Finitely repeated games. *Econometrica* 53: 905–922.

Binmore, Ken, and Larry Samuelson. 2006. The evolution of focal points. *Games and Economic Behavior* 55: 21–42.

Carlsson, Hans, and Eric van Damme. 1994. Global games and equilibrium selection. *Econometrica* 61: 989–1018.

Crawford, Vincent P., and Hans Haller. 1990. Learning how to cooperate: Optimal play in repeated coordination games. *Econometrica* 58: 571–595.

Daley, Brendan, and Philipp Sadowski. 2017. Magical thinking: A representation result. *Theoretical Economics* 12(2): 909–956.

Ellison, Glenn. 1993. Learning, local interaction, and coordination. *Econometrica* 61: 1047–1071.

Fudenberg, Drew, and Eric Maskin. 1986. The Folk theorem in repeated games with discounting or with incomplete information. *Econometrica* 54: 533–554.

Gautier, David. 1975. *Coordination*. Cambridge: Cambridge University Press.

Harsanyi, John and Reinhard Selten. 1988. *A general theory of equilibrium selection in games*. Cambridge: MIT Press.

Janssen, Maarten C.W. 2001a. On the principle of coordination. *Economics and Philosophy* 17: 221–234.

Janssen, Maarten C.W. 2001b. Rationalizing focal points. *Theory and Decision* 50: 119–148.

Kandori, Michihiro, George J. Mailath, and Rafael Rob. 1993. Learning, mutation, and long run equilibria in games. *Econometrica* 61: 29–56.

Kreps, David, Paul Milgrom, John Roberts, and Robert Wilson. 1982. Rational cooperation in the finitely repeated prisoners' dilemma. *Journal of Economic Theory* 27: 245–252.

Lewis, David. 1969. *Convention*. Cambridge, MA: Harvard University Press.

Mehta, Judith, Chris Starmer, and Robert Sugden. 1994. Focal points in pure coordination games: An experimental investigation. *Theory and Decision* 36: 163–185.

Morris, Stephen, and Hyun Song Shin. 2003. Global games: Theory and applications. In *Advances in economics and econometrics (Proceedings of the Eighth World Congress of the Econometric Society)*, ed. M. Dewatripont, L. Hansen, and S. Turnovsky. Cambridge, England: Cambridge University Press.

Schelling, Thomas. 1960. *The strategy of conflict*. Cambridge: Harvard University Press.

Young, H. Peyton. 1993. The evolution of conventions. *Econometrica* 61: 57–84.

Part II
Economic Analysis of Government and Public Sector

Chapter 10
Public Debt, Budget Deficits, Fertility, and Endogenous Growth

Jun-ichi Maeda

10.1 Introduction

In this paper, we study the effects of budget deficits, public debt, and fertility on economic growth referring to Bräuninger (2003, 2005), Carlberg and Hansen (2013), and Groezen et al. (2003). The analysis is based on an endogenous growth model as developed in Romer (1986) and Lucas (1988). For simplicity, we assume an *AK* production structure that captures the basic idea of these models. The microfoundation of individual consumption-saving decisions is given in an overlapping generations model in the tradition of Diamond (1965).

We consider a fixed deficit ratio in an endogenous growth model as in Bräuninger (2003, 2005) and Carlberg and Hansen (2013). It is shown that for a given deficit ratio, there are two steady states, in which the debt-output ratio stays constant. One of these steady states is stable and the other is unstable. However, there is a critical deficit ratio. If the deficit ratio exceeds the critical level, then there is no steady state. Importantly, time preferences for consumption (hereafter, patience) and the utility gained from having children (hereafter, joy) affect the existence of steady state.

The rest of the paper is organized as follows. Section 10.2 presents the model. Section 10.3 analyzes the steady state. Section 10.4 analyzes stability and the effect of deficit ratio changes. Section 10.5 concludes the paper.

J.-i. Maeda (✉)
Hiroshima Shudo University, Hiroshima, Japan
e-mail: maeda-j@shudo-u.ac.jp

T. Naito et al. (eds.), *Applied Approaches to Societal Institutions and Economics*, New Frontiers in Regional Science: Asian Perspectives 18,
DOI 10.1007/978-981-10-5663-5_10

10.2 The Model

10.2.1 Individuals

Individuals live for two periods. In the first period of life, that is, when young, individuals give birth to a certain number of children, employ resources for rearing them, earn income in the labor market, consume part of their income, and save for old age. In the second period of life, that is, when old, individuals enjoy the fruits of the savings.

The representative individual being young at time t consumes c_t^y when young, gives birth to n_t children, supplies one unit of labor inelastically in the labor market, and transfers a fraction z of his income for rearing children. Then, the individual saves the remainder of his income, s_t, for old age consumption. At time $t+1$, the old individual consumes c_{t+1}^o using the proceeds of his savings.

Lifetime utility of the representative individual born at time t is given by:

$$u(c_t^y, n_t, c_{t+1}^o) = \log\ c_t^y + \gamma\ \log\ n_t + \beta\ \log\ c_{t+1}^o, \tag{10.1}$$

where β is an intertemporal discount factor measuring the felicity of own consumption when old. The parameter γ is associated with the consumption aspect of children; it measures the joy of having them.

The representative individual faces an intertemporal budget constraint. Net income in the working period is given by the net wage $(1-\tau_t)w_t$, where w_t is the wage rate and τ_t is the income tax rate. It can be used for consumption in the working period, for rearing children, and for saving. Therefore, the constraint in the first period of life is given by:

$$c_t^y = (1-\tau_t - zn_t)w_t - s_t \tag{10.2}$$

The individual earns net interest rate $(1-\tau_{t+1})r_{t+1}$ on savings, where r_{t+1} is the interest rate at time $t+1$. So, consumption in the retirement period is given by:

$$c_{t+1}^o = \{1 + (1-\tau_{t+1})r_{t+1}\}s_t \tag{10.3}$$

As a consequence, the intertemporal budget constraint can be stated as:

$$c_t^y + \frac{1}{1+(1-\tau_{t+1})r_{t+1}}c_{t+1}^o + zn_tw_t = (1-\tau_t)w_t \tag{10.4}$$

The individual chooses present and future consumption and the number of children so as to maximize utility subject to his intertemporal budget constraint. Maximization of (10.1) under the restriction of (10.4) gives the following conditions:

$$c_{t+1}^o = \beta\{1 + (1-\tau_{t+1})r_{t+1}\}c_t^y \tag{10.5}$$

$$zw_t n_t = \gamma c_t^y \tag{10.6}$$

Inserting (10.3) and (10.4) into (10.2) yields:

$$c_t^y = \frac{1-\tau_t}{1+\beta+\gamma} w_t \tag{10.7}$$

$$c_{t+1}^o = \frac{\beta\{1+(1-\tau_{t+1})r_{t+1}\}(1-\tau_t)}{1+\beta+\gamma} w_t \tag{10.8}$$

$$n_t = \frac{\gamma(1-\tau_t)}{(1+\beta+\gamma)z} \tag{10.9}$$

10.2.2 Government

The government raises loans and levies an income tax in order to finance government purchases and interest payments on public debt. The government spends a fixed share of national income on goods and services:

$$G_t = gY_t, \tag{10.10}$$

Here, G_t is government spending and purchase ratio g is constant. Further, the government borrows a specified proportion of national income:

$$B_t = bY_t, \tag{10.11}$$

Here, B_t is government borrowing and deficit ratio b is constant. The budget deficit of this period adds up to the public debt of this period D_t to give the public debt of the next period D_{t+1}:

$$D_{t+1} = D_t + B_t \tag{10.12}$$

Interest rate r_t has to be paid on public debt D_t, so that the public interest payment is given by $r_t D_t$. The government levies a tax at the flat rate τ_t on factor income and debt income:

$$T_t = \tau_t(Y_t + r_t D_t) \tag{10.13}$$

Accordingly, the government budget constraint can be written as follows:

$$B_t + T_t = G_t + r_t D_t \tag{10.14}$$

Taking account of the functional relationships, the identity can be reformulated in the following way:

$$bY_t + \tau_t(Y_t + r_tD_t) = gY_t + r_tD_t \tag{10.15}$$

The government fixes both the purchase ratio and the deficit ratio and has to accept interest payments on public debt. Then, the tax rate has to be adjusted accordingly.

10.2.3 Firms

A large number of identical firms denoted by i manufacture a single commodity. Firms employ the available labor force which equals the size of the young generation, denoted by N_t^i at time t and the capital stock K_t^i. The production function is of the Cobb-Douglas type:

$$Y_t^i = A(K_t^i)^{\alpha}(E_tN_t^i)^{\beta}, \tag{10.16}$$

where $A > 0$, $\alpha > 0$, $\beta > 0$, $\alpha + \beta = 1$, and E_t are an exogenously given index of labor productivity. Each firm maximizes profits under perfect competition. Each firm adjusts capital to equate the marginal product to the interest rate, and labor is adjusted to equate the marginal product to the wage rate.

The aggregate production function is as follows:

$$Y_t = AK_t^{\alpha}(E_tN_t)^{\beta} \tag{10.17}$$

It is assumed that labor productivity is proportional to capital per worker and is therefore endogenous to the economy:

$$E_t = \frac{K_t}{N_t} \tag{10.18}$$

According to Eq. (10.18), the aggregate production function is simplified as follows:

$$Y_t = AK_t \tag{10.19}$$

The markets for capital and labor are perfectly competitive. In each period, the supply of capital and labor is given exogenously. Given a competitive market, the interest rate and the wage rate adjust to equate the supply and the demand of capital and labor. Hence, the interest rate corresponds to the marginal product of capital and the wage rate corresponds to the marginal product of labor:

$$r_t = \alpha A \tag{10.20}$$

$$w_t = \frac{\beta Y_t}{N_t} \tag{10.21}$$

10.3 Steady State

Net labor income minus consumption and child-rearing costs gives the savings of the representative young individual:

$$s_t = (1 - \tau_t)w_t - c_t^y - zn_t w_t \tag{10.22}$$

The aggregate savings of the working generation are given by $S_t = s_t N_t$. Inserting equation (10.7) and (10.9) into (10.22) yields:

$$s_t = \frac{\beta(1 - \tau_t)}{1 + \beta + \gamma} w_t \tag{10.23}$$

Insert (10.21) into (10.23) to reveal the aggregate savings:

$$S_t = \frac{\beta^2(1 - \tau_t)}{1 + \beta + \gamma} Y_t \tag{10.24}$$

These savings of the young generation are used to finance public debt and private capital of the following period:

$$D_{t+1} + K_{t+1} = \frac{\beta^2(1 - \tau_t)}{1 + \beta + \gamma} Y_t \tag{10.25}$$

The model can be represented by a system of five equations:

$$D_{t+1} = D_t + bY_t \tag{10.12}$$

$$bY_t + \tau_t(Y_t + r_t D_t) = gY_t + r_t D_t \tag{10.15}$$

$$Y_t = AK_t \tag{10.19}$$

$$r_t = \alpha A \tag{10.20}$$

$$D_{t+1} + K_{t+1} = \frac{\beta^2(1 - \tau_t)}{1 + \beta + \gamma} Y_t \tag{10.25}$$

Here, α, β, γ, b, g, A, D_t, and K_t are exogenous, whereas r_t, τ_t, D_{t+1}, K_{t+1}, and Y_t are endogenous.

For further analysis, it is convenient to consider growth factors. First, we focus on the growth factor of public debt. Divide (10.12) by D_t to obtain $D_{t+1}/D_t = bY_t/D_t$. Then, replace the output by invoking (10.19) and insert $x_t \equiv D_t/K_t$ for the debt-capital ratio:

$$\frac{D_{t+1}}{D_t} = 1 + \frac{bA}{x_t} \tag{10.26}$$

Now, we analyze output growth. As is obvious from (10.19), output growth corresponds to capital growth. To obtain the growth factor of capital, we first have to solve for the endogenous tax rate. We observe $\tau_t = \{(g-b)Y_t + r_t D_t\}/(Y_t + r_t D_t)$ from (10.15). Replace Y_t by AK_t and r_t by αA to reveal $\tau_t = \{(g-b)K_t + \alpha D_t\}/(K_t + \alpha D_t)$. Finally, divide the numerator and denominator by K_t, and then substitute $x_t = D_t/K_t$ to obtain:

$$1 - \tau_t = \frac{1 + b - g}{1 + \alpha x_t} \tag{10.27}$$

Further, insert (10.19) and (10.27) into (10.25), to reach $D_{t+1} + K_{t+1} = \beta^2(1 + b - g)AK_{t+1}/\{(1 + \beta + \gamma)(1 + \alpha x_t)\}$. Then, replace debt in the next period by invoking (10.12), solve for K_{t+1}, divide by K_t, and use $x_t = D_t/K_t$ to obtain the growth factor of capital:

$$\frac{K_{t+1}}{K_t} = A\left\{\frac{\beta^2(1 + b - g)}{(1 + \beta + \gamma)(1 + \alpha x_t)} - b\right\} - x_t \tag{10.28}$$

The growth factor of capital as well as of public debt depends on the debt-capital ratio. Both growth factors are constant if the debt-capital ratio is constant. Hence, in the steady state, public debt has to grow at the same rate as capital, so that the debt-capital ratio is constant. Now, equate (10.26) and (10.28) to obtain:

$$1 + \frac{bA}{x_t} = A\left\{\frac{\beta^2(1 + b - g)}{(1 + \beta + \gamma)(1 + \alpha x_t)} - b\right\} - x_t \tag{10.29}$$

Analysis of (10.29) gives rise to the following consideration vis-à-vis the steady state. Denote $F(x_t, b) \equiv 1 + \frac{bA}{x_t}$, $G(x_t, b) \equiv A\left\{\frac{\beta^2(1+b-g)}{(1+\beta+\gamma)(1+\alpha x_t)} - b\right\} - x_t$. In the steady state, we have $F(x_t, b) = G(x_t, b)$. The function F goes to 1 for x_t converging to infinity and goes to infinity for x_t converging to zero. The function G is declining monotonically with x_t from $G(0, b)$. Three cases might occur: (1) the functions F and G have two intersections, so there are two steady states; (2) F and G are just tangent and there is a unique steady state; (3) F and G do not intersect and therefore there is no steady state. Figure 10.1 illustrates these cases.

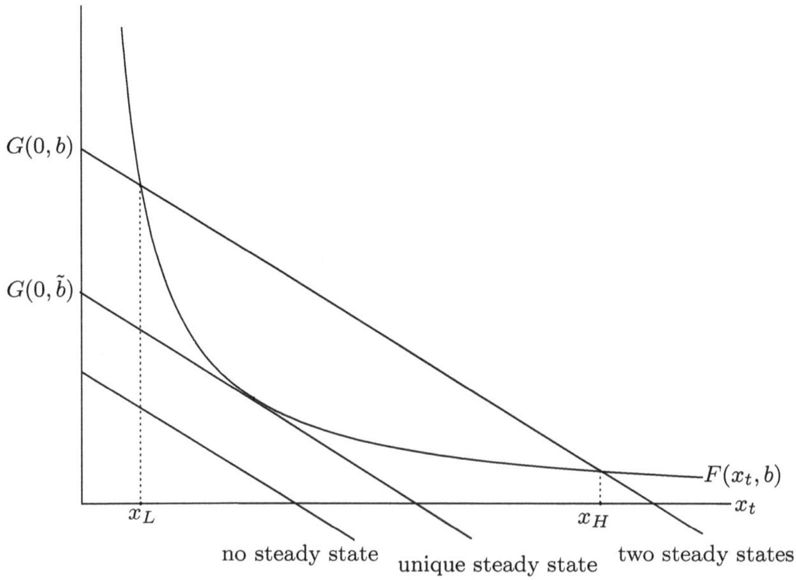

Fig. 10.1 Three cases of steady states

We can notice that $\partial F/\partial \beta = 0$ and $\partial G/\partial \beta > 0$. Hence, an increase in patience has no effect on F but increases G. So, for a sufficiently large level of β, there will be two steady states. Further, notice that $\partial F/\partial \gamma = 0$ and $\partial G/\partial \gamma < 0$. Hence, an increase in the joy of having children has no effect on F but decreases G. So for a sufficiently small level of γ, there will be two steady states.

Assume that β is sufficiently large and γ is sufficiently small. Notice that $\partial F/\partial b > 0$ and $\partial G/\partial b < 0$. Hence, an increase in b leads to an increase in F and a decline in G. So, there will be two steady states for low levels of b. Then, there will be a critical level $\tilde{b}$ where there is only a unique steady state. There is no steady state for $b > \tilde{b}$. An increase in β and a decrease in γ lead to an increase in $\tilde{b}$.

10.4 Stability and Deficit Ratio

10.4.1 Stability

The dynamics of the model are completely described by two equations for the growth factors of public debt and capital. For convenience, they are repeated here:

$$\frac{D_{t+1}}{D_t} = 1 + \frac{bA}{x_t} \tag{10.26}$$

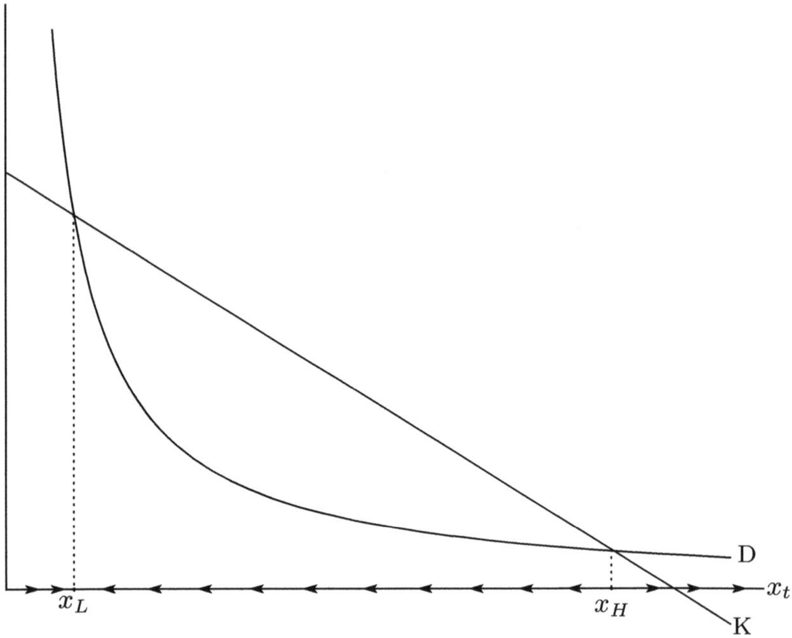

Fig. 10.2 Stability of two steady states

$$\frac{K_{t+1}}{K_t} = A\left\{\frac{\beta^2(1+b-g)}{(1+\beta+\gamma)(1+\alpha x_t)} - b\right\} - x_t \tag{10.28}$$

Both growth factors depend on the debt-capital ratio. First we consider public debt growth. As Eq. (10.26) shows, the growth factor of public debt goes to infinity when the debt-capital ratio approaches zero. For a very large debt-capital ratio, that is, when x_t goes to infinity, the growth factor converges to one. Figure 10.2 displays the downward-sloping D line, representing Eq. (10.26). Equation (10.28) confirms that the growth factor of capital is a declining function of the debt-capital ratio. Thus, the K line, representing Eq. (10.28), is falling.

Figure 10.2 presents the growth diagram. It illustrates that there are two steady states. At an initial debt-capital ratio below x_L, debt grows faster than capital. Therefore, the debt-capital ratio increases toward x_L. Given an initial debt-capital ratio between x_L and x_H, capital grows faster than debt and the debt-capital ratio declines toward x_L. Given an initial debt-capital ratio above x_H, debt grows faster than capital. Therefore, the debt-capital ratio increases.

To confirm the stability of the model, we consider the growth factor of the debt-capital ratio:

$$\frac{x_{t+1}}{x_t} = \frac{\frac{D_{t+1}}{D_t}}{\frac{K_{t+1}}{K_t}} \tag{10.30}$$

Hence, the debt-capital ratio growth factor corresponds to the ratio of the debt growth factor and the capital growth factor. Denote the growth factors with a subscript g:

$$x_{t+1} = \frac{D_g}{K_g} x_t \tag{10.31}$$

The differential is as follows:

$$\frac{dx_{t+1}}{dx_t} = \frac{dD_g}{dx_t}\frac{1}{K_g} + \frac{D_g}{K_g} - \frac{dK_g}{dx}\frac{D_g}{K_g^2} x_t \tag{10.32}$$

Close to the steady states, we have $D_g = K_g$ and $x_{t+1} = x_t$, so (10.32) simplifies to (10.33):

$$\frac{dx_{t+1}}{dx_t} = 1 + \frac{1}{K_g}\left(\frac{dD_g}{dx_t} - \frac{dK_g}{dx_t} x_t\right) \tag{10.33}$$

Use (10.26) and (10.28) to obtain:

$$\frac{dD_g}{dx_t} = -\frac{bA}{x_t^2} \tag{10.34}$$

$$\frac{dK_g}{dx_t} = -1 - \frac{\beta^2(1+b-g)A}{1+\beta+\gamma}\frac{\alpha}{(1+\alpha x_t)^2}. \tag{10.35}$$

Thus, we have:

$$\frac{dx_{t+1}}{dx_t} = 1 + \frac{1}{K_g}\left[-\frac{bA}{x_t^2} + \left\{1 + \frac{\alpha\beta^2(1+b-g)A}{(1+\beta+\gamma)(1+\alpha x_t)^2}\right\} x_t\right] \tag{10.36}$$

When x_t converges to zero, the term in the brackets goes to minus infinity. When x_t goes to infinity, the term in the brackets goes to infinity. As a result, the derivative $dx_{t+1}/dx_t < 1$ for low levels of x_t and $dx_{t+1}/dx_t > 1$ for high levels of x_t. Therefore, if there are two steady states, it must be the case that $dx_{t+1}/dx_t < 1$ holds at the low-level equilibrium and $dx_{t+1}/dx_t > 1$ holds at the high-level equilibrium. Hence, x_L is locally stable, whereas x_H is unstable.

10.4.2 An Increase in the Deficit Ratio

Consider the dynamics of an increase in the deficit ratio. At the start, the economy is in the steady state. The budget deficit and public debt grow at the same rate as capital and output. Then, the government increases the deficit ratio. In the short run, due to the higher budget deficit, debt growth increases as in (10.26). At the same time, capital growth declines as in (10.26). This reduces output growth and budget deficit growth. In the medium run, due to lower deficit growth, debt growth declines as in (10.12). The debt-capital ratio increases. This reduces capital growth further. In the long run, debt growth and capital growth converge. In the new steady state, debt and capital grow at the same constant rate. Compared to the original steady state, capital growth and debt growth are reduced.

10.5 Conclusions

In this paper, we study the effects of budget deficit, public debt, and fertility on endogenous growth in an overlapping generations model. The government fixes the budget deficit ratio. If the deficit ratio stays below a critical level, then there are two steady states where capital, output, and public debt grow at the same constant rate. In this case, one of them is locally stable and the other is unstable. Importantly, patience vis-à-vis consumption and the joy of having children affect the existence of the steady state. An increase in patience and a decrease in joy expand the possibilities of two steady states. An increase in the deficit ratio reduces the growth rate. If the deficit ratio exceeds the critical level, then there is no steady state. If the economy is in the stable steady state, an increase in the deficit ratio leads to a new steady state, where public debt growth and capital growth are lower than those in the original steady state.

References

Bräuninger, M. 2003. *Public debt and endogenous growth*. Heidelberg: Physica-Verlag.

Bräuninger, M. 2005. The budget deficit, public debt, and endogenous growth. *Journal of Public Economic Theory* 7: 827–840.

Carlberg, M., and A. Hansen 2013. *Sustainability and optimality of public debt*, 2nd ed. Heidelberg: Physica-Verlag.

Diamond, P. 1965. National debt in a neoclassical growth model. *American Economic Review* 55: 1126–1150.

Groezen, B., T. Leers, and L. Meijdam 2003. Social security and endogenous fertility: Pensions and child allowances as Siamese twins. *Journal of public Economics* 87: 233–251.

Lucas, R. 1988. On the mechanics of economic development. *Journal of Monetary Economics* 22: 2–42.

Romer, P. 1986. Increasing returns and long-run growth. *Journal of Political Economy* 94: 1002–1035.

Chapter 11
Optimal Income Tax Structure with Favoritism

Hideki Sato

11.1 Introduction

How should a government impose income tax? Since Mirrlees (1971), the standard answer to this question is that the government, to secure the necessary income tax revenue, should impose income taxes that maximize utilitarian economic welfare.

Under such a framework, Sato (2015) examined the income tax structure by weighing the government's value judgment of favoritism toward the poor. That study examined cases where fines for tax evasion were sufficiently low. However, in the present paper, I examine cases where the fines are sufficiently high. Sato (2015) found that sufficiently strong government favoritism toward the poor creates tax exemptions for the poor. In contrast, the results from the present study show that when sufficiently high fines are imposed on tax evaders, tax exemptions for the poor do not emerge, despite the increase in bias toward the poor.

This tax exemption for the poor is the government's choice, or, in other words, a complete self-realization by the government. The results of the present study show that governmental self-realization is affected by whether penalties are strict or tolerant.

The remainder of this paper is organized as follows. In the next section, we set up a game theory model. In Sect. 11.3, we utilize the Nash equilibrium to derive the tax revenues envisioned by the government. In Sect. 11.4, we consider tax structures that would secure the necessary tax revenue. Finally, in Sect. 11.5, we summarize our conclusions.

H. Sato (✉)
Fukuoka Women's University, Fukuoka, Japan
e-mail: h.sato@fwu.ac.jp

T. Naito et al. (eds.), *Applied Approaches to Societal Institutions and Economics*,
New Frontiers in Regional Science: Asian Perspectives 18,
DOI 10.1007/978-981-10-5663-5_11

11.2 Basic Model

The following three phases occur before tax revenue is collected by the government:

i. All taxpayers file their income tax return, and at this point in time, a taxpayer's income level is known only to himself/herself.
ii. Tax authorities conduct a random tax audit of taxpayers. During this audit, the taxpayer's earned income is revealed.
iii. At this time, if the revealed income is different from the declared income, the tax authorities impose a fine on the taxpayer.

This shows that governmental tax revenue comprises income tax and fines. We will set up a model below to depict the three phases described above.

All taxpayers have either high income (I^H) or low income (I^L). The information on each taxpayer's income level is asymmetrical between the taxpayer and tax authorities. In other words, all taxpayers know their own income level, but tax authorities only know the probability distribution: a particular taxpayer holds I^H (or (I^L)) with probability $q \in (0, 1)$ (or $1 - q$).

All taxpayers file their income tax return under these circumstances. The income tax paid by individual taxpayers depends on the declared income level. In other words, when taxpayers file a return as I^H (or (I^L)), we expect the income tax paid to be T^H (or T^L), where $T^L < T^H$.

At this time, if a taxpayer who owns I^H only declares I^L, it is possible to avoid income taxes with $T \equiv T^H - T^L$. In this study, in line with previous research on the theory of tax evasion (e.g., Greatz et al. 1986; Andreoni et al. 1998), we assume a zero cost for the taxpayer to conceal his/her income by $I \equiv I^H - I^L$ to evade taxes.

Even if the taxpayer conceals part of his/her income, we assume that the concealed income will be found if the tax authorities spend C (investigation costs) on tax auditing. At this time, the tax authorities may impose a fine F on the tax evader.

11.3 Nash Equilibrium

For simplicity, I assume the taxpayer and tax authorities are both risk-neutral. I express the probability of tax evasion by the taxpayer to be α and the probability that the tax authorities will carry out tax auditing as β. The following equation shows the taxpayer's expected income:

$$U^H(\alpha, \beta) = \alpha(\beta(I^H - T^H - F) + (1 - \beta)(I^H - T^L)) + (1 - \alpha)(I^H - T^H). \quad (11.1)$$

In contrast, by Bayes' Rule, tax authorities can discover tax evaders with the probability $\mu = q\alpha/(q\alpha + 1 - q)$, obtaining outcomes for $I \equiv I^H - I^L$. Therefore, the expected reward for the tax authorities (Π) is expressed in the following equation in relation to arbitrary α:

$$\Pi(\alpha,\beta) = \beta(\mu(\alpha)I - C). \tag{11.2}$$

The partial derivative relating to α in Eq. (11.2) is linear with respect to β. Because $\frac{\partial U^H(\alpha,1)}{\partial\alpha} = -F$, therefore, $\beta^0 \in (0,1)$ by the intermediate value theorem, that is,

$$\beta^0 = \frac{T}{T+F}. \tag{11.3}$$

At this time, the best response for a taxpayer with I^H is expressed by the following equation:

$$\alpha(\beta)\begin{cases} = 1 & \textit{if } \beta < \beta^0 \\ \in [0,1] & \textit{if } \beta = \beta^0 \\ = 0 & \textit{if } \beta > \beta^0 \end{cases} \tag{11.4}$$

Similarly, we obtain the following best response of the tax authorities:

$$\beta(\alpha)\begin{cases} = 1 & \textit{if } \mu(\alpha) > \mu^0 \\ \in [0,1] & \textit{if } \mu(\alpha) = \mu^0 \\ = 0 & \textit{if } \mu(\alpha) < \mu^0 \end{cases} \tag{11.5}$$

where $\mu^0 = C/I$. Because probability μ has already been defined, we obtain the following:

$$\alpha^0 = \frac{(1-q)C}{q(I-C)}. \tag{11.6}$$

When $I > C/q$, then $\alpha^0 \in (0,1)$. Therefore, the best response of the tax authorities is represented by the following equation:

$$\beta(\alpha)\begin{cases} = 1 & \textit{if } \alpha > \alpha^0 \\ \in [0,1] & \textit{if } \alpha = \alpha^0 \\ = 0 & \textit{if } \alpha < \alpha^0 \end{cases} \tag{11.7}$$

The optimal reactions represented by Eqs. (11.4) and (11.7) show that if $I > C/q$, the Nash equilibrium becomes the interior solution (i.e., a mixed strategy pair).

In the Nash equilibrium, the government's expected revenue (R^e) is represented by the following equation:

$$R^e = \frac{T}{T+F} q\alpha^0(T+F-I) + (q\alpha^0 + 1 - q)T^L + q(1-\alpha^0)(T+T^L). \quad (11.8)$$

Rewriting the left-hand side as $R^e = \bar{R}$ (where $\bar{R}$ is a positive constant), we obtain the following:

$$\overline{R} = \frac{T}{T+F}(T+F-T)q\alpha^0 + T^L + q(1-\alpha^0)T \quad (11.9)$$

To solve T^L, we obtain the following:

$$T^L = \overline{R} - \frac{qT}{T+F}(T + \alpha^0 I + F). \quad (11.10)$$

This equation represents a tax structure that generates the necessary tax revenue.

If we keep all other conditions the same (i.e., *ceteris paribus*) and differentiate T^L with T, we obtain

$$dT^L/dT = -q\frac{F}{(T+F)^2}(T + \alpha^0 I + F) - \frac{qT}{T+F}. \quad (11.11)$$

And it can be seen that T^L is a decreasing function of T. Furthermore, if we differentiate dT^L/dT by T, we obtain the following:

$$d^2T^L/dT^2 = \frac{2qT(T+F)^2 + 2q(F(\alpha^0 I + F) - T^2)(T+F)}{(T+F)^4}. \quad (11.12)$$

The sign of this equation is dependent on the sign of the second term of the numerator. Writing the formula as

$$\begin{aligned} \overline{U} &= F(\alpha^0 I + F) - T^2 \\ &= F^2 + \alpha^0 IF - T^2 \end{aligned} \quad (11.13)$$

we find that $\overline{U} > 0$ if F is sufficiently large. In this case, the set of tax structures (T, T^L) leading to the necessary expected tax revenue is expressed in a strict convex function with respect to T.

11.4 Tax Structure

Of the tax structures shown in Sect. 11.3 capable of obtaining tax revenues, which should the government choose? The standard answer to this question is that the government should impose an income tax to maximize utilitarian economic welfare.

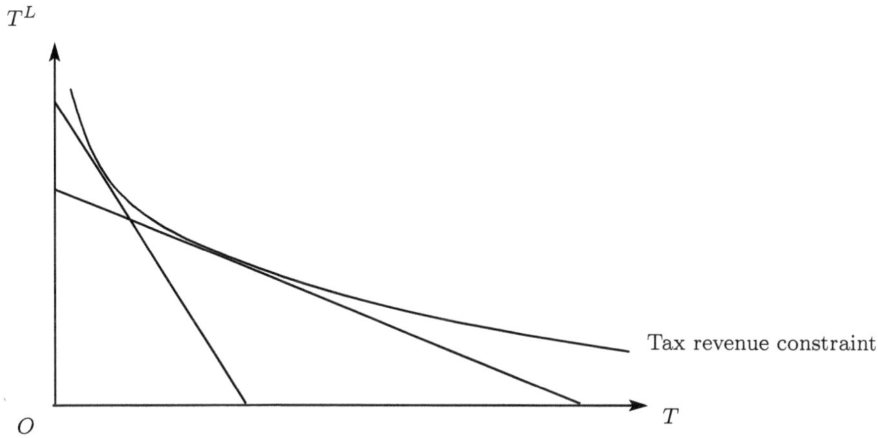

Fig. 11.1 Optimal taxation

To solve this problem, in this study we define economic welfare as the honest tax filer's expected income (W). This is represented in the following equation:

$$W = (1-\alpha)q(I^H - T^H) + s(1-q)(I^L - T^L), \tag{11.14}$$

where $s > 1$ represents the government's degree of favoritism toward low-income earners. A similar idea is cited in Cramer and Gahvari (1995). As Sato (2015, p. 1) pointed out, in their model, the government places a positive weight on the welfare of the high-income earners. When the weight is less than one, this study follows Cramer and Gahvari's economic welfare definition. However, Cramer and Gahvari's result is established under the condition that the weight is fixed, unlike the weighting in this study.

Writing $W = \overline{W}$ (where $\overline{W}$ is a positive constant), then substituting $T^H = T^L + T$, and solving T^L,we obtain the linear function with respect to T as follows:

$$T^L = (\hat{I} - \overline{W} - (1-\alpha)qT)/((1-\alpha)q + s(1-q)), \tag{11.15}$$

where $\hat{I} = (1-\alpha)qI^H + s(1-q)I^L$. The graph of Eq. (11.15) is in the first quadrant of the coordinates (T, T^L); as $\overline{W}$becomes larger (smaller), it is positioned further southwest (northeast).

In Fig. 11.1, $T^H > T^L > 0$ in equilibrium. If we consider the coefficient of T as an increasing function of s as s increases, T^L decreases but never becomes 0.

Therefore, the government can reduce the income tax imposed on low-income earners but cannot provide an income tax exemption to the poor.

11.5 Conclusions

The result obtained in this research infers the following point. In any given society, when stricter penalties for tax evasion are sought based on the permeation of the idea that high-income earners should not be permitted to evade taxes for their personal gain, the government inadvertently creates a larger tax burden on the poor.

This result suggests that a policy decision giving preferential treatment or favoritism to the poor is not compatible with stricter penalties.

Finally, we must be wary of the actions of governments who rely solely on income tax as its chief source of revenue. This is because, as pointed out in some authors (e.g., Zafer 2005 and Baunsgaard and Keen 2010), domestic taxes are not sufficient to be treated as the main financial resource of middle-income and developing countries; such countries also must rely heavily on trade tax revenues.

References

Andreoni, J., B. Erand, and J. Feinstein. 1998. Tax compliance. *Journal of Economic Literature* 36(2): 818–860.

Baunsgaard, T., and M. Keen. 2010. Tax revenue and (or?) Trade liberalization. *Journal of Public Economics* 94(9–10): 563–577.

Cramer, H., and F. Gahvari. 1995. Tax evasion and the optimum general income tax. *Journal of Public Economics* 60(2): 235–249.

Greatz, M.J., J.F. Reinganum, and L.L. Wilde. 1986. The tax compliance game: Toward an interactive theory of law enforcement. *Journal of Law, Economics, and Organization* 2(1): 1–31.

Mirrlees, J.A. 1971. An exploration in the theory of optimum income taxation. *The Review of Economic Studies* 38(2): 175–208.

Sato, H. 2015. Favouritism towards the poor and a discontinuous tax structure. *Applied Economics* 48(3): 222–226.

Zafer, A. 2005. Revenue and the fiscal impact of trade liberalization: The case of Niger. *World Bank Policy Research Working Paper*, 3500.

Chapter 12
Regional Agglomeration and Social Security Policies in OLG Model

Tohru Naito

12.1 Introduction

This chapter presents construction of a simple overlapping generations model (OLG model) that includes multiplicate regions or nursing care probability. Using it, we analyze how social security policies affect regional agglomeration or dispersion. The declining fertility and the progress of aging in Japan present the most severe situation in the world. Japan has already entered a period of declining population. In 2010, Japan's aging rate reached 23.1%. Its social security-related expenditures accounted for 29.5% of all national expenditures. Japan's declining fertility and progressive aging are expected to decrease labor as a factor of economic growth and to destabilize the sustainability of social security. Therefore, it is extremely important, even urgent, for countries facing declining fertility and aging society to adopt policies to overcome such issues. Although most countries regard these issues as severe and important, it is difficult for them to derive adequate policies to resolve the various associated difficulties because the real state of affairs related to these issues differs among countries. For instance, the rates of population increase are not uniform among prefectures in Japan in 2010 (Fig. 12.1).[1] As Fig. 12.1 shows, the rates of population increase in most Japanese prefectures decreased in 2010, but not in some prefectures such as Tokyo and Kanagawa. Therefore, the population is not necessarily decreasing in all Japanese prefectures.

---

[1](See **Source**): Ministry of Internal Affairs and Communications Bureau of Statistics Homepage "National census 2010."

T. Naito (✉)
Doshisha University, Kyoto, Japan
e-mail: tnaito@mail.doshisha.ac.jp

T. Naito et al. (eds.), *Applied Approaches to Societal Institutions and Economics*,
New Frontiers in Regional Science: Asian Perspectives 18,
DOI 10.1007/978-981-10-5663-5_12

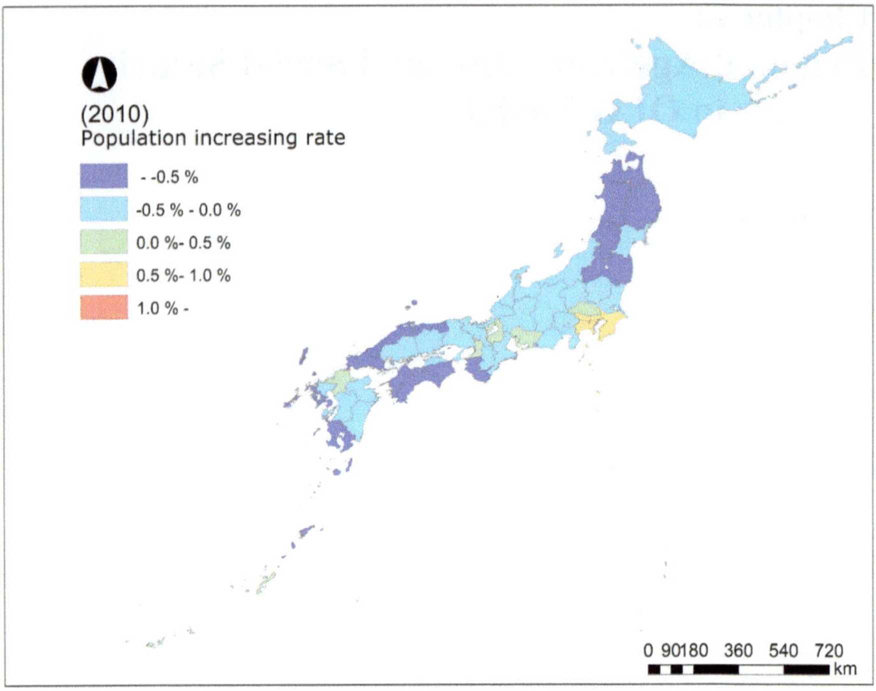

Fig. 12.1 Population increase rate (2010)

Next we refer to nursing care services in Japan. We define that nursing care service is supplied to seniors who are over 65 years old and who have impaired daily living. Figure 12.2 presents the nursing certification rate of Japanese prefectures in 2010.[2] As Fig. 12.2 shows, the nursing care certification rate and the population increase rate differ among prefectures in Japan. In Fig. 12.2, the nursing certification rate of some prefectures in Chugoku area and Shikoku area is shown to be higher than those of other prefectures. Finally, we examine the relation between the rate of population increase and the nursing certification rate. Figure 12.3 shows that their mutual relation exhibits negative correlation. Most seniors tend to stay in the region in which they lived during their working years. Because the social security system in Japan is managed using a pay-as-you-go method, we must consider migration of working generations among regions to maintain sustainability of the social security system.

We have used an overlapping generations (OLG) model constructed by Diamond (1965) to describe income relocation between generations. Although OLG models have been used in economic growth theory and to assess social security like

[2](**Source**): Ministry of Health, Labour, and Welfare Homepage "Survey on Long-Term Care Insurance 2010."

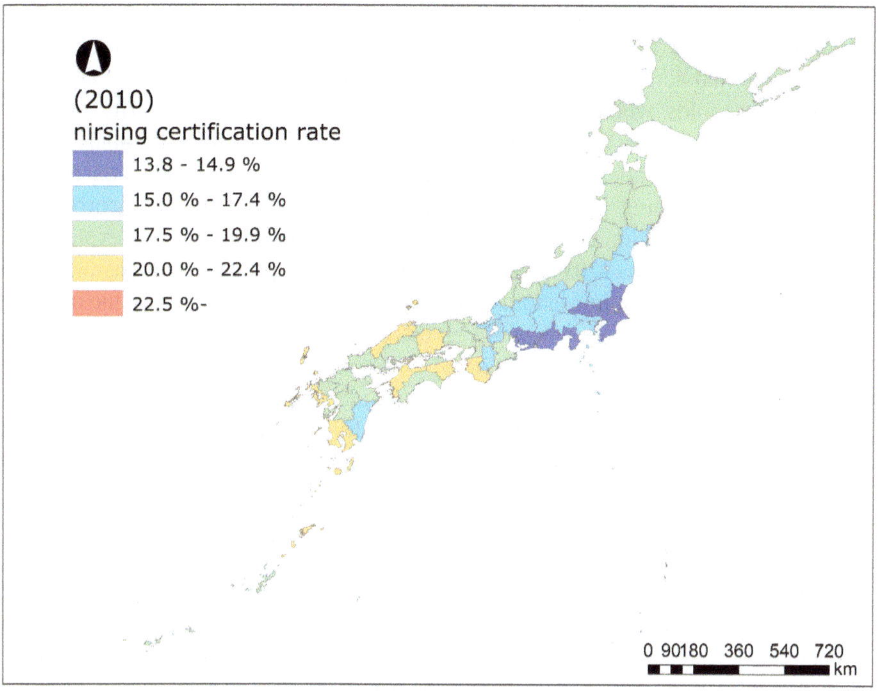

Fig. 12.2 Nursing certification rate (2010)

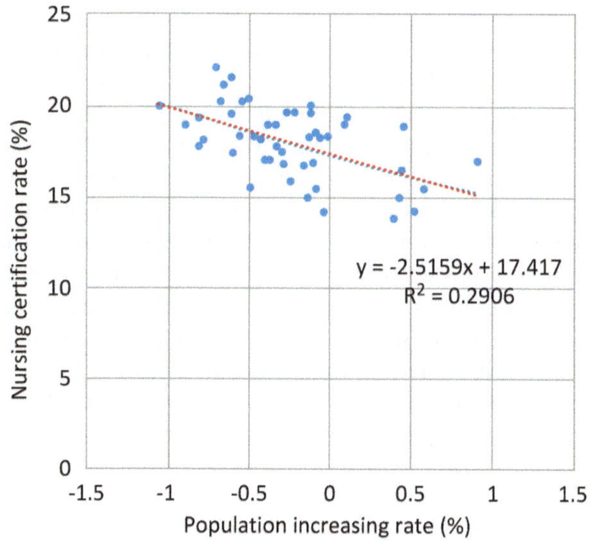

Fig. 12.3 Population increase rate and nursing care certification rate (2010)

pensions, spatial factors have not been given much attention in many studies. Nevertheless, it is necessary to analyze a model including spatial factors and intergenerational activities because we cannot ignore spatial factors such as migration of households when we adopt costlier sustainable social security systems. Sato (2007) introduces regional migration into an OLG model and analyzes the relations among economic geography, fertility, and migration. He constructs a two-period overlapping generations model of endogenous fertility, incorporating n regions, agglomeration economies, and congestion diseconomies to explain this negative relation. Yakita (2011) extends a simple overlapping generations model by introducing migration of households between regions. Results show that the increase of spillover effects of regional public goods influence the population distribution in equilibrium. Naito and Omori (2014) combine the Yakita (2011) model with trans-boundary pollution caused by the manufactured goods sector in an urban area and analyze the effect of environmental policy on the population distribution in equilibrium. Although these studies constructed OLG models including spatial factors or intergenerational activities, they lack survival probability: an extremely important factor. Yakita (2001) or Omori (2009) introduced an uncertain lifetime into an OLG model and analyzed the relation between life expectancy and fertility. However, their models do not include migration between regions.

We consider social security policies of two kinds: child care policy and nursing care policy. It is necessary to increase tax revenue or restrain expenditure to maintain a sustainable social security system. The shortage of nurseries and additional educational expenses engenders increases of household expenditures for child care. However, preventive nursing care attracts attention for decreasing social security cost and maintaining susceptibility. The decrease in demand of nursing care service reduces social security costs. Therefore, preventive nursing care policy is necessary for a sustainable social security system. Although Yakita (2001) and Omori (2009) consider survival probability in their models, they do not incorporate the probability of nursing care in them. We extend the OLG model including survival probability by introducing nursing care probability and preventive nursing care into previous models as a social security policy. Consequently, the model in this chapter complements the gaps in knowledge that have been left by earlier studies.

The organization of this chapter is the following. The next section presents the basic model, which describes the respective behaviors of households, production sectors, and government. In Sect. 12.3, we derive the equilibrium and deal with qualitative analysis of it. Moreover, we analyze the effects of social security policy on equilibrium with comparative statics. Finally we present concluding remarks.

12.2 The Model

12.2.1 Households

We consider a simple OLG model with two regions. Households exist for three periods, which are young generation, working generation, and retirement generation, and survive to the retirement generation. Although nobody does anything for economic activities in the young generation, they decide whether they reside at the top of the working generation and decide their number of children and level of saving. Here we define p as the probability to survive to the retirement generation. Households that survive in the retirement generation consume their savings as they buy consumption goods and nursing care services. Presuming that all households had common preferences in an economy, they have the same utility function. Therefore, we specify household utility functions in region i as presented below.

$$U_t^i = \gamma \ln n_t^i + p\left\{(1-\gamma)\ln C_{t+1}^i + q_t \ln e_{t+1}^i\right\}, \quad (i = u, r) \tag{12.1}$$

Therein, n_t^i, C_{t+1}^i, and e_{t+1}^i, respectively, denote the number of children, consumption for consumption goods, and consumption for nursing care services. Moreover, q_t denotes the probability of demanding nursing care services in the retirement generation. Its value is between zero and one, i.e., $q \in [0, 1]$. Next we refer to the budget constraint of households. Households supply their labor to the production sector in the region, where they choose residence at the top of the working generation. Consequently, they allocate their wage income for the children and saving in the working generation. The budget constraint of households in region u is given as

$$(1-\tau)(1-\sigma-z_t n_t^u)w_t^u = s_t^u, \tag{12.2}$$

where τ, σ, z_t, w_t^u, and s_t^u, respectively, denote the income tax rate, additional residential cost, child care cost, wage in region u at period t, and saving. Although they consume their savings to purchase consumption goods or nursing care services, it is not necessary for every household to receive savings. This is true because we assume that a part of them in the working generation can survive in the retirement generation. Moreover, we define q_t as the probability of demanding the nursing care services in the retirement generation. Therefore, no households in the retirement generation need the expenditure for nursing services. Their budget constraint in the retirement generation is given as

$$\frac{(1+R_{t+1})s_t^u}{p} = C_{t+1}^u + q_t h e_{t+1}^u \tag{12.3}$$

where R_{t+1}, h, and q_t, respectively, denote the interest rate, the nursing care service fee, and the probability of receiving nursing care services. Combining (12.2) with (12.3), the lifetime budget constraint of households in region u is given as

$$(1 + R_{t+1})(1 - \sigma - z_t n_t^u) w_t^u = pC_{t+1}^u + pq_t h e_{t+1}^u. \tag{12.4}$$

Maximizing (12.1) subject to (12.4), we derive the number of children, consumption for goods, and demand of nursing care service as described below.

$$n_t^{u*} = \frac{\gamma(1 - \sigma)}{z_t [\gamma(1 - p) + p(1 + q_t)]} \tag{12.5}$$

$$C_{t+1}^{u*} = \frac{(1 + R_{t+1})(1 - \gamma)(1 - \sigma)(1 - \tau) w_t^u}{\gamma(1 - p) + p(1 + q_t)} \tag{12.6}$$

$$e_{t+1}^{u*} = \frac{(1 + R_{t+1})(1 - \sigma)(1 - \tau) w_t^u}{[\gamma(1 - p) + p(1 + q_t)] h} \tag{12.7}$$

Next we consider household behavior in region r. Because we assume that all households have a common preference, the utility function of households in region r is also given as (12.1). However, the budget constraint of households in region r is not the same as that in region u. Although households in region u must absorb additional residential costs, signified by σ, to reside there, those in region r need not do it. Moreover, households of the working generation in region r supply for their labor inelastically and gain wage income from the production sector in region r. Let w_t^r represent the wage rate in region r at period t. Consequently, the budget constraint of households in region r at period t is given as shown below.

$$(1 - \tau)(1 - z_t n_t^r) w_t^r = s_t^r \tag{12.8}$$

Similar to households in region u at period t, no household at the period in the working generation can survive in the retirement generation. For simplification, we assume that the survival probability is common among all residential regions. It is assumed that saving at period t is distributed for surviving households in retirement generation.[3] Therefore, the budget constraint of households in the retirement generation is given as

$$\frac{(1 + R_{t+1}) s_t^r}{p} = C_{t+1}^r + q_t h e_{t+1}^r. \tag{12.9}$$

[3]We assume that each region has a private pension system. Consequently, the total savings of households in region i at period t are redistributed to households to survive during the retirement period.

Combining (12.8) with (12.9), the lifetime budget constraint of households in region r is given as

$$(1 + R_{t+1})(1 - z_t n_t^r)w_t^r = pC_{t+1}^r + pq_t he_{t+1}^r. \tag{12.10}$$

Maximizing (12.1) subject to (12.10), we derive the number of children, consumption of goods, and demand for nursing care services in region r as shown below.

$$n_t^{r*} = \frac{\gamma}{z_t\left[\gamma(1-p) + p(1+q_t)\right]} \tag{12.11}$$

$$C_{t+1}^{r*} = \frac{(1 + R_{t+1})(1-\gamma)(1-\tau)w_t^r}{\gamma(1-p) + p(1+q_t)} \tag{12.12}$$

$$e_{t+1}^{r*} = \frac{(1 + R_{t+1})(1-\tau)w_t^r}{\left[\gamma(1-p) + p(1+q_t)\right]h} \tag{12.13}$$

The savings of households in region i are given as shown below.

$$s_t^{u*} = (1-\tau)(1-\sigma)\left(\frac{p(1-\gamma+q_t)}{\gamma(1-p)+p(1+q_t)}\right)w_t^{u*} \tag{12.14}$$

and

$$s_t^{r*} = (1-\tau)\left(\frac{p(1-\gamma+q_t)}{\gamma(1-p)+p(1+q_t)}\right)w_t^{r*} \tag{12.15}$$

Let V_t^{i*} represent the indirect utility function of households in region i at period t. Substituting (12.5), (12.6), and (12.7) for (12.1), the indirect utility function of households in region u is given as

$$V_t^{u*} = \ln(n_t^{u*})^{\gamma}(C_{t+1}^{u*})^{p(1-\gamma)}(e_{t+1}^{u*})^{pq_t}. \tag{12.16}$$

Similarly to (12.16), the indirect utility function of households in region r is also derived as

$$V_t^{r*} = \ln(n_t^{r*})^{\gamma}(C_{t+1}^{r*})^{p(1-\gamma)}(e_{t+1}^{r*})^{pq_t}. \tag{12.17}$$

Because households have no incentive to migrate to the other region in equilibrium, the indirect utility in both regions is a common level. Therefore, we derive the migration equilibrium condition as presented below.

$$V_t^{u*} = V_t^{r*} \Longleftrightarrow \frac{w_t^r}{w_t^u} = (1-\sigma)^{\eta}. \tag{12.18}$$

Therein, η is defined as follows.

$$\eta \equiv \frac{\gamma(1-p)+p(1+q_t)}{p(1-\gamma+q_t)}.$$

Next we refer to the population dynamics. We have already derived the number of children in equilibrium as (12.5) and (12.11). Let N_{t+1} and N_t, respectively, represent the total population in an economy at periods $t+1$ and t.

$$N_t = [\phi_t n_t^u + (1-\phi_t)n_t^r]N_t \tag{12.19}$$

In that equation, ϕ_t denotes the total households of working generation at period t and the ratio of households in region u. Substituting (12.5) and (12.11) for (12.19), the fertility m_t is derived as follows.

$$m_t \equiv \frac{\gamma\left[(1-\sigma)\phi_t+(1-\phi_t)\right]}{z_t\left[\gamma(1-p)+p(1+q_t)\right]}. \tag{12.20}$$

From (12.20), the equilibrium fertility at period t depends on σ, ϕ_t, p, q_t, and z_t. Differentiating (12.20) with respect to σ and p, we derive the following results of comparative statics, i.e.,

$$\frac{\partial m_t}{\partial \sigma} < 0, \quad \frac{\partial m_t}{\partial p} < 0.$$

Therefore, we derive the following lemma as to fertility.

Lemma 12.1 *Increase in the additional residential costs and survival probability decrease fertility.*

As for economic interpretation of this lemma, increases in additional residential costs engender expenditures for savings and child care. Consequently, they decrease the number of children. However, households increase incentives to save wage income because increased survival probability engenders an increase in expenditures for consumption and nursing care services.

12.2.2 Production

12.2.2.1 Consumption Goods

Next we refer to the production sectors in this section. Here we consider production of two kinds in an economy. One of them is consumption goods, which are consumed by households during the retirement period. Although these goods are produced in both regions, the production technology differs between regions. Although the production sector in region u requires labor and capital to produce these goods, that in region r requires only labor as a production input. Considering this situation and following Yakita (2011) and Naito and Omori (2014), we specify the production function of consumption goods as follows.

$$Y_t = A\left[(K_t)^{\alpha}(L_t^u)^{1-\alpha} + bL_t^r\right], \quad \alpha \in (0, 1). \tag{12.21}$$

Therein, A, K_t, L_t^u, b, and L_t^r, respectively, denote the technology parameter, the capital input and labor input in region u, and the productivity of production sector and labor input in region r. We regard consumption goods as numeraire and assume that the consumption market is competitive. Consequently, the wage rate in each region is equal to the marginal product of labor in the production sector there. Because the number of children of households in region i is given as (12.5) and (12.11), the labor supply in region i is

$$L_t^{u*} = \frac{p\,(1-\sigma)\,(1-\gamma+q_t)\,\phi_t N_t}{\gamma(1-p)+p(1+q_t)} \tag{12.22}$$

and

$$L_t^{r*} = \frac{p\,(1-\gamma+q)\,(1-\phi_t)N_t}{\gamma(1-p)+p(1+q)}. \tag{12.23}$$

Differentiating (12.21) with respect to L_t^i, the wage rate in region i is derived as

$$w_t^u = A(1-\alpha)\left(\frac{K_t}{L_t^u}\right)^{\alpha} = A(1-\alpha)\left(\frac{[\gamma(1-p)+p(1+q_t)]k_t}{p\,(1-\sigma)\,(1-\gamma+q_t)\,\phi_t}\right)^{\alpha} \tag{12.24}$$

and

$$w_t^r = Ab, \tag{12.25}$$

where k_t stands for per capita capital, $k_t = K_t/N_t$. From (12.24) and (12.25), we know that the wage rate in region u depends on capital accumulation. However, that in region r is independent of it and is constant. Consequently, the wage rate difference between regions expands as capital accumulation progresses. Combining (12.24) and (12.25), the relative wage is given as shown below.

$$\frac{w_t^r}{w_t^u} = \left(\frac{b}{1-\alpha}\right)\left[\frac{p\,(1-\sigma)\,(1-\gamma+q_t)\,\phi_t}{\gamma(1-p)+p(1+q_t)k_t}\right]^{\alpha} \tag{12.26}$$

12.2.2.2 Nursing Care Service

Next we examine nursing care service goods. We assume that one unit of nursing services requires one unit of consumption goods. Because we deal with consumption goods as numeraire, the price of nursing services is also given as one, h is equal to one.

12.2.3 Government

The government administers region u and region r. An income tax is imposed on households in both regions and expends tax revenue for social security of two kinds, which are child care policy for households in the working generation and nursing care service policy for them in the retirement generation. Let δ represent the share of expenditures for child care policy. Because total tax revenue is given as $\tau(w_t^u N_t^u + w_t^r N_t^r)$, the expenditures for child care and for nursing service are represented as $\delta\tau N_t$ and $(1-\delta)\tau N_t$.

$$\tau(w_t^u N_t^u + w_t^r N_t^r) = \begin{cases} \delta\tau(w_t^u N_t^u + w_t^r N_t^r) & \textit{(Child care)} \\ (1-\delta)\tau(w_t^u N_t^u + w_t^r N_t^r) & \textit{(Nursing care)} \end{cases} \tag{12.27}$$

Now we define δ as the share of expenditure for child care policy. We consider child care policy and nursing care policy as public goods. Because nobody has an incentive to migrate to the other region in equilibrium, (12.18) must hold in equilibrium. The total income tax revenue, which is denoted by T_t, is given by combining (12.18), (12.24), and (12.25) with (12.18).

$$T_t = \tau Ab[\phi_t(1-\sigma)^{-\eta} + (1-\phi_t)]N_t \tag{12.28}$$

Because the share of expenditure for each social security policy is given as (12.27), the following equations hold:

$$G_t^c = \delta\tau Ab[\phi_t(1-\sigma)^{-\eta} + (1-\phi_t)]N_t \tag{12.29}$$

and

$$G_t^n = (1-\delta)\tau Ab[\phi_t(1-\sigma)^{-\eta} + (1-\phi_t)]N_t, \tag{12.30}$$

where G_t^c and G_t^n, respectively, denote the expenditures for child care policy and for nursing care policy. For simplification of the analysis of model, we specify z_t and q_t as

$$z_t = \exp\{-G_t^c\} \tag{12.31}$$

and

$$q_t = \exp\{-G_t^h\}. \tag{12.32}$$

We assume that no household can control z_t and q_t because every household deals with them as given. From (12.31) and (12.32), the increases in G_t^c and G_t^n, respectively, decrease z_t and q_t. Differentiating (12.31) and (12.32) with respect to δ, the signs of $\frac{\partial G_t^c}{\partial \delta}$ and $\frac{\partial G_t^c}{\partial \delta}$ are given as

$$\frac{\partial G_t^c}{\partial \delta} < 0, \quad \frac{\partial G_t^n}{\partial \delta} > 0.$$

12.3 Equilibrium

In the previous section, we referred to the behavior of households and production sectors in each region and government. Considering these behaviors, we derive the equilibrium in this section. Because no household in the working generation has any incentive to migrate between regions in equilibrium, the migration equilibrium condition has already been derived as (12.18). However, the relative wage between regions u and r is also given as (12.26). Combining (12.18) with (12.26), the following equation is obtained:

$$\phi_t = \Omega k_t. \tag{12.33}$$

Here we define Ω as follows.

$$\Omega \equiv \left(\frac{1-\alpha}{b}\right)\eta\,(1-\sigma)^{\frac{\eta-\alpha}{\alpha}}.$$

Because ϕ_t is a ratio, it exists from zero to one and depends on per capita capital accumulation. When k_t is sufficiently large, we assume that ϕ_t is equal to one. All households agglomerate in region u under $\phi_t = 1$. Therefore, we define this distribution between regions as "agglomeration equilibrium." However, some households reside in region u. Others reside in region r when k_t is less than one. We designate this distribution between them as "dispersion equilibrium." Consequently, ϕ_t is given as

$$\phi_t = \begin{cases} 1 & (k_t > \bar{k}) \\ \Omega k_t & (k_t \leq \bar{k}) \end{cases} \tag{12.34}$$

When we define $\bar{k}$ as the per capita capital stock to hold (12.33) under $\phi = 1$, $\bar{k}$ is given as $1/\Omega$. Because the relative wage between region u and region r depends on capital accumulation, capital accumulation, which is denoted by k_t, engenders increased differences of relative wage.[4] Because the fertility is given as (12.20). We can rewrite the following total fertility in an economy by combining (12.20) with (12.34), i.e.,

$$m_t = \begin{cases} \frac{\gamma(1-\sigma)}{z_t[\gamma(1-p)+p(1+q_t)]} & (k_t > \bar{k}) \\ \frac{\gamma(1-\Omega\sigma k_t)}{z_t[\gamma(1-p)+p(1+q_t)]} & (k_t \leq \bar{k}) \end{cases} \tag{12.35}$$

[4]Here we specify (12.21) as the production function, in which production technology in region u differs from that in region r. Although the wage rate in region r is constant irrespective of capital accumulation, the wage increases because of capital accumulation. However, the increase of additional residential cost in region u decreases the relative wage between them.

We assume that the savings of households in each region are invested in the production sector in region u. Because savings of households are given as (12.14) and (12.15), respectively, the capital accumulation function is derived as follows.

$$K_{t+1} = \left[\phi_t s_t^u + (1-\phi_t) s_t^r\right] N_t. \tag{12.36}$$

Substituting (12.14), (12.15), and (12.20) for (12.36), we derive per capita capital accumulation as shown below.

$$k_{t+1} = \left[\phi_t s_t^u + (1-\phi_t) s_t^r\right] / m_t. \tag{12.37}$$

We know that the accumulation function of per capita capital depends on the population distribution between regions, i.e.,

$$k_{t+1} = \begin{cases} \Psi_1(k_t) & (k_t > \bar{k}) \\ \Psi_2(k_t) & (k_t \leq \bar{k}), \end{cases} \tag{12.38}$$

where $\Psi_1(k_t)$ and $\Psi_2(k_t)$ are defined as shown below.

$$\Psi_1(k_t) = A(1-\tau)(1-\alpha)(1-\sigma)^{1-\alpha}\eta^{\alpha-1}k_t^{\alpha} \tag{12.39}$$

and

$$\Psi_2(k_t) = \frac{Az_t\left[\gamma(1-p) + p(1+q_t)\right]}{\gamma(1-\sigma\Omega k_t)} \times \left[\Omega^{1-\alpha}(1-\tau)(1-\sigma)^{1-\alpha}\eta^{-\alpha}(1-\alpha)k_t + (1-\Omega k_t)b\right]. \tag{12.40}$$

Differentiating (12.39) with respect with k_t, $\frac{\partial \Psi_1(k_t)}{\partial k_t}$ is positive. Moreover, differentiating $\frac{\partial k_{t+1}}{\partial k_t}$ with respect with k_t, $\frac{\partial^2 \Psi_1(k_t)}{\partial k_t^2}$ is negative because of $\alpha \in (0,1)$. Therefore, we know $\Psi_1(k_t)$ is concave. Similarly, differentiating (12.40) with respect with k_t, $\Psi_2(k_t)$ is positive. However, $\frac{\partial^2 \Psi_2(k_t)}{\partial k_t^2}$ is also positive when the productivity in region r is small. Consequently, $\Psi_1(k_t)$ is convex. When k_t is equal to zero, $\Psi_2(0)$ is given as shown below.

$$\Psi_2(0) = \left(\frac{Abz_t}{\gamma}\right)\left[\gamma(1-p) + p(1+q_t)\right] > 0 \tag{12.41}$$

Next, we focus our analysis on the steady state. Although the steady state is described by the intersection points of $\Psi_i(k_t)(i=1,2)$ and the 45° line, the location and shape of $\Psi_i(k_t)$ depend on each parameter. As Fig. 12.4 shows, it is possible that multiplicate steady states exist.

In case 1, there is a unique steady state in which population disperse between region u and region r. In case 2, there are three intersection points of $\Psi_i(k_t)(i=1,2)$

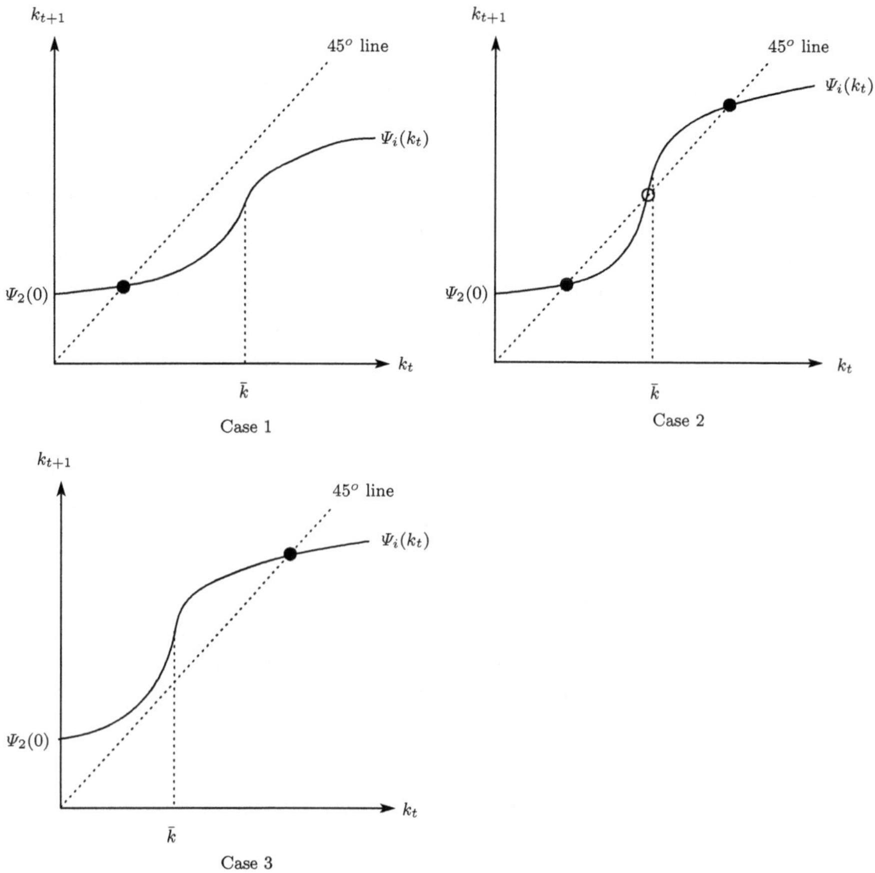

Fig. 12.4 Steady state

and the 45° line, in which black points are stable and the other point is unstable. Because the 45° line intersects $\Psi_1(k_t)$ and $\Psi_2(k_t)$, there are population distributions of two kinds between regions. The intersection point of the 45° line and $\Psi_1(k_t)$ shows the agglomeration equilibrium, in which all households concentrate in region u. However, that of the 45° line and $\Psi_2(k_t)$ show the dispersion equilibrium, in which some households reside in each region. In case 3, the agglomeration equilibrium is a unique equilibrium because the 45° line intersects only $\Psi_1(k_t)$. All households concentrate in region u. Nobody resides in region r under this case.

Because we deal with some parameters or policy variables as given in this section, we do not refer to the effect of these parameters or variables on a steady state. Therefore, we analyze their effects on the steady state in the next section.

12.4 Comparative Statics

12.4.1 *Effects of the Survival Probability on Steady State*

To begin with, we consider the effect of survival probability on equilibrium. Because of partial differentiation of $\Psi_1(k_t)$ with respect to p, $\frac{\partial \Psi_1}{\partial p}$ is positive, the increase of survival probability makes $\Psi_1(k_t)$ shift upward. Next, we partially differentiate $\Psi_2(k_t)$ with respect to p to analyze the effect of survival probability on $\Psi_2(k_t)$. Presuming that the additional residential cost was high, $\frac{\partial \Omega}{\partial p}$ is positive. When $\frac{\partial \Omega}{\partial p}$ is positive, then $\frac{\partial \Psi_2}{\partial p}$ is also positive. Consequently, the increase of survival probability also makes $\Psi_2(k_t)$ shift upward. When we assume that $\frac{\partial \Omega}{\partial p}$ is positive, then $\Psi_i(k_t)$ shifts upward. It increases capital accumulation at the steady state in every case. Consequently, the ratio of population in region u to the total population denoted by ϕ_t increases. The increase of survival probability strengthens agglomeration of households in region u. Regarding the economic mechanism, we present the following economic interpretation. Extending the survival probability, households in both regions have an incentive to save their wage income for consumption and nursing care service in the retirement generation. Because we assume that the savings of households are invested in capital of the production sector in region u, the increasing savings engender increased capital accumulation. Although the wage in region r does not depend on capital accumulation, the wage in region u is raised by it. Consequently, the wage differential between regions expands, as does the incentive to reside and work in region u.

Lemma 12.2 *The increase of survival probability engenders agglomeration in region u.*

12.4.2 *Effect of Changing Share of Expenditure for Social Security*

Finally we consider how social security policy affects the population distribution between the regions. In the previous section, we show that steady states of three types can appear in our model (Fig. 12.4). Therefore, we analyze the effect of the share of expenditure for child care policy on a steady state by case division with agglomeration equilibrium and dispersion equilibrium. First, we consider the steady state under agglomeration equilibrium. Because all households agglomerate in region u under agglomeration equilibrium, ϕ_t is equal to one. Consequently, the capital accumulation equation under agglomeration equilibrium is given as s_t^{u*}/m_t.

$$\frac{\partial \Psi_1(k_t)}{\partial \delta} = \frac{1}{\{m_t\}^2} \cdot \left\{ \frac{\partial s_t^{u*}}{\partial \eta} \cdot \frac{\partial \eta}{\partial \delta} \cdot m_t - s_t^{u*} \cdot \frac{\partial m_t}{\partial \delta} \right\} \gtreqless 0 \tag{12.42}$$

As we know from (12.42), it is apparent that there are effects of the two kinds caused by increasing δ, which denotes the share of expenditure for child care policy. Next, we describe the first term and second term in brackets of the right side of (12.42), respectively, as "*saving effect*" and "*fertility effect*." Because the direction of shift of this function depends on the relation among these effects, the sign of $\frac{\partial \Psi_1(k_t)}{\partial \delta}$ is ambiguous.[5] When the saving effect is sufficiently greater than fertility effect, then the sign of $\frac{\partial \Psi_1(k_t)}{\partial \delta}$ is positive. Because per capita capital accumulation is promoted by increased saving, the agglomeration force into region u is more reinforced.

Next we consider the effect of the share of expenditures for child care policy on the other steady states. Although the steady state under the agglomeration equilibrium is given by the intersection of $\Psi_1(k_t)$ and 45° in Fig. 12.4, the steady state under dispersion equilibrium is derived by the intersection of $\Psi_2(k_t)$ and 45° in Fig. 12.4. The effect of the share of expenditure for child care policy on $\Psi_2(k_t)$ is more complex than in the case of $\Psi_1(k_t)$ because we must incorporate consideration of the trade-off among three effects: the saving effect, fertility effect, and "*migration effect*." Differentiating $\Psi_2(k_t)$ with respect to δ, the effect of δ on $\Psi_2(k_t)$ is given as

$$\frac{\partial \Psi_2(k_t)}{\partial \delta} = \left\{ \left[\left(s_t^{u*} - s_t^{r*}\right) \frac{\partial \phi_t}{\partial \Omega} \cdot \frac{\partial \Omega}{\partial \eta} \cdot \frac{\partial \eta}{\partial \delta} + \left(\phi_t \frac{\partial s_t^{u*}}{\partial \eta} \frac{\partial \eta}{\partial \delta} + (1-\phi_t) \frac{\partial s_t^{r*}}{\partial \eta} \frac{\partial \eta}{\partial \delta} \right) \right] m_t \right.$$
$$\left. - \left[\phi_t s_t^{u*} + (1-\phi_t) s_t^{r*}\right] \frac{\partial m_t}{\partial \delta} \right\} \cdot \frac{1}{\{m_t\}^2}$$
$$\gtreqless 0. \tag{12.43}$$

The first term, second term, and third term of the middle bracket on the right-hand side of (12.43), respectively, represent migration effects, saving effects, and fertility effects. As confirmed already, the sign of $\frac{\partial m_t}{\partial \delta}$ is ambiguous because the fertility effect depends on the decreasing effect of child care cost and the increasing effect of nursing care probability effects. Next we analyze the migration effect. The population distribution between regions is nonuniform because the number of households in region u differs from that in region r in our model. Therefore, the total saving of households in region i depends on ϕ_t, which is given as (12.33).

[5]Differentiating (12.14) with respect to η, $\frac{\partial s_t^{u*}}{\partial \eta} = -A(1-\tau)(1-\sigma)^{1-\alpha}(1-\alpha)^2\eta^{\alpha-2}k^{\alpha} < 0$. Moreover, differentiating η with respect to δ, $\frac{\partial \eta}{\partial \delta} = -\frac{\gamma p}{\{p(1-\gamma+q_t)\}} \cdot \frac{\partial q_t}{\partial \delta} < 0$. Consequently, $\frac{\partial s_t^{u*}}{\partial \delta} = \frac{\partial s_t^{u*}}{\partial \eta} \cdot \frac{\partial \eta}{\partial \delta} > 0$. Therefore, we know that the saving effect is positive. As for the effect of δ on m_t, which is the fertility effect, differentiating m_t with respect to δ, $\frac{\partial m_t}{\partial \delta} = -\frac{\gamma(1-\sigma)}{\{p(1-\gamma+q_t)\}^2} \cdot \left\{ \frac{\partial z_t}{\partial \delta}[\gamma(1-p) + p(1+q_t)] + pz_t \frac{\partial q_t}{\partial \delta} \right\} \gtreqless 0$. Consequently, the sign of $\frac{\partial m_t}{\partial \delta}$ is also ambiguous because there are two effects of δ on m_t. One is a positive effect, in which the increase in δ decreases the child care cost z_t. Decreasing z_t increases a household's incentive to have children. However, the other is a negative effect, in which the increase in δ increases the nursing care probability q_t. Consequently, its effect decreases incentives to have children by increasing saving for the retirement generation.

Differentiating (12.33) with respect to δ, the following equation is derived:

$$\frac{\partial \phi_t}{\partial \delta} = \frac{\partial \phi_t}{\partial \Omega} \cdot \frac{\partial \Omega}{\partial \eta} \cdot \frac{\partial \eta}{\partial \delta}$$
$$= k_t \cdot \left(\frac{1-\alpha}{b\alpha} \frac{\alpha + \eta \ln(1-\sigma)}{(1-\sigma)^{\frac{\alpha-\eta}{\alpha}}} \right) \cdot \left(-\frac{\gamma p}{\{p(1-\gamma+q_t)\}} \cdot \frac{\partial q_t}{\partial \delta} \right)$$
$$\gtreqless 0. \tag{12.44}$$

From (12.44), the effect of δ on ϕ_t is ambiguous. When the additional residential cost in region u is sufficiently large, the sign of $\frac{\partial \Omega}{\partial \eta}$ is negative. Consequently, we know that the migration effect is positive. However, the sign of $\frac{\partial \Omega}{\partial \eta}$ is negative when it is not sufficiently large. Consequently, the migration effect is negative.

Finally we consider the saving effect. The effect of the share of expenditure for child care policy on saving in region u under dispersion equilibrium is more complicated than that under agglomeration equilibrium because saving in region u depends not only on wage income but also on the population distribution between regions. To begin with, we refer to the saving effect in region u. We differentiate (12.14) with respect to δ to analyze the effect of δ on saving effect, as

$$\frac{\partial s_t^{u*}}{\partial \delta} = \left\{ \frac{\partial s_t^{u*}}{\partial \eta} + \frac{\partial s_t^{u*}}{\partial \phi_t} \cdot \frac{\partial \phi_t}{\partial \eta} \right\} \cdot \frac{\partial \eta}{\partial \delta} \gtrless 0. \tag{12.45}$$

When the additional residential cost in region u is sufficiently large, we know that the effect of δ on saving effect in region u is positive, i.e., $\frac{\partial s_t^{u*}}{\partial \delta} > 0$. Moreover, we confirm the effect of δ on saving effects. Differentiating (12.15) with respect to δ, we derive the following equation:

$$\frac{\partial s_t^r}{\partial \delta} = \frac{\partial s_t^r}{\partial \Omega} \cdot \frac{\partial \Omega}{\partial \delta} > 0. \tag{12.46}$$

Summarizing (12.45) and (12.46), we know that the increase in share of expenditure for child care policy produces a positive saving effect when the additional cost to reside in region u is sufficiently large. When the sum of saving effects and migration effects is larger than the fertility effect under the case in which the additional residential cost in region u, the increase in the share of government expenditure for child care policy increases the per capita capital accumulation at steady state.

Theorem 12.3 *Increasing the share of government expenditure for child care policy intensifies agglomeration in region u when the sum of the saving effect and migration effect is greater than the fertility effect under the case in which an additional cost is necessary to reside in region u.*

12.5 Concluding Remarks

For the analyses described in this chapter, we constructed a simple OLG model with two regions. After consideration of the child care policy in the working generation and nursing care policy in the retirement generation as social security policy in this model, we analyze the effect of central government's social security policy on the population distribution between regions. Results show that per capita capital accumulation at the steady state depends in this model on a trade-off among saving effects, migration effects, and fertility effects. When the sum of saving effects and migration effects is greater than the fertility effect and the additional residential cost in region u, per capita capital accumulation exacerbates the wage difference between regions and strengthens agglomeration force. Consequently, the increase in the share of government expenditure for child care policy increases per capita capital accumulation in a steady state when we consider the effect of social security policy on population distribution in a steady state.

For simplification of the analysis, we omitted some factors from this model. We assume that the production technologies of region u and region r are extraneous. Because we assume this production heterogeneity between regions, we ignore which production technology each production sector chooses. Moreover, we do not consider the social security system as a pension. Because it is extremely important to take account of sustainable pension system, a model with this point must be constructed to support future analysis.

References

Diamond, P.A. 1965. National debt in a neoclassical growth model. *The American Economic Review* 55: 1126–1150.

Naito, T., and T. Omori. 2014. Can urban pollution shrink rural districts? *Letters in Spatial and Resources Science* 7(2): 73–83.

Omori, T. 2009. Effects of public education and social security on fertility. *Journal of Population Economics* 22(3): 585–601.

Sato, Y. 2007. Economic geography, fertility and migration. *Journal of Urban Economics* 61(2): 372–387.

Yakita, A. 2001. Uncertain lifetime, fertility and social security. *Journal of Population Economics* 14(4): 635–640.

Yakita, S. 2011. Regional public goods, migration, and growth. *Letters in Spatial and Resources Science* 4(2): 129–138.

Chapter 13
Can Migration Affect the Decision of Governmental Fiscal Bailout?

Woohyung Lee

13.1 Introduction

In general, it has been revealed that grants from the central government to local government, which does not undertake responsibility for local finance, cannot guarantee efficient financial management. This observation is based on the recognition through experiments that the central government bails out local governments when they face a default caused by their lax management. This problem is called a soft budget constraint, which was defined by Kornai (1979, 1980, 1986) as occurring when a bailout from the central government incurs local financial management that allows for ex post bailout to the local governments.[1] In the case of Korea, Oh (2008) analyzed the circumstance of Korean local finance and concluded that the soft budget constraint problem arises readily in Korea because local finance has a high level of dependence on the central government due to the serious local tax revenue imbalance, and this high dependence impedes the autonomy and responsibility of the local government.

Considering the status of local finance in Japan and Korea, over 30% of revenue in local finance depends on the central government. According to the White Paper on Local Public Finance Japan (2016), of the total revenue in the 2014 fiscal year, national treasury disbursements account for 15%, local allocation taxes account for 17.1%, and local taxes account for 36.0%. According to the Summary of Local

[1] Akai (2006) summarizes previous theoretical studies on soft budget constraint in detail.

W. Lee (✉)
Keimyung University, Daegu, South Korea
e-mail: iuh1231@kmu.ac.kr

T. Naito et al. (eds.), *Applied Approaches to Societal Institutions and Economics*, New Frontiers in Regional Science: Asian Perspectives 18,
DOI 10.1007/978-981-10-5663-5_13

Budget for FY 2015 in Korea (2015), of the total revenue in 2015 fiscal year, national treasury disbursements account for 24.1%, local allocation taxes account for 18.2%, and local taxes account for 34.3%.

The concept of a soft budget constraint has been examined in various research fields and has generally been applied to local finance theory. Many studies have been conducted that apply soft budget constraint to local finance theory, such as Wildasin (1997), Qian and Roland (1998), Caplan et al. (2000), Goodspeed (2002), etc. Qian and Roland (1998) insist that the soft budget constraint problem occurs due to the possibility of the moral hazard of the local government under a centralized regime, while competition between local governments under a decentralized regime could realize a hard budget constraint. Goodspeed (2002) analyzes the relationship between local governments' borrowing and central governments' grants using a two-period model and shows that a grant by national tax restrains local borrowing in the first period since national tax places the cost burden on all the households in the economy.

On the other hand, Facchini and Testa (2008) investigate the effectiveness of selective bailout. They consider the case when the central government faces a situation for bailout of the local government and insist that only the bailout in a large state can be socially desirable since the social cost of default is less than the bailout cost in a small state. Lee (2016) analyzed the case of an asymmetric region which is similar to the study by Facchini and Testa (2008) and concluded that if the population is not densely concentrated in a particular region, a soft budget constraint might be able to improve social welfare rather than a hard budget constraint.

These studies, however, do not consider the migration of households. If a region faces default or is under financial difficulty and bailout from the central government is not expected, households in the region must bear all of the financial cost. This results in the decline of welfare in the region, forcing some households to move to other regions. Free mobility plays a very important role when we consider the soft budget constraint for multi-regions. In this paper, we consider four cases of bailout under a two-region model, whereby both regions are asymmetric in the productiveness of firms, i.e., firms are symmetric on their production technology in the same region but asymmetric between regions. In the first case, hard budget constraint is applied to both regions, so each local government must solely finance the cost of overprovision of local public goods. In the second case, central government bails out both regions, while in the third case, it only bails out the relatively productive region. Finally, in the fourth case, we consider the case where the central government only bails out the relatively less productive region.

The aim of this paper is twofold: (i) to compare these four cases under the assumption of no migration in the context of social welfare to determine the most socially desirable case and (ii) to investigate the effect of migration on the bailout policy of the central government through a comparison of social welfare under free migration.

This paper is organized as follows. Section 13.2 describes the basic model for our analysis. In Sect. 13.3, we investigate the behaviors of local governments in terms of their provision of local public goods under a decentralization regime. This section corresponds to the first case. Cases 2, 3, and 4 are then analyzed in Sect. 13.4. In Sect. 13.5, we compare the social welfare conditions among the four cases under with and without migration. Finally, Sect. 13.6 concludes the paper.

13.2 The Model

We consider an economy which is composed of two regions: region i ($i = 1, 2$). The households in both regions are assumed to be the only labor suppliers to the firms in their region. They are employed by the firms which are located at their region and earn labor income by providing one unit of labor inelastically. Firms in the economy produce a homogeneous consumption good x with n units of labor as the only input. The good x is a numeraire good of which price is unit. The production function of a firm in region i is given as

$$f(n_i) = n_i - \frac{\gamma_i}{2} n_i^2, \quad \gamma_i > 0, \; i = 1, 2, \tag{13.1}$$

where n_i is the population of region i. It holds $n_1 + n_2 = N$, where N refers the total population in the economy. Households can migrate across regions but cannot move to the outside of the economy, so n_i is flexible but N is fixed. We assume that firms have different technologies on their production between regions while firms in the same region are identical, i.e., γ_i is not the same as that in the region j, $\gamma_j \quad (i, j = 1, 2, i \neq j)$.[2] We assume that the consumption goods produced by the firms are private consumption goods, x_i, and public goods, g_i, and that the marginal rate of transformation between private consumption goods and public goods is in units, MRT = 1; therefore, the marginal cost for the provision of public goods is in units.

All the households have identical utility function which is composed of private consumption goods x and local public goods g. Assuming quadric utility function, the utility function of a household in region i can be given as

$$u_i = x_i + g_i - \frac{\alpha}{2} g_i^2, \quad \alpha > 0. \tag{13.2}$$

Using the traditional way for obtaining optimal resource distribution, e.g., Flatters et al. (1974), the problem of optimal resource allocation is given as

$$\begin{aligned} \max_{\{x_i, g_i, n_i\}} \quad & u_i \\ s.t. \quad & u_i = u_j \\ & f(n_i) + f(n_j) = n_i x_i + n_j x_j + g_i + g_j \\ & N = n_i + n_j. \\ & i.j = 1.2, \quad i \neq j \end{aligned}$$

[2] We assume that firms in region 1 is more productive than those in region 2, i.e., $\gamma_1 < \gamma_2$.

From this, the optimal solutions of this model can be obtained.

$$g_i = \frac{n_i - 1}{\alpha n_i}, \ i = 1, 2, \tag{13.3}$$

$$1 - \gamma_1 n_1 - x_1 = 1 - \gamma_2 n_2 - x_2. \tag{13.4}$$

Equation (13.3) indicates the Samuelson condition for the optimal provision of public goods, that is, marginal benefit equals to marginal cost. Equation (13.4) is the condition for the optimal population distribution.

13.3 Behaviors of Local Governments

In this section, we investigate the behaviors of local governments under the decentralization regime. Each government provides local public goods to maximize its social welfare by local tax which is levied from households in its region. At this stage, we do not consider the case that the local governments overprovide the public goods since they expect the bailout of the central government. It means that each government does not have any motivations for overprovision if the central government commits a hard budget constraint and the commitment is credible.

First, under the conditions of full employment and zero profit, the income for a household in region i is given as

$$w_i = \frac{2 - \gamma_i n_i}{2}. \tag{13.5}$$

We can easily confirm that $dw_i/dn_i < 0$. We also assume $\gamma_i < 2/n_i$ to consider the case $w_i > 0$ only in this paper. If the local government of region i levies proportional income tax, t_i, to provide local public good, g_i, the budget constraint for a household in region i is

$$x_i = (1 - t_i)w_i = \frac{1}{2}(1 - t_i)(2 - \gamma_i n_i). \tag{13.6}$$

Accordingly, the provision of public goods can be written as

$$g_i = t_i n_i w_i = \frac{1}{2} t_i n_i (2 - \gamma_i n_i). \tag{13.7}$$

Substituting Eqs. (13.6) and (13.7) into Eq. (13.2), the utility function of Eq. (13.2) can be rewritten as

$$W_i = \frac{1}{2}(1-t_i)(2-\gamma_i n_i) + \frac{1}{2}t_i n_i(2-\gamma_i n_i) - \frac{\alpha}{2}\left(\frac{1}{2}t_i n_i(2-\gamma_i n_i)\right)^2. \quad (13.8)$$

As the households in the economy are identical, we can define the utility function of a representative household as social welfare, W_i. From the first order condition for social welfare maximization, the optimal tax is given as

$$t_i = \frac{2(n_i - 1)}{\alpha n_i^2(2-\gamma_i n_i)}. \quad (13.9)$$

To investigate the case that t_i is positive only, we assume $n_i \geqslant 1$. Substituting Eq. (13.9) into Eqs. (13.6) and (13.7), the amount of consumption goods and public goods are given as[3]

$$x_i = \frac{\alpha n_i^2(2-\gamma_i n_i) - 2(n_i - 1)}{2\alpha n_i^2}, \quad (13.10)$$

$$g_i = \frac{n_i - 1}{\alpha n_i}. \quad (13.11)$$

We can confirm that the provision of public goods in Eq. (13.11) satisfies the Pareto optimal condition in Eq. (13.3). As Oates (1972) suggests at his "Decentralization theorem," the behavior of local governments under the decentralization regime realizes the optimal resource allocation if there is no externality. Equations (13.3) and (13.11) indicate this point is valid.

Using Eqs. (13.10) and (13.11), we can obtain the indirect utility function as follows:

$$V_i = \frac{\alpha n_i^2(2-\gamma_i n_i) - 2(n_i - 1)}{2\alpha n_i^2} + \frac{n_i - 1}{\alpha n_i} - \frac{\alpha}{2}\left(\frac{n_i - 1}{\alpha n_i}\right)^2. \quad (13.12)$$

13.4 Behaviors of Locals Governments Under Soft Budget Constraint

13.4.1 The Case That Bail Out Both Regions (Case SS)

If the commitment of hard budget constraint by the central government is not credible, local governments would have motivations to overprovision of their local public goods because they believe that the central government will aid them

[3] To obtain positive values, it must be $n_i > 1$.

financially. In the real world, we can find a lot of cases that local governments take these kinds of behavior such as a luxurious city hall, unnecessarily large local roads or facilities, etc.

In this section, we explore the case that the central government bails out the overprovision of local public goods. The finance for bailout is burdened by all the households in the economy evenly through national tax. If the commitment of the central government is incredible, the local government in region i would take overprovision of public goods, B_i. If credible, it becomes $B_i = 0$. If $B_i > 0$, total cost in the economy is $B_1 + B_2$. Same to local income tax, the national tax for bailout is $(B_1 + B_2)/(n_1 w_1 + n_2 w_2)$.

Referring the local tax and optimal level of local public goods that we have obtained in the previous section t_i^* and g_i^*, the budget constraint of a households in region i is given as

$$x_i = \left(1 - t_i^* - \frac{B_i + B_j}{n_i w_i + n_j w_j}\right) w_i, \; i, j = 1, 2, \; i \neq j. \tag{13.13}$$

Using Eqs. (13.2) and (13.13), social welfare function is given as

$$W_i = \left(1 - t_i^* - \frac{B_i + B_j}{n_i w_i + n_j w_j}\right) w_i + (g_i^* + B_i) - \frac{\alpha}{2}\left(g_i^* + B_i\right)^2. \tag{13.14}$$

From the first order condition for welfare maximization, we can obtain B_i as

$$B_i = \frac{n_j(2 - \gamma_j n_j)}{\alpha n_i \left(n_i(2 - \gamma_i n_i) + n_j(2 - \gamma_j n_j)\right)} > 0. \tag{13.15}$$

From the assumption $2 - \gamma_i n_i > 0$, we can know that each local government takes positive overprovision of its public goods. The amount of overprovision is different between regions since it depends on population, n_i, and productivity of firms, γ_i.

$$B_1 - B_2 = \frac{-n_1^2(2 - \gamma_1 n_1) + n_2^2(2 - \gamma_2 n_2)}{\alpha n_1 n_2 \left(n_1(2 - \gamma_1 n_1) + n_2(2 - \gamma_2 n_2)\right)}.$$

The denominator of above equation is positive while the sign of the numerator is ambiguous. Using Eq. (13.5), the numerator can be rewritten as $-2n_1^2 w_1 + 2n_2^2 w_2$. Consequently, if $n_1 > n_2\sqrt{w_2/w_1}$, it becomes $B_1 < B_2$. The intuition of this is straightforward. As all the households bear tax burden evenly to bail out both regions, the region with a small population would increase the amount of overprovision, B, because that total tax burden of the region is relatively small so that it can enjoy a large benefit with a small burden. Goodspeed (2002) addresses this effect, that is, national tax has the effect to lessen the local borrow. Also Crivelli (2011) identifies two effects of bailout on the state governments' behavior, and one of them is this common pool effect on taxpayers.

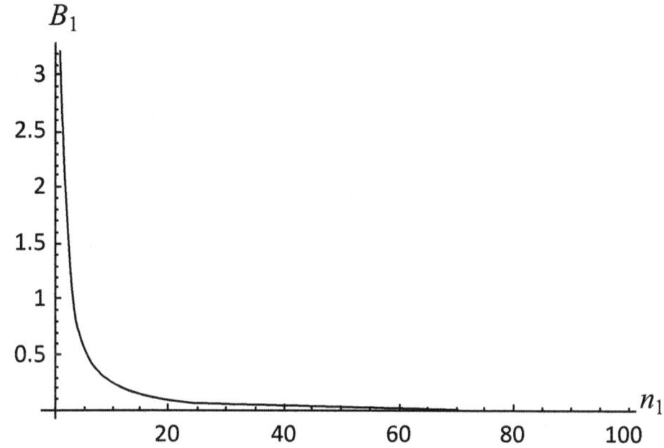

Fig. 13.1 The change of B_1 along with increasing n_1

Moreover, although it is difficult to confirm the sign of $\partial B_i/\partial n_i$ explicitly, we can deduce B_i is decreasing function with respect to n_i from the relationship of $B_1 - B_2$. As we have seen above, the region with large population bears relatively more national tax burden than the region with small population. Due to this effect, a region with large population would reduce the amount of overprovision, $\partial B_i/\partial n_i < 0$.

A simple numerical example supports this point at Fig. 13.1.[4] Thus, we can conclude that $\partial B_i/\partial n_i < 0$ and $\partial B_j/\partial n_i > 0$, $i, j = 1, 2, i \neq j$ We can summarize these results as Lemma 13.1.

Lemma 13.1 *Under the case SS,*

1. *The amount of overprovision of local public goods in the region with a small population is larger than that in the region with large population.*
2. *Local governments tend to decrease the amount of overprovision along with the increase of population since national tax burden in the region becomes high.*

13.4.2 The Case That Bail Out One Region (Case SH or HS)

In this subsection, we investigate the case that the central government bails out only one region. Facchini and Testa (2008) analyze this asymmetric bailout case and conclude that bailout of relatively large state in a federation is socially desirable

[4]We set $\alpha = 0.3$, $\gamma_1 = 0.01$, $\gamma_2 = 0.015$, $N = 100$.

while bailout of a small state will never be optimal since the cost of bailout is larger than the cost of default.[5]

At first, we consider case SH, i.e., the central government bails out only region 1 which has relatively productive firms and applies hard budget constraint to region 2. In this case, the budget constraints of households are different between both regions.

$$x_1 = \left(1 - t_1^* - \frac{B_1 + B_2}{n_1 w_1 + n_2 w_2}\right) w_1,$$

$$x_2 = \left(1 - t_2^* - \frac{B_2}{n_2 w_2} - \frac{B_1 + B_2}{n_1 w_1 + n_2 w_2}\right) w_2.$$

Accordingly, social welfare functions are also different between both regions.

$$W_1 = \left(1 - t_i^* - \frac{B_1 + B_2}{n_1 w_1 + n_2 w_2}\right) w_1 + (g_1^* + B_1) - \frac{\alpha}{2}\left(g_1^* + B_1\right)^2,$$

$$W_2 = \left(1 - t_2^* - \frac{B_2}{n_2 w_2} - \frac{B_1 + B_2}{n_1 w_1 + n_2 w_2}\right) w_2 + (g_2^* + B_2) - \frac{\alpha}{2}\left(g_2^* + B_2\right)^2.$$

From the first order condition for welfare maximization, we can obtain

$$B_1 = \frac{n_2(2 - \gamma_2 n_2)}{\alpha n_1 \left(n_1(2 - \gamma_1 n_1) + n_2(2 - \gamma_2 n_2)\right)} > 0, \tag{13.16}$$

$$B_2 = -\frac{2 - \gamma_2 n_2}{\alpha \left(n_1(2 - \gamma_1 n_1) + n_2(2 - \gamma_2 n_2)\right)} < 0. \tag{13.17}$$

We can know that Eq. (13.16) coincides with Eq. (13.15). This can be explained by the assumption of quasilinear utility function. Comparing to case HH, it is true that the tax burden of households increased because of national tax to bail out. Generally, decrease of disposable income affects both consumption of private consumption goods, x, and public goods, g. In the case of quasilinear utility function, the income effect of public goods is zero so that the decrease of disposable income only affects the consumption of x. That is the reason why Eq. (13.16) coincides with Eq. (13.15) even though the disposable incomes are different between two cases.

Equation (13.17), however, becomes negative since region 2 could not receive bailout from the central government. It should finance by itself if B_2 is positive. Moreover, it should burden a part of cost for B_2. The same reason as the assumption of quasilinear utility function, we can regard $B_2 = 0$ when $B_2 < 0$.

On the other hand, in case of HS, $B_1 = 0$ in equilibrium and B_2 becomes as follows:

---

[5]Although it is true that the default of a region accompanies social cost, we neglect this social cost since we do not consider the case of default.

$$B_2 = -\frac{n_1(2-\gamma_1 n_1)}{\alpha\,(n_1(2-\gamma_1 n_1)+n_2(2-\gamma_2 n_2))} > 0. \tag{13.18}$$

We can confirm that Eq. (13.18) also coincides with Eq. (13.15) by the same reason of Eq. (13.16).

13.5 The Effect of Migration on Bailout Policy

In the previous sections, we considered four cases of bailout by central government: cases HH, SS, SH, and HS. Case HH is the case that each local government behaves under hard budget constraint. In this case, it chooses Pareto optimal level of public goods as we have seen at Sect. 13.3. Although the central government commits no bailout, if social welfare under soft budget constraint is higher than that under hard budget constraint, the commitment becomes incredible. This gives some motivations for overprovision of public goods to local governments.

In this section, we compare the social welfares between four cases to see whether the commitment is credible or not. We define the social welfare as the sum of both regions' utility level, i.e., $W = V_1 + V_2$. As we have seen in the previous sections, it is difficult to compare social welfare among cases, as it is very complicated. We use, therefore, a numerical analysis to obtain concrete results. At first, we set $\alpha = 0.3$, $N = 100$. As we know from Eq. (13.5), γ_i should be $\gamma_i < 2/n_i$ so that γ_i must not exceed 0.02 when $N = 100$. Also as we assume that region 1 has relatively more productive firms than region 2, we set $\gamma_1 = 0.01$ and $\gamma_2 = 0.015$.

On the other hand, if the migration cost does not occur, each household moves to the region where he or she attains the higher utility level. In general, a policy of government affects the utility of households in the region. While some policies improve the utility level, it is exacerbated by other policies. We should consider, therefore, the migration of households between regions when we analyze the policy effects in this paper.

To obtain the optimal population distribution, it should satisfy the condition of Eq. (13.4). Through our parameters setting, we can obtain $n_1 = 62.88$ that satisfies the condition of Eq. (13.4). Even though migration is very important to see how the bailout affects each household's utility level, we fix the population at the optimal level first, i.e., $n_1 = 62.88$. Next, we will investigate the migration effect. Table 13.1 shows the utility levels without consideration of migration under four cases.

Table 13.1 The utility levels without consideration of migration

	V_1^{HH}	V_2^{HH}	V_1^{SS}	V_2^{SS}	V_1^{SH}	V_2^{SH}	V_1^{HS}	V_2^{HS}
$n_1 = 62.88$	2.29968	2.29968	2.29936	2.30011	2.29974	2.29947	2.29913	2.30014
$W = V_1 + V_2$	4.59936		4.59947		4.59921		4.59927	

Let us have case HH as an initial state where $B_1 = B_2 = 0$ and $n_1 > n_2$. If the central government takes case SS, it becomes that $B_1 > 0$, $B_2 > 0$, and $B_1 < B_2$ from Eq. (13.15). So the households in region 1 bear relatively the larger cost burden for the provision of $B_1 + B_2$, and the utility level is decreased, $V_1^{SS} < V_1^{HH}$, while the utility level of region 2 is increased, $V_2^{SS} > V_2^{HH}$. From the same reason, we can draw that $V_1^{SH} > V_1^{HH}$, $V_2^{SH} < V_2^{HH}$, $V_1^{HS} < V_1^{HH}$, and $V_2^{HS} > V_1^{HH}$. Also we can confirm that $W^{SS} > W^{HH} > W^{HS} > W^{SH}$. Under no migration, the bailout of both regions (case SS) improves social welfare, and the commitment of no bailout becomes incredible. Different from Facchini and Testa (2008), case SH or HS does not improve social welfare, i.e., asymmetric bailout is not beneficial for the economy.[6] If the central government takes the bailout due to some reasons, it is better to support the region with less population.

Next, we consider the migration problem. As seen in Table 13.1, the bailout policy makes the utility level different between both regions. In general, when few population reside in a region, the utility level rises along with the increasing of population through the agglomeration effect. However, if the population continues to grow and exceeds a threshold, the utility level decreases because the agglomeration economy changes to diseconomy. Figure 13.2 shows the utility level in equilibrium when migration is occurred. Migration makes the utility levels between both regions the same. If not, migration does not stop until they become the same.

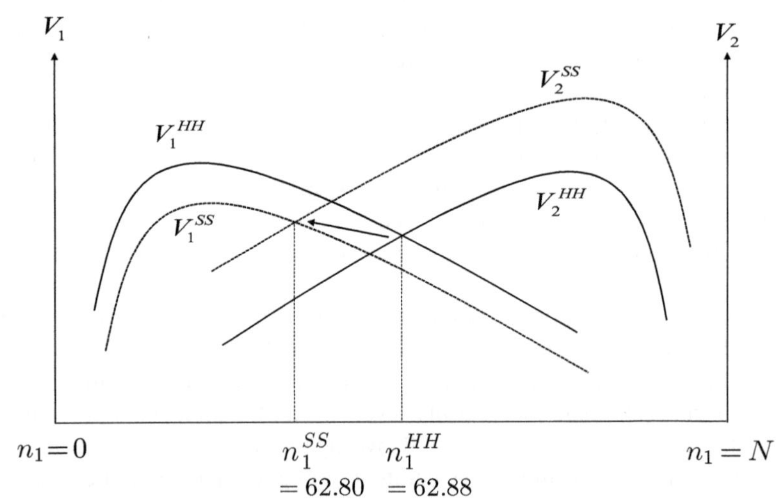

Fig. 13.2 Utility level in equilibrium when migration is occurred

[6]This result depends on the definition of social welfare. The social welfare function in this paper is typical utilitarian welfare function. If we raise the weight of region 1, the result will be changed. To do so, however, it is necessary to provide reasonable evidence.

Table 13.2 The utility levels with consideration of migration

	W^{HH}	W^{SS}	W^{SH}	W^{HS}
	4.59936	4.5994	4.59924	4.59916
n_1	62.88	62.80006	62.90911	62.77291

The results of numerical analysis are summarized in Table 13.2. As seen in Table 13.1, the utility in region 1 decreases and that in region 2 increases in case SS. V_1^{SS} curve moves downward and V_2^{SS} moves upward, so the population in new equilibrium is decreased, $n_1^{SS} < n_1^{HH}$. Moreover, since the increase of V_2^{SS} overweighs the decrease of V_1^{SS}, social welfare is increased in equilibrium. Figure 13.2 shows this mechanism.

In case SH, the increase of V_1^{SH} does not overweigh the decrease of V_2^{SH} even though households in region 1 do not burden the cost of overprovision in region 2 since $B_2 = 0$. As V_1^{SH} curve moves upward and V_2^{SH} curve moves downward, the population in new equilibrium becomes large, and social welfare is decreased. Different from the case of no migration, although some households in region 2 can move to region 1 and they also enjoy the benefit of overprovided public goods, this positive effect could not offset the negative effect in region 2. Thus, social welfare is decreased. Finally, since the decrease of V_1^{HS} overweighs the increase of V_2^{HS} under case HS, social welfare is decreased.

It is socially more desirable that the central government takes the SH type of bailout rather than stick to hard budget constraint under free mobility.

We can summarize these results as Proposition 13.1.

Proposition 13.1

1. *When migration of households between regions is impossible, although the bailout of both regions (case SS) decreases utility in the region with large population while it increases utility in the region with less population, total effect is positive so that social welfare is improved.*
2. *If free migration is possible, some households in the region with large population move to the region with less population in case SS so that the population in the region with large population is decreased ($n_1^{SS} < n_1^{HH}$). Moreover, the social welfare is improved.*
3. *Asymmetric bailout such as case SH and case HS does not improve social welfare, irrespective of the possibility of migration.*

13.6 Concluding Remarks

Generally, even though the central government does not commit to financial aid, the soft budget constraint problem occurs because the commitment is not credible. If it is, local governments will not have any motivation for their overborrow and excessive public expenditure.

This paper studies the effect of households' migration on the fiscal bailout policy of the central government. We focus on two points: one is asymmetric bailout such as Facchini and Testa (2008), the other is the effect of migration on the bailout policy. On the bailout, we consider four cases under a two-region model that both regions are asymmetric in productiveness of firms. The first case is applying hard budget constraint to both regions (case HH). In this case, the local government must finance the cost of overprovision of local public goods by itself. The second case is that the central government bails out both regions (case SS), and the third case is it bails out relatively productive region only (case SH). The last case is that it bails out relatively less productive region only (case HS).

The main results are as follows. First, the amount of overprovision of local public goods in the region with small population is larger than that in the region with large population under case SS. And local governments tend to decrease the amount of overprovision along with increase of population since the national tax burden in the region becomes high. Second, when migration of households between regions is impossible, although the bailout of both regions (case SS) decreases utility in the region with large population while it increases utility in the region with less population, total effect is positive so that social welfare is improved. Third, if free migration is possible, some households in the region with large population move to the region with less population in case SS so that the population in the region with large population is decreased. Moreover, the social welfare is improved. Finally, asymmetric bailout such as case SH and case HS does not improve social welfare, irrespective of the possibility of migration.

Actually, it is difficult for the central government to stick to hard budget constraint. If a local financial bankruptcy is occurred, it accompanies serious social costs including opportunity cost. Some residents who belong to highly skilled labor or high-income class might move to the other region to avoid worsening public service. This may be possible to cause the spiral of economic recession in the region. As we do not consider the case of default in this paper, these kinds of costs are not considered in our model. It is important to identify these kinds of costs. When the central government considers whether or not to bail out a local government, it might be necessary to compare the social costs for default with those for bailout. This is another interesting topic for future work.

Acknowledgements This work was supported by the National Research Foundation of Korea Grant funded by the Korean government (NRF-2014S1A3A2044643).

References

Akai, N. 2006. Contractual problems in inter-governmental relationships (central & regional) – With focus on problems of soft budget constraint. *Financial Review* 82: 79–101 (In Japanese).

Caplan, A., R. Cornes, and E. Silva. 2000. pure public goods and income redistribution in a federation with decentralized leadership and imperfect labor mobility. *Journal of Public Economics* 77: 265–284.

Facchini, G., and C. Testa. 2008. Fiscal decentralization, regional inequality and bail-out: Lessons from Brazil's debt crisis. *The Quarterly Review of Economics and Finance* 48: 333–344.
Flatters, F., V. Henderson, and P. Mieszkowski. 1974. Public goods, efficiency, and regional fiscal equalization. *Journal of Public Economics* 3: 99–112.
Goodspeed, T.J. 2002. Bailouts in federation. *International Tax and Public Finance* 9(4): 409–421.
Kornai, J. 1979. Resource constraints versus demand constraint systems. *Econometrica* 47: 801–820.
Kornai, J. 1980. *Economics of shortage*. Amsterdam: North-Holland.
Kornai, J. 1986. The soft budget constraint. *Kyklos* 39: 3–30.
Lee, W. 2016. Fiscal decentralization and soft budget constraint. *The Journal of Social science* 23(1): 261–278 (In Korean).
Ministry of the Interior, Korea. 2015. Summary of Local Budget for FY.
Ministry of Internal Affairs and Communications, Japan. 2016. FY 2014 Settlement White Paper on Local Public Finance.
Naito, T., and T. Omori. 2016. Household's disaster prevention activities, agglomeration, and economic growth. *Regional Science Policy and Practice* 8(4): 177–195.
Oates, W.E. 1972. *Fiscal federalism*. New York: Harcourt Brace Jovanovich.
Oh, Y. 2008. A study of fiscal decentralization and the soft budget constraint. *Korean Journal of Public Administration* 46(3): 121–143 (In Korean).
Qian, Y., and G. Roland. 1998. Federalism and the soft budget constraint. *American Economic Review* 88: 1143–1162.
Wildasin, D.E. 1997. Externalities and bailouts: Hard and soft budget constraints in intragovernmental fiscal relations. Mimeo, Vanderbilt University.

Chapter 14
Delegation of Policy Tasks from Politician to the Bureaucrat

Masayuki Kanazaki

14.1 Introduction

Originally, the agenda setting is the task in legislature. However, we often see that the politician and the bureaucrat contend with this task cooperatively although the politician has accountability in policy implementation as Maskin and Tirole (2004) examined. This implies that the politician delegates a part of his tasks to the bureaucrat. Why does the politician delegate his tasks? Does the bureaucrat who is delegated the politician's tasks make an effort sufficiently for the policy implementation?

To analyze this problem, we must clarify the role of the bureaucrat's tasks and the motivation of effort. We can consider that the politician's motivation of effort for the policy is to win the next electoral competition by leaving good policy outcome. The agenda setting, the tasks which the politician must do, needs much information of the citizens' preferences to the public service.

As for such information, the bureaucrat can collect easily because his administrative routine is the window of public service for the citizens. Therefore, if the politician wants to make a policy which is agreeable to the citizens' preferences, it is essential for the politician to use the information which the bureaucrat obtained from the citizens in his routine. This fact causes that the politician consigns his tasks to the bureaucrat.

Now, what are the bureaucrat's incentives to effort? Does the bureaucrat take on the politician's tasks? In Niskanen (1971), he considered the bureaucrats' object is their organization make larger and they obtain more budget. The bureaucrat is often argued in the framework of career concern. The career concern means that

M. Kanazaki (✉)
Kyushu Sangyo University, Fukuoka, Japan
e-mail: kanazaki@ip.kyusan-u.ac.jp

T. Naito et al. (eds.), *Applied Approaches to Societal Institutions and Economics*,
New Frontiers in Regional Science: Asian Perspectives 18,
DOI 10.1007/978-981-10-5663-5_14

the bureaucrat is interested in his future career path (including the post after his retirement) and profit. To obtain these career and profit, the bureaucrat must know his ability and appeal it to the others.

If the bureaucrat could lead the delegated tasks from the politician to success, the others recognize that this bureaucrat's ability is likely high. Therefore, to lead the delegated tasks' success is appeal of his ability to the others and incentives to effort.

These are the differences of incentives to effort between the politician and the bureaucrat. So, what is the difference of employment between the politician and the bureaucrat? The politician can be in office only when he wins the election. If he fails the policy implementation in his term, he will lose his office in the next election. Needless to say, the politician is not ensured tenure. However, as for the bureaucrat, although he must pass the examination to be recruited, once he passes this examination, he is ensured tenure. Therefore, as long as the bureaucrat does not perpetrate serious failure, he will not be fired. The bureaucrat is ensured stable environment of employment better than the politician.

How do these differences affect the policy outcome and the interaction between the politician and the bureaucrat?

In recent research of new political economy, which is represented by Persson and Tabellini (2000), we can see the development of theoretical analysis about the behavior of the politician and the bureaucrat. Especially, as for the problem whether the voter reelects the incumbent politician by his performance in term or not, Carillo and Mariotti (2001), Gersbach (2004), Besley and Smart (2007), Borgne and Lockwood (2006), and Alesina and Tabellini (2008) analyzed.

Carillo and Mariotti (2001) examined influence between the election and the political turnover. Gersbach (2004) analyzed incentive contract to motivate the politician. Besley and Smart (2007) analyzed how the fiscal constraint affects voters' reelection strategy. In Borgne and Lockwood (2006), they examined what adoption system is desirable to make the politician adequate effort. Moreover, as for the behavior of the politician and the bureaucrat, we mention Alesina and Tabellini (2008). In their paper, they studied whether the politician or the bureaucrat should implement the policy tasks and, moreover, how the bribe and the lobbying activity affect the politician and the bureaucrat.

Not only in economics but also in the field of political science, there exist many research of the interaction between the politician and the bureaucrat. We can mention Epstein and O'Halloran (1999) as typical analysis. They describe the bureaucrat as an agent who can overcome the uncertainty of outcome of policy implementation better than the politician.

They focused on the degree of the delegation of authority from the politician to the bureaucrat. If the politician delivers too much authority to the bureaucrat, the politician's utility is declined because the bureaucrat implements the policy which is based on his ideology. However, if the politician does not deliver too much authority to the bureaucrat, the politician cannot obtain the policy outcome which he had expected because the politician cannot overcome such an uncertainty as well as the bureaucrat does, and he will face the risk of losing in the next electoral competition.

In the field of economics, Bennedsen and Feldmann (2006) analyze the interaction between the politician, the bureaucrat, and the special interest group by using the method of analysis of Epstein and O'Halloran (1999). Swank and Visser (2002) analyzed comparison between delegation and voting in decision making.

On such related works and motivation of research, we examine why and when the politician delegates his tasks to the bureaucrat and whether such a delegation is desirable for the citizens or not. Moreover, when such a delegation is desirable for the citizens, we discuss what incentives we should assign to the bureaucrat. The bureaucrat makes an effort to lead public works to success when he is delegated the politician's tasks. Consequently, depending on success or failure of public works, the reputation (about ability) of the bureaucrat is formed by all the players. This reputation affects the bureaucrat's future career, wage, and the post after his retirement. So, the bureaucrat is interested in the appeal of his ability to the others.

In such a framework of career concern, as for which the bureaucrat or politician makes more effort, we compare the reelection rent which is the politician's incentive to effort with the scheme of future profit which is the bureaucrat's incentive to effort.

As a result, when the citizens' anticipation value of the bureaucrat's effort rises, the actual bureaucrat's effort rises, too. These mechanism is introduced in Rasmusen (1996). In rational expectation equilibriums where the citizens' anticipation value coincides to the actual bureaucrat's effort, the equilibriums where the highest and the lowest anticipation value coincide with actual one are stable.

As for the politician's effort and delegation, when the politician's reelection rent is small, by operating the bureaucrat's incentive for effort adequately, the bureaucrat makes an effort more than the politician and the politician delegates his tasks to the bureaucrat. Such a delegation is desirable for the citizens.

When the reelection rent is intermediate, although the politician makes an effort more than the bureaucrat, the politician delegates tasks to the bureaucrat, and this delegation is not desirable for the citizens. Moreover, when the reelection rent is large, the politician makes an effort much more than the bureaucrat, the politician does not delegate his tasks, and such a situation is desirable for the citizens.

14.2 The Model

Now, we consider an economy which consists of three agents, the politician, the bureaucrat, and the citizens. The task of politician is to make an effort to implement the public works. Let this effort be e_p and $e_p \in (0, 1)$. These public works have two cases; the first one is the good project case which yields some benefits to the citizens, and the other is bad project case which does no benefits to the citizen. We can consider this public works as success when the politician or the bureaucrat can access the good project.

For the access of good project, the politician must make an effort and let the cost of effort be $c = c(e_p)$ and $c', c'' > 0$. Moreover, to ensure interior solution, we assume $c'(0) = 0, c'(1) = \infty$. Also, the politician's effort level is his private information. Depending on his effort, whether the public works succeed or not decide stochastically. Now, we define the benefit of this public works as follows.

$$g = \begin{cases} 1 & \text{when the project is success.} \\ 0 & \text{when the project is failure} \end{cases} \quad (14.1)$$

The another factor of success is the politician's ability. We can interpret this ability in several ways. One of them is how much knowledge about the policy, including academic one, the politician has. The other is considered as the degree by which the politician can access the citizens' demand to public works. In these ways, though we can consider several factors in which the policymaker can access the good project, we express these as only "ability."

This ability θ_p has two cases, $\theta_p \in \{\theta_p^l, \theta_p^h\}$; we assume $0 < \theta_p < 1$ and $\theta_p^l < \theta_p^h$. All players (including the politician) are unknown to the politician's ability and have initial belief $\text{Prob}(\theta_p = \theta_p^h) = 1/2$. This belief is common knowledge among all players.

Now, let the probability of success of public works be $\theta_p e_p$. The politician can obtain the reelection rent R as the monetary reward and nonmonetary benefits which, to some or all authority, are generated only when he is reelected. We define the politician's utility which consists of effort cost and reelection rent R as follows.

$$U_p = \begin{cases} E(\theta_b)e_b R - c(e_p) & \text{delegation cases} \\ E(\theta_p)e_p R - c(e_p) & \text{non-delegation case} \end{cases} \quad (14.2)$$

Here, $E(\theta_i)e_i, (i = p, b)$ is expressed as the reelection probability of the politician. As for this reelection probability, we argue later in detail.

Subsequently, the politician can delegate the tasks to lead the success of public works to the bureaucrat. In this case, the bureaucrat makes an effort, and then success of public works depends on the bureaucrat's ability and effort. Let this effort be $e_b(\in (0, 1))$.

The bureaucrat's effort in case of delegation is the one which the politician, who belongs to legislative, should do basically. Note that this bureaucrat's effort is additional effort for legislative except for his ordinary administrative effort.[1] Namely, the bureaucrat always makes an effort to the administrative tasks regardless of whether he is delegated the tasks from the politician or not.

[1] In this paper, we consider that the tasks which the politician can delegate to the bureaucrat are not the ones that only the politician can fulfill, for example, attendance in congress and vote for the passing of the bill. The tasks which can be delegated by the politician are the ones that this delegation does not cause some problems such as basic agenda setting. Therefore, as same as the bureaucrat, we consider the situation in which the politician fulfills their own tasks in legislative and makes an effort. However, as for the ambiguous boundary between the tasks of politician and the one of the bureaucrat, we must discuss more whether this boundary becomes the contestation in election.

Also, the bureaucrat's effort is his private information, and it is unobservable by the politician and the citizens. As same as politician's ability, all players do not know the bureaucrat's effort and have the information and belief about the bureaucrat's ability, $\theta_b \in \{\theta_b^l, \theta_b^h\}$ and $\text{Prob}(\theta_b = \theta_b^h) = 1/2$. We assume $0 < \theta_p^l < \theta_b^l < \theta_p^h < \theta_b^h < 1$. From this assumption, we obtain $E(\theta_p) < E(\theta_b)$ and note that the average ability of the bureaucrat is higher than the politician's.

In case of delegation, all players update the belief about the bureaucrat's ability after observing the project's outcome. We assume that the politicians and citizens update the belief of the bureaucrat's ability based on a given anticipation value for the bureaucrat's effort. Let their anticipation value be e^a.

Their anticipation does not need to coincide with an effort which the bureaucrat actually made, but this anticipation affects effort level which the bureaucrat decides.

Because, when the public works succeed, the bureaucrat is recognized by all agents that his average ability is higher than the average ability based on initial belief. Such an update forms the bureaucrat's high reputation and, consequently, affects the bureaucrat's career and wage, moreover, the post after his retirement (which is often called "AMAKUDARI"). This anticipation value is common knowledge among all players.

Depending on the result of public works, the politician can understand how they update the belief and what the bureaucrat's future career and wage are. Therefore, the politician can anticipate correctly how much effort the bureaucrat makes based on his future profit. If the bureaucrat's effort is sufficiently close to politician's effort or higher than one, the politician will delegate his tasks to the bureaucrat for the reduction of effort cost.

However, when the politician does not delegate his tasks, the update of belief is not done. So all players estimate the bureaucrat's expected ability based on initial belief.

In the framework of career concern, we define the bureaucrat's expected ability based on updated belief as $E(\theta_b^{ud})$ and his future profit as $X(E(\theta_b^{ud})), X'' < 0 < X'$. From this, the bureaucrat's utility is described as follows:

$$U_b = \begin{cases} X(E(\theta_b^{ud})) - c(e_b) & \text{delegation case} \\ X(E(\theta_b)) - c(e_b) & \text{non-delegation case.} \end{cases} \tag{14.3}$$

Finally, we define the citizens' utility. The citizens can observe whether the politician delegates the tasks to the bureaucrat or not. Therefore, only when the citizens observed delegation from the politician to the bureaucrat, they update their belief for the bureaucrat's ability. The citizens are voters and decide whether they reelect the politician or not after observing the result of public works. However, the citizens cannot observe the bureaucrat's effort.

The citizens can obtain the size 1 benefit when the public works succeed. But they cannot obtain any benefit when these public works fail. Then, we define the following citizens' expected utility:

$$U_r = \begin{cases} E(\theta_p)e_b & \text{delegation case} \\ E(\theta_b)e_b & \text{non-delegation case.} \end{cases} \tag{14.4}$$

Subsequently, we assume the citizens adopt the following voting rule; they reelect the politician if the public works are a success and do not reelect him if it is a failure.[2] Therefore, the reelection probability of politician coincides with the one of success of public works. The timing of the game is as follows. In the first stage, θ_p, θ_b, and e^a decide. In the second stage, the politician decides whether he delegates tasks to the bureaucrat or not. In the third stage, the politician or the bureaucrat makes an effort depending on delegation. In the fourth stage, the public works outcome is realized depending on effort and ability. In the fifth stage, the citizens decide whether they reelect the politician or not. In the final stage, the bureaucrat obtains future profit X and the politician does reelection rent R.

14.3 The Benchmark (Without AMAKUDARI)

In this case, so if there is no increase of future profit by update of belief, the bureaucrat does not make an effort, namely, $e_b = 0$. Therefore, in the case without AMAKUDARI, the politician does not delegate tasks to the bureaucrat so that he will always lose the election because the bureaucrat does not make any effort, namely, reelection probability is 0.

14.3.1 The Politician's Behavior

In this case, the politician implements his tasks by himself. The optimal effort level of the politician is decided by following maximization problem:

$$\max_{e_p} U_p = E(\theta_p)e_pR - c(e_p). \tag{14.5}$$

From first-order condition, we obtain the optimal effort of politician e_p^* which satisfies the following equation:

$$E(\theta_p)R = c'(e_p^*). \tag{14.6}$$

[2] We can consider such a situation as the one that the citizens who have reservation utility V such as $0 < V < 1$ reelect the politician when the benefit of the public works exceeds his reservation utility, not reelect when it does not exceed his one.

The optimal effort level for the politician increases with the reelection rent R and the expected ability of politician based on initial belief. This is led by the fact that the effort and the ability complement each other so that the expected benefit for the politician consists of the product of the politician's effort and ability.

14.4 The Case That There Is AMAKUDARI

In this case, only when the bureaucrat is delegated with tasks from the politician that the belief of the bureaucrat's ability is updated by the citizens and the politician after observing the result of public works. If his effort leads to the higher assignment of probability to high ability, the bureaucrat has incentives to effort to appeal of his high ability to the social.

14.4.1 The Bureaucrat's Behavior

Even the case of AMAKUDARI, when the politician does not delegate tasks to the bureaucrat, his ability is evaluated as initial expected ability so that there is no update of his ability. Consequently, as same as the previous analysis, it is optimal for the bureaucrat not to make an effort. Now we consider the case that the politician delegates to the bureaucrat.

Then, under some anticipation value of the bureaucrat's effort, the probability by which he is recognized as high-ability person is by Bayes rule:

$$Prob(\theta_b = \theta_b^h | success) = \frac{\frac{1}{2}\theta_b^h e^a}{\frac{1}{2}\theta_b^l e^a + \frac{1}{2}\theta_b^h e^a} = \frac{\theta_b^h}{\theta_b^l + \theta_b^h}\left(> \frac{1}{2}\right). \tag{14.7}$$

If public works succeed, the expected ability of the bureaucrat based on ex post belief is higher than ex ante expected one. Moreover, note that this ex post belief does not depend on the citizens' anticipation about the bureaucrat's effort. Also, we define the ex post expected ability of the bureaucrat $E(\theta_b^{ud})$ as θ_b^{es}. Then,

$$\theta_b^{es} = \frac{\theta_b^h}{\theta_b^l + \theta_b^h}\theta_b^h + \frac{\theta_b^l}{\theta_b^l + \theta_b^h}\theta_b^l = \frac{(\theta_b^h)^2 + (\theta_b^l)^2}{\theta_b^l + \theta_b^h}. \tag{14.8}$$

Subsequently, we analyze the ex post belief in the case of failure. Then,

$$Prob(\theta_b = \theta_b^h | failure) = \frac{\frac{1}{2}(1 - \theta_b^h e^a)}{\frac{1}{2}(1 - \theta_b^h e^a) + \frac{1}{2}(1 - \theta_b^l e^a)}$$
$$= \frac{(1 - \theta_b^h e^a)}{(1 - \theta_b^h e^a) + (1 - \theta_b^l e^a)}(\equiv A). \quad (14.9)$$

As same as above,

$$Prob(\theta_b = \theta_b^l | failure) = \frac{(1 - \theta_b^l e^a)}{(1 - \theta_b^h e^a) + (1 - \theta_b^l e^a)}(\equiv B). \quad (14.10)$$

As for the ex post belief in case of failure,

$$\frac{dA}{de^a} = -\frac{1}{4}\frac{(\theta_b^h - \theta_b^l)}{\left(1 - \frac{(\theta_b^h + \theta_b^l)e^a}{2}\right)^2}(< 0) \quad (14.11)$$

and

$$\frac{dB}{de^a} = \frac{1}{4}\frac{(\theta_b^h - \theta_b^l)}{\left(1 - \frac{(\theta_b^h + \theta_b^l)e^a}{2}\right)^2}(> 0). \quad (14.12)$$

In case of failure, the ex post belief of high ability decreases with the citizens' anticipation value. On the contrary, the one of low ability increases with it. This fact is a risk for the bureaucrat to make an effort.

Let the expected ability when public works fail be $E(\theta_b^{ud}) = \theta_b^{ef}(e^a)$. Then,

$$\theta_b^{ef}(e^a) = A\theta_b^h + B\theta_b^l,$$

and

$$\frac{d\theta_b^{ef}(e^a)}{de^a} = \theta_b^h \frac{dA}{de^a} + \theta_b^l \frac{dB}{de^a} = -\frac{1}{4}\frac{(\theta_b^h - \theta_b^l)^2}{\left(1 - \frac{(\theta_b^h + \theta_b^l)e^a}{2}\right)^2}(< 0). \quad (14.13)$$

From this equation, we see that, when the public works fail, the ex post expected ability of the bureaucrat decreases with the citizens' anticipation of bureaucrat's effort level. Also, from (14.13), we can easily check that $\frac{d^2\theta_b^{ef}}{de^2} < 0$ in $0 < e < 1$. Moreover, the interval of the ex post expected ability of the bureaucrat between the success and the failure is

$$\theta_b^{es} - \theta_b^{ef}(e^a) = \frac{(\theta_b^h - \theta_b^l)^2}{(\theta_b^h + \theta_b^l)((1 - \theta_b^h e^a) + (1 - \theta_b^l e^a))}(> 0). \quad (14.14)$$

Lemma 14.1 *The higher the citizens' anticipation value to the bureaucrat's effort is, in the case of failure, the lower the bureaucrat's ability is regarded. Moreover, as the citizens' anticipation value to the bureaucrat's effort is getting higher, the interval of the ex post expected ability of the bureaucrat between the success and the failure is getting larger.*

Subsequently, the success probability of public works in ex ante stage is $\frac{1}{2}\theta_b^h e_b + \frac{1}{2}\theta_b^l e_b = E(\theta_b)e_b$, and the failure probability is $1 - E(\theta_b)e_b$.

Therefore, we can define the bureaucrat's expected utility as follows:

$$\begin{aligned} EU_b &= E(\theta_b)e_b(X(\theta_b^{es}) - c(e_b)) + (1 - E(\theta_b)e_b)(X(\theta_b^{ef}(e^a)) - c(e_b)) \\ &= (X(\theta_b^{es}) - X(\theta_b^{ef}(e^a)))E(\theta_b)e_b + X(\theta_b^{ef}(e^a)) - c(e_b) \end{aligned} \quad (14.15)$$

From the first-order condition, we obtain the optimal effort level for the bureaucrat e_b^* from the following equation:

$$(\bar{X} - X(\theta_b^{ef}(e^a)))E(\theta_b) = c'(e_b^*) \qquad (\bar{X} = X(\theta_b^{es})) \quad (14.16)$$

Also, we can easily check if the second-order condition is satisfied. Here, we draw the following figure to describe the relation of the citizens' anticipation value to the bureaucrat's effort and the actual bureaucrat's effort.

The left-hand side of Eq. (14.16) corresponds to horizontal line in Fig. 14.1. The height of this line denotes the magnitude of the bureaucrat's incentive to effort which

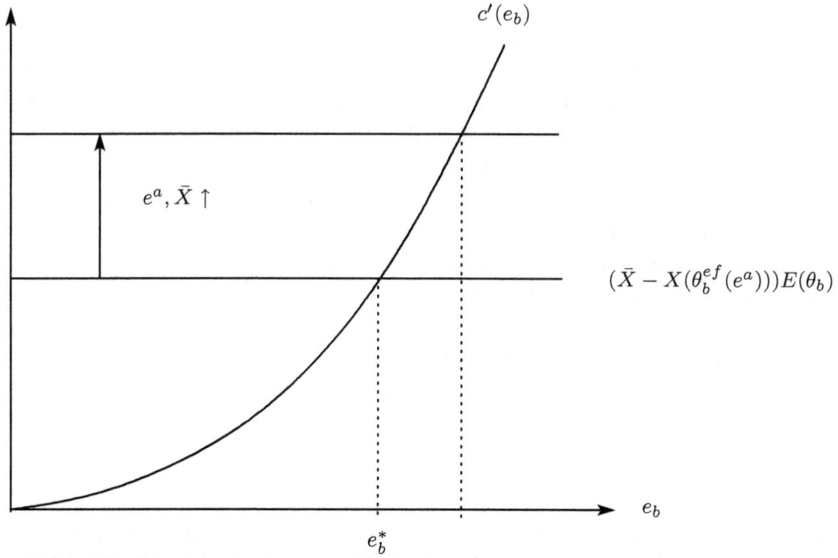

Fig. 14.1 The bureaucrat's decision of effort

makes the increase of bureaucrat's future profit by leading the success of public works possible.

As we see in Lemma 14.1, the rise of the citizens' anticipation value has an effect which makes the interval of future profit of the bureaucrat between success and failure increase.

The more this interval increases, the more the bureaucrat makes an effort, so that the bureaucrat's incentive to lead success rises to get his increasing future profit. Such an increase of bureaucrat's effort is based on selfish reason that the bureaucrat wants to make sure to increase future profit, not to live up to citizens' expectation.

Moreover, if $\bar{X}$ which is the future profit of the bureaucrat by success of public works rises, the bureaucrat raises his effort level. This is a very intuitive result as we have seen in ordinary incentive theory.

Now, we focus on the rational expectation equilibrium in which the actual effort of the bureaucrat corresponds to the citizens' anticipation. At first, from (14.16) which denotes the decision of bureaucrat's optimal effort, we see that

$$\frac{de_b^*}{de^a} = -\frac{E(\theta_b) \cdot X'(\theta_b^{ef}(e^a))(\theta_b^{ef}(e^a))'}{c''(e_b^*)}(> 0). \tag{14.17}$$

Also,

$$\begin{cases} \theta_b^{ef}(0) = E(\theta_b) & \text{when } e^a = 0 \\ \theta_b^{ef}(1) = \frac{\theta_b^h(1-\theta_b^h)+\theta_b^l(1-\theta_b^l)}{(1-\theta_b^h)+(1-\theta_b^l)} & \text{when } e^a = 1. \end{cases} \tag{14.18}$$

From this Eq. (14.16), we see that the left-hand side of Eq. (14.16) is finite for any $e^a \in [0, 1]$. And taking into account continuity of Eq. (14.16) in $e^a \in [0, 1]$, $e^a = e_b$ which is the condition of rational expectation equilibrium and Eq. (14.16) has a solution (e^a,e_b) in (0,1). Although this fact implies the existence of rational expectation equilibrium in (0,1), this equilibrium is not always unique.

Now we draw the case that there exist three rational expectation equilibriums.

The curve in Fig. 14.2 corresponds to Eq. (14.16) which denotes the relation of the citizens' anticipation and the bureaucrat's actual effort. From Eq. (14.17), this curve is increasing with e^a. The intersections of this curve and 45 line are given by the points A, B, and C. These points are the rational expectation equilibriums. Examining the stability of these equilibriums, we can consider that the point A and C are stable, but the point B is unstable.[3] Both of the equilibriums at the

[3]To start the argument of stability, since the actual effort of the bureaucrat is his private information, it needs to add some assumptions including the process of adjustment of anticipation. At first, we assume that this game between the politician and the bureaucrat is repeated over many terms and the effort level of bureaucrat in some term is revealed at the beginning of the next term, namely, in the beginning of the next term; all players know the bureaucrat's effort level in the previous term. This is possible in some measure by the investigation and report of some organization and

highest and the lowest effort level which the citizens anticipate are stable rational expectation equilibriums, and the middle one is unstable.[4] Moreover, when the ex ante bureaucrat's expected ability $E(\theta_b)$ rises, the curve in this Fig. 14.2 shifts upward in the range that e_b does not exceed 1 when $e^a = 1$. In the rational expectation equilibrium, we see that the bureaucrat's actual effort increases with the ex ante bureaucrat's expected ability.

When the ex ante expected bureaucrat's ability goes on rising, the middle and lowest rational expectation equilibriums are getting close. Thereafter, the number of equilibriums decreases to two, and, finally, the highest rational expectation equilibrium becomes a stable and unique one.

From these discussions, we obtain the following proposition.

Theorem 14.2 *(1) The actual bureaucrat's effort increases with the citizens' anticipation value to the bureaucrat's effort and his future profit in case of success.*

(2) When there exist multiple rational expectation equilibriums, the highest and lowest ones are stable. When the ex ante expected bureaucrat's ability goes on

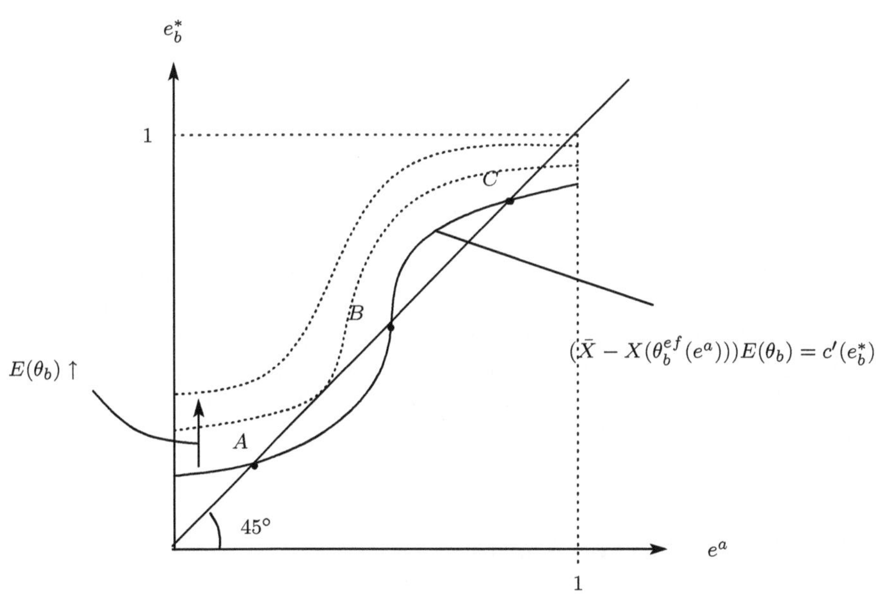

Fig. 14.2 Rational expectation equilibriums

mass communication. Second, we assume that the citizens and the politician adopt the adjustment mechanism of anticipation which the citizens adopt the actual bureaucrat's effort in term t as the anticipation in term $t+1$, namely, myopic adjustment as $e_{bt}^*(e_t^a) = e_{t+1}^a$. By these assumptions, the points A and C are stable.

[4]As for stability, the result is same in the case that the number of equilibriums is more than four, too.

rising, the middle and lowest rational expectation equilibriums disappear and the highest one becomes unique and stable one.

14.4.2 The Politician's Behavior

Considering the bureaucrat's behavior in previous section, the politician decides whether he delegates tasks to the bureaucrat or not. When he does not delegate, the politician efforts at the level that is given in Eq. (14.6). In this case, the politician's expected utility is

$$EU_p^{nd} = E(\theta_p)e_p^* R - c(e_p^*). \tag{14.19}$$

Also, when he delegates, the politician cannot control the bureaucrat's effort and the bureaucrat efforts at the level that is given in Eq. (14.16). In this delegation case, the politician does not have to pay the effort cost.

Therefore, his expected utility is

$$EU_p^d = E(\theta_b)e_b^* R. \tag{14.20}$$

If $EU_p^{nd} < EU_p^d$ is satisfied, the politician delegates the tasks to the bureaucrat. We can rewrite this condition of delegation as follows.

$$R(E(\theta_p)e_p^* - E(\theta_b)e_b^*) < c(e_p^*) \tag{14.21}$$

The left-hand side of this equation denotes the increase of benefit that the controlling the reelection probability by fulfilling tasks by himself generates. The right-hand side of this equation denotes the effect of effort cost reduction.

When $e_p^* = e_b^*$, namely, the bureaucrat efforts as much as the politician does, this condition is always satisfied. This is why the politician reduces the effort cost without decline of his reelection probability.

14.5 An Equilibrium Analysis

In this section, we examine how the reelection rent R and the bureaucrat's future profit in success $\bar{X}$ affect the effort level of the bureaucrat and the politician. At first, for a given $\bar{X}$, we analyze how the change of reelection rent affects the politician's effort and delegation behavior. Subsequently, we do how the change of $\bar{X}$ affects the delegation behavior and whether such a delegation is desirable for the citizens or not.

Seeing the sign of the Eq. (14.21) that is the condition of the politician's delegation for R, we can draw following Fig. 14.3 by using envelope theorem.

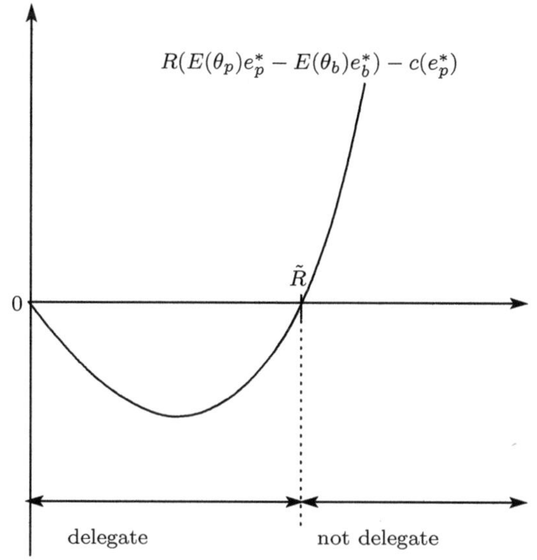

Fig. 14.3 Delegate or not

The slope of $R(E(\theta_p)e_p^* - E(\theta_b)e_b^*) - c(e_p^*)$ in this figure is decided by the value of $E(\theta_p)e_p^* - E(\theta_b)e_b^*$. Now, since e_p^* increases with R, $R(E(\theta_p)e_p^* - E(\theta_b)e_b^*) - c(e_p^*)$ decreases until R derives $E(\theta_p)e_p^* = E(\theta_b)e_b^*$ and thereafter increases with R. Therefore, for some R which is smaller than $\tilde{R}$ in the figure, the politician delegates, but for the one which is larger than it, he does not delegate.

Moreover, since this $\tilde{R}$ depends on the size of $E(\theta_b)e_b^*$ and the size of $E(\theta_b)e_b^*$ depends on e_b^*, $\tilde{R}$ depends on $\bar{X}$. Namely, the larger $\bar{X}$ is, the larger $\tilde{R}$ is.

From these arguments, we obtain the following lemma.

Lemma 14.3 *Under the sufficiently small reelection rent, the politician delegates his tasks to the bureaucrat. Conversely, under the sufficiently large reelection rent, the politician implements his tasks by himself. Also, when the bureaucrat will be allocated his post after his retirement in order to reflect his ability more, the threshold of reelection rent such as the politician delegate is getting larger.*

When the reelection rent is sufficiently large, so the politician has large incentive to effort, he can raise the reelection probability by implementing his tasks by himself in spite of his lower expected ability to the bureaucrat. This effect exceeds the effort cost reduction effect. Therefore, he does not delegate. This is so intuitive result.

On the contrary, when the slope of the bureaucrat's incentive scheme is large, namely, $\bar{X}$ is large, he delegates his tasks to the bureaucrat so that the bureaucrat makes more effort.

Here, we set the following assumption for the bureaucrat's incentive scheme.

Assumption 1 *As for the bureaucrat's incentive scheme,* $K \geq \bar{X}$. *(K is constant.)*

This assumption reflects the fact that there is limit of the post after retirement which is allocated to the bureaucrat.

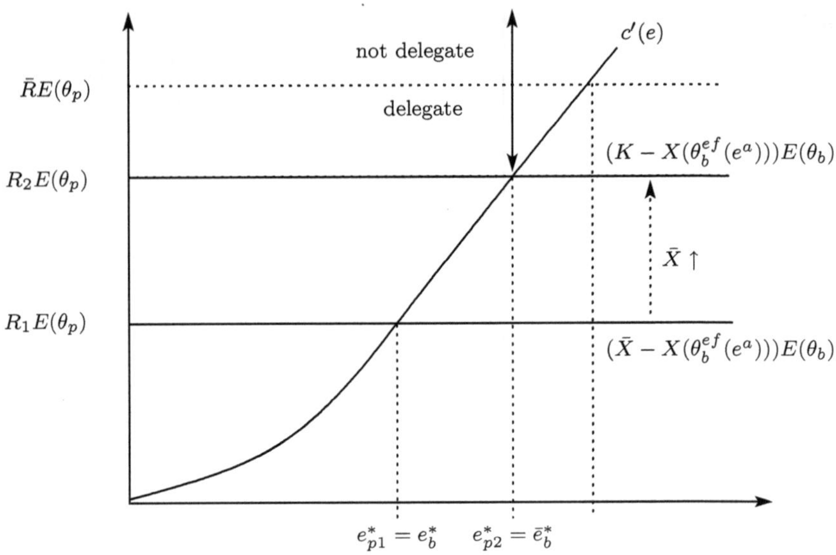

Fig. 14.4 The relation of effort and delegation

Subsequently, let R_2 be the reelection rent that derives the same level of the bureaucrat's effort, when the bureaucrat's incentive is K, to the politician. When the reelection rent is larger than R_2, the politician always makes an effort more than the bureaucrat.

Now we examine the relation of the delegation and the effort level of the politician and the bureaucrat in following Fig. 14.4.

We define the following notations: the bureaucrat's effort level for some X is e_b^*, the reelection rent which derives this bureaucrat's effort level to the politician is R_1, and the politician's effort level under this R_1 is e_{p1}^*; moreover, the bureaucrat's effort level when his incentive is $\bar{X}$ is $\bar{e}_b^*$, the reelection rent which derives this bureaucrat's effort level to the politician is R_2, and the politician's effort level under this R_2 is e_{p2}^*. In addition, let the reelection rent which is indifferent for the politician between the delegation and non-delegation be $\bar{R}$. As we can see from this figure, it is obvious that, under some $\bar{X}$, the equilibrium effort level of the bureaucrat is higher than the politician's one for any R satisfies $R < R_1$. The politician always delegates in this case.

Also, for $R(> R_2)$, the politician's effort is higher than the bureaucrat's for any incentive scheme to the bureaucrat. Moreover, for $R_1 < R < R_2$, by operating $\bar{X}$ well, it makes possible that the bureaucrat makes an effort more than the politician.

Therefore, in the range $R < R_2$, the bureaucrat, who has higher expected ability than the politician, makes more effort than the politician; this delegation is desirable for the citizens because this one generates higher success probability of public works.

Subsequently, we consider the situation that the bureaucrat's incentive scheme is raised to the limit $\bar{X}$. Then, the bureaucrat's effort level is equal to e^*_{p2} which the politician does under R_2 and any incentive scheme cannot make the bureaucrat to exert more effort. Let the bureaucrat's effort level here be $\bar{e}^*_b$.

Also, it is obvious that $\tilde{R}$ is larger than R_2 because, under the reelection rent which is slightly larger than R_2, the politician can reduce his effort cost without declining his reelection probability as the interval between the politician's effort and the bureaucrat's is sufficiently small. Accordingly, under such a reelection rent, the politician delegates his tasks to the bureaucrat.

Defining the threshold of delegation when the bureaucrat's incentive is $\bar{X}$ as $\bar{R}$, in $R_2 < R < \bar{R}$, although the politician makes an effort more than the bureaucrat if he does not delegate, he delegates his tasks to the bureaucrat for the reduction of effort cost.

The following proposition is derived from these arguments.

Theorem 14.4 *(1) In $R < R_2$, by raising the bureaucrat's incentive scheme $\bar{X}$, the bureaucrat makes an effort more than the politician if the politician delegates. In a view of success of public works, it is desirable because the bureaucrat who has higher expected ability than the politician makes an effort more than the politician.*

(2) In $R_2 < R < \bar{R}$, the politician delegates his tasks to the bureaucrat although the politician makes an effort more than the bureaucrat if he does not delegate.

(3) In $R > \bar{R}$, the politician's effort level is sufficiently higher than the bureaucrat's and the politician does not delegate.

Here, we examine whether such a delegation is desirable for the citizens or not. When $R < R_2$, by designing incentive scheme to the bureaucrat adequately, the bureaucrat who has higher expected ability than the politician is delegated the tasks and makes an effort more than the politician. Therefore, such a delegation is desirable for the citizens.

Subsequently, we analyze in case of $R_2 < R < \bar{R}$. We can rewrite the definition of $\bar{R}$ as

$$E(\theta_p)e^*_p - \frac{c(e^*_p)}{\bar{R}} = E(\theta_b)e^*_b.$$

From this equation, we obtain $E(\theta_p)e^*_p > E(\theta_b)e^*_b$. This inequality is held when R is slightly smaller than $\bar{R}$. In the area of $R_2 < R < \bar{R}$, though the politician delegates his tasks to the bureaucrat, as for the success probability of public works in ex ante stage, $E(\theta_p)e^*_p > E(\theta_b)e^*_b$ is held. Then, we see that there exists some area where the undesirable delegation for the citizens is implemented. In such an area, the success probability when the politician implements his tasks by himself is higher than the one when he delegates.

Also, in the area of $R > \bar{R}$, the delegation is not implemented and $E(\theta_p)e_p^* > E(\theta_b)e_b^*$ is always satisfied. Therefore, this situation is desirable in a view of the citizens.

Theorem 14.5 *(1) In $R < R_2$, the desirable delegation for the citizens, such as the bureaucrat makes an effort more than the politician, is implemented.*
(2) In $R_2 < R < \bar{R}$, there exists some area for R where the undesirable delegation for the citizens is implemented.
(3) In $R > \bar{R}$, the delegation is not implemented and this is desirable for the citizens.

14.6 Concluding Remarks

In this paper, we have examined about reelection which is the politician's incentive to effort and the future profit which is the bureaucrat's incentive to do. At first, as for the bureaucrat's effort, the higher the citizens' anticipation value is, the more the bureaucrat makes an effort to obtain his future profit. In rational expectation equilibriums, the ones where the highest and lowest anticipation value corresponds to actual effort are stable.

Subsequently, for the politician's effort and delegation, when the politician's incentive to reelection is sufficiently small or large, by operating the bureaucrat's incentive scheme adequately, the bureaucrat makes more effort, and this situation is desirable for the citizens. In this case, to assign the better post for the bureaucrat who showed his higher ability is not contrary to the citizens' benefit.

Also, when the politician's incentive to reelection is intermediate, any operation of incentive scheme of the bureaucrat cannot make the bureaucrat to exert more effort. In this case, the interval between the politician's effort and the bureaucrat's is close. Therefore, the reduction effect of effort cost by delegation exceeds the decline effect of reelection probability. Thus, the politician delegates his tasks to the bureaucrat. However, the success probability of public works by the politician is higher than the one by the bureaucrat. Such a delegation is obviously undesirable for the citizens. In the view of the citizens, it would seem the default of the politician.

To avoid such a situation, the politician's reelection rent has to be raised more. However, in this paper, we did not consider the fact that this politician's rent and the bureaucrat's AMAKUDARI generate the distortion of resource allocation and it decreases social welfare. Especially, AMAKUDARI is often argued that it leads fiscal distortion. To examine this problem, we must modify the model by focusing more on the bureaucratic organization.

As the problem that we have not analyzed yet, we must consider who design the bureaucrat's incentive scheme. If the politician can design it, he has incentive to approve AMAKUDARI when his reelection rent is not large. Also, if the bureaucrat can design it, he may do it as it derives excessive future profit to him. Such incentive scheme is obviously socially undesirable, and only the politician and the bureaucrat can amend such a scheme. However, they may not have incentive to improve it.

In the political and administrative reform, all we have to do is not only the submission of reform. The politician and the bureaucrat may not have incentive to this reform which may harm their interests. Especially, when public works are a failure, they may not fulfill the accountability to the citizen. To make an implementation of this reform easier, we must maintain the transparency of political and administrative tasks and establish the accomplishment evaluation system which has externality.

However, this reform that deprives the politician and the bureaucrat of their interest has possibility that it distorts the talent allocation in labor market. Namely, for high-ability individual, the politician and the bureaucrat, especially the politician, it becomes a high-risk occupation. This may prevent the high-ability individual from entering in this section. We must discuss carefully how this possibility affects the citizens' welfare.

Even if the public sector needs high-ability person, the protection of their interest needs to employ such individuals. If this protection decreases the citizens' welfare, we may obtain the result that such an individual should be put in the private sector, not public sector. Therefore, we would need to extend the model to the individuals' occupation selection stage through labor market.

References

Alesina, A., and G. Tabellini. 2008. *Bureaucrats or politicians?* Part II: Multiple policy tasks. Journal of Public Economics 92:426–447.

Bennedsen, M., and S.E. Feldmann. 2006. *Lobbying bureucrats*. The Scandinavian Journal of Economics 108:643–668.

Besley, T., and M. Smart 2007. *Fiscal restraints and voter welfare*. Journal of Public Economics 91:755–773.

Borgne, I.E., and B. Lockwood. 2006. *Do elections always motivate incumbents? Learning vs. re-election concerns*. Public Choice 129:41–60.

Carillo, J., and T. Mariotti. 2001. Electoral competition and politicians' turnover". *European Economic Review* 45: 1–25.

Epstein, D., and S. O'Halloran. 1999. Asymmetric information, delegation, and the structure of policy making. *Journal of Theoretical Politics* 11: 37–56.

Gersbach, H. 2004. *Compensation of politicians for incentive contracts and elections*. Public Choice 121:157–177.

Maskin, E., and J. Tirole. 2004. The politician and the judge: accountability in government. *American Economic Review* 94: 1034–1054.

Niskanen, W.A. (1971) *Bureaucracy and representative government*. New Brunswick: Aldine-Atherton.

Persson, T., and G. Tabellini. 2000. *Political economics: explaining economic policy*. Cambridge: MIT Press.

Rasmusen, E. 1996. Stigma and self-fulfilling expectations of criminality. *Journal of Law and Economics* 39: 519–544.

Swank, H.O., and B. Visser. 2002. Delegation or Voting. Tinbergen Institute Discussion Papers, No.02-005/1.

Chapter 15
Measurement of Ideology Based on Per Capita Vote Versus Money Count Vote in Korea

Hang Keun Ryu, Eunju Chi, and Hyeok Yong Kwon

15.1 Introduction

This paper studies political confrontation developed through ideological differences as well as economic confrontation developed by income inequality. Political confrontation is a shadow of human history. The French Revolution was an uprising against the inheritance of the royal class; subsequently, the Marxist revolution tried to remove inheritance through wealth. Many countries have recently adopted liberal democracy as a political system; it is a phenomenon described by Huntington (1991) as Third Wave democracy. Larry Diamond (2013) explained the expansion of liberal democracy as (1) electoral competition described as institutionalized, fair, and open; (2) civil liberties protected by law; (3) the rule of law that is dependable; and (4) low levels of political violence and hard power (or impunity) indicative of a repressive state apparatus.

Income inequality has been the major element of social distrust and political instability in human economic history. Humans are not born equal; someone can always be found to be stronger, smarter, and with a better emotional quotient. People born rich can succeed with less effort. The economic development and globalization of Korea generated new opportunities for the well educated; subsequently, a new front of wealth confrontation was developed. Income inequality increased with the adoption of a free market system.

H.K. Ryu (✉)
Chung Ang University, Seoul, South Korea
e-mail: hangryu@cau.ac.kr

E. Chi • H.Y. Kwon
Korea University, Seoul, South Korea

T. Naito et al. (eds.), *Applied Approaches to Societal Institutions and Economics*,
New Frontiers in Regional Science: Asian Perspectives 18,
DOI 10.1007/978-981-10-5663-5_15

Korea abolished the military dictatorship after democratization in 1987 and the enactment of the 1988 Constitution of the Sixth Republic. Before democratization, there were two competing groups of pro-military leadership and pro-democratization leadership; however, new political cleavages were established immediately after the democratization of Korea. Progressives and conservatives have peacefully shared the political leadership of Korea back and forth for the last thirty years (Ryu 2005), with full acceptance by the civil service and the military. Historically, the progressive group was a minority group with a small voice, but it has succeeded in the presidential elections of 1997 (Kim Dae-jung) and 2002 (Roh Moo-hyun). The emergence of viable progressive governments led to expectations that pro-poor policies would be introduced. However, surprisingly, Kim Dae-jung and Roh Moo-hyun (two former progressive presidents) adopted the market clearing system which is the economic policy of the conservatives. Former president Kim Dae-jung supported new liberalism and successfully revived the Korean economy from a near default during the foreign currency crisis of 1998. President Kim adopted and followed the monetarist advices of the International Monetary Fund (IMF). President Roh later initiated the KORUS FTA with the USA despite opposition from fellow progressive members critical of unregulated market-oriented policies. There have now been substantial discussions on who the real progressives are (Kang 2010). Two progressive presidents and three conservative presidents are indicated by an asterisk that denotes the elected candidate.

A. Korean presidential election result (1992.12.18)
* Kim Young-sam (Conservative, 42%)
Kim Dae-jung (Progressive, 33.8%)
Chung Ju-young (Conservative, 16%)
B. Korean presidential election result (1997.12.18)
* Kim Dae-jung (Progressive, 40.3%)
Lee Hoi-chang (Conservative, 38.7%)
Rhee In-Je (Conservative, 19.2%)
C. Korean presidential election result (2002.12.19)
* Roh Moo-hyun (Progressive, 48.9%)
Lee Hoi-chang (Conservative, 46.6%)
D. Korean presidential election result (2007.12.19)
* Lee Myung-bak (Conservative, 48.7%)
Chung Dong-young (Progressive, 26.1%)
Lee Hoi-chang (Conservative, 15.1%)
E. Korean presidential election result (2012.12.19)
* Park Geun-hye (Conservative, 51.6%)
Moon Jae-in (Progressive, 48.0%)

We have explained that the economic policies of past governments were more or less similar despite the ideological differences of the presidents. We now show the relationship between income and ideology at the individual level. The difference in income will be shown to have negligible impact on the formation of individual ideology. There are no polarized groups made of many poor progressive persons and a small number of rich conservative persons. This paper shows that confrontation originating from income inequality has a negligible influence on individual choices of ideology.

About the social cleavages in Korea, Choi (2010) claims the quality of life worsened after democratization. The income inequality gap increased, the possibility of social class mobility and transition from poor class to rich has decreased, and Korean politics were controlled by a handful of individuals holding a conservative ideology. However, strangely, ideology is not divided between the haves and the have-nots. Many Korean scholars agree on two confrontation fronts. Different attitudes toward the method for North and South Korea unification are the first front. Supporting liberalism and allowing the intervention of a state in economic policies are the second front. Lee and Lee (2014) provided detailed analysis of political cleavages in region, class, generation, and ideology in Korea. Individual opinions on the political, social, or economic issues can be very different if such cleavages exist; however, this topic is to be discussed in detail in a subsequent paper.

This paper asks several questions. Does income difference cause influence on political decisions at the individual level? The per capita vote and money count vote will collide on many political and economic issues if a small number of persons are rich, support a free market system, and encourage fast economic growth and minimum welfare policy in contrast to if a majority of population are poor and support a progressive idea of a more comprehensive welfare policy and higher minimum wage. Ideology histograms of different income groups are tabulated, and the null hypothesis of no influence of income to ideology is tested in this paper.

Several statistical methods are used to answer the above questions. The correlation coefficient matrix is used to check the linearity of the two variables. A conditional histogram is plotted to check varying composition when income has changed. The null hypothesis of the random sample generation that checks no correlation among variables is considered and tested with Pearson's chi-square test. Data was collected by the KBS (2012) broadcasting company survey project team from the general election of 2012. The sample number consisted of 3739 observations.

An overview of this paper is as follows. Section 15.2 examines the influence of income difference and ideology belief. Section 15.3 explains how the money count vote is established. Section 15.4 presents the summary and concluding remarks.

15.2 The Relationship Between Income and Ideology

This paper shows that individual political choice can be independent of income. The fundamental departure comes from two distinct objectives. Capitalism pursues the achievement of equilibrium and market system efficiency, while democracy pursues the determination of social choice through majority rule. Buchanan (1954) distinguished the selection of the choice mechanism and the selection of the power structure among individual choosers. Market freedom and market power should be differentiated conceptually. A redistributive decision cannot be made in isolation because a power structure cannot be modified independently. Market freedom and market power need not be distinguished if the ideology distribution of the rich and the ideology distribution of the poor are similar. We have the following 3739 observations collected by the KBS (2012) broadcasting company survey team. The survey question was a self-declaration of ideology, and survey participants were able to choose one of the following to declare their ideological disposition.

(1) Very conservative (ideology = 2)
(2) Somewhat conservative (ideology = 1)
(3) Neither conservative nor progressive (ideology=0)
(4) Somewhat progressive (ideology = −1)
(5) Very progressive (ideology = −2)

Another question was about monthly household income divided into 14 brackets; however, I put the brackets as follows for the sake of simplicity:

(1) No reply
(2) One million won or less
(3) Above 1 million won but less than or equal to 2 million won
(4) Above 2 million won but less than or equal to 3 million won
(5) Above 3 million won but less than or equal to 4 million won
(6) Above 4 million won but less than or equal to 5 million won
(7) Above 5 million won but less than or equal to 6 million won
(8) Above 6 million won but less than or equal to 7 million won
(9) Above 7 million won but less than or equal to 8 million won
(10) Above 8 million won but less than or equal to 9 million won

Table 15.1 indicates the observed frequencies. For example, 13 persons reported an income of 7–8 million won and declared the ideology level to be −2.

Many people have neutral ideology level, but the income distribution is right fat tailed. There are many persons above 8 million won, but we do not keep detailed income distribution of the rich group in order to simplify exposition.

Table 15.1 Table of ideology with respect to monthly income intervals (income unit: million won)

Ideology income	Ideology: −2	Ideology: −1	Ideology: 0	Ideology: +1	Ideology: +2	Sum
7.01–8	13	52	111	39	23	238
6.01–7	11	31	35	19	6	102
5.01–6	7	77	115	68	20	287
4.01–5	20	116	205	98	23	462
3.01–4	26	137	321	130	30	644
2.01–3	34	133	320	142	55	684
1.01–2	24	85	248	105	41	503
−1	15	48	238	76	32	409
Sum	150	679	1593	577	230	3329

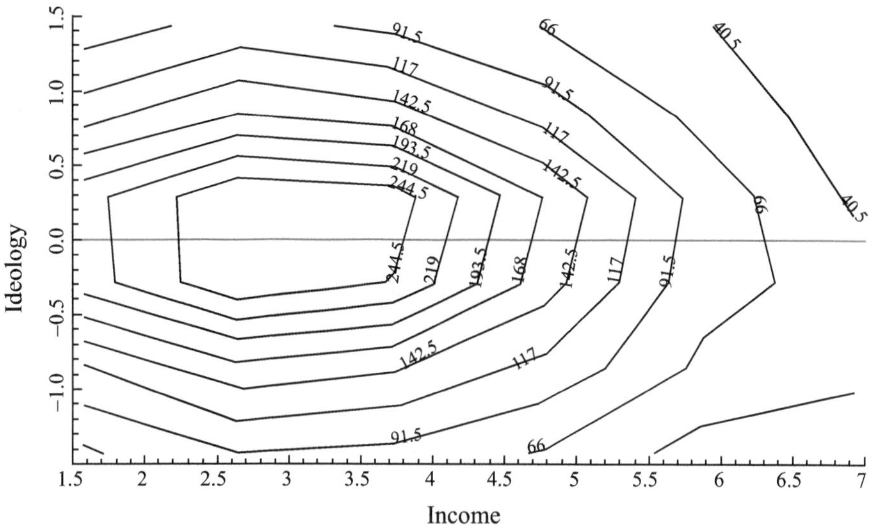

Fig. 15.1 Contour plot of ideology and income frequencies

15.2.1 Contour Plot and Volume Plot of Income and Ideology

The basic structure of a two-dimensional histogram can be examined with a contour plot and a volume plot consisting of income and ideology. Figure 15.1 has a single peak with fairly circular contours. This means no ideological polarization is found, and the correlation between income and ideology is small. Figure 15.2 shows the volume plot of income and ideology. The height is the number of observation at each cell. All high-income individuals are added together and shown at an income of 8 million won; therefore, a small peak develops when ideology equals zero and income is above 7 million.

15.2.2 Correlation Coefficient Analysis

The observed correlation coefficient between income and ideology is small with $\rho = -0.0535$. Income and ideology do not go together; therefore, ideology dispositions of the rich are more or less the same with the ideology dispositions of the poor. Income difference has negligible influence on ideology difference. Though small in number, the correlation coefficient was negative, which means the poor have a small and well-known trend to become conservative. Elderly persons are poor and are known to support conservative ideology in Korea.

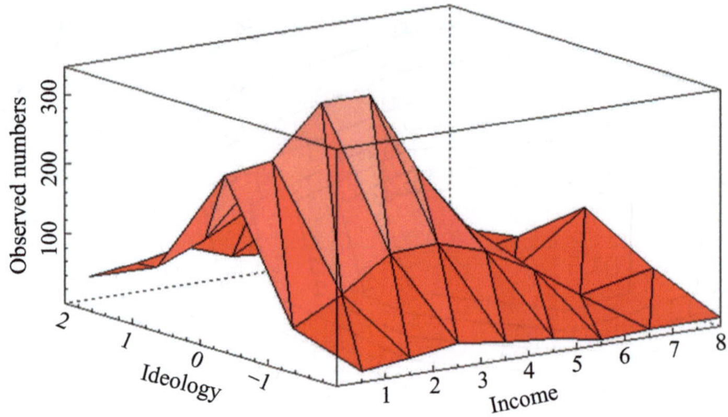

Fig. 15.2 Volume plot of observed numbers for ideology and income

15.3 Conditional Histogram

For different income groups, conditional histogram is plotted in Fig. 15.3.

Figure 15.3 shows the lowest income group with less than 1 million won; there are:

15 persons with ideology $= -2$
48 persons with ideology $= -1$
238 persons with ideology $= 0$
76 persons with ideology $= 1$
32 persons with ideology $= 2$

The composition of the ideology spectrum seems similar for all income ranges. The proportions of ideology =2 (very conservative) for the poor and low middle-income class with incomes less than 3 million won are higher than the proportions of ideology =2 of high income above 6 million won.

If monthly income is below 0–1 million won, then the proportion of ideology = 2 is $32/(15 + 48 + 238 + 76 + 32) = 0.0782$.
If monthly income is between 1 and 2 million won, then the proportion of ideology = 2 is $41/(24 + 85 + 248 + 105 + 41) = 0.0815$.
If monthly income is between 2 and 3 million won, then the proportion of ideology = 2 is $55/(34 + 133 + 320 + 142 + 55) = 0.0804$.
If monthly income is between 6 and 7 million won, then the proportion of ideology = 2 is $6/(11 + 31 + 35 + 19 + 6) = 0.0588$.
If monthly income is between 7 and 8 million won, then the proportion of ideology = 2 is $23/(13 + 52 + 111 + 39 + 23) = 0.0435$.

Therefore, a proportion of ideology that equals 2 at a different income level is more or less the same. The poor range is from 7.82 to 8.15% and the rich range is

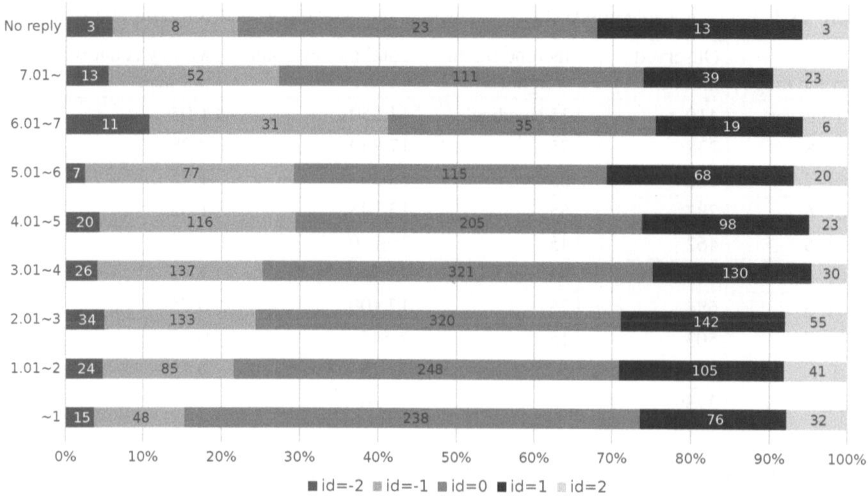

Fig. 15.3 Conditional histogram

from 4.35 to 5.88%. Again, the poor are slightly more conservative compared to the rich.

15.4 Measurement of Ideology by Money Count Vote

15.4.1 Definition of Money Count Vote

The equilibrium determined by the market clearing system balances the total demand with the total supply which is measured by the amount of money. The number of buyers and sellers is inconsequential, but the total amount of money offered to sell and buy matters. Similarly, a different number of votes can be considered for each individual based on income level. The purpose of this experiment is to check any departure between the results measured by the per capita vote and money count vote.

For simplicity, assume 1 million won offered results in ten votes. If monthly income is below 1 million won, assume it corresponds to a half million won, and people within this range receive five votes. Similarly, if monthly income is located:

between 1 and 2 million won, the person receives 15 votes
between 2 and 3 million won, the person receives 25 votes
between 3 and 4 million won, the person receives 35 votes
between 4 and 5 million won, the person receives 45 votes
between 5 and 6 million won, the person receives 55 votes
between 6 and 7 million won, the person receives 65 votes

Table 15.2 Per capita vote observations and income inflated vote weight (unit: million won)

Income range	Observed number (A)	Income-based weight (B)	Total money count (A*B)	Money count weight per head
No answer	410	35 (median)	14,350	1.05
7.01–8	238	75	17,850	2.25
6.01–7	102	65	6,630	1.95
5.01–6	287	55	15,785	1.65
4.01–5	462	45	20,790	1.35
3.01–4	644	35	22,540	1.05
2.01–3	684	25	17,100	0.75
1.01–2	503	15	7,545	0.45
0–1	409	5	2,045	0.15
Sum	3739		124,635	

Table 15.3 Histogram of per capita vote and money count vote

	Observed number	Population histogram	Income-adjusted number	Income-adjusted histogram
Ideology = −2	165	4.41%	170.8	4.56%
Ideology = −1	752	20.1%	826.8	22.1%
Ideology = 0	1,813	48.5%	1739.8	46.5%
Ideology = +1	754	20.2%	751.8	20.1%
Ideology = +2	255	6.82%	249.7	6.67%
Sum	3739	100	3738.9	100

above 7 million won, the person receives 75 votes

If no reply, use a medium income of 3.5 million won, and the person receives 35 votes.

The median income belongs to the 3–4 million won interval (Table 15.2).

Median=1870th person

Total money weight for the income group less than 1 million won is 2045 for 409 persons.

Multiply each money vote by 3739/124,635 to make sum of weight equal to 3739. Money count weight for less than 1 million won is 5*(3739/124,635) =0.15. This means that the per capita vote for the income group of less than 1 million won has one vote in the per capita vote, but the same individual has 0.15 vote in the money count vote. This means 100 votes are counted as 15 votes. Similarly, the per capita vote of an income group of more than 7 million won is inflated to 225%; therefore, 100 votes are counted as 225 votes.

To read Table 15.3, 165 persons declared their ideology as very progressive (−2); therefore, the per capita vote proportion becomes 165/3739=0.0441. Similarly, 752 persons are declared as somewhat progressive (−1) and the per capita vote proportion becomes 752/3,739=0.201. A total of 5,695 votes was given to very progressive (−2) if everyone has a different number of vote inflated according to

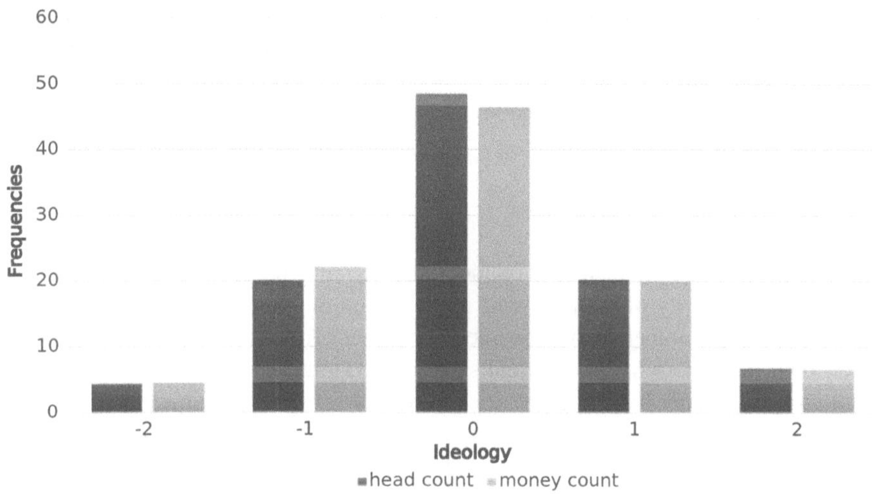

Fig. 15.4 Histograms of ideology by per capita vote versus money count

income level; therefore, money count proportion becomes 5,695/124,635=0.0456. Figure 15.4 compares two histograms; consequently the per capita vote and money count vote seem to produce similar results.

15.4.2 Pearson's Chi-Square Test of No Influence

The χ^2–test will help verify if the categories of money count and per capita vote are equal and likely. Freedman et al. (1988) explain several examples of this test.

Pearson's chi-square test is performed to indicate that the two categories are equal.

$$\chi^2 = \sum_{i=1}^{n} \frac{(\text{head count frequency}_i - \text{money count frequency}_i)^2}{\text{head count frequency}_i} \tag{15.1}$$

$$\chi^2 = \sum_{i=1}^{n} \frac{(165 - 170.8)^2}{165} + \cdots + \frac{(255 - 249.7)^2}{255} = 6.9 \tag{15.2}$$

Chi-square statistics =6.9; tail area 10% at DF=4 is 7.78. Therefore, both histograms (per capita vote histogram and money count histogram) can be assumed to share the same categories.

The income inequality issue and ideology conflict issue do not influence each other. We may assume that the poor will demand progressive policies to establish changes in social and economic systems, such that the poor can choose to take better positions due to the changes in economic and political systems. But poor people in Korea are commonly considered to support conservative policies and market clearing economic system.

15.5 Conclusion

This paper analyzed the impact of income inequality on ideology distribution in Korea. The majority of the poor will not agree on the policies chosen for the rich if only a small number of rich people choose economic and political policies for their own interest. A stable political system encourages social cohesion when the majority of the poor have opportunities to realize self-interest. This paper tests the existence of polarized groups of a small number of rich persons versus a large number of poor persons. Table 15.1 indicates the observed numbers with respect to income groups and ideology groups. In Fig. 15.1 the contour plot of frequencies of ideology and income is shown to have a single peak with smooth graduation. Figure 15.2 shows the volume plot of observations with respect to ideology and income with no reason to believe in the conflict between two polarized groups. In addition, there is no linear trend to follow because the correlation coefficient between income and ideology was very low at −0.0535. Conditional histograms are plotted along with conditional tabulations of ideology plotted for specific income groups. The proportions of the progressives and conservatives were similar for all income groups. Section 15.3 explained the measurement of ideology with money count. One million won corresponds to ten votes, and each individual receives different votes depending on income. The Pearson's chi-square test shows that both categories (observations of per capita vote and observations made of money count) are equal and likely.

Politicians often exaggerate conflicts of income inequality and ideology conflict. However, Fig.15.1 contour shows that the presidential candidate has an incentive to stay near the peak point with income near 3 million won and an ideologically neutral stance. The shortest distance between the candidate and the public will only be the at the peak point; consequently, anyone away from the peak will receive support from fewer persons.

Acknowledgements This research was supported by the National Research Foundation of Korea (2014S1A3A2044032).

References

Buchanan, J. 1954. Individual choice in voting and the market. *Journal of Political Economy* 62(4): 334–343.

Choi, J. 2010. *Democracy after democratization in Korea*. Seoul: Humanitas (Korean Book).

Diamond, L. 2013. Democratic development. https://www.coursera.org/.
Freedman D., R. Pisani, and R. Purves. 1988. *Statistics*. 3rd ed. New York: Norton.
Huntington, S. 1991. *The third wave*. Norman: University of Oklahoma Press.
Kang, S. 2010. *Real progressive*. Seoul: Redian Books (Korean Book).
KBS. 2012. National survey performed on April 11 for the general election of Korea.
Lee, K., and H. Lee. 2014. *Political cleavages in Korea, region, class, generation and ideology*. Seoul: Oruem Publishing House (Korean Book).
Ryu, H. 2005. National survey for Korean economic advancement by Gallup Korea (Korean Report).

Part III
Applied Approaches to Current Economic Issues

Chapter 16
Externalities of Network Formation and Economic Growth

Tomoya Sakagami, Yasuhiko Kato, Hiroki Inoue, and Hiroki Unoki

16.1 Introduction

The purpose of this paper is to clarify the influence of network formation among countries on the economies of those countries. This is accomplished through theory and simulation using an economic growth model with network externalities.

In recent years, economic partnership networks among countries such as the Economic Partnership Agreement (EPA) and the Trans-Pacific Partnership (TPP) have generated much heated discussion. Furthermore, the European Union (EU), which is the chief representative of such economic integration networks, has several countries seeking to join, while the United Kingdom has decided to withdraw. This issue, so-called Brexit, is the cause of much attention around the world.

In these economic partnerships and integration, there are movements to try to advance them and other movements to prevent or dilute them. The reason is that there are advantages and disadvantages for economic partnership and integration among countries. Taking the EU as an example, joining the EU completely liberalizes the movement of people and capital between states, and a positive external effect by economic integration is expected. On the other hand, member

T. Sakagami (✉) • Y. Kato
Kumamoto Gakuen University, Kumamoto, Japan
e-mail: tomoya@kumagaku.ac.jp

H. Inoue
Kyoto University, Kyoto, Japan

H. Unoki
Nakakyushu Junior College, Yatsushiro, Japan

T. Naito et al. (eds.), *Applied Approaches to Societal Institutions and Economics*, New Frontiers in Regional Science: Asian Perspectives 18,
DOI 10.1007/978-981-10-5663-5_16

countries need to pay contributions in proportion to their economic power.[1] Thus, each country compares the advantages and disadvantages of economic partnership and integration and decides to join or leave it.

Although the EU is subject to such conflicting influences, it has steadily expanded its scale from its establishment in 1993 until the expected Brexit in 2018. One of the reasons behind this is considered to be the existence of endogenous economic growth theory which had gathered great attention before the establishment of the EU. The endogenous decision model of technological progress by Romer (1990) has indicated that the population has a scale effect on economic growth. Rivera-Batiz and Romer (1991) applied this model to economic integration, arguing that the scale effect of the integration would boost the long-term economic growth rate.[2]

Economic partnership and economic integration can also be analyzed as network formation among countries. Research on network formation like this has developed with Jackson and Wolinsky (1996) and Inoue et al. (2013), and today it is well known as network economics. In their model, a "network maintenance cost" is required to connect the network, while the profit from other nodes (other countries) is brought to the home node (home country) as a "network externality" through the network. In the network formation game by Jackson and Wolinsky (1996), the node of the network becomes the player, and the player decides the strategy of whether or not to connect the network.

For these reasons, this paper introduces "network externalities" to conventional growth theory and clarifies the impact of economic partnership and integration networks on capital stock, under dynamic economic analysis. In particular, after incorporating "network externalities" of capital stock into economic growth models, we analyze the relationship between a network with three nodes and their economic growth. As for the network maintenance cost, we follow the EU type and make it proportional to the production level of each country.

In addition, we examine the dynamic change of capital stock and consumption between the hub country is the other countries by theoretical analysis and simulation. As a result, it is shown that becoming the hub of the network may cause a country to be overtaken by other countries in the long term, even if the initial capital stock and consumption level of the hub country is higher than those of the other countries.

The remainder of this paper is organized as follows: In Sect. 16.2, the network externalities are given, and steady-state and policy functions in the economic growth model are derived. Section 16.3 formulates the network externalities. In Sect. 16.4,

[1]According to the official website of the European Union, member countries are required to pay about 0.7% of GDI.

[2]After that, this scale effect was modified from various angles. For example, there is a model that suppresses scale effects (see Jones 1995) and a model where the scale effect does not occur depending on the character of knowledge capital (see Takahashi and Sakagami 1998).

we obtain a steady-state that satisfies the match condition on network externalities. Finally, simulation analysis is performed under two different parameter sets in Sect. 16.5.

16.2 The Model

The model in this paper is a discrete Ramsey model[3] incorporating network externalities. There are three countries in this model, and a set of countries is $N = \{a, b, h\}$. We assume that the production function and the utility function of the three countries are the same. Let $L_{i,0} > 0$ be the initial value of the labor force in country $i (i \in N)$, n_i the labor force growth rate, $K_{i,0} > 0$ the initial capital stock, $L_{i,t}$ the population at period$t$, and $K_{i,t}$ the capital stock. There is one kind of goods produced in each country, and the output at the t period of these goods is represented by $Y_{i,t}$. The production function of these goods is given by the following Cobb-Douglas production function:

$$Y_{i,t} = A\hat{K}^{\gamma}_{i,t}K^{\alpha}_{i,t}L^{\beta}_{i,t}, \text{ and } \alpha + \beta = 1$$

where $A > 0$ represents production technology and is assumed to be constant through time. Also, $\hat{K}_{i,t}$ is the "network externality" that the country i gains from the network with other countries in period t. From the primary homogeneity of the production function, the production function per labor in country i is expressed as follows:

$$y_{i,t} = A\hat{K}^{\gamma}_{i,t}k^{\alpha}_{i,t} \tag{16.1}$$

where $y_{i,t}$ is the GDP per labor in country i in period t and $k_{i,t}$ is the capital stock per labor in country i in period t, respectively.

The transient utility function of a representative individual in the country i is given by the discount rate $\rho > 0$ and the per-capita consumption $c_{i,t}$ in each period, as follows:

$$U_i = \sum_{t=0}^{\infty} \left(\frac{1}{1+\rho} \right)^t \ln c_{i,t}. \tag{16.2}$$

On the other hand, the budget constraint equation of representative individuals in country i is as follows:

$$k_{i,t+1} = \frac{1}{1+n_i} \left[y_{i,t} + (1-\delta)\, k_{i,t} - c_{i,t} - g_{i,t} \right]. \tag{16.3}$$

[3]See Ramsey (1928), Cass (1965) and Koopmans (1965).

where n_i is the population growth rate of country i and $\delta \in [0, 1]$ is the capital depletion rate, respectively. Also, $g_{i,t}$ is the network maintenance cost per labor in country i. The network maintenance cost per link depends on the per capita GDP of the country $y_{i,t}$ forming the link and is formulated as follows:

$$g_{i,t} = l_i g y_{i,t},$$

where l_i is the number of links formed by country i and is a constant.[4] g is the GDP burden rate per link and it is assumed to be $0 < g < 0.5$.[5] In the following, we will solve the optimization problem using the externality sequence $\left\{\hat{K}_{i,t}\right\}_{t=1}^{\infty}$ as given. $\hat{K}_{i,t}$ is specified in the next section. To simplify the model, let $n_i = 0, \delta = 1$ to calculate the solution of the optimization problem consisting of Eq. (16.2) and Eq. (16.3).

The steady-state is defined as a state in which capital stock, consumption level, and externality are constant, and each of the values in the steady-state are indicated by k_i^*, c_i^*, and $\hat{K}_i^*$. We obtain the following results:

$$c_i^* = \frac{1+\rho-\alpha}{\alpha} D_i^{\frac{1}{1-\alpha}} \hat{K}_i^{*\frac{\gamma}{1-\alpha}} , \tag{16.4}$$

$$k_i^* = \left[\frac{(1-l_i g)\alpha A \hat{K}_i^{*\gamma}}{1+\rho}\right]^{\frac{1}{1-\alpha}} \tag{16.5}$$

where $D_i = (1 - l_i g)\,\alpha A/(1 + \rho)$. Also, $c_{i,t}$ and $k_{i,t+1}$ on the optimal path are obtained as follows:

$$k_{i,t+1} = \left[\frac{(1-l_i g)\,\alpha}{1+\rho}\right] y_{i,t} = \left[\frac{(1-l_i g)\,\alpha}{1+\rho}\right] A\hat{K}_{i,t}^{\gamma} k_{i,t}^{\alpha}, \tag{16.6}$$

$$c_{i,t} = \left[1 - \frac{(1-l_i g)\,\alpha}{1+\rho} - l_i g\right] y_{i,t} = \left[1 - \frac{(1-l_i g)\,\alpha}{1+\rho} - l_i g\right] A\hat{K}_{i,t}^{\gamma} k_{i,t}^{\alpha}. \tag{16.7}$$

Equation (16.6) is a policy function and expresses the optimal capital accumulation process. Equation (16.7) shows that we will consume a certain percentage of income every period on the optimal path. From Eq. (16.6), if the externality sequence is constant, the economy will converge stably to a stationary solution because $0 < \alpha < 1$. In this model, $\left\{\hat{K}_{i,t}\right\}_{t=1}^{\infty}$ fluctuates (is not constant), but the stability of the steady-state solution in this case is confirmed by simulation analysis using Eqs. (16.6) and (16.7) in Sect. 16.5.

[4]This means that, in this paper, each country does not try to form additional links or delete links.

[5]In general, it is $0 < g < 1$, but in Proposition 16.1 later we discuss it in the area of $g < 0.5$.

16.3 Network Externality

Each country can obtain positive network externality through the network. This network externality can be interpreted as a positive effect on production activity brought about by collaboration among countries.[6] In the case where a link is formed between two countries, network externalities propagate mutually between them.

In this paper, it is assumed that there are three countries, and a star network,[7] shown in Fig. 16.1, is formed between them. Country h is the hub in the network, meaning direct links are formed between country a and country h, and country b and country h. In the star network shown in Fig. 16.1, country h can obtain the network externality from countries a and b. Meanwhile, country a does not form a direct link with country b, so network externalities propagate from country b to country a via country h (and *vice versa*). In other words, even if no direct links are formed between the two countries, network externalities propagate via links formed between other countries. However, by going through many links, the value of the network externality gradually diminishes.[8] Let η be the propagation rate of network externalities when passing through a link $(0 < \eta < 1)$. For example, considering an information transmission network, accuracy of information (or the value of information) will be lost by passing through many people. Therefore, though paying increased network maintenance costs, forming a direct link with many countries can acquire more network externalities.

We assume that network externality in period t depends on capital stock per capita in period $t-1$ of other countries. Then, the network externalities of each country, given the star network of Fig. 16.1, are as follows:

$$\hat{K}_{a,t} = 1 + \eta k_{h,t-1} + \eta^2 k_{b,t-1}, \quad (16.8)$$

$$\hat{K}_{b,t} = 1 + \eta k_{h,t-1} + \eta^2 k_{a,t-1}, \quad (16.9)$$

$$\hat{K}_{h,t} = 1 + \eta k_{a,t-1} + \eta k_{b,t-1}. \quad (16.10)$$

Fig. 16.1 Star network

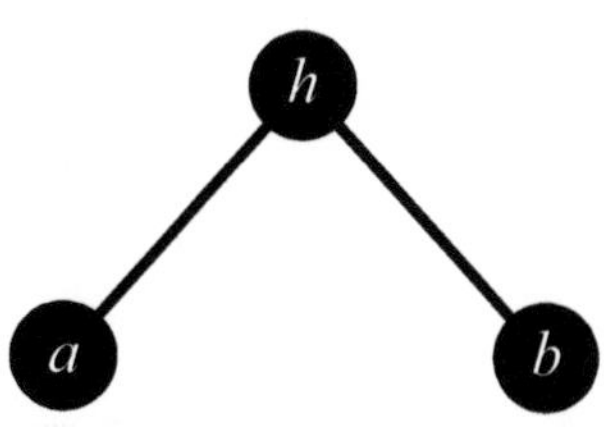

[6]Such network externality can be interpreted as the effect of propagation of imitation where similar products are produced in other countries a while after new products have been developed in the first.

[7]A star network or a hub and spoke-type network is a network in which a hub country (h), which is the center of the network, forms a link with all other countries (countries a and b), but the other countries do not form links with each other.

[8]The assumption that the value of network externality is discounted every time it goes through the link has also been introduced in Jackson and Wolinsky (1996) and Bala and Goyal (2000).

The network maintenance costs of each country in the star network of Fig. 16.1 are as follows:

$$g_{a,t} = gy_{a,t}, \quad g_{b,t} = gy_{b,t}, \quad g_{h,t} = 2gy_{h,t}. \tag{16.11}$$

16.4 Steady-State in a Star Network

In this section, we identify the network as a star network composed of the three countries shown in Fig. 16.1 and give $g_{i,t}$ as Eq. (16.11). Then by substituting c_i^* and k_i^* obtained in Sect. 16.2 and $\hat{K}_{i,t}$ specified in Sect. 16.3 as the consistency condition into Eqs. (16.4) and (16.5), we will derive each variable of the stationary solution under a rational expectation equilibrium. From now on, we will analyze the solutions that meet this consistency condition. Also, in order to obtain the solutions analytically, $1 - \alpha = \gamma$ is assumed below. By expressing countries other than hub with $j \in \{a, b\}$, the network externalities, the per capita stocks, the consumption levels, and the production levels of each country in the stationary solution are as follows:

$$\hat{K}_h^* = \frac{1 - \eta^2 D_j^{1/\gamma} + 2\eta D_j^{1/\gamma}}{X}, \quad \hat{K}_j^* = \frac{1 + \eta D_h^{1/\gamma}}{X}, \tag{16.12}$$

$$k_h^* = \frac{\left(1 - \eta^2 D_j^{1/\gamma} + 2\eta D_j^{1/\gamma}\right) D_h^{1/\gamma}}{X}, \quad k_j^* = \frac{\left(1 + \eta D_h^{1/\gamma}\right) D_j^{1/\gamma}}{X}, \tag{16.13}$$

$$c_h^* = \frac{(1 + \rho - \alpha)\left(1 - \eta^2 D_j^{1/\gamma} + 2\eta D_j^{1/\gamma}\right) D_h^{1/\gamma}}{\alpha X},$$

$$c_j^* = \frac{(1 + \rho - \alpha)\left(1 + \eta D_h^{1/\gamma}\right) D_j^{1/\gamma}}{\alpha X}, \tag{16.14}$$

$$y_h^* = \frac{(1 + \rho)\left(1 - \eta^2 D_j^{1/\gamma} + 2\eta D_j^{1/\gamma}\right) D_h^{1/\gamma}}{\alpha (1 - 2g) X},$$

$$y_j^* = \frac{(1 + \rho)\left(1 + \eta D_h^{1/\gamma}\right) D_j^{1/\gamma}}{\alpha (1 - g) X}, \tag{16.15}$$

where $D_h \equiv (1 - 2g)\alpha A/(1 + \rho)$, $D_j \equiv (1 - g)\alpha A/(1 + \rho)$, and $X \equiv 1 - \eta^2 D_j^{1/\gamma} - 2\eta^2 (D_j D_h)^{1/\gamma}$. As can be confirmed from the denominator of Eqs. (16.12), (16.13), (16.14), and (16.15) below, $X > 0$ is assumed as a condition for various variables in the steady-state to take a positive value. The next proposition concerns the magnitude relation of each variable of the hub country and the other countries in the steady-state.

Proposition 16.1 *If* $1 - \alpha = \gamma$, *then for hub country h and for other countries j, the following relations hold:*

(i) $\hat{K}_h^* > \hat{K}_j^*$.

(ii) If

$$\eta(1-\eta) > (<) \frac{(1-g)^{1/\gamma} - (1-2g)^{1/\gamma}}{(1-g)^{1/\gamma}(1-2g)^{1/\gamma}} \left(\frac{1+\rho}{\alpha A}\right)^{\frac{1}{\gamma}} \tag{16.16}$$

is true, then $c_h^* > (<)\, c_j^*$ *and* $k_h^* > (<)\, k_j^*$.

(iii) If

$$\eta\left[1-(1-g)\eta\right] > (<) \frac{(1-g)\left[(1-g)^{1/\gamma} - (1-2g)^{1/\gamma}\right] - g(1-g)^{1/\gamma}}{\left[(1-g)(1-2g)\left(\frac{\alpha A}{1+\rho}\right)\right]^{1/\gamma}} \tag{16.17}$$

is true, then $y_h^* > (<)\, y_j^*$.

See Appendix.

From Proposition 16.1, despite the fact that each country is homogeneous in this paper,[9] there is a difference between the hub country of the network and the other countries. The hub country is getting more network externality from the network than other countries by contributing more expenses than other countries. Nevertheless, if LHS <RHS is established in Eq. (16.16), both the consumption level and the capital stock level of the hub country will be smaller than in other countries. The reason for this is that the network externalities do not compensate for the increased network maintenance costs.

16.5 Simulation Analysis

In this section, we simulate how k_i^*, c_i^* and $\hat{K}_i^*$ in the hub country and other countries converge to stationary solutions, respectively. We also check how the magnitude relationship between stationary solutions k_i^*, c_i^* in the hub country and other countries varies depending on the combination of parameters in Proposition 16.1.

The network is in the form of a star network. Therefore, given the initial value of the capital stock, the magnitude of the externality of the first phase is determined by Eqs. (16.8), (16.9), and (16.10). From these externalities and Eq. (16.6), each country can determine the optimal level of capital stock (investment) in the next

[9] Homogeneity here means that each country's preference (utility function) and technology (production function) are the same.

period. By repeating this process until the 30th period, we simulate the convergence process to a stationary solution. The software used for the simulation is "Maxima."

First, the values of each parameter are set as follows:

[Case 1]

$$A=3,\ \rho=2,\ \alpha=0.6,\ g=0.01,\ \gamma=0.4,\ \eta=0.5,\ k_{h,0}=0.1,\ k_{a,0}=k_{b,0}=0.05.$$

In this case, the theoretical values of stationary solutions are as follows:

$$\begin{array}{llll} k_h^* = 0.3562, & k_j^* = 0.3437, & c_h^* = 1.4250, & c_j^* = 1.3749 \\ \hat{K}_h^* = 1.3437, & \hat{K}_j^* = 1.2640, & y_h^* = 1.8176, & y_j^* = 1.7360 \end{array}$$

In case 1, the initial value of capital stock is set higher for the hub country than for other countries, and as a result of the simulation, it can be confirmed that the economy converges to the stationary solution of the theoretical value. Moreover, it can be confirmed that the steady-state solution and the convergence process always have higher values of each variable in the hub country than in other countries (Fig. 16.2).

[Case 2]

$$A=2,\ \rho=2,\ \alpha=0.6,\ g=0.04,\ \gamma=0.4,\ \eta=0.7,\ k_{h,0}=0.08,\ k_{a,0}=k_{b,0}=0.05.$$

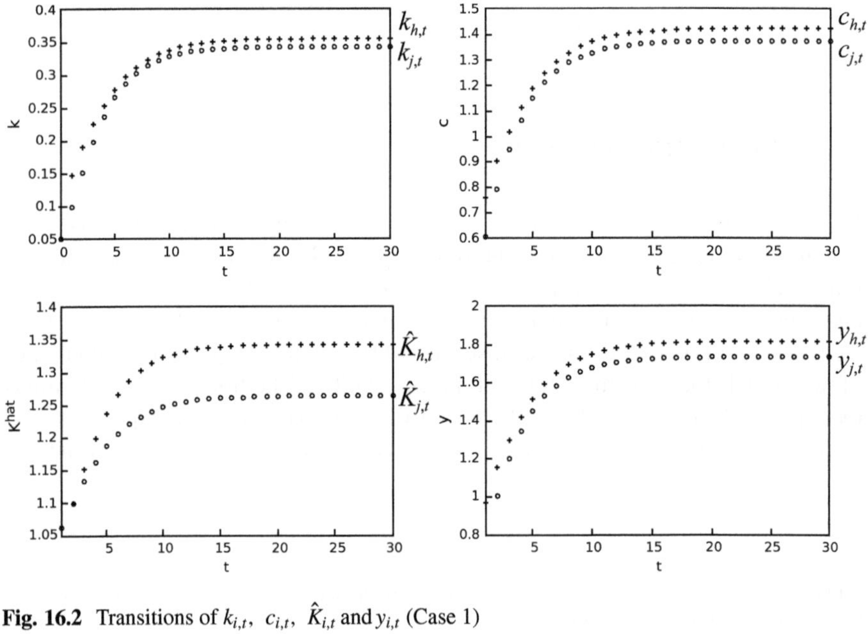

Fig. 16.2 Transitions of $k_{i,t}$, $c_{i,t}$, $\hat{K}_{i,t}$ and $y_{i,t}$ (Case 1)

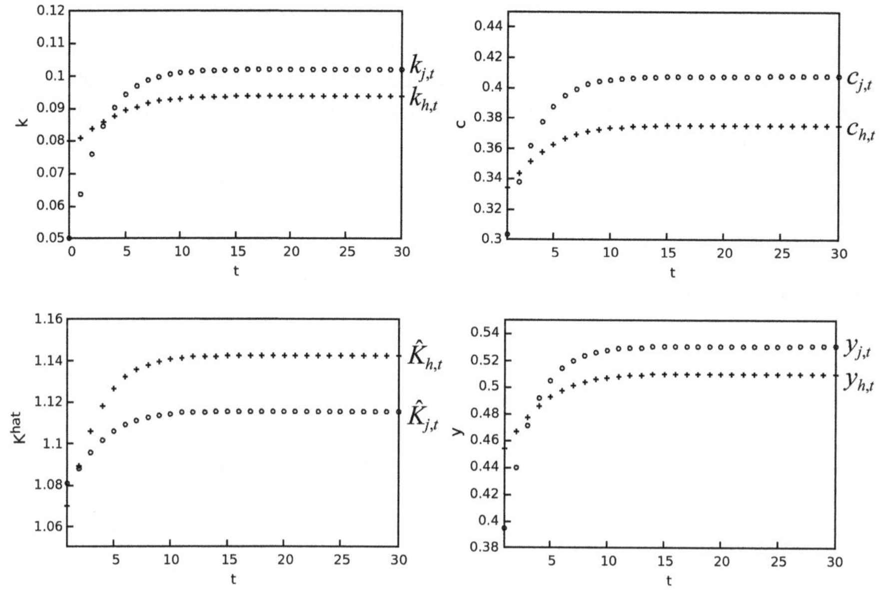

Fig. 16.3 Transitions of $k_{i,t}$, $c_{i,t}$, $\hat{K}_{i,t}$ and $y_{i,t}$ (Case 2)

In this case, the theoretical values of stationary solutions are as follows:

$$k_h^* = 0.0938, \;\; k_j^* = 0.1019, \;\; c_h^* = 0.3755, \;\; c_j^* = 0.4077$$
$$\hat{K}_h^* = 1.1427, \;\; \hat{K}_j^* = 1.1156, \;\; y_h^* = 0.5102, \;\; y_j^* = 0.5309$$

In case 2,

$$\text{LHS of Eq. (16.16)} = 0.21 < \text{RHS of Eq. (16.16)} = 1.2286,$$
$$\text{LHS of Eq. (16.17)} = 0.2296 < \text{RHS of Eq. (16.17)} = 0.6925.$$

For this reason, it is expected that the stationary solutions $k_{i,t}$, $c_{i,t}$, $y_{i,t}$ from Proposition 16.1 will be higher in country j than in country h. In fact, we can confirm that this prediction is correct by simulation. Furthermore, the initial value of capital stock of country h is higher than that of the other countries, but $k_{i,t}$, $c_{i,t}$, $y_{i,t}$ are reversed in countries other than the hub in the process of convergence to a steady-state (Fig. 16.3).

The reason why the reversal of the magnitude relation of the variables occurs in the convergence process is because cases g and η are higher in case 2 than in case 1. Since g corresponds to the network maintenance cost per link, in case 2 where g is high, the hub country places a greater burden of contributing network maintenance costs compared with other countries. Therefore, despite being able to acquire a lot of network externalities, consumption, and investment, every period will be reduced. Also, since η is the propagation rate of network externalities, the higher the value of η, the more countries can acquire greater network externality. In that sense, the hub country benefits, unlike the increase in η as g increases. However, when η is sufficiently large, there is almost no difference in network externalities between the hub country and the other countries.[10] In other words, if it is sufficiently high, there is little merit in forming more links than other countries. For these reasons, the hub country is considered to be lower in $k_{i,t}$, $c_{i,t}$, $y_{i,t}$ than the other countries.

16.6 Conclusion

In this paper, we analyzed how the network externality affects the steady-state of each country and the transitional path, when the three countries are connected by a star network. As a result, it was revealed that the ranks of the capital stock per capita and the consumption level in the steady-state may be reversed between the hub country and the other countries depending on the parameters. Simulation analysis also showed that even if the initial capital stock of the hub country is great, the capital stock of the hub may be overtaken by that of the other countries in the middle of the transitional path.

Finally, we will discuss future work. Although in this paper the network was fixed, if each country can strategically determine link formation and deletion, the shape of the network may change dynamically. As the result, it is likely that a difference occurs between the initial network and the final, stable network. At this time, if it can be confirmed that a country with a large initial capital stock leaves the network, it will lead to explaining Brexit.

In addition, this time, we discussed the situation when the network externalities depended on the capital stock of other countries in the previous term. By endogenizing those externalities, we can also suppose a planner who maximizes the welfare of the whole world. Due to externalities, it is likely that the social optimal path derived by this planner is different from the dynamic path of this paper. However, the setting at this time is too complicated to analyze the endogeneity externalities so this will be a future task.

Since it seems that it is comparatively easy to analyze how the parameter changes influence the steady-state and the rank of each variable, we would like to work on this as soon as possible.

[10]For example, when η is sufficiently close to 1, there is almost no difference in Eqs. (16.8), (16.9), and (16.10).

A Proof of Proposition 16.1

First, we analyze the magnitude relation between $\hat{K}_h^*$ and $\hat{K}_j^*$. The following result can be obtained by paying attention to the assumption of $X > 0$ and $D_j^{1/\gamma} > D_h^{1/\gamma}$.

$$\hat{K}_h^* - \hat{K}_j^* = \frac{(1-\eta)\,\eta D_j^{1/\gamma} + \eta\left(D_j^{1/\gamma} - D_h^{1/\gamma}\right)}{X} > 0$$

Next, the magnitude relationship between c_h^* and c_j^* is analyzed.

$$c_h^* - c_j^* = \frac{1+\rho-\alpha}{\alpha X}\left[D_h^{1/\gamma} - D_j^{1/\gamma} + \eta(1-\eta)\left(D_j D_h\right)^{1/\gamma}\right].$$

The necessary and sufficient conditions for $c_h^* - c_j^* > 0$ are as follows:

$$D_h^{1/\gamma} - D_j^{1/\gamma} + \eta(1-\eta)\left(D_j D_h\right)^{1/\gamma} > 0 \tag{A1}$$

$$\Leftrightarrow \eta(1-\eta) > \frac{(1-g)^{1/\gamma} - (1-2g)^{1/\gamma}}{(1-g)^{1/\gamma}(1-2g)^{1/\gamma}}\left(\frac{1+\rho}{\alpha A}\right)^{\frac{1}{\gamma}}. \tag{A2}$$

Let's analyze the magnitude relation between k_h^* and k_j^* next.

$$k_h^* - k_j^* = \frac{1}{X}\left[D_h^{1/\gamma} - D_j^{1/\gamma} + \eta(1-\eta)\left(D_j D_h\right)^{1/\gamma}\right].$$

Obviously, the necessary and sufficient condition for $k_h^* - k_j^* > 0$ is that Eq. (A1) holds.

Finally, the magnitude relationship between y_h^* and y_j^* is analyzed.

$$y_h^* - y_j^* = \frac{1+\rho}{\alpha(1-g)(1-2g)X}\Big\{(1-g)\left(D_h^{1/\gamma} - D_j^{1/\gamma}\right) + gD_j^{1/\gamma} + \eta\left(D_j D_h\right)^{1/\gamma}\left[1-(1-g)\eta\right]\Big\}.$$

The necessary and sufficient conditions for $y_h^* - y_j^* > 0$ are as follows:

$$(1-g)\left(D_h^{1/\gamma} - D_j^{1/\gamma}\right) + gD_j^{1/\gamma} + \eta\left(D_j D_h\right)^{1/\gamma}\left[1-(1-g)\eta\right] > 0$$

$$\Leftrightarrow \eta\left[1-(1-g)\eta\right] > \frac{(1-g)\left[(1-g)^{1/\gamma} - (1-2g)^{1/\gamma}\right] - g(1-g)^{1/\gamma}}{(1-g)^{1/\gamma}(1-2g)^{1/\gamma}}\left(\frac{1+\rho}{\alpha A}\right)^{\frac{1}{\gamma}}.$$

Q.E.D.

References

Bala, V., and S. Goyal. 2000. A non-cooperative model of network formation. *Econometrica* 68: 1181–1229.

Cass, D. 1965. Optimum growth in an aggregative model of capital accumulation. *Review of Economic Studies* 32: 233–240.

European Union, Official website, How is the EU funded? https://europa.eu/european-union/about-eu/money/revenue-income_en.

Inoue, H., Y. Kato, and T. Sakagami. 2013. Airline network optimization using evolutionary computation. *Electronics and Communications in Japan* 96(11): 16–25.

Jackson, M.O., and A. Wolinsky. 1996. A strategic model of social and economic networks. *Journal of Economic Theory* 71: 44–74.

Jones, C.I. 1995. R&D-based models of economic growth. *Journal of Political Economy* 103: 759–784.

Koopmans, T.C. 1965. On the concept of optimal economic growth. In *Econometric Approach to Development Planning*. Amsterdam: North-Holland.

Ramsey, F. 1928. A mathematical theory of saving. *Economic Journal* 38: 543–559.

Rivera-Batiz, L.A., and P.M. Romer. 1991. Economic integration and endogenous growth. *Quarterly Journal of Economics* 106(2): 531–555.

Romer, P.M. 1990. Endogenous technological change. *Journal of Political Economy* 98(5): S71–S102.

Takahashi, H., and T. Sakagami. 1998. Transitional dynamics of economic integration and endogenous growth. *Journal of Economic Behavior and Organization* 33: 63–79.

Chapter 17
Environmental Policy and the Excess Entry Theorem

Hajime Sugeta

17.1 Introduction

During the past decades, market liberalization and environmental protection have been salient features of economic policy trend in the industrialized countries. However, relatively few economic analyses have focused on how an environmental policy interacts with an antitrust or a competition policy.[1] This paper is aimed at examining the effects of these two policies on pollution control and social welfare.

Various studies have explored the optimal pollution taxation in imperfectly competitive markets. The literature is concerned about whether the optimal emission tax rate exceeds the marginal environmental damage. In a perfectly competitive market, the traditional Pigouvian tax rule suggests that the optimal rate is equal to the marginal environmental damage. In a monopolistic market, which is the other polar case, the polluting firm supplies less and thus the optimal rate falls short of the marginal damage.[2]

As we have seen in the aforementioned argument, when the firm exerts monopoly power in the product market, the environmental damage to a society tends to be under-internalized. In an oligopolistic industry, which has a more realistic market

[1] Matsumoto and Sugeta (2007) showed that an antitrust policy banning an input price discrimination reduces pollution emission and improves social welfare.

[2] Buchanan (1969) was the first to point out this monopoly result. Barnett (1980) extended his result by incorporating the monopolist's abatement technology.

H. Sugeta (✉)
Kansai University, Osaka, Japan
e-mail: sugeta@kansai-u.ac.jp

T. Naito et al. (eds.), *Applied Approaches to Societal Institutions and Economics*,
New Frontiers in Regional Science: Asian Perspectives 18,
DOI 10.1007/978-981-10-5663-5_17

structure, this assertion may not be true.[3] Allowing free entry in a symmetric Cournot model with a linear demand, Katsoulacos and Xepapadeas (1995) showed that the optimal pollution tax can be greater than the marginal environmental damage if the marginal abatement costs are independent of the level of output. Lee (1999) abstracted firms' abatement activities and assumed a general inverse demand function in a free-entry Cournot oligopoly to establish the same result for the concave demand. Simpson (1995) set up a model of heterogenous Cournot duopoly to show that the optimal rate is greater than the marginal environmental damage when the two firms have sufficiently different costs. These contributions were summarized in a survey by Requate (2007) under a unified framework.

This paper uses a symmetric Cournot oligopoly model with free entry and derives the conditions for the optimal pollution tax to exceed the marginal environmental damage. The policy direction, that is, whether the optimal tax rate is greater or smaller than the marginal damage depends, especially, on the curvature of the inverse demand curve[4] and the output elasticity of emissions. Previous models studied by Lee (1999) and Requate (2007) rely on the assumption that pollution emissions are proportional to output. This assumption implies that the elasticity of emissions with respect to output becomes unity.[5] We generalize it to the case in which the elasticity of emission can be either greater or smaller than unity. Such generalization leads to the emergence of the perverse comparative static effects on environment: Entry of a new firm may reduce total emission, while an increase in the emission tax may expand it at the long-run free-entry equilibrium. We then show that the policy direction is reversed according to whether the elasticity of emissions is greater or smaller than unity and that the optimal tax rate can be greater than the marginal damage even in the case of convex demand.

In the antitrust literature, it is well-established that there may exist too many firms at the free-entry Cournot equilibrium from the viewpoint of social welfare. This is called the excess entry theorem, whose pioneering works include von Weizsäcker (1980), Mankiw and Whinston (1986), and Suzumura and Kiyono (1987). The last two specifically show that if the business-stealing effect is present, that is, entry of a new firm reduces output of an incumbent firm, then the social welfare is improved by reducing the number of firms from the long-run free-entry equilibrium level. The second purpose of the paper is to see how the environmental taxation affects the theorem.

[3]Even in monopoly, the optimal tax rate can be greater than the marginal damage. Misiolek (1988) shows that such over-internalization can occur when a monopolist engages in rent seeking.

[4]The curvature of the inverse demand curve can be interpreted as the degree of convexity of the demand, which is measured by the elasticity of the slope of the inverse demand curve. The characteristics of comparative statics and optimal policies are affected crucially by this parameter in most oligopoly models.

[5]The linear specification of output-emission relation has the weakness that the analysis of an emission tax is almost identical to that of an output tax.

We propose the traditional Pigouvian tax rule, rather than the optimal tax formula, which is complex and thus causes the informational problem. It is shown that under the traditional Pigouvian tax rule, the business-stealing effect is more likely to be realized than under the exogenously given tax rate. This implies that even though the regulator does not have full information about the curvature of demand and the output elasticity of emissions, holding the tax rate at the marginal damage level and reducing the number of firms from the free-entry equilibrium level enhance the social welfare. Hence, the joint use of the Pigouvian tax and the entry regulation resolves the informational problem.

The rest of the paper is organized as follows. Section 17.2 sets up a model of symmetric Cournot oligopoly. Section 17.3 derives the optimal pollution taxation both in the short-run and long-run equilibria, respectively. The traditional Pigouvian tax rule is proposed and the validity of the Excess Entry Theorem is explored under this tax rule.

17.2 The Model

Consider an oligopolistic industry in which n identical firms produce a homogenous good and emit pollution. Let q^i be the output of firm $i \in \{1, \cdots, n\}$. The price of the good, p, is given by the inverse demand function, $p = p(Q)$, where $Q \equiv \sum_{i=1}^{n} q^i$ is the aggregate output. We assume $p' \equiv dp/dQ < 0$. However, $p'' \equiv d^2p/dQ^2$ is allowed to be either positive or negative.[6] Let ϵ denote the curvature of the inverse demand function, which is defined as $\epsilon \equiv -Qp''/p'$. ϵ measures the convexity of the market demand. This is also interpreted as the output elasticity of the slope of the demand curve.

Let e^i be firm i's emission level. It is given by the emission generating function, $e^i = e(q^i)$, with $e(0) = 0$, $e' > 0$, and $e'' \gtreqless 0$. In the literature, the function e is frequently assumed to take the linear form, for example, $e^i = \gamma q^i$ for a constant $\gamma > 0$. However, we relax this common assumption. We define the output elasticity of emission level as $\mu \equiv qe'/e > 0$. The aforementioned linear form possesses the property of $\mu = 1$. We deal with more general cases, that is, $\mu \gtreqless 1$.

The regulator sets an emission tax rate, τ, per unit of pollutant prior to the firms' output decision. Firm i's tax payments are thus $\tau e(q^i)$. Let $c(q^i)$ be firm i's production costs with $c(0) > 0$, $c' > 0$, and $c'' \gtreqless 0$.[7] Firm i's profits are therefore given by $\pi^i(q^i, Q^{-i}, \tau) \equiv p(q^i + Q^{-i})q^i - c(q^i) - \tau e(q^i)$, where $Q^{-i} \equiv \sum_{j \neq i} q^j$ is the total output of firm i's rivals. Firm i decides its own output so as to maximize π^i, taking the others' output and the emission tax rate as given. The first-order condition

[6] In what follows, primes denote differentiation.

[7] We allow decreasing marginal production costs, which may cause instability of a Cournot-Nash equilibrium. Later, we impose that $c'' + \tau e'' > p'$ for the stability of the equilibrium (see Seade 1980).

for profit maximization is therefore $\pi^i_{q^i} \equiv \partial\pi^i/\partial q^i = p'q^i + p - c' - \tau e' = 0$. The second-order condition is assumed to be satisfied[8]: $\pi^i_{q^i q^i} \equiv \partial^2\pi^i/\partial\left(q^i\right)^2 = p''q^i + 2p' - c'' - \tau e'' < 0$.

We assume the existence and uniqueness of a Cournot-Nash equilibrium. Focusing on the symmetric equilibrium, $q^i \equiv q$ for all i and dropping the superscripts that indicate the firm index, we write the first-order condition as

$$\pi_q = p'(nq)\,q + p(nq) - c'(q) - \tau e'(q) = 0. \tag{17.1}$$

Following Seade (1980) and Mankiw and Whinston (1986), we treat the number of firms as a continuous variable. In the long-run equilibrium, the profits must be driven to zero owing to free entry and exit. Thus, the number of firms, n, is endogenously determined by the zero-profit condition:

$$\pi = p(nq)\,q - c(q) - \tau e(q) = 0. \tag{17.2}$$

This implies that $p = \frac{c+\tau e}{q}$, which can be substituted into (17.1). After some manipulations, we have

$$q = \frac{(c' + \tau e') - \frac{c+\tau e}{q}}{p'}. \tag{17.3}$$

It should be noted that $(c' + \tau e') < (c + \tau e)/q$ is required for the long-run free-entry equilibrium to exist, that is, for the right-hand side of (17.3) to be positive. This inequality means that overall costs must exhibit scale economies, that is, average costs exceed marginal costs. Define the output elasticity of production cost as $\lambda \equiv qc'/c \in (0, 1)$. Then the above existence condition places the upper bound for μ, that is, $\mu < \frac{c}{\tau e}(1 - \lambda) + 1 \equiv \bar{\mu}$. Since we allow $\mu > 1$, it is necessary for at least one of the both elasticity λ and tax payment τe or both to be sufficiently small.

In what follows, we perform comparative statics for the short-run and long-run equilibria. For that purpose, it is necessary to assume the stability of each equilibrium. First, we present the short-run stability conditions with regard to Eq. (17.1). As in Seade (1980) and Dixit (1986), $\pi_{qq} \equiv \partial\pi_q/\partial q < 0$ and $\kappa \equiv 1 - (c'' + \tau e'')/p' > 0$ are assumed to be satisfied. Note that κ measures the relative slope of the marginal cost curve and the demand curve. We now utilize ϵ and κ to express the former condition as[9]

$$\pi_{qq} = \left(-p'\right)(\epsilon - n - \kappa) < 0 \quad \Leftrightarrow \quad \epsilon < n + \kappa \equiv \bar{\epsilon}.$$

This places the upper bound for ϵ, which is denoted by $\bar{\epsilon}$.

---

[8]In what follows, subscripts denote partial differentiation.

[9]These conditions also ensure that the second-order condition for profit maximization is satisfied at the symmetric equilibrium: $p''q + 2p' - c'' - \tau e'' = p' \cdot (1 + \kappa - \epsilon/n) < 0 \Leftrightarrow \epsilon < n + n\kappa$. The last inequality is implied by $\kappa > 0$ and $\epsilon < \bar{\epsilon} \equiv n + \kappa < n + n\kappa$.

Next, the long-run stability condition is introduced. The long-run equilibrium is then characterized by Eqs. (17.1) and (17.2). Appendix shows that the stability condition can be expressed as

$$H \equiv \pi_{qq}\pi_n - \pi_{qn}\pi_q = \frac{1}{n}\left(p'q\right)^2(n + n\kappa - \epsilon) > 0.$$

It is also shown in Appendix that $H > 0$ is automatically implied by the short-run stability conditions.

17.2.1 Short-Run Equilibrium

The number of firms, n, is exogenously given in the short-run equilibrium. Then, in view of Eq. (17.1), we write the Cournot-Nash equilibrium output as $\tilde{q} = \tilde{q}(\tau, n)$. Accordingly, from Appendix, the effects of an increase in the emission tax and entry of a new firm are

$$\frac{\partial \tilde{q}}{\partial \tau} = \frac{e'}{\pi_{qq}} < 0, \qquad \frac{\partial \tilde{q}}{\partial n} = \frac{\epsilon - n}{\bar{\epsilon} - \epsilon}\frac{\tilde{q}}{n} \lesseqgtr 0 \quad \Leftrightarrow \quad \epsilon \lesseqgtr n. \tag{17.4}$$

The effect of entry is worth mentioning. In the antitrust literature, $\partial\tilde{q}/\partial n < 0$ is named as the business-stealing effect (see Mankiw and Whinston 1986). It is related with the concept of strategic substitutes (see Bulow et al. 1985). This means $\pi^i_{q^iQ^{-i}} \equiv \partial\pi^i_{q^i}/\partial Q^{-i} = p''q^i + p' < 0$, that is, firm i's marginal profits decrease with its rivals' output. The entry of a new rival firm reduces the marginal profits, and thus the existing firms cut back their own output. In the symmetric equilibrium, we have $\pi^i_{q^iQ^{-i}} = (-p')(\epsilon/n - 1) < 0 \Leftrightarrow \epsilon < n$. If the demand is too convex (i.e., $\epsilon \in (n, \bar{\epsilon})$), the outputs become strategic complements, and thus the entry of a new firm expands the individual output.

The effects on total output $\tilde{Q} \equiv n\tilde{q}$ are found immediately by

$$\frac{\partial \tilde{Q}}{\partial \tau} = \frac{ne'}{\pi_{qq}} < 0, \qquad \frac{\partial \tilde{Q}}{\partial n} = \frac{\kappa}{\bar{\epsilon} - \epsilon}\tilde{q} > 0. \tag{17.5}$$

The short-run equilibrium price is defined as $\tilde{p} \equiv p(\tilde{Q})$, and the short-run equilibrium emission level is denoted by $\tilde{e} \equiv e(\tilde{q})$. Clearly, $\partial\tilde{p}/\partial\tau > 0$ and $\partial\tilde{e}/\partial\tau < 0$, that is, an increase in emission tax rate, raise the price, while it reduces the emission level.

We next examine whether the net price of the product given by $\tilde{p} - \tau\tilde{e}/\tilde{q}$ would increase. Seade (1985) was the first to point out that the net price may be raised by an increase in the output or commodity tax. We confirm his price over-shifting argument in our emission tax framework. For this, we differentiate the net price and evaluate its derivative at $\tau = 0$, which yields the following relationship[10]:

$$\frac{\partial\left(\tilde{p} - \tau\tilde{e}/\tilde{q}\right)}{\partial\tau} = \frac{\epsilon - \epsilon_2}{\bar{\epsilon} - \epsilon}\frac{\tilde{e}}{\tilde{q}} \gtreqless 0 \quad \Leftrightarrow \quad \epsilon \gtreqless \epsilon_2 \equiv \kappa - n\left(\mu - 1\right). \tag{17.6}$$

If $\epsilon > \epsilon_2$, then an increase in the tax would be over-shifted into the price (so-called price over-shifting). When the emission is output-elastic (or inelastic), that is, $\mu >$ (or $<$) 1, the emission tax is more (less) likely to induce the price over-shifting than the output tax, whose result is generated by setting $\mu = 1$. Moreover, when $\mu >$ (or $<$) 1, more (fewer) firms in the industry are more (less) likely to cause the price over-shifting.

We find the effects on the short-run equilibrium profits denoted by $\tilde{\pi} \equiv p\left(n\tilde{q}\right)\tilde{q} - c\left(\tilde{q}\right) - \tau e\left(\tilde{q}\right)$. Straightforward differentiations give[11]

$$\frac{\partial\tilde{\pi}}{\partial\tau} = \frac{\epsilon - \epsilon_3}{\bar{\epsilon} - \epsilon}\tilde{e} \lesseqgtr 0 \quad \Leftrightarrow \quad \epsilon \lesseqgtr \epsilon_3 \equiv \kappa + 1 - (n-1)\left(\mu - 1\right), \tag{17.7a}$$

$$\frac{\partial\tilde{\pi}}{\partial n} = \frac{n + n\kappa - \epsilon}{n\left(\bar{\epsilon} - \epsilon\right)}p'\tilde{q}^2 < 0, \tag{17.7b}$$

where the last inequality is due to the stability conditions: $\kappa > 0$ and $\epsilon < \bar{\epsilon} \equiv n + \kappa < n + n\kappa$. Therefore, we conclude that the profit would be over-shifted by an increase in the emission tax for the sufficiently convex demand with $\epsilon \in (\epsilon_3, \bar{\epsilon})$. Furthermore, from $\epsilon_3 - \epsilon_2 = \mu > 0$, we establish that the profit over-shifting is less likely than the price over-shifting. This is because as shown by Seade (1985), the price over-shifting is necessary for the profit over-shifting to occur.

The effects on total emission $\tilde{E} \equiv ne\left(\tilde{q}\right)$ are derived by simple differentiations:

$$\frac{\partial\tilde{E}}{\partial\tau} = \frac{n\left(e'\right)^2}{\pi_{qq}} < 0, \qquad \frac{\partial\tilde{E}}{\partial n} = \frac{\left(\mu - 1\right)\left(\epsilon - n\right) + \kappa}{\bar{\epsilon} - \epsilon}\tilde{e} \gtreqless 0 \quad \Leftrightarrow \quad \left(\mu - 1\right)\epsilon + \epsilon_2 \gtreqless 0. \tag{17.8}$$

As expected, an increase in the emission tax reduces total emission. However, this assertion is not always true in the long-run equilibrium.

The effects of entry should be intensively discussed. The term, $\left(\mu - 1\right)\left(\epsilon - n\right)$, in the middle expression of the numerator of Eq. (17.8) can be called the emission divisionalization effect. Dividing up a firm causes the individual output to shrink (i.e., business-stealing) or expand (i.e., business-augmenting), given that $\epsilon < n$ or $> n$. On the other hand, the emission change can be greater or smaller than the output change depending upon $\mu > 1$ or < 1.[12] When the emission is output-

[10]By inspection, we have $\bar{\epsilon} - \epsilon_2 = \mu n > 0$. Hence ϵ_2 is below the upper bound for ϵ.

[11]Note that ϵ_3 lies below the upper bound for ϵ, that is, $\bar{\epsilon} - \epsilon_3 = \mu\left(n-1\right) > 0$ holds except for the natural monopoly case.

[12]When $\mu = 1$, that is, the emission is proportional to the output, the effect will be vanished. In this case, the allocation of total output among the firms does not matter for the amount of emissions,

elastic (i.e., $\mu > 1$) and the business-stealing effect is present (i.e., $\epsilon < n$), the divisionalization effect is negative. Thus the entry of a firm reduces the individual output, and thus the emission will lower, to a lesser extent, the output reduction. Therefore, total emission may increase in the event of entry.

Now we establish the first proposition:

Proposition 17.1 *In the short-run equilibrium in which the number of firms is exogenously given, (1) an increase in the emission tax rate always reduces total emission.*

(2) If the emission is elastic with respect to output (i.e., $\mu > 1$) and the inverse demand function is sufficiently concave (i.e., $\epsilon < n - \kappa/(\mu - 1)$), entry of a new firm reduces total emission. Otherwise, the entry of a new firm raises total emission.

Proof See Appendix.

17.2.2 Long-Run Equilibrium

In the long-run equilibrium in which all the profits are driven to zero by free entry, the number of firms is endogenously determined as a function of the tax rate, that is, $n = n(\tau)$, and thus $q = q(\tau) \equiv \tilde{q}(\tau, n(\tau))$. Therefore, the effect of a change in the emission tax is found by totally differentiating the equilibrium conditions, (17.1) and (17.2). In Appendix, the long-run equilibrium comparative static results are derived as follows[13]:

$$\frac{dq}{d\tau} = \frac{p'qe}{Hn}(\epsilon - \epsilon_1) \lesseqgtr 0 \quad \Leftrightarrow \quad \epsilon \gtreqless \epsilon_1 \equiv -n(\mu - 1), \tag{17.9a}$$

$$\frac{dn}{d\tau} = \frac{p'e}{H}(\epsilon_3 - \epsilon) \lesseqgtr 0 \quad \Leftrightarrow \quad \epsilon \lesseqgtr \epsilon_3 \equiv \kappa + 1 - (n-1)(\mu - 1), \tag{17.9b}$$

where $H > 0$ is the stability condition in the long-run equilibrium.

It should be noted that if $\mu = 1$, then $\frac{dq}{d\tau} = \frac{p'qe}{Hn}\epsilon \lesseqgtr 0 \Leftrightarrow p'' \gtreqless 0$. In particular, when the demand is linear, there is no impact of environmental tax on the individual output. The intuition for this result is from the fact that a change in the emission tax behaves the same as in the output tax. The residual demand faced by a representative firm has a constant slope, and it is always tangent to the average overall cost curve. An increase in the tax shifts the average cost curve parallelly without changing its slope. Therefore, the tangency point moves upward, keeping the equilibrium output constant.

---

and thus the effect of entry on the total emission is almost same as that on the total output described in Eq. (17.5).

[13]Note that $\bar{\epsilon} > \epsilon_3 > \epsilon_2 > \epsilon_1$. To prove these inequalities, we calculate: $\epsilon_3 - \epsilon_1 = \kappa + \mu > 0$ and $\epsilon_2 - \epsilon_1 = \kappa > 0$. Combining these with $\epsilon_3 - \epsilon_2 = \mu > 0$, we have $\epsilon_3 = \epsilon_2 + \mu = \epsilon_1 + \kappa + \mu$.

The long-run equilibrium results are related with the short-run counterparts in the following way:

$$\frac{dq}{d\tau} = \frac{\partial \tilde{q}}{\partial \tau} + \frac{\partial \tilde{q}}{\partial n}\frac{dn}{d\tau}. \tag{17.10}$$

The first term is the direct effect of a tax hike and is negative. However, an increase in the emission tax may reduce the profitability per firms and so does the number of firms in the long run. It creates the negative business-stealing effect, and thus it expands the output per firm. This long-run or indirect effect may increase the firm's output. However, total output declines with an increase in emission tax:

$$\frac{dQ}{d\tau} = \frac{p'qe}{H}(\kappa + \mu) < 0. \tag{17.11}$$

We next check the price over-shifting in the long-run equilibrium. We calculate and evaluate the derivative at $\tau = 0$ yields the following relationship:

$$\frac{d(p - \tau e/q)}{d\tau} = \frac{\epsilon - \epsilon_1}{n + n\kappa - \epsilon}\frac{e}{q} \gtreqless 0 \quad \Leftrightarrow \quad \epsilon \gtreqless \epsilon_1. \tag{17.12}$$

Since the price is equal to average overall costs $\frac{c+\tau e}{q}$ owing to free entry, the net price is the same as the average production cost $\frac{c}{q}$. Scale economies imply that the average production cost falls with output. Thus, the direction of a net price change is opposite to that of an output change.

The effect of an increase in the emission tax on the total emission, $E \equiv ne(q)$, is given by

$$\frac{dE}{d\tau} = ne'\frac{dq}{d\tau} + e\frac{dn}{d\tau} = \frac{p'e^2}{H}\left[\kappa + 1 + (\epsilon + 1)(\mu - 1) + n(\mu - 1)^2\right]. \tag{17.13}$$

As in Lee (1999) and Requate (2007), suppose that $\mu = 1$. This implies that $\frac{dE}{d\tau} = \frac{p'e^2}{H}[\kappa + 1] < 0$, and thus an increase in the emission tax always raises the level of total pollution. To the contrary, suppose $\mu \neq 1$, which is the overlooked case in the previous literature. Then the following relationship is immediate:

$$\frac{dE}{d\tau} \lesseqgtr 0 \quad \Leftrightarrow \quad \epsilon \left\{ \begin{matrix} \gtreqless \\ \lesseqgtr \end{matrix} \right\} \epsilon_4 \equiv -1 - n(\mu - 1) - \frac{\kappa + 1}{\mu - 1} \text{ if } \mu \left\{ \begin{matrix} > \\ < \end{matrix} \right\} 1. \tag{17.14}$$

It can be shown that $\bar{\epsilon} - \epsilon_4 = \mu(n - n_0) \gtreqless 0 \Leftrightarrow n \gtreqless n_0 \equiv \frac{\kappa+1}{1-\mu}$. The following lemma is useful for the remaining analyses.[14]

Lemma 17.2 *(1) If $\mu > 1$, then $\epsilon_4 < \epsilon_1 < \epsilon_2 < \epsilon_3 < \bar{\epsilon}$, where ϵ_4 and ϵ_1 are both negative. (2) If $\mu < 1$, then (a) $0 < \epsilon_1 < \epsilon_2 < \epsilon_3 < \bar{\epsilon} < \epsilon_4$ for $n < n_0$; (b) $0 < \epsilon_1 < \epsilon_2 < \epsilon_3 < \epsilon_4 < \bar{\epsilon}$ for $n > n_0$.*

We are interested in identifying under what circumstances total emission increases with the emission tax. We use Lemma 17.2 to explore the sign patterns in (17.14) in Appendix. Thus, the following result is obtained:

Proposition 17.3 *Consider the long-run equilibrium in a free-entry Cournot oligopoly. An increase in the emission tax rate raises total emission in the following two types of industry: (1) For an industry with the elastic emission (i.e., $\mu > 1$ and thus $\epsilon_4 < 0$), the market demand has concavity with $\epsilon \in (-\infty, \epsilon_4)$. (2) Conversely, for an industry with the inelastic emission (i.e., $\mu < 1$ and thus $\epsilon_4 > 0$), the demand has convexity with $\epsilon \in (\epsilon_4, \bar{\epsilon})$, and the equilibrium market structure is sufficiently competitive (i.e., $n > n_0$).*

17.3 Optimal Environmental Taxation

This section derives the optimal tax rate under the short-run and the long-run equilibria. Let $D(E)$ denote the environmental damage to the economy. It is assumed to satisfy $D' > 0$ and $D'' \geq 0$. The social welfare is then defined as

$$W = \int_0^{nq} p(z)\,dz - nc(q) - D(ne(q)). \tag{17.15}$$

The short-run welfare function, $\widetilde{W}$, is defined as W evaluated at $q = \tilde{q}(n, \tau)$. The welfare change expression is then given by

$$dW = n\left(p - c' - D'e'\right)dq + \left(pq - c - D'e\right)dn. \tag{17.16}$$

The first-best solution is obtained by setting the coefficients of both dq and dn to zero. These two equations yield $p = c' + D'e'$ and $p = (c + D'e)/q$, and thus, the first-best solution implies that $\mu = \frac{c}{D'e}(1 - \lambda) + 1 > 1$.[15] The first-best solution can be achieved only in the industry with output-elastic emissions.

[14] If $\mu > 1$, then n_0 becomes negative and thus $\bar{\epsilon} > \epsilon_4$ holds always. It is also shown that $\epsilon_4 - \epsilon_1 = (\kappa + \mu)/(1 - \mu)$, $\epsilon_4 - \epsilon_2 = \mu(\kappa + 1)/(1 - \mu)$, and $\epsilon_4 - \epsilon_3 = \mu(\kappa + \mu)/(1 - \mu)$. Using the relationship in Footnote 13, we obtain the lemma.

[15] Upon equating the right-hand side of the two conditions, we have $c' + D'e' = \frac{c+D'e}{q}$ or, equivalently, $D'e(qe'/e - 1) = c(1 - qc'/c)$. Then, using $\mu \equiv qe'/e$ and $\lambda \equiv qc'/c$ yields the result.

Suppose that the regulator sets the emission tax rate so as to maximize (17.15) but that he cannot control the firms' behavior directly. In the short-run equilibrium, n is exogenously given and thus $dn = 0$. Therefore, the first-order condition for short-run welfare maximization is

$$\frac{\partial \widetilde{W}}{\partial \tau} = n\left(-p'\tilde{q} + \left(\tau - D'\right)e'\right)\frac{\partial \tilde{q}}{\partial \tau} = 0, \tag{17.17}$$

where $p - c' = -p'\tilde{q} + \tau e'$ was substituted from Eq. (17.1). Solving this for the tax rate, we get

$$\tilde{\tau} - D' = \frac{p'\tilde{q}}{e'} < 0. \tag{17.18}$$

The short-run optimal taxation falls short of the marginal environmental damage. The intuition for this result is straightforward. Oligopoly distortion induces firms to produce less, and thus the regulator has an incentive to subsidize them. Therefore, the regulator undercuts the tax rate from the traditional Pigouvian rule.

In the long-run equilibrium, n is endogenously determined and is affected by the tax rate. Therefore the first-order condition for long-run welfare maximization is

$$\frac{dW}{d\tau} = \left(\tau - D'\right)\frac{dE}{d\tau} - p'nq\frac{dq}{d\tau} = 0, \tag{17.19}$$

where $pq - c = \tau e$ and $p - c' = -p'q + \tau e'$ from the equilibrium conditions, (17.1) and (17.2), were substituted. Solving the above condition gives

$$\tau - D' = np'q\frac{dq}{d\tau}/\frac{dE}{d\tau} = \frac{p'q^2}{e}\psi; \tag{17.20a}$$

$$\psi \equiv \frac{n(\mu - 1) + \epsilon}{\kappa + 1 + (\epsilon + 1)(\mu - 1) + n(\mu - 1)^2}. \tag{17.20b}$$

If $\psi < 0$, the optimal emission tax exceeds the marginal environmental damage. First, we consider a special case of $\mu = 1$. Then $\psi = \frac{\epsilon}{1+\kappa}$. Since $\kappa > 0$, if the demand is concave ($\epsilon < 0$), the optimal emission tax exceeds the marginal environmental damage. Otherwise, the optimal emission tax falls short of the marginal environmental damage. This is a well-known result (see Lee 1999 and Requate 2007).

We extend the analyses by Lee (1999) and Requate (2007) into the more general framework where μ can be greater or smaller than unity. The condition for the optimal rate to exceed the marginal environmental damage is, therefore

$$\frac{dq}{d\tau}\cdot\frac{dE}{d\tau} = \frac{(p')^2 qe^3}{H^2 n}(\mu - 1)(\epsilon - \epsilon_1)(\epsilon - \epsilon_4) < 0. \tag{17.21}$$

This condition implies that $(i)\epsilon_4 < \epsilon < \epsilon_1$ for $\mu > 1$ and, conversely, $(ii)\epsilon > \epsilon_4$ or $\epsilon < \epsilon_1$ for $\mu < 1$. As for Case (ii), when $n < n_0$ holds, Lemma 17.2 excludes the condition of $\epsilon > \epsilon_4$.

In summary, our first main result is as follows:

Proposition 17.4 *In the long-run equilibrium in a free-entry Cournot oligopoly, the optimal emission tax rate exceeds the marginal environmental damage in the following three cases: (1) For an industry with elastic emission (i.e., $\mu > 1$ and thus $\epsilon_4 < \epsilon_1 < 0$), the market demand must have concavity with $\epsilon \in (\epsilon_4, \epsilon_1)$. (2) Conversely, for an industry with inelastic emission (i.e., $\mu < 1$ and thus $\epsilon_4 > \epsilon_1 > 0$), (a) the demand must have concavity or convexity with $\epsilon \in (-\infty, \epsilon_1)$, and the equilibrium market structure must be sufficiently concentrated (i.e., $n < n_0$); or (b) the demand must not have convexity with $\epsilon \in (\epsilon_1, \epsilon_4)$ and the equilibrium market structure must be sufficiently competitive (i.e., $n > n_0$).*

17.4 Excess Entry Theorem Under the Pigouvian Tax Rule

The previous section derives the optimal pollution tax rate and shows under what conditions the optimal rate exceeds the marginal environmental damage. To find the sign of the deviation term, $\tau - D'$, we need to investigate the sign of ψ, which is defined as in Eq. (17.20b). It contains the terms ϵ, μ, κ, and n. However, exact information on the first three terms can hardly be obtained. Such informational requirements may discourage the regulator to implement the right but complicated policy rule. Recently, Requate (2007) proposed that, in Cournot models with free entry, it is a good strategy to stick to the traditional Pigouvian tax rule and encourage more competition through tough antitrust laws. This section investigates the validity of his proposal, that is, whether the joint use of the Pigouvian rule and competition policy is subject to the informational problem.

The analysis of this section relies on the seminal contributions by Mankiw and Whinston (1986) and Suzumura and Kiyono (1987). In a symmetric Cournot oligopoly, they established that the number of firms at a long-run free-entry equilibrium can be larger than the socially optimal number of firms. This is the so-called "excess entry theorem". More specifically, reducing the number of firms from the free-entry equilibrium level leads to a welfare gain if and only if the business-stealing effect is present. In what follows, we examine the validity of the theorem under the traditional Pigouvian tax rule.

The sequence of the game is as follows. First, the antitrust authority selects the number of firms in the industry. Second, the firms make an entry decision. Third, the environmental regulator sets the emission tax equal to the marginal damage. Lastly, the firms decide output in a Cournot manner. Following Mankiw and Whinston (1986), we assume that neither regulator can control firms' behavior directly after their entry.

In our framework, the Pigouvian tax rate is given by the marginal damage:

$$\tau = D'\left(ne\left(q\right)\right) \equiv \tau\left(n\right). \tag{17.22}$$

Under this rule, the marginal production costs become $c'\left(q\right) + D'\left(ne\left(q\right)\right)e'\left(q\right)$, which can be interpreted as the marginal social costs of individual production. Then the relative slope of these social marginal costs is modified into

$$\kappa_s \equiv 1 - \frac{c'' + D'e'' + D''n\left(e'\right)^2}{p'} > 0,$$

which constitutes one of the short-run stability conditions under the Pigouvian tax rule. The additional condition for the short-run stability is then expressed as $\epsilon < n + \kappa_s \equiv \bar{\epsilon}_s$.

We now write the short-run equilibrium condition as

$$\pi_q|_{\tau=\tau(n)} = p'\left(nq\right)q + p\left(nq\right) - c'\left(q\right) - D'\left(ne\left(q\right)\right)e'\left(q\right) = 0. \tag{17.23}$$

Assuming that $D'' = 0$ is identical to the analysis in which the tax rate is exogenously given, it is, therefore, assumed that this is not the case. Totally differentiating Eq. (17.23) to obtain the comparative statics result yields

$$\frac{dq}{dn}|_{\tau=\tau(n)} = \frac{\epsilon - n - \delta/\mu}{\bar{\epsilon}_s - \epsilon}\frac{q}{n} \lesseqqgtr 0 \quad \Leftrightarrow \quad \epsilon \lesseqqgtr n + \delta/\mu, \tag{17.24}$$

where $\delta \equiv -\frac{D''n(e')^2}{p'} > 0$. If the elasticity of the slope of demand, ϵ, lies below $n + \delta/\mu$, then the individual output falls because of entry of a new firm, that is, the business-stealing effect prevails. Compared to the result in Eq. (17.4), we see that the cutoff value in Eq. (17.24) has the extra term, $\delta/\mu > 0$. Therefore, we can say that for a wider range of the demand parameter ϵ, the Pigouvian tax rule generates the business-stealing effect. In summary, we claim the following:

Lemma 17.5 *The business-stealing effect is more likely to be observed under the traditional Pigouvian tax rule than under the exogenously given tax rate.*

We next evaluate the welfare effect of changing the number of firms at the free-entry, zero-profit equilibrium. From Eqs. (17.16), (17.1), and (17.2), we calculate

$$\frac{dW}{dn} = n\left(-p'q + e'\left(\tau - D'\right)\right)\frac{dq}{dn} + e\left(\tau - D'\right).$$

Evaluating the above expression at the Pigouvian tax rate (17.22) , we have the following relationship:

$$\frac{dW}{dn}|_{\tau=\tau(n)} = \left(-p'nq\right)\frac{dq}{dn}|_{\tau=\tau(n)}. \tag{17.25}$$

Consequently, we establish our second main result:

Proposition 17.6 *The excess entry theorem is more likely to hold under the traditional Pigouvian tax rule than under the exogenously given tax rate.*

17.5 Concluding Remarks

In this paper, we identified the effects of pollution taxation and a firm's entry in a Cournot oligopoly model. Introducing free entry and a general functional form relating output to pollution emission, we showed that the optimal emission tax rate exceeds or falls short of the marginal environmental damage to the society, depending upon the curvature of the inverse demand as well as the output elasticity of pollution emission. To implement such a complex policy rule, the regulator faces tremendous informational requirements. Therefore, as suggested by Requate (2007), it is a good strategy to stick to the traditional Pigouvian tax rule: the emission tax rate is equal to the marginal damage.

In light of informational feasibility, our policy recommendation is a joint use of the Pigouvian rule with an antitrust or competition policy that reduces the number of firms from the free-entry equilibrium level. To support this, we showed that the business-stealing effect is more likely to be observed under the Pigouvian rule than under the exogenously given tax rate. Judging whether the business-stealing effect prevails does not require much information. Hence, we established that the Pigouvian rule advocates the validity of the excess entry theorem.

Appendix

A.1 Comparative Statics

Totally differentiating the system described by Eqs. (17.1) and (17.2) yields

$$\pi_{qq}dq + \pi_{qn}dn + \pi_{q\tau}d\tau = 0, \qquad \pi_q dq + \pi_n dn + \pi_\tau d\tau = 0,$$

where $\pi_{qq} \equiv \partial\pi_q/\partial q$, $\pi_{qn} \equiv \partial\pi_q/\partial n$, $\pi_{q\tau} \equiv \partial\pi_q/\partial\tau$, etc. and these partial derivatives are thus:

$$\pi_q = p'nq + p - c' - \tau e' = p'(n-1)q, \qquad \pi_n = p'q^2, \qquad \pi_\tau = -e,$$
$$\pi_{qq} = p''nq + (1+n)p' - c'' - \tau e'', \qquad \pi_{qn} = q\left(p''q + p'\right), \qquad \pi_{q\tau} = -e'.$$

The short-run comparative static results are obtained by the first equation alone. Writing it as $\pi_{qq}dq = -\pi_{qn}dn - \pi_{q\tau}d\tau$ yields the following results: $\frac{\partial \tilde{q}}{\partial\tau} = \frac{e'}{\pi_{qq}} < 0$

and $\frac{\partial \tilde{q}}{\partial n} = -\frac{q(p''q+p')}{\pi_{qq}}$. From $\epsilon \equiv -Qp''/p'$ and $\kappa \equiv 1 - \frac{c''+\tau e''}{p'}$, it follows that $\pi_{qq} = (-p')(\epsilon - n - \kappa)$ and $p''q + p' = p'(1 - \epsilon/n)$, and thus upon substitution, we obtain Eq. (17.4).

The comparative statics results for the long-run equilibrium are found by writing the above system as $\begin{bmatrix} \pi_{qq} & \pi_{qn} \\ \pi_q & \pi_n \end{bmatrix} \begin{bmatrix} dq/d\tau \\ dn/d\tau \end{bmatrix} = \begin{bmatrix} -\pi_{q\tau} \\ -\pi_\tau \end{bmatrix}$, where $H \equiv \begin{vmatrix} \pi_{qq} & \pi_{qn} \\ \pi_q & \pi_n \end{vmatrix} > 0$ is the stability condition in the long-run equilibrium. Thus, upon substitution, we have $H = p'q^2\left(\pi_{qq} - (n-1)(p''q + p')\right)$. From $\pi_{qq} = (-p')(\epsilon - n - \kappa)$ and $p''q + p' = p'(1 - \epsilon/n)$, we obtain the following relationship:

$$H = \frac{(p'q)^2}{n}(n + n\kappa - \epsilon) > 0 \quad \Leftrightarrow \quad \epsilon < n + n\kappa.$$

Hence, from $\kappa > 0$ and $\bar{\epsilon} \equiv n + \kappa < n + n\kappa$, it follows that the short-run stability implies the long-run stability.

We now obtain the long-run comparative static results: $\frac{dq}{d\tau} = \frac{1}{H}\begin{vmatrix} -\pi_{q\tau} & \pi_{qn} \\ -\pi_\tau & \pi_n \end{vmatrix} = \frac{1}{H}\left(-\pi_{q\tau}\pi_n + \pi_{qn}\pi_\tau\right) = \frac{1}{H}q\left(qe'p' - e\left(p''q + p'\right)\right)$ and $\frac{dn}{d\tau} = \frac{1}{H}\begin{vmatrix} \pi_{qq} & -\pi_{q\tau} \\ \pi_q & -\pi_\tau \end{vmatrix} = \frac{1}{H}\left(-\pi_{qq}\pi_\tau + \pi_{q\tau}\pi_q\right) = \frac{1}{H}(\pi_{qq}e - e'p'(n-1)q)$. Substituting $qe' = \mu e$, $\pi_{qq} = (-p')(\epsilon - n - \kappa)$, and $p''q + p' = p'(1 - \epsilon/n)$ into these results yields the ones in Eq. (17.9).

A.2 *Proof of Proposition 17.1*

When $\mu = 1$, we have $\frac{\partial \tilde{E}}{\partial n} = \frac{\kappa}{\bar{\epsilon}-\epsilon}\tilde{e} > 0$ from $\kappa > 0$ and $\bar{\epsilon} > \epsilon$. However, in the case of $\mu > 1$, we have the sign patterns of $\frac{\partial \tilde{E}}{\partial n} \gtreqless 0 \Leftrightarrow \epsilon \gtreqless -\frac{\epsilon_2}{\mu-1}$. If the case of $\mu < 1$, it follows that $\frac{\partial \tilde{E}}{\partial n} \gtreqless 0 \Leftrightarrow \epsilon \lesseqgtr -\frac{\epsilon_2}{\mu-1}$. Note that $\bar{\epsilon} - (-\frac{\epsilon_2}{\mu-1}) = \frac{\kappa\mu}{\mu-1} \gtrless 0 \Leftrightarrow \mu \gtrless 1$. If $\mu > 1$, then $\bar{\epsilon} > -\frac{\epsilon_2}{\mu-1}$ is obtained. Therefore, if $\epsilon < -\frac{\epsilon_2}{\mu-1}$, that is, the demand is sufficiently concave, then we observe $\frac{\partial \tilde{E}}{\partial n} < 0$, that is, the entry of a firm reduces the pollution level. On the other hand, if $\mu < 1$, then $\bar{\epsilon} < -\frac{\epsilon_2}{\mu-1}$ holds and thus the stability condition rules out the case of $\frac{\partial \tilde{E}}{\partial n} < 0$, that is, the entry always increases the pollution level.

A.3 *Proof of Proposition 17.3*

First, Suppose that $\mu > 1$. Then we have $\bar{\epsilon} > \epsilon_4$. Therefore, we have the following sign pattern: $\frac{dE}{d\tau} < 0$ for $\epsilon \in (\epsilon_4, \bar{\epsilon})$ and $\frac{dE}{d\tau} > 0$ for $\epsilon \in (-\infty, \epsilon_4)$. To the contrary, suppose that $\mu < 1$. In the case of $n < n_0$, ϵ_4 exceeds $\bar{\epsilon}$, and thus the stability condition implies $\frac{dE}{d\tau} < 0$. On the other hand, in the case of $n > n_0$, ϵ_4 falls short of $\bar{\epsilon}$. Therefore, the sign pattern is reversed from that in the case of $\mu > 1$: $\frac{dE}{d\tau} > 0$ for $\epsilon \in (\epsilon_4, \bar{\epsilon})$ and $\frac{dE}{d\tau} < 0$ for $\epsilon \in (-\infty, \epsilon_4)$.

Acknowledgements I would like to thank Editage (www.editage.jp) for English language editing.

References

Barnett, A. 1980. The Pigouvian tax rule under monopoly. *American Economic Review* 70: 1037–1041.

Buchanan, J.M. 1969. External diseconomies, corrective taxes, and market structure. *American Economic Review* 59: 174–177.

Bulow, J.I., J.D. Geanakoplos, and P.D. Klemperer. 1985. Multimarket oligopoly: Strategic substitutes and complements. *Journal of Political Economy* 93: 488–511.

Dixit, A. 1986. Comparative statics for oligopoly. *International Economic Review* 27: 107–122.

Katsoulacos, Y., and A.P. Xepapadeas. 1995. Pigouvian taxes for under oligopoly. *Scandinavian Journal of Economics* 97: 411–420.

Lee, S.-H. 1999. Optimal taxation for polluting oligopolists with endogenous market structure. *Journal of Regulatory Economics* 15: 293–308.

Mankiw, N.G., and M.D. Whinston. 1986. Free entry and social inefficiency. *RAND Journal of Economics* 17: 48–58.

Matsumoto, S., and H. Sugeta. 2007. Antitrust policy and environmental protection. *Economics Bulletin* 17: 1–10.

Misiolek, W. 1988. Pollution control through price incentives: The role of rent seeking costs in monopoly markets. *Journal of Environmental Economics and Management* 15: 1–8.

Requate, T. 2007. Environmental policy under imperfect competition. In *The International Yearbook of Environmental and Resource Economics 2006/2007*, ed. T. Tietenberg, and H. Folmer. Northampton: Edward Elgar.

Seade, J. 1980. On the effects of entry. *Econometrica* 48: 479–489.

Seade, J. 1985. Profitable cost increases and the shifting of taxation: Equilibrium responses of markets in oligopoly. The Warwick economics research paper series (TWERPS) No. 260, University of Warwick, Department of Economics.

Simpson, D. 1995. Optimal pollution taxation in a Cournot duopoly. *Environmental and Resource Economics* 6: 359–369.

Suzumura, K., and K. Kiyono. 1987. Entry barriers and economic welfare. *Review of Economic Studies* 54: 157–167.

von Weizsäcker, C.C. 1980. A welfare analysis of barriers to entry. *Bell Journal of Economics* 11: 399–420.

Chapter 18
Bilateral Cooperation for Transboundary Pollution Problems

Toshiyuki Fujita

18.1 Introduction

Global or transboundary pollution problems caused by specific pollutants such as carbon dioxide, nitrogen oxides, sulfur oxides, and chlorofluorocarbon started to receive significant public attention almost 30 years ago. We have to abate the emission of pollutants that cause externalities, at the cost of restricting economic growth to some extent. The optimal emission or abatement level is determined theoretically, taking into account the balance of costs and benefits. Basically, the optimal level can be realized by implementing various government policies that target domestic problems.

Because of the public good nature of pollution abatement by an individual country, international cooperation is essential for solving global environmental issues, and a number of international conferences and negotiations are being held to achieve this goal. A well-enforced international environmental agreement would ensure efficient abatement by all participating countries. However, a globally efficient international environmental agreement to tackle some global problems such as climate change is yet to be concluded.

In the Paris Agreement, which was concluded in 2015 and made effective in 2016, all countries have agreed to work on greenhouse gas emission abatement. The use of financial and technological aid or the market mechanism is also specified. However, each country's abatement target, which is called "Intended Nationally Determined Contribution (INDC)," is being set voluntarily, and there is no rule on compliance. Developed countries' INDCs submitted in 2015 are generally ambitious, but developing countries are generally reluctant to commit to the

T. Fujita (✉)
Kyushu University, Fukuoka, Japan
e-mail: tfujita@econ.kyushu-u.ac.jp

T. Naito et al. (eds.), *Applied Approaches to Societal Institutions and Economics*, New Frontiers in Regional Science: Asian Perspectives 18,
DOI 10.1007/978-981-10-5663-5_18

abatement.[1] As a result, it seems that developing countries' plans are insufficient to help realize the world's long-run target of limiting the temperature rise to 2.0 degrees from the preindustrial level. As can be seen from this example, the differences in the situations under which the countries are placed are considered to be a significant factor preventing a consensus in actual negotiations about transboundary environmental problems.

In this study, we model bilateral cooperation to solve pollution problems between two asymmetric countries as a game played by a developed country (country N) and a developing country (country S). We first introduce the outline of the model proposed by Hoel (1991) in a seminal paper, which provides a framework of noncooperative and cooperative games of pollution abatement between two countries. He shows a paradoxical outcome that an ex ante unilateral action by one country before international negotiations can result in decreasing ex post-total welfare of the two countries. In this study, we apply the framework of the noncooperative game in Hoel (1991), considering the financial and technological aid from country N to country S as international cooperation and analyze the effect of cooperation by comparing the Nash equilibria.

A number of game theoretic studies consider international environmental agreements among many countries concerning the global environmental issues (Carraro and Siniscalco 1993; Barrett 1994; Hoel and Schneider 1997; Barrett 2001; Lange and Vogt 2003; Diamantoudi and Sartzetakis 2006). Certain studies also focus on the effect of international cooperation schemes, such as Breton et al. (2006) and Matsueda et al. (2006, 2007).

Clean Development Mechanism (hereafter, CDM) is a flexibility mechanism specified in the Kyoto Protocol for mitigating climate change. Any country in Annex I Parties can invest in emission abatement projects called CDM projects in any country in non-Annex I Parties as an alternative to abating emissions domestically, and the investing country can obtain certain emission permits by realizing the abatement in non-Annex I countries.[2]

A similar scheme is also specified in the Paris Agreement, which says "Parties recognize that some Parties choose to pursue voluntary cooperation in the implementation of their nationally determined contributions..." (Article 6-1), and "the use of internationally transferred mitigation outcomes to achieve nationally determined contributions under this Agreement shall be voluntary and authorized by participating Parties" (Article 6-3).[3] Thus, the scheme specified in the Paris Agreement can be designed more freely than CDM schemes in a bilateral agreement.

[1]For example, China has submitted INDCs stating they will "achieve the peaking of carbon dioxide emissions around 2030 and lower carbon dioxide emissions per unit of GDP by 60% to 65% from the 2005 level."

[2]Annex I Parties consists of developed countries and countries with economies in transition. Most countries in Annex I Parties had emissions reduction targets in the Kyoto Protocol.

[3]See United Nations (2015, p. 7).

In what follows, we first introduce the model of Hoel (1991) as a reference model. Then, we incorporate international cooperation into the base model and examine the effects on the model results. We show that both types of cooperation can increase the total abatement at the equilibrium, and in the technological aid case, both countries abate more than in the base case under certain conditions. These results imply the effectiveness of bilateral cooperative relationships. Finally, we present some conclusive remarks.

18.2 The Basic Model

We introduce the basic model of noncooperative games concerning pollutant abatement, following Hoel (1991).

Players of the game are two countries, a developed country and a developing country, termed as countries N and S, respectively. We focus on a specific pollutant that causes damage to society. Each country i's ($i = N, S$) abatement of pollutant emissions is denoted by $X_i(\geq 0)$. The payoff to country i is expressed as

$$\pi_i = B_i(X_N + X_S) - C_i(X_i), \tag{18.1}$$

where B_i is the benefit function which depends on the total abatement, and C_i is the cost function which depends on the abatement of country i. We assume that $B'_N > B'_S > 0, B''_i < 0, C'_i > 0$, and $C''_i > 0 (i = N, S)$. Differentiating (18.1) with respect to X_i leads to the following first-order conditions for the optimal decisions:

$$\frac{\partial \pi_i}{\partial X_i} = B'_i(X_N + X_S) - C'_i(X_i) = 0 \ (i = N, S). \tag{18.2}$$

If we regard the optimal response X_i^* which satisfies (18.2) as a function of $X_j (j \neq i)$ and denote it by $X_i^* = R_i(X_j)$, we obtain

$$\frac{dR_i(X_j)}{dX_j} = \frac{B''_i}{C''_i - B''_i} \in (-1, 0) \tag{18.3}$$

by differentiating (18.2) with respect to X_j.

A set of strategies (X_N^*, X_S^*) which satisfies $R_N(X_S^*) = X_N^*$ and $R_S(X_N^*) = X_S^*$ is the Nash equilibrium of the game. Throughout this study, we assume that there exists a unique equilibrium as an interior solution.

From (18.3) we can see that the decision makings of the two countries are strategic substitutes, that is, if one country unilaterally increases its abatement, the other country will decrease its abatement as a response. A unilateral policy of country i which increases above the equilibrium level would be followed by the decrease of the other country's abatement, and the effect would be canceled.

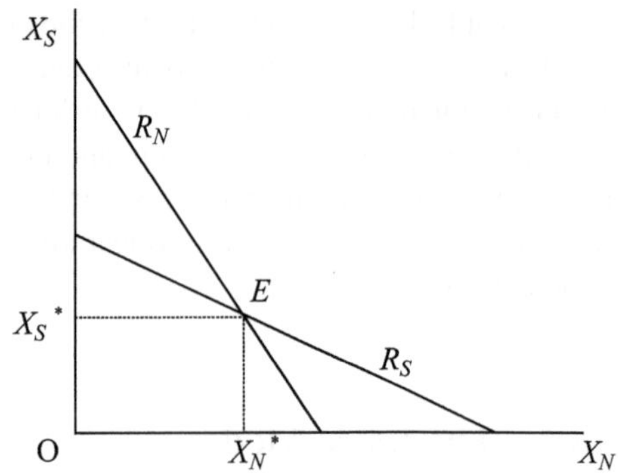

Fig. 18.1 Nash equilibrium in the base case

However, since both of the absolute values of $\frac{dR_N}{dX_S}$ and $\frac{dR_S}{dX_N}$ are smaller than 1, the total abatement will increase by the unilateral action. Figure 18.1 illustrates the optimal response functions, and their intersection (point E) is the Nash equilibrium.

The condition to be satisfied by the set of Pareto efficient abatement combinations (X_N, X_S) is

$$(B'_N - C'_N)(B'_S - C'_S) = B'_N B'_S, \tag{18.4}$$

which is obtained as a solution of maximization problem: $\max_{X_N, X_S} \pi_N$ s.t. $\pi_S \geq \overline{\pi}_S$, where $\overline{\pi}_S$ is a specific payoff level. It is clear that the equilibrium (X_N^*, X_S^*) does not satisfy (18.4) since $B'_N - C'_N = B'_S - C'_S = 0$. Increases in both X_N and X_S from the equilibrium are necessary for Pareto improvement.

18.3 The Effects of Bilateral Cooperation

18.3.1 Financial Aid

In the case of financial aid, country N supports a portion of the abatement cost of country S. This aid can be regarded as the side payment given to country S on the condition that it abates pollution. Let us assume that the support ratio is denoted by $\alpha \in [0, 1]$. The payoff functions become

$$\pi_N^F = B_N(X_N + X_S) - C_N(X_N) - \alpha C_S(X_S),$$
$$\pi_S^F = B_S(X_N + X_S) - (1 - \alpha) C_S(X_S).$$

The first-order conditions for the countries' optimal decisions are

$$\frac{\partial \pi_N^F}{\partial X_N} = B_N'(X_N + X_S) - C_N'(X_N) = 0, \tag{18.5}$$

$$\frac{\partial \pi_S^F}{\partial X_S} = B_S'(X_N + X_S) - (1-\alpha)C_S'(X_S) = 0. \tag{18.6}$$

Let $(X_N^F(\alpha), X_S^F(\alpha))$ denote the Nash equilibrium in the financial aid case which satisfies (18.5) and (18.6). We obtain the following proposition by comparative statics.

Proposition 18.1 *In the financial aid case, as the support ratio* α *increases, the abatement of country S in equilibrium increases, whereas that of country N decreases. The total abatement of two countries increases.*

Proof By differentiating (18.5) and (18.6) with respect to α, we have $B_N''(X_N'+X_S') - C_N''X_N' = 0$ and $B_S''(X_N'+X_S') + C_S' - (1-\alpha)C_S''X_S' = 0$, where $X_i' \equiv \frac{dX_i^F(\alpha)}{d\alpha} (i = N, S)$. Solving these equations for X_N' and X_S', we obtain $X_S' = C_S'\left((1-\alpha)C_S'' - \frac{B_S''C_N''}{C_N''-B_N''}\right) > 0$ and $X_N' = \frac{B_N''X_S'}{C_N''-B_N''} < 0$. As for the total abatement $X^F \equiv X_N^F + X_S^F$, we have $\frac{dX}{d\alpha} = X_N' + X_S' = \frac{C_N''X_S'}{C_N''-B_N''} > 0$.

Let R_i^α be the optimal response function of country i in the financial aid case with the support ratio α. Since (18.5) coincides with (18.2), R_N^α also coincides with R_N in the base case, and it is not affected by the value of α. On the other hand, R_S^α takes a larger value than R_S for a given value of X_N. See Fig. 18.2 for the graphical depiction of the equilibrium movement. The equilibrium moves to point E', and the increase in X_S would normally be canceled by the decrease in X_N. However, the total abatement $X_N^F(\alpha) + X_S^F(\alpha)$ is larger than in the base case, since the slope of R_N is larger than -1.

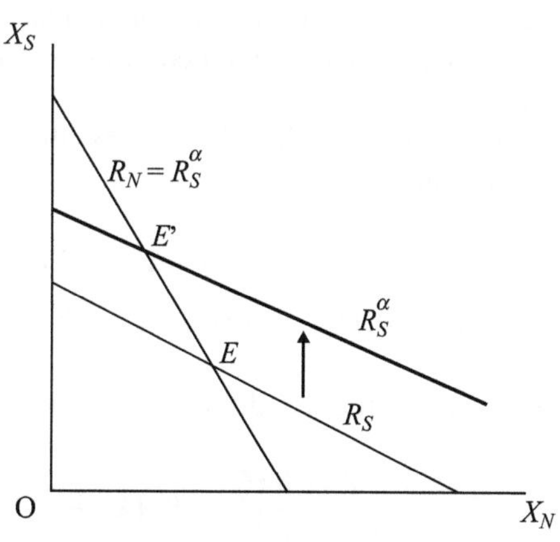

Fig. 18.2 Nash equilibrium in the financial aid case

Let us check the welfare effects of the financial aid.

Proposition 18.2 *Introduction of financial aid increases the total payoff to the two countries.*

Proof By differentiating π_N^F and π_S^F with respect to α and using (18.5) and (18.6), we have $\frac{d\pi_N^F}{d\alpha} = C_N'X_S' - C_S - \alpha C_S'X_S'$ and $\frac{d\pi_S^F}{d\alpha} = (1-\alpha)C_S'X_N' + C_S$. Although the signs of these derivatives are not certain, it follows that $\left.\frac{d(\pi_N^F+\pi_S^F)}{d\alpha}\right|_{\alpha=0} = (C_N' - C_S')X_S' + C_S'(X_S' + X_N') > 0$.

The proof of Proposition 18.2 is based on the relationship $C_N' > C_S'$ at the equilibrium in the base case. It is also noted that Proposition 18.2 usually does not hold when $C_N' < C_S'$, that is, the aid from the developing country to the developed country is not effective.

18.3.2 Technological Aid

Next, we consider a system of technological aid from the developed country to the developing country which is similar to CDM. First we assume that country N is committed to an abatement level and regard it as country N's strategy. We also assume that the extent to which country N undertakes the abatement of country S is fixed and denote it by the ratio β. This means that if country S decides to set its abatement at X_S, country N should offer the technology to country S to realize the abatement βX_S at the cost $C(\beta X_S)$. We assume that C is strictly increasing and convex and also assume $C < C_S$ and $C' < C_S'$. The rest, $(1-\beta)X_S$, is abated by country S. Strategies of countries are assumed to be determined simultaneously.

The abatement activities by country N are assumed to create $\gamma(X_S - X_S^*)$ of the credit for pollution emissions. Here X_S^* is the abatement of country S in the equilibrium of the base case ($= R_S(X_N^*)$), and γ is the ratio by which an additional abatement is certified for the credit. Country N is awarded the credit for creating the incentive for country S to decide X_S that is higher than the business-as-usual level. Since country N is committed to its abatement X_N, it must abate $X_N - \gamma(X_S - X_S^*)$ domestically.

From the preceding discussions, the payoff functions in the technological aid case become

$$\pi_N^T = B_N(X_N - \gamma(X_S - X_S^*) + X_S) - C_N(X_N - \gamma(X_S - X_S^*)) - C(\beta X_S),$$
$$\pi_S^T = B_S(X_N - \gamma(X_S - X_S^*) + X_S) - C_S((1-\beta)X_S),$$

and the first-order conditions for the countries' optimal decisions are

$$\frac{\partial \pi_N^T}{\partial X_N} = B_N'(X_N - \gamma(X_S - X_S^*) + X_S)$$

$$-C_N'(X_N - \gamma(X_S - X_S^*)) = 0, \tag{18.7}$$

$$\frac{\partial \pi_S^T}{\partial X_S} = (1-\gamma)B_S'(X_N - \gamma(X_S - X_S^*) + X_S)$$
$$-(1-\beta)C_S'((1-\beta)X_S) = 0. \tag{18.8}$$

If we regard the Nash equilibrium X_N^T and X_S^T which satisfy (18.7) and (18.8) as functions of β and γ, and denote them by $X_i^T(\beta,\gamma)(i = N, S)$, we have following results.

Proposition 18.3 *In the technological aid case, as the support ratio β increases, the abatement of country S in equilibrium always increases, and that of country N increases if the credit certification ratio γ is sufficiently large. Total abatement always increases.*

Proof By differentiating (18.7) with respect to β, we have $B_N''(X_{N\beta} + (1-\gamma)X_{S\beta}) - C_N''(X_{N\beta} - \gamma X_{S\beta}) = 0$, where $X_{i\beta} \equiv \frac{\partial X_i^T(\beta,\gamma)}{\partial \beta}(i = N, S)$. Solving this for $X_{N\beta}$, we have

$$X_{N\beta} = \left(\gamma + \frac{B_N''}{C_N'' - B_N''}\right) X_{S\beta}. \tag{18.9}$$

Next, by differentiating (18.8) with respect to β, we have $(1-\gamma)B_S''(X_{N\beta} + (1-\gamma)X_{S\beta}) + C_S' - (1-\beta)C_S''(-X_S + (1-\beta)X_{S\beta}) = 0$. Solving this for $X_{S\beta}$ using (18.9), we have

$$X_{S\beta} = \left\{(1-\beta)^2 C_S'' - (1-\gamma)\frac{B_S'' C_N''}{C_N'' - B_N''}\right\}^{-1} (C_S' + (1-\beta)C_S'' X_S) > 0. \tag{18.10}$$

From (18.9) and (18.10), $X_{N\beta}$ and $X_{S\beta}$ are both positive if the value of γ is sufficiently large such that it satisfies:

$$\gamma + \frac{B_N''}{C_N'' - B_N''} > 0. \tag{18.11}$$

The total abatement is defined as $X^T \equiv X_N^T - \gamma(X_S^T - X_S^*) + X_S^T$, and a simple calculation leads to $\frac{\partial X^T}{\partial \beta} = \frac{C_N'' X_{S\beta}}{C_N'' - B_N''} > 0$.

Figure 18.3 illustrates how this phenomenon occurs. If (18.11) holds, the optimal response of country N is an upward sloping curve. The equilibrium moves from E to E'' following the increase of β. The parameter β denotes the ratio of technological aid, so its increase strengthens the incentive for country S to abate more. The parameter γ denotes the ratio by which the additional abatement is certified, so if it is not too small, country N is willing to be committed to large X_N and realize the considerable amount of abatement by investing in country S.

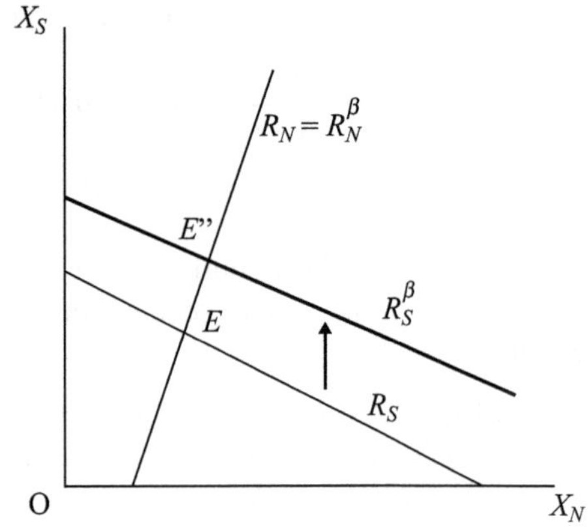

Fig. 18.3 Nash equilibrium in the technological aid case

Proposition 18.4 *In the technological aid case, as the credit certification ratio γ increases, the abatement of country S and the total abatement in equilibrium always decrease.*

Proof By differentiating (18.7) with respect to γ, we have

$$X_{N\gamma} = X_S^T - X_S^* + \left(\gamma + \frac{B_N''}{C_N'' - B_N''}\right) X_{S\gamma}, \tag{18.12}$$

where $X_{i\gamma} \equiv \frac{\partial X_i^T(\beta,\gamma)}{\partial \gamma}(i = N, S)$. Next, by differentiating (18.8) with respect to γ and using (18.12), we have

$$X_{S\gamma} = -\left\{(1-\beta)^2 C_S'' - (1-\gamma)\frac{B_S'' C_N''}{C_N'' - B_N''}\right\}^{-1} B_S' < 0.$$

As for the total abatement X^T, we have $\frac{\partial X^T}{\partial \gamma} = \frac{C_N'' X_{S\gamma}}{C_N'' - B_N''} < 0$.

Proposition 18.4 shows that the increase of the value of γ always leads to lower X_S. This is because higher credit certification ratio means that the environmental benefit with the abatement of country S is weakened by country N's credit acquisition. As (18.12) shows, the sign of X_N depends on the parameter values, but it is remarkable that both X_N and X_S can decrease with a higher value of γ. In order to make technological aid effective, the increase of only the credit certification ratio or only the support ratio would be insufficient.

Concerning the welfare effects, we have the following result.

Proposition 18.5 *Introduction of the technological aid increases the total payoff to two countries if the credit certification ratio γ is sufficiently large.*

Proof By differentiating π_N^T and π_S^T with respect to β and using (18.7) and (18.8), we have $\frac{\partial \pi_S^T}{\partial \beta} = C_S'\left(\frac{1-\beta}{1-\gamma}X_{N\beta} + X_S\right) > 0$ and $\frac{\partial \pi_N^T}{\partial \beta} = C_N' X_{S\beta} - C' X_S - \beta C' X_{S\beta}$. Although the sign of $\frac{\partial \pi_N^T}{\partial \beta}$ is not certain, it follows that $\left.\frac{\partial(\pi_N^T + \pi_S^T)}{\partial \beta}\right|_{\beta=0} = \frac{C_S' X_{N\beta}}{1-\gamma} + (C_S' - C')X_S + C_N' X_{S\beta}$. This is positive if γ is large enough such that $X_{N\beta} > 0$.

18.4 Conclusions

We modeled pollution abatement games between a developed country and a developing country and examined how the equilibrium changes with international cooperation.

In the financial aid case, the developed country abates less, and the developing country abates more than in the base case. The total abatement, however, increases and the total payoff to two countries also increases.

In the technological aid case, when the credit certification ratio is sufficiently large, both countries abate more with the introduction of a positive support ratio than in the base case, and thus, the total payoff increases. This outcome is because the incentive to abate more works for both countries; the developing country chooses higher abatement if the other country will realize a substantial amount, and the developed country chooses higher abatement if a large amount of emission credits are certified by abatement activities abroad. However, we must note that this is not the case when the value of the credit certification ratio is small.

Matsueda et al. (2007) assumes that the strategy of the developed country is to change the level of technology and shows that the decisions of a developed country and a developing country are strategic complements. We have fixed the technology level and still observe cooperative behavior. Our results imply the effectiveness of the bilateral environmental cooperation, such as the credit transfer scheme in the Paris Agreement, for mitigating climate change.

Future topics for consideration include the framework of dynamic games, the outcome of cooperative games, and the empirical analyses using the actual data.

References

Barrett, S. 1994. Self-enforcing international environmental agreements. *Oxford Economic Papers* 46: 878–894.

Barrett, S. 2001. International cooperation for sale. *European Economic Review* 45: 1835–1850.

Breton, M., G. Zaccour, and M. Zahaf. 2006. A game-theoretic formulation of joint implementation of environ-mental projects. *European Journal of Operational Research* 168: 221–239.

Carraro, C., and D. Siniscalco. 1993. Strategies for the international protection of the environment. *Journal of Public Economics* 52: 309–328.

Diamantoudi, E., and E.S. Sartzetakis. 2006. Stable international environmental agreements: An analytical approach. *Journal of Public Economic Theory* 8: 247–263.

Hoel, M. 1991. Global environmental problems: The effects of unilateral actions taken by one country. *Journal of Environmental Economics and Management* 20: 55–70.

Hoel, M., and K. Schneider. 1997. Incentives to participate in an international environmental agreement. *Environmental and Resource Economics* 9: 153–170.

Lange, A., and C. Vogt. 2003. Cooperation in international environmental negotiations due to a preference for equity. *Journal of Public Economics* 87: 2049–2067.

Matsueda, N., K. Futagami, and A. Shibata. 2006. Environmental transfers against global warming: A credit-based program. *International Journal of Environmental Issues* 6: 47–72.

Matsueda, N., K. Futagami, and A. Shibata. 2007. Dynamic analyses of international environmental aid. In *The mechanism design for protecting the global environment*, ed. K. Kiyono, and K. Shinpo, 311–340. Tokyo University Press, Tokyo (in Japanese).

United Nations. 2015. *Paris Agreement*. Available at UNFCCC (United Nations Framework Convention on Climate Change) website. http://unfccc.int/files/essential_background/convention/application/pdf/english_paris_agreement.pdf.

Chapter 19
Social Capital, Resource Boom, and Underdevelopment Traps

Nobuaki Hori and Peseth Seng

19.1 Introduction

The most serious and challenging issues in the field of economic development have always involved explaining the persistent differences of economic development between different countries, generally known as "underdevelopment traps." For a long time, economists have devoted considerable effort in explaining the causes and mechanism of these traps. In economic theories, the concept of underdevelopment traps is usually modeled by multiple equilibria. Many models and a rich array of concepts in both static and dynamic settings have been proposed in the literature. We construct a dynamic model of intergenerational cultural transmission to analyze the cause of underdevelopment traps from the perspectives of cultural economics.

The fundamental mechanism of our model is the interaction between the cultural norms and material incentives of individual agents. The authors of a number of recent studies have argued that cultural factors can provide new insights into understanding economic development (e.g., Tirole 1996; Francois and Zabojnik 2005; Sindzingre 2007; Tabellini 2008, 2010; Aghion et al. 2009). The notion of cultural effects on economic development can be tracked back at least to the work of Weber ([1902] 1958), who links the Protestant reformation and ethic to the rise of industrialized society in Western Europe.

Formal economic models in this field have become increasingly attractive to development economists in the last 2 decades. Indeed, Aghion and Howitt (2009) point out that cultures and beliefs may be the most fundamental layer of

N. Hori (✉)
Kyushu University, Fukuoka, Japan
e-mail: hori@econ.kyushu-u.ac.jp

P. Seng
Orkide Villa Co., Ltd, Phnom Penh, Cambodia

T. Naito et al. (eds.), *Applied Approaches to Societal Institutions and Economics*, New Frontiers in Regional Science: Asian Perspectives 18,
DOI 10.1007/978-981-10-5663-5_19

the economic development process. Culture may be considered as the cognitive dimensions of institutions (Sindzingre 2007). In this sense, cultural factors, such as social norms, which move slowly and are hard to change, may be considered the supporting factors of different institutions (Acemoglu and Robinson 2012). It can be perceived that the development process works as follows: cultural factors support the existence of different institutions, and different institutions lead individual agents to have different incentives and make different choices in the market, which eventually brings about multiple equilibria.

However, some researchers, such as Tabellini (2010), even argue that insights from cultural hypothesis may help us understand why the same institutions function differently in different economies. He raises the example of the Italian judicial system, which works very differently in Northern and Southern Italy, where legal and economic institutions (legal system, judges' career paths, and human capital) are very similar. He concludes that historical differences of the two regions, which shape different cultures and norms, can explain this puzzle.

The concepts that are most commonly used in the modeling of culture and economic development literature are perhaps those of trust and trustworthiness. These two concepts are interrelated and inseparable. Trustworthy behavior among members of society induce higher social trust in the society. Aghion et al. (2009) develop a model to show that distrust among agents predominating in an economy creates public demand for regulations. Too many regulations in turn discourage social capital accumulation, which eventually leads to multiple equilibria of development. Similarly, Tirole (1996) shows that lack of trust among different economic agents, particularly that generated by existing bad reputations of the group to which the agents belong, induce them to behave dishonestly toward one another, which eventually creates persistent corruption and underdevelopment traps.

Culture or social norms are always viewed as persistent and changing very slowly over time compared to other economic phenomena. Culture and social norms are transferred from one generation to another. The process of intergenerational transmission of culture is formalized by Bisin and Verdier (2001), who conceptualize intergenerational cultural transmission as the results of two interactions between vertical direct socialization and horizontal socialization. The former refers to intentional socialization within the family, in particular, from parents to their offspring, while the latter is imitation and learning from other members in the society, for example, friends, colleagues, and teachers.

Incorporating the ideas of cultural transmission pioneered by Bisin and Verdier (2001), Francois and Zabojnik (2005) develops a model to show the complementarity between social capital, particularly trustworthiness, and more efficient modern production. The basic argument behind this model is that modern production is more vulnerable to expropriation than less efficient traditional production. Firms choose modern production only if they believe their partner contractors are trustworthy. Similarly, parents try to socialize their offspring to be trustworthy if it increases their chances of employment compared to opportunistic characteristics. While the cultural transmission process moves slowly in response to change, firm decisions are quick to change. Therefore, the model of Francois and Zabojnik (2005) emphasizes that quick reform that increases the profitability of modern production, for example, globalization, trade openness, or access to new technology, may become favorable for more opportunistic behavior, which in turn causes the economy to become caught in underdevelopment traps.

Francois and Zabojnik (2005) provide a good framework for understanding the effects of social capital on development from the cultural transmission perspectives. Their analysis is useful for the explanation of least developed countries that have been trying to adopt more open and globalized policies to gain access to modern production but have failed to move beyond underdevelopment traps. However, in some least developed countries, development occurs in traditional production instead of modern production. For example, globalization and free-trade agreements may lead to a boom in the price of primary products, such as agricultural products and other natural resources. It would be equally important to investigate the interaction between the development of social capital and traditional production. The model of Francois and Zabojnik (2005) focuses only on analyzing the development of modern production and treats traditional production as inactive. In their model, contractors are completely unemployed if they are not hired in modern production. This, of course, implies that the effects of development of the traditional production sector are not taken into account by parents when making decisions about socializing their offspring. Further analysis concentrating on the traditional side of production may offer more useful insights.

By following the setting pioneered by Bisin and Verdier (2001) and Francois and Zabojnik (2005), we develop a new cultural transmission model of underdevelopment traps, incorporating the role of the development of an economy's traditional sector. Our model is different from Francois and Zabojnik (2005) in several ways. First, while their focus is on the effects of the modern production development, ours is on the effects of traditional production. Second, unlike their model, the key features of our model are the characteristics of traditional production, in which we assume possible monitoring on contractors, leaving no room for opportunistic behavior. Traditional production usually involves simple and routine jobs that are easier to monitor and control than those in modern production, which usually involve sophisticated jobs, high skills, and more discretionary power of contractors. Therefore, opportunistic contractors may be hired to work in traditional production firms if they are not employed in the modern firms. This, of course, affects the incentives and process of cultural development. Such mechanisms do not exist in the model of Francois and Zabojnik (2005).

The subsequent sections proceed as follows. Section 19.2 presents the setting of the model. Section 19.3 describes the cultural transmission in the model, and Sect. 19.4 shows the production side reactions to the gradual changes in cultural traits. Section 19.5 solves the steady state, and Sect. 19.6 presents some comparative dynamics. Section 19.7 concludes.

19.2 Model

In this model, the economy lives infinitely, and each period is denoted by a subscript, t. For each period, 1 unit measure of homogenous potential entrepreneurs is born, and 1 unit measure of their trading partners, called "contractors," is born. Both entrepreneurs and contractors live for one period only. The entrepreneurs are purely economic agents; they do not have any cultural traits or norms. Each entrepreneur can set up a production firm by hiring a contractor to work for him, and they share the total production output as follows: the entrepreneur obtains a share $\alpha \in (0, 1)$ of the total output, and the remaining proportion $(1 - \alpha)$ of the total output is allocated to the partner contractor.

The contractors may have different cultural traits or hold different cultural norms, which is discussed later. They are of overlapping generations, in which a young child is born when his adult parent is still alive. However, only adult contractors are active in economic transactions, and the young child learns cultural norms and is influenced by the cultural norms of his parent. The young child becomes an adult when his parent dies and then starts to become involved in economic transactions, holding the cultural norms he obtained when he was young. This process is repeated infinitely. Moreover, we assume that the entrepreneur is matched with only one adult contractor once in his life. Since the numbers of entrepreneurs and adult contractors in each period are equal, all entrepreneurs are able to find a partner.

19.2.1 Cultural Norms

Before providing a detailed discussion on production and profitability, we first illustrate the two different norms of contractors. We assume that the contractors can be of two types: trustworthy and opportunistic. Trustworthy contractors are those who behave in accordance with the promise and contracts made with the entrepreneurs who hire them. On the other hand, opportunistic contractors are those who break promises or violate the contracts made with their trading partners, particularly the entrepreneurs, if they consider they will be better off doing so.

We draw attention to the fact that although we use the terms "trustworthy" and "opportunistic," they do not generally refer to honest (good) and dishonest (bad) agents, and we do not intend to imply that opportunistic agents are always bad. These two types of agents should be considered as two competing norms or beliefs in the society. For example, following Tabellini (2008), these two competing norms can be thought of as the distinction between norms of limited and generalized morality. In this sense, "trustworthy agents" can be considered as those who hold norms of general morality, in which they always keep their promises and obey the formal contracts made with all partners, for example, outsiders, strangers, or foreign partners, regardless of their familiarity with them. On the other hand, "opportunistic agents" can be interpreted as those who hold norms of limited morality, in which they keep promises only within a narrow circle of people in their individual group, community, village, or family. Outside this circle, cheating is permitted and regularly committed. These agents may not be bad people, taking into account the different values and definition of morality and justice. For example, they may violate formal contracts with outsiders, as long as such behavior is beneficial to their own communities. The points we emphasize here about the difference between the two norms are not about which is morally better than the other. However, we emphasize that these two competing norms are favorable for different kinds of production. For example, while opportunistic (or limited morality) may be favorable for small and traditional production in a local village, trustworthy (or general morality) is necessary for large-scale and modern production, which usually involves more discretion and larger ranges of cooperation between many unfamiliar partners.

We denote subscript T for the trustworthy type, and subscript O for the opportunistic type, and denote $\beta_t \in [0, 1]$ for the proportion of trustworthy contractors and $(1 - \beta_t)$ for the proportion of the opportunistic ones in period t. If cheating is possible, a contractor of either type can behave opportunistically, particularly by cheating the entrepreneur, and earn a financial benefit $b > 0$, in addition to the total production output share he can obtain. However, while there is no utility loss for the intrinsically opportunistic contractor to cheat, the intrinsically trustworthy contractor has a disutility of γ if he cheats. This can be considered as feelings of guilt for breaking promises, which occurs only for trustworthy contractors. The contractors do not have any other outside options besides working for the entrepreneurs.

These two types of norms or preferences of the contractors are transferred from one generation to another in the way formalized by Bisin and Verdier (2001). The intergenerational transmission is that of asexual one-for-one reproduction with only two possible types, trustworthy and opportunistic. Bisin and Verdier (2001) formulates two types of transmission process: (1) direct vertical socialization (effort of parents to directly transmit their own preferences to their offspring) and (2) horizontal socialization (social interaction, imitation, and learning from others in the society). For simplicity, we focus on only the vertical socialization process. We denote P_t^{ij} as the probability that a child of a type-i parent becomes the contractor of type-j trait, with the subscripts i and $j \in \{T, O\}$, and assume the following transmission system:

$$\begin{aligned} P_t^{TT} &= 1 - (q^{TO} - d_t) \\ P_t^{TO} &= q^{TO} - d_t \\ P_t^{OO} &= 1 - q^{OT} \\ P_t^{OT} &= q^{OT} \end{aligned} \tag{19.1}$$

where $q^{TO} < 1/2$ and $q^{OT} < 1/2$ are fixed variables. We assume that only the trustworthy parent can make effort to intentionally transfer his preferences to his child and call such efforts the *education effort* inside the family. The probability that his child becomes trustworthy is augmented via this education effort by $d_t \in$

$[0, q^{TO}]$. However, this direct vertical socialization incurs cost C, where C is an increasing function of d_t and is given as $C(d_t) = d_t^2/(2\phi), \phi > 0$. This cost function implies that $C(0) = 0, C'(d_t) \geq 0$ and $C''(d_t) > 0$.

Moreover, we assume that the trustworthy parent is altruistic and always tries to choose d_t to maximize the expected utility of his child, by considering the perspective of his own intrinsic type. This means that the trustworthy parent takes into account the utility loss of feeling guilty from cheating, γ, when considering the utility of his potential opportunistic child, even though the potential opportunistic child does not face this loss. This kind of assumption is common in the cultural transmission literature. Since our analysis is on the development of social capital, we focus only on the education effort made by trustworthy parents to educate their offspring and simply assume that there is no education effort made by the opportunistic parents. The education effort of the opportunistic parents does not change our qualitative results but only adds more complexity to the model.

19.2.2 Production

Next, we discuss the production side of the economy. There are two types of production that the entrepreneur can choose: to enter modern production or stay in traditional production. Modern production is more productive and yields higher output but is also more sophisticated and difficult to monitor, making it vulnerable to opportunistic behavior on the part of the trading partners, particularly the contractor. This could be an industrialized and modern production that involves high skills and technologies. The opportunistic behavior in this kind of production can be considered as a case in which producers hire contractors to contribute necessary inputs or parts for the final products, and the contractors do not contribute qualified inputs in accordance with the specification of the contracts. Due to the sophistication of the intermediate goods, which is difficult to verify, and the necessary discretion given to the contractors, such kind of production is very vulnerable to cheating. The contractor gains by providing cheaper and low-quality inputs, but the entrepreneur loses. On the other hand, traditional production is less productive but is engaged only with simple and routine work. Thus, it could be almost perfectly monitored and controlled and is not vulnerable to any opportunistic behavior on the part of the contracting partners. This may refer to production activities in agriculture and natural resource sectors, which do not involve high skills and technologies. In this kind of production, the work of the contractors can be monitored almost perfectly, leaving it almost no room for any opportunistic behavior, compared to that of modern production. The assumption that opportunistic behavior does not occur in traditional production can be considered a case in which the contractor is simply a normal worker who provides labor to the producer and works in simple routine jobs that are easy to monitor and control.

We denote $p_t \in [0, 1]$ as the proportion of entrepreneurs who enter modern production and $(1-p_t)$ as the proportion of those who choose traditional production in period t. We call the former "the modern producer" and the latter "the traditional producer." We denote Π_H and Π_L as the notations for production output from modern and traditional production, respectively, where $\Pi_H > \Pi_L$. In either case, the entrepreneur has to hire a contractor to work for him. The entrepreneur does not know perfectly the types of the contractors, but with probability $\theta \in (0, 1)$, he can detect the opportunistic type of the contractor before making production choices.

If the entrepreneur wants to enter modern production, the entrepreneur has to first invest in the entry sunk cost $k(p_t) = \kappa p, \kappa > 0$. The assumption that $k'(p_t) > 0$ implies that the cost of entering modern production is increasing in the number of modern producers. For example, when more firms want to hire office space in a capital city, the office rentals in that city become more expensive. In addition to the entry cost, if the entrepreneur is cheated by the contractor in modern production, the associated loss will amount to $\delta\Pi_H, \delta \in (0, 1)$. On the other hand, if the entrepreneur chooses traditional production, he does not need to invest any entry cost and is never subject to any loss of opportunistic behavior. The only disadvantage is lower output compared to that of modern production. Lastly, for simplicity, we assume that the utility of all agents—both entrepreneurs and contractors—is only linear in consumption or that utility is only equal to income.

19.2.3 Timing of Events

The timing of events at the production stage in each period is given as follows. First, entrepreneurs decide on the types of production to choose based on their expectations about the types of the contractors they meet, taking into account the contractor's cheating behavior. Second, entrepreneurs meet with contractors. At this stage, if an entrepreneur meets with an opportunistic agent, the entrepreneur finds that fact ("the contractor is opportunistic type") with probability θ and decides whether to continue the match or not. Next, if the production is actually taken place, contractors decide whether to cheat the entrepreneur. Finally, each T type contractor (parent) of the current period decides on the education effort, considering the expected utility and behavior of his offspring as well as the entrepreneurs' strategies in the next period. Before we proceed to the solution, in order to simplify the model, we introduce the following two assumptions:

Assumption 1 $b - \gamma < 0$

Assumption 2 $\alpha - \delta < 0$

Since opportunistic contractors always gain from cheating, they always cheat, if possible. Assumption 1 assures that trustworthy contractors never cheat at all. In this sense, the strategies of the contractors in the production partnership are straightforward. Considering these behaviors of the contractors, Assumption 2 implies the entrepreneur with the modern production never chooses to enter the production if he meets an opportunistic contractor and can detect her type, because doing so leads to a negative profit.

Considering these two assumptions, the main mechanism of this dynamic model lies only in the strategic interaction between the education efforts of the trustworthy parents and the entrepreneurs' choices of production in each period. The dynamic interaction of these two strategies derives the steady-state solutions of the two key endogenous variables of this model, β and p, which are denoted as β^* and p^*, respectively.

Moreover, note in advance that we assume the entrepreneur can switch quickly between the two types of production to adapt to any changes in β_t. Therefore, the dynamic parameter p_t is a jump variable that moves quickly in response to a change in β_t. However, β_t evolves slowly in adaptation to the change in p_t due to the gradual effect of the cultural socialization process.

19.3 Evolution of Cultural Preferences

Now, we consider the trustworthy parent's decision on his education effort. Based on our assumptions about the intergenerational cultural transmission process, the proportion of offsprings who become the trustworthy type in period $t+1$ is given by

$$\beta_{t+1} = [1 - (q^{TO} - d_t)]\beta_t + q^{OT}(1 - \beta_t). \tag{19.2}$$

From equation (19.2), a difference equation for β can be obtained as follows:

$$d\beta_t = \beta_{t+1} - \beta_t = q^{OT}(1 - \beta_t) - (q^{TO} - d_t)\beta_t. \tag{19.3}$$

Next, denote U_t^{TT} and U_t^{TO} as the expected utility of the trustworthy and the opportunistic child (contractor), respectively, for the trustworthy parent, from the perspective of the trustworthy parent. These two utility functions are given as follows:

$$U_t^{TT} = (1 - \alpha)[p_t \Pi_H + (1 - p_t)\Pi_L] \tag{19.4}$$

$$U_t^{TO} = p_t(1 - \theta)[(1 - \alpha)\Pi_H + (b - \gamma)] + (1 - p_t)(1 - \alpha)\Pi_L \tag{19.5}$$

The trustworthy parent chooses the education effort or equivalently the probability d_t, so as to maximize his child's expected utility. Then, this maximization problem is given by

$$d(p_t) = \arg\max_{d_t} 1 - (q^{TO} - d_t)U_t^{TT} + (q^{TO} - d_t)U_t^{TO} - d_t^2/(2\phi) \tag{19.6}$$

Here we introduce another assumption.

Assumption 3

$$\phi \leq \frac{q^{TO}}{\theta(1-\alpha)\Pi_H + (1-\theta)(\gamma - b)}.$$

Assumption 3 puts a restriction on the maximum values of the parameter ϕ to assure an interior solution of the optimal education effort level, that is, $d(p_t) < q^{TO}$. From the equation (19.4), and (19.5), the solution of the maximization problem in (19.6) can be derived as the function of p_t,

$$d(p_t) = \phi p_t[\theta(1-\alpha)\Pi_H + (1-\theta)(\gamma - b)]. \quad (19.7)$$

From, equation (19.7), it is shown easily that $d'(p_t) > 0$, implying that the equilibrium education effort is always increasing in the (expected) number of the modern producers. The reason for this result is that an increase in p_t raises the chance of employment of the trustworthy child (contractor) in the modern production. Thus, the expected utility of the trustworthy child also increases in p_t, making it better off for the trustworthy parent to put more education effort on his child. Under Assumption 3, the minimum and maximum equilibrium values of $d(p_t)$ evaluated at $p_t = 0$ and $p_t = 1$ are given as follows.

$$d(0) = 0 \quad (19.8)$$

$$d(1) = \phi[\theta(1-\alpha)\Pi_H + (1-\theta)(\gamma - b)] < q^{TO} \quad (19.9)$$

In the next step, we derive the motion equation of the endogenous parameter β_t, which is the proportion of trustworthy contractors in the economy in each period. First, note from the difference equation (19.3) that the motion of β_t for a given initial value of β_t is represented by the sign of $d\beta_t$. Define $\beta(p) = \frac{q^{OT}}{q^{OT}+q^{TO}-d(p)}$ which satisfies $d\beta = 0$ for a given p. This threshold value $\beta(p)$ determines the direction of the motion of β_t which is given as follows

$$\begin{cases} d\beta_t > 0 & \text{when } \beta_t < \beta(p) \\ d\beta_t < 0 & \text{when } \beta_t > \beta(p) \\ d\beta_t = 0 & \text{when } \beta_t = \beta(p) \end{cases} \quad (19.10)$$

By inserting the equilibrium value of $d(p)$ from equation (19.7) into $\beta(p) = \frac{q^{OT}}{q^{OT}+q^{TO}-d(p)}$, we obtain the threshold value $\beta^*(p)$ as a direct function of p.

$$\beta(p) = \frac{q^{OT}}{q^{OT} + q^{TO} - \phi p[\theta(1-\alpha)\Pi_H + (1-\theta)(\gamma - b)]} \quad (19.11)$$

Subsequently, the minimum and maximum values of β^* evaluated at $p = 0$, and $p = 1$ are given as follows

$$\begin{cases} \beta(0) = \frac{q^{OT}}{q^{OT}+q^{TO}} \\ \beta(1) = \frac{q^{OT}}{q^{OT}+q^{TO}-\phi[\theta(1-\alpha)\Pi_H+(1-\theta)(\gamma-b)]} \leq 1 \end{cases} \quad (19.12)$$

Note that $\beta(1) \leq 1$ is directly derived from Assumption 3.

The sign of the first derivatives of equation (19.11) can be confirmed as follows

$$\frac{\partial \beta(p)}{\partial p} = \frac{\phi[\theta(1-\alpha)\Pi_H + (1-\theta)(\gamma-b)]q^{OT}}{\{q^{OT} + q^{TO} - \phi p[\theta(1-\alpha)\Pi_H + (1-\theta)(\gamma-b)]\}^2} > 0 \quad (19.13)$$

Equation (19.13) indicates that $\beta(p)$ is an increasing function, implying that the number of trustworthy contractors is increasing in the number of modern producers. The reason for this result comes directly from $d'(p_t) > 0$, which we mentioned earlier. The existence of more modern producers implies that the trustworthy child has more chance of employment in modern production, which yields higher utility for him. For a given education cost, this induces the trustworthy parent to put more education effort into his child, which eventually results in an increase in the number of trustworthy contractors in the new generation. Next, from equation (19.13), we can check the sign of the second derivatives of $\beta(p)$.

$$\frac{\partial^2 \beta(p)}{\partial p^2} = \frac{2\phi^2[\theta(1-\alpha)\Pi_H + (1-\theta)(\gamma-b)]^2 q^{OT}}{\{q^{OT} + q^{TO} - \phi p[\theta(1-\alpha)\Pi_H + (1-\theta)(\gamma-b)]\}^3} \quad (19.14)$$

From Assumption 3, it can be confirmed that $q^{OT} + q^{TO} > \phi p[\theta(1-\alpha)\Pi_H + (1-\theta)(\gamma-b)]$, implying that $\partial^2\beta(p)/\partial p^2 > 0$. Then, equation (19.13) and (19.14) indicate that $\beta(p)$ is a concave and increasing function of p. For ease of reference in the subsequent analyses, we state this result in the following Lemma.

Lemma 19.1 *$\beta(p)$ is a concave and increasing function of p, and*

$$\begin{cases} \beta(0) = \frac{q^{OT}}{q^{OT}+q^{TO}} \\ \beta(1) = \frac{q^{OT}}{q^{OT}+q^{TO}-\phi[\theta(1-\alpha)\Pi_H+(1-\theta)(\gamma-b)]} \leq 1 \end{cases}$$

19.4 Adjustment of Entrepreneurs

Now, we turn to consider the entrepreneurs' decisions about which production type to choose. Denote V_H and V_L as the payoffs of the entrepreneur who chooses modern and traditional production, respectively, in each period. We omit the subscript t from these two variables, as it does not cause any confusion. If the entrepreneur enters modern production, his payoff in each period, excluding the entry cost $k(p_t)$, is given by $V_H = [\beta\alpha + (1-\beta)(1-\theta)(\alpha-\delta)]\Pi_H$, which can be rearranged as follows

$$V_H = \{[1-(1-\beta)\theta]\alpha - (1-\beta)(1-\theta)\delta]\}\Pi_H \tag{19.15}$$

On the other hand, if he chooses to stay in traditional production, his payoff is given as

$$V_L = \alpha\Pi_L \tag{19.16}$$

In addition, note that all entrepreneurs engage in either one of the two production types, and no entrepreneur chooses to stay inactive, because at least they can earn positive payoffs of $\alpha\Pi_L$ in the traditional production.

Let $W(\beta_t)$ denote $V_H - V_L$;

$$W(\beta_t) \equiv \alpha(\Pi_H - \Pi_L) - \eta(1-\beta_t)\Pi_H,$$

where $\eta = \theta\alpha + (1-\theta)\delta > 0$. The equilibrium free-entry volume of modern sector entrepreneurs $p(\beta_t)$ satisfies the following conditions:

$$\begin{cases} p(\beta_t) = 0 & \text{if } W(\beta_t) < k(0) = 0 \\ 0 < p(\beta_t) < 1 & \text{if } W(\beta_t) = k(p(\beta_t)) = \kappa p(\beta_t) \\ p(\beta_t) = 1 & \text{if } W(\beta_t) > k(1) = \kappa \end{cases} \tag{19.17}$$

These equations, along with the assumption about the speed of the entrepreneur's movement, implies that $p(\beta_t)$ is a jump variable, meaning that the entrepreneur is always in equilibrium, switching quickly between the two production types in order to adapt to the changes. Here, we introduce another assumption:

Assumption 4 $\alpha(\Pi_H - \Pi_L) > k(1) = \kappa$

Assumption 4 is to assure that the output from modern production is high enough relative to Π_L and $k(1)$, such that the profitability in modern production remains always strictly higher than that in the traditional production, even when all entrepreneurs choose modern production (i.e., the economy with full modern producer is possible). Under this assumption, $p(\beta_t)$ is finally given in the following lemma:

Lemma 19.2

$$p(\beta_t) = \begin{cases} 0 & when\ \beta_t \le \underline{\beta} \\ \frac{\alpha(\Pi_H - \Pi_L) - \eta(1-\beta_t)\Pi_H}{\kappa} & when\ \underline{\beta} < \beta_t < \overline{\beta} \\ 1 & when\ \beta_t \ge \overline{\beta} \end{cases}, \tag{19.18}$$

Fig. 19.1 Steady states

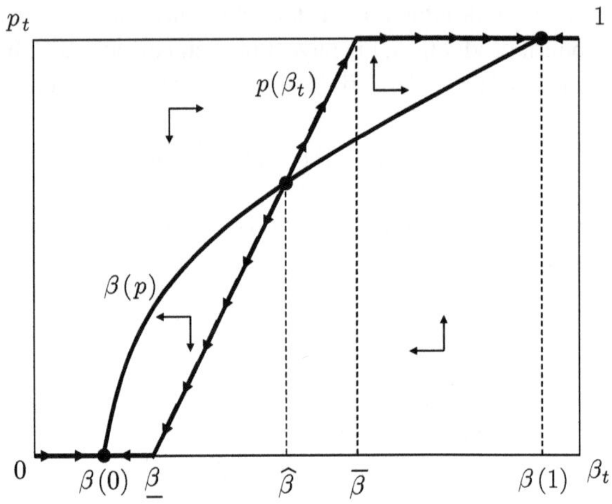

where

$$\underline{\beta} \equiv 1 - \frac{\alpha(\Pi_H - \Pi_L)}{\eta \Pi_H},$$

$$\overline{\beta} \equiv 1 - \frac{\alpha(\Pi_H - \Pi_L) - \kappa}{\eta \Pi_H}.$$

Note that $W(\beta_t)$ is linear and increasing in β_t. This result, along with the free-entry condition and the assumption that $k(p)$ is a linear and increasing function, implies that $p(\beta_t)$ is also a linear and increasing function of $\beta_t \in [\underline{\beta}, \overline{\beta}]$. $p'(\beta_t) > 0$ implies that an increase in the number of trustworthy contractors induces more entrepreneurs to choose modern production instead of traditional production. The reason behind this result is that more trustworthy contractors lead to more expected payoffs from the modern production compared to the traditional production for a given k.

The results from Lemmas 19.1 and 19.2 indicate that the numbers of modern producers and trustworthy contractors are complimentary to each other. More trustworthy contractors mean higher profits for modern producers, and more modern producers lead to more education effort of trustworthy parents, and thereby, an increase in the number of trustworthy contractors. As we already have derived the dynamic equations of the two key variables $p(\beta_t)$ and $\beta(p)$, we are almost ready to solve for the steady-state equilibrium points (p^*, β^*).

19.5 Steady States

We solve for the steady-state equilibrium points (p^*, β^*) by using the graphical analyses, particularly, Fig. 19.1. This figure combines the dynamics equations (19.11) and (19.18) together in (β, p) space. The steady-state equilibrium points (p^*, β^*) are derived from the intersection of the two dynamic equations (19.11) and (19.18). Since p_t is the jump variable and β_t adjusts slowly, the economy suddenly moves to the equilibrium point $p(\beta_t)$, then starts to adjust slowly to the equilibrium point β^* along the $\underline{dp} = 0$ locus. Note that Fig. 19.1. corresponds to the case in which $\underline{\beta} < \beta(0)$ and $\overline{\beta} < \beta(1)$. For the subsequent analyses, we study only this interesting case.

Note that the $p(\beta_t)$ line intersects with the $\beta(p)$ three times, determining three possible equilibria: two corner equilibria and one interior equilibrium. However, only the two corner equilibria are the stable equilibria in the steady state. These two corner stable equilibria are located at points $(\beta^* = \beta(1), p^* = 1)$ and $(\beta^* = \beta(0), p^* = 0)$, in which both β^* and p^* are higher in the former than the latter. Therefore, we call the former the *high social capital/modern production equilibrium* and the latter the *low social capital/traditional production equilibrium*. The interior equilibrium shown as the point $(\widehat{\beta}, p(\widehat{\beta}))$ in Fig. 19.1 is not stable. However, $\widehat{\beta}$ is the border point of β_t, which separates the economies into two different stable equilibria. For example, if a country begins with $\beta_t > \widehat{\beta}$, it moves to the *high social capital/modern production equilibrium at points* $(\beta(1), 1)$. On the other hand, the country with initial values of $\beta_t < \widehat{\beta}$ converges to the *low social capital/traditional production equilibrium at points* $(\beta(0), 0)$. We formally summarize these results in the following proposition.

Proposition 19.3 *Under Assumption 1–4, there are two corner stable equilibria points* $(\beta(1), 1)$ *and* $(\beta(0), 0)$ *in the steady state. In addition, there is an unstable interior equilibrium that determines the threshold value,* $\widehat{\beta} \in \left(\underline{\beta}, \overline{\beta}\right)$, *such that the economies beginning with* $\beta_t > \widehat{\beta}$ *converge to the "high social capital/modern production equilibrium," while those with initial value* $\beta_t < \widehat{\beta}$ *end up in the "low-social capital/traditional production equilibrium."*

Proposition 19.3 indicates that cultural factors that support different kinds of production predominating in economies can be the root of divergence of different economies. Only economies that have already accumulated sufficiently high social capital to support new and more efficient modern production may be able to take advantage of this new technological advance. Without enough social capital, the economies remain in low social capital and traditional production.

The fundamental mechanism behind this result is the complimentary strategic interaction between the trustworthy parents' education effort and the entrepreneurs' choices of productions. Due to the risk of opportunistic behavior in modern production and uncertainty of the contractors' types, an initially insufficient number of trustworthy contractors induces some entrepreneurs to choose traditional production that is not vulnerable to opportunistic behavior. In turn, a lower number of modern producers discourage trustworthy parents from educating their offspring, leading to a lower number of trustworthy contractors. Again, this causes more modern producers to switch to traditional production. This cycle is repeated continuously until the economies end up in the *low social capital/traditional production equilibrium*. The opposite movement toward the *high social capital/modern production equilibrium* occurs in economies with sufficiently high social capital.

Next, we investigate the total income in an economy in the two possible stable equilibrium points. From Assumption 4, it can be noted that the entrepreneurs can always obtain higher net profits from choosing modern production than from engaging in traditional production, as long as the number of trustworthy contractors is high enough. Moreover, since $\Pi_H > \Pi_L$ and cheating are possible only in modern production, both trustworthy and opportunistic contractors are always better off when employed in the modern production. Therefore, the total income in the economy is always the highest at the corner steady-state equilibrium points $(\beta(1), 1)$. From this, we obtain the following result.

Proposition 19.4 *Under Assumption* 1–4, *the total income of the economy in the corner stable equilibrium points* $((\beta(1), 1))$ *always exceeds that in the corner stable equilibrium points* $(\beta(0), 0)$ *in the steady state.*

Since the *high social capital/modern production equilibrium* is associated with the highest total incomes, it may be referred to as *high development equilibrium*. Similarly, the *low social capital/traditional production equilibrium* can be referred to as *low development equilibrium* or *underdevelopment traps*. Propositions 19.3 and 19.4 indicate that while countries with sufficient social capital are converging to the high development equilibrium, economies whose predominant cultural norms are favorable only for less efficient traditional production are left behind and become stuck in the *low development equilibrium*. These results clearly show that the causes of underdevelopment traps can be explained by cultural factors, such as social norms and preferences.

19.6 Comparative Dynamics

19.6.1 Development of Traditional Production

Now, we investigate the effects of the development of the traditional production on the dynamics of the two key variables (β^*, p^*). Some kinds of policies or reforms, such as globalization or free-trade agreements, may lead to increases in the profits of traditional production, instead of the development of modern production. For example, trade openness might lead to an increase in the price of natural resources or primary products, such as agricultural products or raw material products. In this model, this effect is captured by the increase in Π_L.

Now suppose that Π_H remains the same, and Π_L increases, but in the ranges of values that still satisfy all our previous Assumptions 1–4. Then, it can be noted from Equations (19.11) and (19.18) that the increase in Π_L affects only $p(\beta_t)$ ($dp = 0$ locus) but does not have any impact on $\beta(p)$ ($d\beta = 0$ locus). In particular, an increase in Π_L shifts the $dp = 0$ locus to the right, while the $d\beta = 0$ locus curve remains unchanged. Figure 19.2 shows the graphical illustration of this effect. When

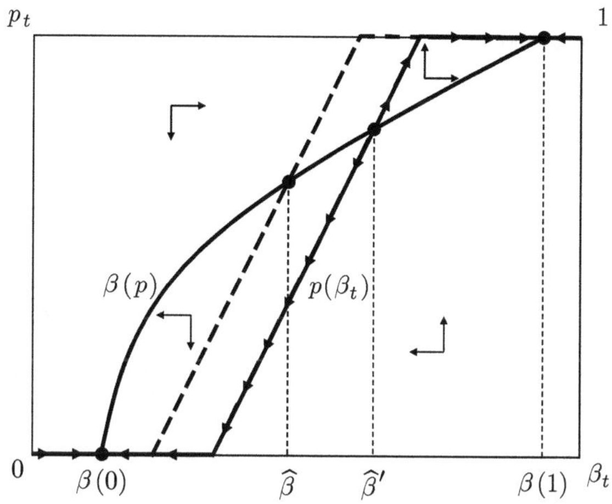

Fig. 19.2 Development of traditional production

Π_L increases, the $dp = 0$ locus moves to the right. Although the two stable equilibria points remain unchanged, the threshold value of β, which separates the paths to the two stable equilibria, increases from $\widehat{\beta}$ to $\widehat{\beta}'$. Then, a country which used to be on the paths to the *high development equilibrium* converges to the underdevelopment traps. This significant result leads us to another Proposition.

Proposition 19.5 *Under Assumption* 1–4*, an increase in* Π_L *shifts the* $dp = 0$ *locus to the right, increasing the threshold level of social capital* $\widehat{\beta}$ *below which the economies converge to underdevelopment traps.*

When the profits of the traditional production suddenly increase relative to those of the modern production, more entrepreneurs find it more profitable to engage in traditional production, and so, they respond to this change by switching quickly to the traditional production. The economy now needs more trustworthy contractors to assure that it remains on the paths to the high development equilibrium. However, the social capital in some economies that used to be sufficient to assure high development paths before an increase in Π_L now may no longer be enough to assure high development paths after the shock.

Since traditional production is usually agricultural and natural resource-based production, an increase in Π_L can be thought of as related to an abundance of natural resources. Regarding the resource curse implication, our result indicates that economies with more abundant natural resources (higher Π_L) are more likely to remain in underdevelopment traps than those with less abundant natural resources. That is, richer natural resources require higher social capital for economies to break free of low development traps and jump to the paths of high development equilibrium.

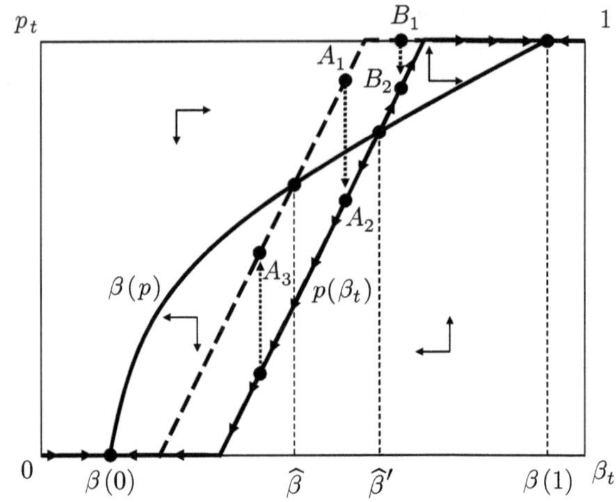

Fig. 19.3 Temporary resource boom

19.6.2 Temporary Resource Boom

In this subsection, we apply the results of our model to explain the resource curse phenomena that exist in some countries but not in others. Many studies in the literature have argued that resource booms, particularly the rise in the price of natural resources, always have boom-and-bust characteristics. This boom-and-bust cycle has been proposed as the cause of resource curses owing to the macroeconomic instability generated from this cycle. Since the boom-and-bust cycles of natural resource prices are a global issue, it should affect resource-rich countries in similar ways. However, while a temporary resource boom may adversely affect many resource-rich countries, such as Nigeria, Indonesia, Iraq, Saudi Arabia, Sierra Leone, Venezuela, and Zambia, other resource-abundant Scandinavian nations, particularly Norway and Sweden, have never experienced these adverse impacts. From the perspectives of cultural economics, our model provides the micro-foundational mechanisms that explain why a temporary resource boom may lead some countries, but not others, to underdevelopment traps.

Again, we use a graphical illustration to explain this phenomenon. Figure 19.3 presents the case of a temporary resource boom and its impacts on the development paths of different economies. There are two countries in this figure: A and B. Initially, Countries A and B are located at points A_1 and B_1, respectively, on the right-hand side of the threshold value of social capital $\widehat{\beta}$, and both countries are moving toward the *high development equilibrium*. Suddenly, at some point of time, a resource boom occurs and shifts the straight line to the right, raising $\widehat{\beta}$ to $\widehat{\beta}'$. Country B has already accumulated sufficient social capital and is now located at point B_2 which is higher than $\widehat{\beta}'$, and so, this country continues on its paths to the *high development equilibrium*. However, Country A has not yet accumulated enough social capital and remains at point A_2 on the left-hand side of the new threshold

$\widehat{\beta}'$, implying that its development paths are now reversed, moving backward to the *low development equilibrium*. Finally, the resource boom finishes, and the prices of natural resources suddenly fall back to their original levels, shifting the $dp = 0$ locus back to its original position. Although the threshold value of social capital falls back from $\widehat{\beta}'$ to $\widehat{\beta}$, Country A has already moved backward to point A_3 on the left-hand side of $\widehat{\beta}$ and, thus, continues on the path to the *low development equilibrium* and becomes caught in underdevelopment traps. Meanwhile, Country B continues on its path to the *high development equilibrium*. This scenario clearly shows that a temporary resource boom may lead different economies that are initially on the same direction of the development paths to diverge if their initial social capital accumulation is different.

19.7 Concluding Remarks

We construct an intergenerational cultural transmission model of underdevelopment traps and the resource curse, under the setting of interaction between the development of social capital and the development of traditional production. We show that economies may converge to different paths of development, given their initial levels of social capital, which support different production types. The economies with sufficient social capital that supports more efficient modern production converge to high development equilibrium, while those with insufficient social capital continue their practice of less efficient traditional production and become caught in underdevelopment traps.

In addition, we investigate the effect of the development of traditional production on the development paths of the economies. Some policies and reforms, or market shocks that may lead to increased profits of traditional production vis-à-vis those of modern production, raise the threshold level of social capital needed for the economies to remain on the paths toward high development equilibrium. Such reforms or sudden shocks may cause some economies that are on the path to high development equilibrium to reverse their development paths toward the low development equilibrium. The implication from this result can be used to explain the resource curse phenomena from the perspective of cultural economics. Countries with more abundant natural resources and, thus, higher profitability of traditional production require higher levels of social capital than those with scarcity of natural resources to get out of low development traps.

Lastly, we apply our result to explain the effect of a temporary resource boom on the development paths of different economies. We show that a temporary resource boom may lead two economies that are initially on the same paths to high development equilibrium to diverge. While economies with initially higher social capital can assure movement to the high development equilibrium, those with initially lower social capital may reverse their paths to the low development equilibrium.

Our model suggests that the development of social capital that supports more efficient modern production is crucial for economies to get out of underdevelopment traps and to join the convergence club of high development countries.

References

Acemoglu, D., and J. Robinson. 2012. *Why nations fail: The origins of power, prosperity, and poverty*. New York: Crown.

Aghion, P., Y. Algan, P. Cahuc, and A. Shleifer. 2009. Regulation and distrust. National Bureau of Economic Research, Working Paper No. 14648.

Aghion, P., and P. Howitt. 2009. *The economics of growth*. Cambridge: MIT Press

Bisin, A., and T. Verdier. 2001. The economics of cultural transmission and the dynamics of preferences. *Journal of Economic Theory* 97(2): 298–319.

Francois, P., and J. Zabojnik. 2005. Trust, social capital, and economic development. *Journal of the European Economic Association* 3(1): 51–94.

Sindzingre, A.N. 2007. Poverty traps: A perspective from development economics. Economix Document de Travail Working Paper, 2007–26.

Tabellini, G. 2008. The scope of cooperation: Values and incentives. *Quarterly Journal of Economics* 123(3): 905–950.

Tabellini, G. 2010. Culture and institutions: Economic development in the regions of Europe. *Journal of the European Economic Association* 8(4): 677–716.

Tirole, J. (1996). A theory of collective reputations. *Review of Economic Studies* 63(1): 1–22.

Weber, M. [1902]. 1958. *The Protestant ethic and the spirit of capitalism*. Reprint. Scribner's.

Chapter 20
Quality-Improving R&D and Semicollusive Production Cartel in Differentiated Cournot Duopoly

Yasunori Ouchida

20.1 Introduction

Innovation does not succeed without efforts for research and development (R&D). Report conducted by Fukuda (2017) emphasizes that firms engaging in R&D tend to locate in northern regions when transportation costs are high and that R&D investment and firms' location influence economic growth. On the other hand, new wave has come from consumer side. In recent years, many green consumers tend to pay a higher price for environmentally friendly products (or green products) rather than nongreen products. Some countries strongly promote a green public procurement. In financial market, the bank carrying out green finance is increasing. One of the reasons of such phenomenon is the change of consumers' preference resulting from environmental higher education and announcement effect of environmental policy. Hence, in order to survive competition, many firms develop an environmental high-quality good or want to establish a green brand. In addition, while the contribution of green innovation to economic growth is expected widely, the antitrust regulator must design the competition policy to achieve the social efficiency of the market.

R&D for environmentally friendly products is categorized into quality-improving R&D (product R&D).[1] The studies on product R&D in oligopolistic market are

[1]Examples of good yielded by quality-improving R&D, markets of LED lights, electric cars, advanced safety vehicle, home air conditioner, refrigerator, digital camera, water purifier, organic soap, detergents, antiaging cosmetics, foods for specified health use (e.g., high-catechin beverage), rare sugar (e.g., D-Psicose), and others.

Y. Ouchida (✉)
Hiroshima University, Higashihiroshima, Japan
e-mail: ouchida@hiroshima-u.ac.jp

T. Naito et al. (eds.), *Applied Approaches to Societal Institutions and Economics*, New Frontiers in Regional Science: Asian Perspectives 18,
DOI 10.1007/978-981-10-5663-5_20

made by Motta (1993), Symeonidis (2000, 2003), Kabiraj and Roy (2004), Yakita and Yamauchi (2011), and others. In particular, Yakita and Yamauchi (2011) provide an investigation of welfare effects of environmental R&D formations in symmetric equilibrium in a setting where Cournot duopolists invest in R&D in order to improve product quality. They analyze the semicollusive R&D when collusion variable is environmental R&D and when competition variable is quantity. The results reveal that higher social welfare, production level, and environmental quality level are yielded by cooperative R&D when the degree of product differentiation is larger relative to R&D spillover.

On the other hand, whereas the antitrust authorities guard the market, cartels still exist in markets. It is very difficult to eradicate cartels. In our real society, there may exist many tacit cartels which are not coming to light. Additionally, some countries are ironized as "cartel paradise".[2] However, some governments may set lawful cartels.[3] Accordingly, it is an unexceptional phenomenon that oligopolistic firms collusively choose its own quantity level after noncooperative quality-improving R&D stage.

Matsui (1989) reveals that, in a setting of a two-stage game where each quantity-setting firm determines its own capital equipment level for cost reduction before production stage, semicollusive production cartel can be beneficial to consumers.[4] The subsequent studies on semicollusion are made by Fershtman and Gandal (1994), Brod and Shivakumar (1999), Steen and Sørgard (1999), Foros et al. (2002), Röller and Steen (2006), Ringbom and Shy (2008), Simbanegavi (2009), Pal (2010), Dewenter et al. (2011), and others.[5] In particular, Brod and Shivakumar (1999) explicitly introduce the parameters of product differentiation and technological spillover and also explore the welfare effects of semicollusive production cartel between Cournot duopolists engaging in noncooperative cost-reducing R&D before production stage. Their main result is that there exist parameter values of product differentiation and technological spillover such that quantity cartel can be either beneficial to both firms and consumers or harmful to both firms and consumers.

However, irrespective of the crucial impact yielded by firm's semicollusive behavior, semicollusion has not been investigated adequately. Furthermore, whereas Brod and Shivakumar (1999) analyze the case of cost-reducing R&D classified into process R&D, no one has examined the welfare effects of semicollusive production cartel in the context of product R&D. Therefore, in accordance with the framework of Yakita and Yamauchi (2011), we develop the scenario of semicollusive production cartel after noncooperative quality-improving R&D and compare our

[2]For an example, postwar Japan in the 1950s and 1960s. For the competition policy of Japan, see Porter and Sakakibara (2004).

[3]For details, see Matsui (1989) and Weinstein (1995). Lawful cartels are feasible through making exceptional rules.

[4]For the definition of semicollusion, see Steen and Sørgard (2009, chapter 2).

[5]Phlips (1995, Chaps. 9 and 10) and Steen and Sørgard (2009) provided detailed and excellent surveys on semicollusion studies.

new scenario with the case of full competition investigated by Yakita and Yamauchi (2011). The aim of this paper is to examine whether such semicollusive production cartel is socially allowable. Moreover, our investigation reveals when production cartel after noncooperative quality-improving R&D is pro-competitive and also derives antitrust implications for Cournot duopolists engaging quality-improving R&D.

This paper is organized as follows. The next section introduces the model. The third section solves the two-stage game and derives the equilibrium outcomes. In the fourth section, we compare two scenarios and derive policy implications. The final section presents conclusions.

20.2 The Model

We imply the framework of a two-stage game in Symeonidis (2003) and Yakita and Yamauchi (2011).[6] Our analysis focuses on symmetric equilibrium. First, consider an industry comprising two firms – firm i and firm j – engaging in a Cournot competition with the same cost structure and R&D technology. Then $x_i(> 0)$ denotes the quantity of variety i. Production cost is $C_i(x_i) = cx_i$, $(0 < c < 1)$.

We assume that there are $S(> 0)$ identical individuals in the market. Each consumer's income is captured by $Y(> 0)$. The price of variety i is given by $p_i(> 0)$. Then, $M = Y-(p_ix_i+p_jx_j)$ means expenditure on outside goods. The utility function of each individual is given as the following quality-augmented quadratic function:

$$U(x_i, x_j, M) = x_i + x_j - \frac{x_i^2}{u_i^2} - \frac{x_j^2}{u_j^2} - 2\sigma\frac{x_i}{u_i}\frac{x_j}{u_j} + M,$$

where $u_i(i,j = 1, 2; i \neq j)$ presents the quality of variety i.[7] Higher u_i increases the consumers' willingness to pay for the firm i's product, whereas it takes R&D expenditures.[8] The exogenous parameter $\sigma \in (0, 1)$ denotes the degree of horizontal product differentiation between two varieties. As $\sigma \to 0$ (1), then the goods become independent (perfect substitutes) when $u_i = u_j$. We assume that an individual consumer spends only a small part of her income on the industry's product. Under that assumption, an interior solution of utility maximization is ensured. In addition, that assumption enables us to ignore the income effects on the industry examined here and to apply the partial equilibrium analysis.

[6]We basically follow the model and notations used by Yakita and Yamauchi (2011) to compare consistently our results and Brod and Shivakumar's (1999) ones.

[7]For this type of utility function, see also Sutton (1997, 1998) and Symeonidis (1999, 2000). As Yakita and Yamauchi (2011), we can regard u_i as the environmental quality of variety i.

[8]In line with Symeonidis (2003), Ouchida and Goto (2016a,b), and others, this paper assumes that there exists no uncertainty regarding the outcome of R&D projects.

The inverse demand function of each consumer for variety i is derived as follows:

$$p_i = 1 - \frac{2x_i}{u_i^2} - \frac{2\sigma}{u_i}\frac{x_j}{u_j}, \ (i, j = 1, 2; i \neq j), \tag{20.1}$$

in the region of quantity spaces where prices are positive.

The direct demand for variety i is

$$x_i = \left(\frac{u_i(1 - p_i) - \sigma u_j(1 - p_j)}{2(1 - \sigma)^2}\right) u_i, \ (i, j = 1, 2; i \neq j), \tag{20.2}$$

in the region of prices paces where quantities are positive. It can be observed with ease that $dx_i/du_i > 0, dx_i/dp_i < 0, dx_i/du_j < 0$, and $dx_i/dp_j > 0$.

The quality level of variety i depends on the level of R&D activities. The relation between quality level and R&D expenditures is specialized by

$$u_i = \alpha\left(R_i^{1/4} + \rho R_j^{1/4}\right), \ (i, j = 1, 2; i \neq j), \tag{20.3}$$

where $R_i(> 0)$ presents firm i's R&D expenditures. Technological spillover effect is captured by $\rho \in (0, 1)$. A positive constant $\alpha(> 0)$ is the efficiency parameter of R&D cost.

The time structure is the following:

Stage 1: Firm i determines the quality level u_i.
Stage 2: Firm i determines its own output level x_i.

In the first stage, each firm noncooperatively and simultaneously decides its own quality level. In the second stage, each firm chooses the output level noncooperatively and simultaneously. This paper examines the two scenarios illustrated in Table 20.1. This paper examines the two scenarios illustrated in Table 20.1. The first scenario is the case of full competition in both stages. The second scenario is the case of noncooperative R&D and semicollusion in production. Throughout this paper social welfare is defined as the sum of consumer surplus and industry net profits.[9] We seek the subgame perfect Nash equilibrium (SPNE) by using backward induction.

Table 20.1 Two scenarios

	Stage 1	Stage 2
	R&D	Production
Full competition	Noncooperative	Noncooperative
Semi-collusion in production	Noncooperative	Cooperative

[9]Net profit function of each firm is defined in Sect. 20.3.

20.3 Analysis of a Two-Stage Game and Equilibrium Outcomes

In this section, we solve the two-stage game under two scenarios defined in Table 20.1 and derive equilibrium outcomes.[10] This section presents brief solution procedures of two scenarios.

First, we deal with the case of full competition. In stage 2, firm i noncooperatively and simultaneously chooses x_i to maximize its own profit $\pi_i = S(p_i - c)x_i$. From the first-order conditions $\partial\pi_i/\partial x_i = 0, (i,j = 1,2; i \neq j)$, we obtain the subgame equilibrium output level:

$$x_i(u_i, u_j) = \frac{(1-c)u_i(2u_i - \sigma u_j)}{2(2+\sigma)(2-\sigma)}, \quad (i,j = 1,2; i \neq j), \tag{20.4}$$

where we assume $u_j/u_i < 2/\sigma$ to satisfy the sufficient condition for $x_i > 0$. Then, the subgame equilibrium profit is derived as:

$$\pi_i(u_i, u_j) = S\left[\frac{(1-c)^2(2u_i - \sigma u_j)^2}{2(2+\sigma)^2(2-\sigma)^2}\right]. \tag{20.5}$$

In stage 1, firm i noncooperatively and simultaneously determines the quality level u_i to maximize its own net profit $\Pi_i(u_i, u_j) \equiv \pi_i(u_i, u_j) - R_i$. From the first-order conditions for firms, the equilibrium quality level and the equilibrium values of other variables are obtained. The results are presented in Table 20.2.[11]

On the other hand, in the case of semicollusion in production stage (semicollusive production cartel), firm i collusively chooses x_i to maximize the joint profits during the second stage. From the first-order conditions $\partial(\pi_i + \pi_j)/\partial x_i = 0 = \partial(\pi_i + \pi_j)/\partial x_j, (i,j = 1,2; i \neq j)$, we obtain the subgame equilibrium output level:

$$\hat{x}_i(u_i, u_j) = \frac{(1-c)(u_i - \sigma u_j)u_i}{4(1+\sigma)(1-\sigma)}, \quad (i,j = 1,2; i \neq j), \tag{20.6}$$

where we assume $u_j/u_i < 1/\sigma$ to satisfy the sufficient condition for the positive output level. The subgame equilibrium profit is derived as:

$$\hat{\pi}_i(u_i, u_j) = \frac{S(1-c)\hat{x}_i(u_i, u_j)}{2}. \tag{20.7}$$

---

[10] Yakita and Yamauchi (2011) have already provided the SPNE under the case of full competition.

[11] In Table 20.2, the subscripts "N" and "S," respectively, denote the two cases of "full competition" and "semicollusion in production".

Table 20.2 Equilibrium outcomes under two scenarios

	Two scenarios	
	Full competition	Semi-collusion in production
Quality level	$u_{\mathrm{N}} = \frac{S^{1/2}\alpha^2(1-c)(1+\rho)^{3/2}(2-\sigma\rho)^{1/2}}{2(2+\sigma)(2-\sigma)^{1/2}}$	$u_{\mathrm{S}} = \frac{\sqrt{2}S^{1/2}\alpha^2(1-c)(1+\rho)^{3/2}[2-\sigma(1+\rho)]^{1/2}}{8(1+\sigma)^{1/2}(1-\sigma)^{1/2}}$
R&D expenditures	$R_{\mathrm{N}} = \left(\frac{S\alpha^2(1-c)^2(1+\rho)(2-\sigma\rho)}{4(2+\sigma)^2(2-\sigma)}\right)^2$	$R_{\mathrm{S}} = \left(\frac{S\alpha^2(1-c)^2(1+\rho)[2-\sigma(1+\rho)]}{32(1+\sigma)(1-\sigma)}\right)^2$
Output level	$x_{\mathrm{N}} = \frac{S\alpha^4(1-c)^3(1+\rho)^3(2-\sigma\rho)}{8(2+\sigma)^3(2-\sigma)}$	$x_{\mathrm{S}} = \frac{S\alpha^4(1-c)^3(1+\rho)^3[2-\sigma(1+\rho)]}{128(1+\sigma)^2(1-\sigma)}$
Price	$p_{\mathrm{N}} = c + \frac{1-c}{2+\sigma}$	$p_{\mathrm{S}} = c + \frac{1-c}{2}$
Net profits	$\Pi_{\mathrm{N}} = \frac{S^2\alpha^4(1-c)^4(1+\rho)^2(2-\sigma\rho)[2(1-\sigma+2\rho)-\sigma\rho]}{16(2+\sigma)^4(2-\sigma)^2}$	$\Pi_{\mathrm{S}} = \frac{S^2\alpha^4(1-c)^4(1+\rho)^2[2-\sigma(1+\rho)] \times [4(1-\sigma)(1+\rho)-[2-\sigma(1+\rho)]]}{1024(1+\sigma)^2(1-\sigma)^2}$
Consumer surplus	$CS_{\mathrm{N}} = \frac{S^2\alpha^4(1-c)^4(1+\rho)^3(1+\sigma)(2-\sigma\rho)}{8(2+\sigma)^4(2-\sigma)}$	$CS_{\mathrm{S}} = \frac{S^2\alpha^4(1-c)^4(1+\rho)^3[2-\sigma(1+\rho)]}{256(1+\sigma)^2(1-\sigma)}$
Social welfare	$W_{\mathrm{N}} = \frac{S^2\alpha^4(1-c)^4(1+\rho)^2(2-\sigma\rho) \times [(1+\rho)(2-\sigma)(3+\sigma)-(2-\sigma\rho)]}{8(2+\sigma)^4(2-\sigma)^2}$	$W_{\mathrm{S}} = \frac{S^2\alpha^4(1-c)^4(1+\rho)^2[2-\sigma(1+\rho)] \times [2(2+3\rho)-5\sigma(1+\rho)]}{512(1+\sigma)^2(1-\sigma)^2}$

At the first stage, firm i noncooperatively and simultaneously chooses u_i to maximize the net profit $\hat{\pi}_i(u_i, u_j) - R_i$. From the first-order conditions for firms, the equilibrium quality level is obtained as:

$$u_S = \frac{\sqrt{2}S^{1/2}\alpha^2(1-c)(1+\rho)^{3/2}[2-\sigma(1+\rho)]^{1/2}}{8(1+\sigma)^{1/2}(1-\sigma)^{1/2}}. \tag{20.8}$$

After some manipulation, the equilibrium outcomes under semicollusive production cartel are calculated as in Table 20.2.

20.4 Comparison of Two Scenarios

This section compares the equilibrium outcomes described in Table 20.2 and derives policy implications.

20.4.1 Quality Level, Production Level, and Market Price

First, we compare the two equilibrium values of quality level. After some manipulation, the difference between u_s and u_n is as follows:

$$u_S - u_N = \frac{S^{1/2}\alpha^2(1-c)(1+\rho)^{3/2}V(\sigma,\rho)}{8(1+\sigma)^{1/2}(1-\sigma)^{1/2}(2+\sigma)(2-\sigma)^{1/2}} > 0, \tag{20.9}$$

where $V(\sigma,\rho) \equiv \sqrt{2}(2+\sigma)(2-\sigma)^{1/2}[2-\sigma(1+\rho)]^{1/2} - 4(1+\sigma)^{1/2}(1-\sigma)^{1/2}(2-\sigma\rho)^{1/2} > 0$. Equation (20.9) states the equilibrium value of quality-improving R&D effort under semicollusive production cartel is invariably larger than the case of full competition. This result is consistent with Fershtman and Gandal's (1994) Proposition 1 and Brod and Shivakumar's (1999) Proposition 1.

Similarly, the difference between two equilibrium production levels is derived as follows:

$$x_S - x_N = \frac{S\alpha^4(1-c)^3(1+\rho)^3 J(\sigma,\rho)}{128(1+\sigma)^2(1-\sigma)(2+\sigma)^3(2-\sigma)} \gtreqless 0, \tag{20.10}$$

where $J(\sigma,\rho) \equiv (2+\sigma)^3(2-\sigma)[2-\sigma(1+\rho)] - 16(1+\sigma)^2(1-\sigma)(2-\sigma\rho) \gtreqless 0$. In the right (left) region of the curve satisfying with $J(\sigma,\rho) = 0$ in Fig. 20.1, $x_S > (<) x_N$.

The following proposition summarizes the above results.

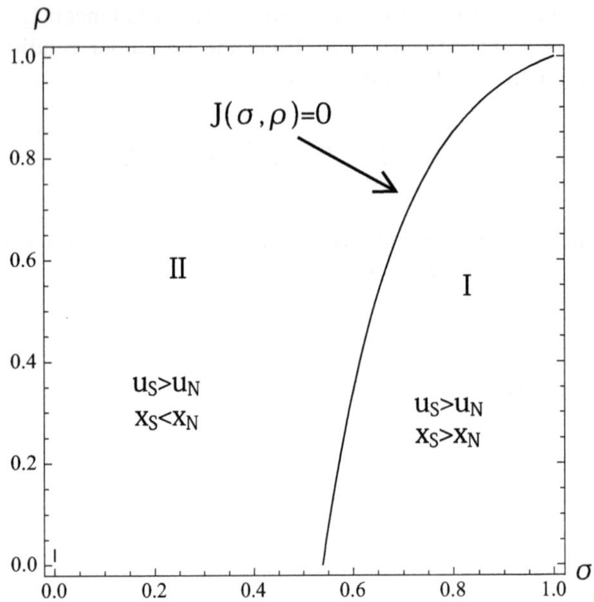

Fig. 20.1 Quality level and production level

Proposition 20.1 *There exist values of the spillover and product differentiation parameters such that:*

(i) $u_S > u_N$ *and* $x_S > x_N$ (Region I).
(ii) $u_S > u_N$ *and* $x_S < x_N$ (Region II).

Proof See Fig. 20.1. □

The intuition behind this proposition is as follows. If both firms form a quantity cartel in only output stage, they fiercely invest in R&D stage in order to enhance the joint profits in output stage.[12] The motivation for R&D investment leads to the result of Eq. (20.9). Furthermore, as reported in Fig. 20.1, there exist the regulatory circumstances where both quality and output levels under semicollusive production cartel are greater than those under full competition. The reason of existence of Region I is that the output-enhancing effect resulting in fierce R&D competition dominates the market inefficiency yielded by quantity cartel.

[12]Matsui (1989, p. 465) and Steen and Sørgard (2009, pp. 22–26) provide the useful explanations in the context of cost-reducing R&D. Their arguments help us to understand the intuition behind Proposition 20.1.

Next, let us focus on the market price. The difference between the two values of the equilibrium price is straightforwardly obtained as follows:

$$p_S - p_N = (1-c)\left[\frac{1}{2} - \frac{1}{2+\sigma}\right] = \frac{\sigma(1-c)}{2(2+\sigma)} > 0. \tag{20.11}$$

Interestingly, Eq. (20.11) insists that the equilibrium price under semicollusive production cartel is always higher than that under full competition even though there exist the circumstances of $x_S > x_N$ (see Region I in Fig. 20.1). This result is sharply contrastive to Brod and Shivakumar (1999) who show that, in the context of cost-reducing R&D, the difference of the equilibrium price between full competition and production cartel depends on values of the spillover and product differentiation parameters and the sign of the price difference is arbitrary. In the present model, whereas the value of p_N does not depend on the parameter of product differentiation, the value of p_S is strictly decreasing in $\sigma \in (0, 1)$. Hence, the difference between p_S and p_N is strictly increasing in $\sigma \in (0, 1)$. We summarize the above investigations as the following proposition.[13]

Proposition 20.2

(i) *Even though there exist the circumstances that output level under semicollusive production cartel is strictly greater than that under full competition, the value of* p_S *is invariably higher than the value of* p_N *for all* $\sigma \in (0, 1)$.
(ii) *The price difference between* p_S *and* p_N *is strictly increasing in* $\sigma \in (0, 1)$.

With regard to Proposition 20.2, Fershtman and Gandal's (1994, p. 148) Corollary 1 shows that semicollusive production cartel results in higher equilibrium price than the case of full competition, in a setting where Cournot duopolists invest in cost-reducing R&D. Equation (20.11) in the present paper seems to be consistent with Fershtman and Gandal's (1994) Corollary 1. However, in Fershtman and Gandal model, the equilibrium output level under semicollusive production cartel is always smaller than the case of full competition.[14] Their results on price and production level are reasonable and consistent with standard textbooks on microeconomics.[15] On the other hand, the part (i) of Proposition 20.2 in this paper is quite counterintuitive. The economic intuition behind Proposition 20.2(i) is as follows. In this model, higher quality level of good i increases the consumers' willingness to pay for the firm i's product. Hence, even though there exist the

[13] Yakita and Yamauchi (2011) show that $p_N = p_C$, where p_C denotes the equilibrium price under R&D cooperation and noncooperative production. For details, see Yakita and Yamauchi (2011, p. 141).

[14] It is straightforward to verify this. For details, see Section 3 in Fershtman and Gandal (1994, pp. 145–149).

[15] Whereas Fershtman and Gandal (1994) model is the case of "no technological spillover" and "no product differentiation," Brod and Shivakumar (1999) extend the Fershtman and Gandal's framework to the case with R&D spillover and product differentiation.

circumstances where output level under semicollusive production cartel is strictly greater than the case of full competition, the price-decreasing effect generated by larger outputs is dominated by the increasing effect of willingness to pay. Consequently, consumers are faced with the higher price.

20.4.2 Consumer Surplus and Net Profits

In this subsection, we examine the consumer surplus and net profits under two scenarios respectively. The difference in consumer surplus between semicollusive production cartel and full competition is given as follows:

$$CS_S - CS_N = \frac{S^2\alpha^4(1-c)^4(1+\rho)^3 H(\sigma,\rho)}{256(1+\sigma)^2(1-\sigma)(2+\sigma)^4(2-\sigma)} \gtreqless 0, \quad (20.12)$$

where $H(\sigma,\rho) \equiv (2+\sigma)^4(2-\sigma)[2-\sigma(1+\rho)] - 32(1+\sigma)^3(1-\sigma)(2-\sigma\rho) \gtreqless 0$. In line with Figure 2 in Brod and Shivakumar (1999), we plot the implicit function $H(\sigma,\rho) = 0$ in (σ,ρ)-space. In the right (left) region of the curve satisfying with $H(\sigma,\rho) = 0$ in Fig. 20.2 in the present paper, $CS_S > (<) CS_N$.

Similarly, the difference of two equilibrium net profits (Π_S and Π_N) is obtained as:

$$\begin{aligned} \Pi_S - \Pi_N &= (\pi_S - R_S) - (\pi_N - R_N) \\ &= \frac{S^2\alpha^4(1-c)^4(1+\rho)^2 G(\sigma,\rho)}{1024(1+\sigma)^2(1-\sigma)^2(2+\sigma)^4(2-\sigma)^2} \gtreqless 0, \end{aligned} \quad (20.13)$$

where $G(\sigma,\rho) \equiv (2+\sigma)^4(2-\sigma)^2[4(1+\rho)(1-\sigma) - [2-\sigma(1+\rho)]][2-\sigma(1+\rho)] - 64(1+\sigma)^2(1-\sigma)^2(2-\sigma\rho)[2(1-\sigma+2\rho)-\sigma\rho] \gtreqless 0$. The implicit function $G(\sigma,\rho) = 0$ is described in Fig. 20.2. In the right (left) region of the curve satisfying with $G(\sigma,\rho) = 0$, $\Pi_S < (>) \Pi_N$. Consequently, with regard to comparisons in the above Eqs. (20.12) and (20.13), we obtain the following proposition.[16]

Proposition 20.3 *There exist values of the spillover and product differentiation parameters such that:*

(i) $CS_S > CS_N$ *and* $\Pi_S > \Pi_N$ (Region A).
(ii) $CS_S < CS_N$ *and* $\Pi_S < \Pi_N$ (Region B).
(iii) $CS_S < CS_N$ *and* $\Pi_S > \Pi_N$ (Regions C_1 and C_2).
(iv) $CS_S > CS_N$ *and* $\Pi_S < \Pi_N$ (Regions D_1 and D_2).

[16]The labeling of six regions in Fig. 20.2 (i.e., A, B, C_1, C_2, D_1, and D_2) approximately follows to that used in Brod and Shivakumar's (1999, p. 228) Fig. 2. The definition of the curve $K(\sigma,\rho) = 0$ in Fig. 20.2 is explained in Sect. 20.4.3.

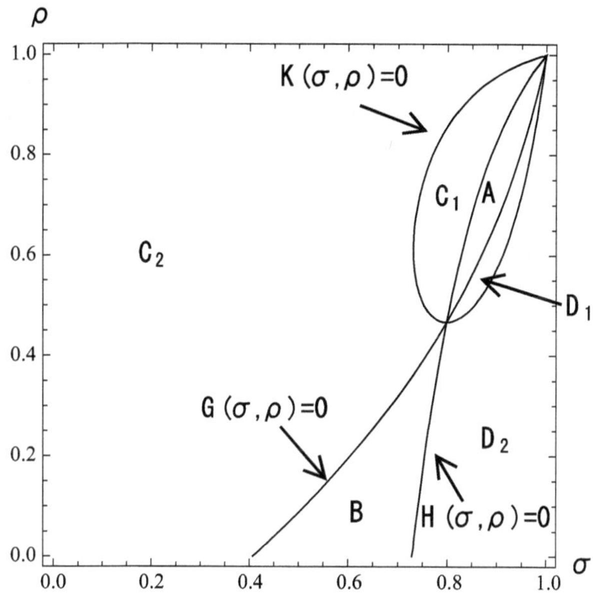

Fig. 20.2 Consumer surplus and net profits

Proof See Fig. 20.2. □

When it is defined that $\sigma_G \equiv \{\sigma | G(\sigma, 0) = 0, \sigma \in (0, 1)\}$ and $\sigma_H \equiv \{\sigma | H(\sigma, 0) = 0, \sigma \in (0, 1)\}$, we have $\sigma_G \approx 0.4075$ and $\sigma_H \approx 0.7292$. These values are straightforwardly identified in Fig. 20.2. Therefore, the following corollary is obtained.

Corollary 20.1

(i) *When* $\sigma < \sigma_G \approx 0.4075$, *then* $\Pi_S > \Pi_N$ *for all* $\rho \in (0, 1)$.
(ii) *When* $\sigma < \sigma_H \approx 0.7292$, *then* $CS_S < CS_N$ *for all* $\rho \in (0, 1)$.

Proof See Fig. 20.2. □

The intuitive explanations for these results are essentially equivalent to ones of Proposition 20.1. If both firms cartelize in only production stage, they fiercely invest in R&D stage in order to enhance the joint profits in production stage. Figure 20.1 reports such a phenomenon. In fact, if the parameter of production differentiation is sufficiently large and if spillover effect is not large, then we find that $u_S > u_N$ and $x_S > x_N$. In the Regions (A+D_1+D_2) in Fig. 20.2, consumer surplus under semicollusive production cartel is greater than that under full competition. The reason is that the consumer surplus-enhancing effect resulting in fierce R&D competition dominates the market inefficiency yielded by quantity cartelization. Next, let us examine the firm profitability. As the degree of product differentiation becomes smaller, market competition becomes fiercer. In addition, as the spillover parameter becomes smaller, firms cannot receive positive external effects. Therefore, when there exists the large value of product differentiation parameter and the small value of spillover parameter, firms' excessive R&D under semicollusion is wasteful, which yields to lower profits. The parameter set (σ, ρ) in Regions ($B+D_1+D_2$) generates such a phenomenon. These results in this Sect. 20.4.2 resemble those of Proposition 2 in Brod and Shivakumar (1999).[17]

20.4.3 Social Welfare

In Matsui (1989), Fershtman and Gandal (1994), and Brod and Shivakumar (1999), the analysis on social welfare is not carried out. Therefore, the comparison with regard to social welfare is significant for semicollusion studies. Additionally, the comparison makes it possible to compare consistently between our results and previous works (e.g., Yakita and Yamauchi (2011)). Social welfare is defined as the sum of industry net profits and consumer surplus. From Table 20.2, the difference in social welfare between two scenarios is calculated as follows:

$$\begin{aligned} W_S - W_N &= (CS_S + 2\Pi_S) - (CS_N + 2\Pi_N) \\ &= \frac{S^2\alpha^4(1-c)^4(1+\rho)^2K(\sigma,\rho)}{512(1+\sigma)^2(1-\sigma)^2(2+\sigma)^4(2-\sigma)^2} \gtreqless 0, \end{aligned} \tag{20.14}$$

where $K(\sigma, \rho) \equiv (2+\sigma)^4(2-\sigma)^2[2-\sigma(1+\rho)][2(2+3\rho)-5\sigma(1+\rho)]-64(1+\sigma)^2(1-\sigma)^2(2-\sigma\rho)[(1+\rho)(2-\sigma)(3+\sigma)-(2-\sigma\rho)] \gtreqless 0$. The result of this comparison (Equation (20.14)) is illustrated in Fig. 20.2. On the curve $K(\sigma, \rho) = 0$, the spillover and product differentiation parameters satisfy with $W_S = W_N$.[18] In the region inside (outside) the curve, $K(\sigma, \rho) = 0$, the equilibrium social welfare under semicollusive production cartel is greater (smaller) than that under full competition. Hence, we have the following proposition:

Proposition 20.4 *There exist values of the spillover and product differentiation parameters such that:*

(i) $W_S > W_N$ (Regions C_1, A, and D_1).
(ii) $W_S < W_N$ (Regions C_2, B, and D_2).

Proof See Fig. 20.2. □

Proposition 20.4 states that if the parameter set (σ, ρ) exists in the Regions (C_1+A+D_1) in Fig. 20.2, semicollusive production cartel is socially allowable.

[17] For details, see Fig. 20.2 in Brod and Shivakumar (1999, p. 228). From the comparison between their Fig. 20.2 and our Fig. 20.2, we straightforwardly grasp that the region where consumers prefer semicollusive production cartel is wider than that of the present paper.

[18] In defined parameter space, the curve $K(\sigma, \rho) = 0$ crosses uniquely at the intersection of $H(\sigma, \rho) = 0$ and $G(\sigma, \rho) = 0$. In fact, $W_S - W_N = (CS_S - CS_N) + 2(\Pi_S - \Pi_N)$.

Table 20.3 Summary of results

Region	Consumers surplus	Net profits	Social welfare
A	$CS_S > CS_N$	$\Pi_S > \Pi_N$	$W_S > W_N$
B	$CS_S < CS_N$	$\Pi_S < \Pi_N$	$W_S < W_N$
C_1	$CS_S < CS_N$	$\Pi_S > \Pi_N$	$W_S > W_N$
C_2	$CS_S < CS_N$	$\Pi_S > \Pi_N$	$W_S < W_N$
D_1	$CS_S > CS_N$	$\Pi_S < \Pi_N$	$W_S > W_N$
D_2	$CS_S > CS_N$	$\Pi_S < \Pi_N$	$W_S < W_N$

Proposition 20.4 provides the following tentative policy implication. If the degree of product differentiation is fairly small and if technological spillover effect is fairly large, then semicollusive production cartel is socially more desirable than the case of full competition. According to previous studies, the value of spillover parameter can be interpreted as the level of intellectual property rights (IPR) protection. Therefore, roughly speaking, if the degree of product differentiation between two goods is fairly small and if the strength of IPR protection is insufficient or production technology itself has a fairly large spillover effect, semicollusive production cartel yields the higher social welfare than the case of full competition. This new finding is contrastive to the usual textbook explanation of cartel prohibition. Furthermore, Proposition 20.4 suggests that the antitrust regulator should precisely investigate the real values of spillover and the degree of product differentiation.

On the other hand, if spillover effect is sufficiently small or if the parameter value of product differentiation is sufficiently small, production cartel after noncooperative R&D should not be socially allowable. That suggests that semicollusive production cartel should not be permitted if the IPR protection level is adequately strong or if the degree of product differentiation is sufficiently large. The above results of our examinations on consumer surplus, net profits, and social welfare are summarized in Table 20.3.[19]

Precisely, there can be two cases of semicollusive behavior (i.e., "semicollusion in upstream stage" and "semicollusion in downstream stage"). Yakita and Yamauchi (2011) focus on the former and show that each equilibrium level of quality, output, consumer surplus, and social welfare under R&D cooperation during stage 1 is greater (smaller) than the case of full competition if $\rho > (<)\sigma/2$. From their results, we understand that, in (σ, ρ)-space, the equilibrium social welfare under full competition (i.e., W_N) is widely dominated by one under R&D cooperation (semicollusion in upstream stage). Proposition 20.4 and Fig. 20.2 show that, in stark contrast to Yakita and Yamauchi (2011), the equilibrium social welfare under full competition is limitedly dominated by one under semicollusion in output stage (i.e., W_S).

Here, let us consider the real-world market corresponding to this model. We can find the Japanese detergent market as a comparatively applicable example. That

[19]Table 20.3 describes Fig. 20.2 in Sect. 20.4.3 of the present paper.

market was largely shared by giant two firms (i.e., Lion and Kao) till 1995. In fact, they have carried out fierce R&D competition. Their quality-improving R&D has led the improvements of water quality, antibacterial effect, water-saving effect, and others. In this research, it is newly shown that there can exist the social superiority of semicollusive production cartel in quality-improving R&D model. Proposition 20.4 is proving a tentative policy implication from a theoretical viewpoint. However, semicollusive behavior in production stage should not be easily permitted. It is hasty and undesirable to dispute production cartel from only theoretical viewpoint. The reason is that many properties are simplified and ignored in this two-stage game model. Further inquiries from other viewpoints should be accumulated for real policy design. The contribution of this paper is providing indispensable theoretical results for competition policy.

20.5 Concluding Remarks

During the past several decades, green innovation and healthcare innovation have received great attentions. In many developed countries, the development of high-quality products in those fields is one of the central themes in science and technology policy. Hence, it is quite necessary for the antitrust authority to enact competition rules with regard to such new innovation fields.

This paper investigates the social superiority of production cartel in a setting where duopolistic firms determine quantity level to maximize the joint net profits after noncooperative quality-improving R&D. The main results from a theoretical viewpoint are the following: First, contrary to previous studies, even though there exist the regulatory circumstances that output level under semicollusive production cartel is strictly greater than that under full competition, the market price under semicollusive production cartel is invariably higher than the case of full competition. Second, we show that there exist values of the spillover and product differentiation parameters such that both consumers and firms prefer semicollusive production cartel to full competition. Furthermore, if the degree of product differentiation is fairly small and if technological spillover effect is fairly large, then semicollusive production cartel has the social superiority rather than the case of full competition.

Finally, some directions for future research are pointed out. First, it is necessary to examine the case of price-setting duopolists' semicollusive behavior. Second, we should add the case of full collusion (joint exploitation) to welfare comparison. Third, further investigations from empirical and experimental sides are also necessary.

Acknowledgements The author is grateful for a Research Grant for Environmental Policy Studies of the Ministry of the Environment of Japan, No. 6, 2009–2011. In addition, this research is partially supported by KAKENHI, No. 22730200 and No. 25380303.

References

Brod, A., and R. Shivakumar. 1999. Advantageous semi-collusion. *Journal of Industrial Economics* 47: 221–230.

Dewenter, R., J. Haucap, and T. Wenzel. 2011. Semi-collusion in media markets. *International Review of Law and Economics* 31: 92–98.

Fershtman, C., and N. Gandal, 1994. Disadvantageous semicollusion. *International Journal of Industrial Organization* 12: 141–154.

Foros, Ø., B. Hansen, and J.Y. Sand. 2002. Demand-side spillover and semi-collusion in the mobile communications markets. *Journal of Industory, Competition and Trade* 2(3): 259–278.

Fukuda, K. 2017. The effects of globalization on regional inequality in a model of semi-endogenous growth and footloose capital. *Asia-Pacific Journal of Accounting & Economics* 24(1–2): 95–105.

Kabiraj, T., and S. Roy. 2004. Demand shift effect of R&D and the R&D organization. *Journal of Econoimics* 83(2): 181–198.

Matsui, A. 1989. Consumer-benefited cartels under strategic capacity investment competition. *International Journal of Industrial Organization* 7: 451–470.

Motta, A. 1993. Engogenous quality choice: Price versus quantity competition. *International Journal of Industrial Organization* 41: 113–131.

Ouchida, Y., and D. Goto. 2016a. Cournot duopoly and environmental R&D under regulator's precommitment to an emissions tax. *Applied Economics Letters* 23(5): 324–331.

Ouchida, Y., and D. Goto. 2016b. Environmental research joint ventures and time-consistent emission tax: Endogenous choice of R&D formation. *Economic Modelling* 55: 179–188.

Pal, R. 2010. Cooperative managerial delagation, R&D and collusion. *Bulletin of Economic Research* 62(2): 155–169.

Phlips, L. 1995. *Competition policy: A game-theoretic perspective*. Cambridge: Cambridge University Press.

Porter, M. E., and M. Sakakibara. 2004. Competition in Japan. *Journal of Economic Perspectives* 18(1): 27–50.

Ringbom, S., and O. Shy. 2008. Refund and collusion in service industries. *Journal of Economics and Business* 60: 502–516.

Röller, L.H., and F. Steen. 2006. On the workings of a cartel: Evidence from the Norwegian cement industry. *American Economic Review* 96(1): 321–338.

Simbanegavi, W. 2009. Informative advertising: Competition or cooperation? *Journal of Industrial Economics* 57(1): 147–166.

Steen, F., and L. Sørgard. 1999. Semicollusion in the Norwegian cement market. *European Economic Review* 43(9): 1775–1796.

Steen, F., and L. Sørgard. 2009. Semicollusion. *Foundations and Trends® in Microeconomics* 5(3): 153–228.

Sutton, J. 1997. One smart agent. *RAND Journal of Economics* 28(4): 605–628.

Sutton, J. 1998. *Technology and market structure*. Cambridge: The MIT Press.

Symeonidis, G. 1999. Cartel stability in advertising-intensive and R&D-intensive industries. *Economics Letters* 62: 121–129.

Symeonidis, G. 2000. Quality heterogeneity and welfare. *Economics Letters* 78: 1–7.

Symeonidis, G. 2003. Comparing Cournot and Bertrand equilibria in a differentiated duopoly with product R&D. *International Journal of Industrial Organization* 21: 39–55.

Weinstein, D.E. 1995. Evaluating administrative guidance and cartels in Japan (1957–1988). *Journal of the Japanese and International Economies* 9(2): 200–223.

Yakita, A., and L. Yamauchi. 2011. Environmental awareness and environmental R&D spillovers in differentiated duopoly. *Research in Economics* 65: 137–143.

Chapter 21
Optimal Commodity Taxation with Tax Brackets Under Vertical Product Differentiation

Kiyoshi Arakawa

21.1 Introduction

Commodity taxation based on product characteristics is widely seen all over the world. However, commodity taxation under a vertically differentiated market has seldom been analyzed in the existing literature—a notable exception being Cremer and Thisse (1994). They analyzed ad valorem commodity taxation under a differentiated duopoly market and showed that it might be optimal to set a higher tax rate on high-quality products, while setting a lower tax rate on low-quality products.[1] They considered a situation in which tax rates are set on products per se; in this case, firms cannot select or change tax rates. In other words, their model considered an endogenous product selection, while the tax rates levied on products were given exogenously. This is similar to charging tariffs on imported products. Otherwise, however, tax rates levied on products are determined according to product characteristics, such as product quality. Thus, in general, firms can select tax rates by determining product characteristics. This implies that firms are allowed an endogenous tax rate selection. More precisely, there are tax brackets that are classified by product characteristics where tax rates are designated for each bracket; firms can determine their product characteristics and tax rates simultaneously.

In such taxation with brackets, there may be notches. A notch is a discontinuity in tax liability as a function of the size of the base, i.e., the tax amounts levied on

[1]Arakawa (2012) compared specific and ad valorem taxation from the welfare perspective by introducing specific taxation in which the amount of tax depended on product quality.

K. Arakawa (✉)
Faculty of Social Information Studies, Otsuma Women's University, Tokyo, Japan

T. Naito et al. (eds.), *Applied Approaches to Societal Institutions and Economics*, New Frontiers in Regional Science: Asian Perspectives 18,
DOI 10.1007/978-981-10-5663-5_21

products change discontinuously when product characteristics cross tax thresholds.[2] Notches are widely found when tax amounts depend on characteristics, including fuel economy of the car, size of the firm, and quantities such as income.[3] For example, Blinder and Rosen (1985) found that when the purpose of a policy is to promote socially preferable goods, compared with a linear subsidy policy, notches might be socially preferable. Slemrod et al. (1994) investigated a two-bracket piecewise income tax structure and showed that a second marginal tax rate was less than the first rate but that progressivity was obtained. Dharmapala et al. (2011) showed that discontinuous tax treatment in firm size is optimal when there are firm-level administrative costs.[4]

Gillitzer et al. (2015) constructed a model of a differentiated product market by recasting the characteristic approach adopted by Lancaster (1975) and showed that tax thresholds that create notches may improve social welfare (SW) and induce product innovation. Arakawa (2014) investigated the effect of a two-bracket piecewise quality-specific tax on SW in a vertically differentiated oligopoly model based on that of Mussa and Rosen (1978), with an endogenous selection of product qualities and tax amounts. He showed that SW is maximized with a taxation system in which each product belongs to a different tax bracket and, thus, is subject to different tax amounts. He also showed that using the notch where one of the products binds to the tax threshold may improve SW. That is, notches may be socially preferable. Considering a duopoly in which each firm produces a differentiated single product, Arakawa (2014) clarified the effects of notches on competition among firms. Because taxation policy with tax brackets affects not only a firm's product strategies against other firms but also the firm's product strategies in terms of their own product lines, it is necessary to analyze the effects of tax brackets on a multiproduct monopoly or a scenario with many firms.

In this paper, we analyze the effects of commodity taxation with tax brackets under a vertically differentiated multiproduct monopoly and show an optimal taxation scheme. The tax brackets are classified by product qualities. A monopolist with two products determines the prices and qualities of the products that will maximize his profit, given the tax brackets. Based on this monopolistic behavior, the government determines taxation using tax brackets that will maximize SW. In such a taxation plan, because there may be notches at different tax thresholds, by analyzing the effects of the notches on SW, we are able to show whether setting notches can improve SW.

This paper is organized as follows. In the next section, we show the model and explain the three locations of product qualities on the tax brackets. In Sect. 21.3,

---

[2] Kinks are conceptually different from notches because kinks are defined as discontinuities in the slope of the choice, while notches are defined as discrete changes in the tax liability.

[3] The literature on notches has been surveyed by Slemrod (2013).

[4] To analyze a missing middle, a bimodal distribution of firm size in poor countries, empirical economic literature dealing with the political effects of notches has recently grown. See also Kleven and Waseem (2013).

we define the SW function. In Sect. 21.4, we analyze the equilibrium under taxation with tax brackets. In Sect. 21.5, we show the optimal level of taxation. Finally, in Sect. 21.6, we conclude.

21.2 Model

In this section, we show a vertically differentiated model based on that of Mussa and Rosen (1978). The structure of the model is as follows. First, the government determines a taxation system, and next the monopolist decides on a product line, determining the price and quality of each product. Here, we explain the relationship between taxation with brackets and the monopolist's strategy.

The monopolist produces one or two kinds of vertically differentiated products to maximize his profit. When he produces one kind of product, let the quality and price of the products be q and p, respectively. When he produces two kinds of products, we denote the quality and price of product i as q_i and $p_i \quad (i = 1, 2)$. Without loss of generality, we assume that $q_2 > q_1$. Thus, hereafter, we identify Product 1 as the low-quality product and Product 2 as the high-quality product.

The government levies a specific commodity tax on the products based on their qualities, and consumers pay the tax. The amount of tax is t when the monopolist offers one kind of product; when the monopolist offers two kinds of products, the tax amounts levied on Products 1 and 2 are t_1 and t_2, respectively.

Each tax is determined as follows. Tax brackets are determined by the quality threshold $\bar{q}$. The amount of tax on the low-quality side of the bracket is t_L and that on the high-quality side is t_H. Because the tax amount changes discontinuously at different tax thresholds, this taxation system creates notches. Thus, the products may bind to the tax threshold. In order to deal with this, we define a range on the low-quality side of the bracket as $q \leq \bar{q}$ if $t_L < t_H$ and as $q < \bar{q}$ if $t_L > t_H$. In a similar fashion, the range on the high-quality side of the bracket is defined as $q > \bar{q}$ if $t_L < t_H$ and as $q \geq \bar{q}$ if $t_L > t_H$. We assume that the amount of tax can be negative, and this situation would be one in which the government grants subsidies.

A continuum of consumers of mass $\bar{\theta}$ is uniformly distributed over the interval $[0, \bar{\theta}]$ with density equal to unity. The total market size is $\bar{\theta}$. Parameter θ identifies each consumer's marginal willingness to pay. If faced with one unit of a vertically differentiated product of quality level q at price p, each consumer maximizes his net surplus, which is $U = \theta q - p$ if he buys, and $U = 0$ otherwise.

Let us obtain the demand for each product. First, we consider the case where the monopolist produces one kind of product. Among consumers whose net surpluses are positive, the consumer θ_1 who has the smallest θ is obtained as follows:

$$\theta_1 = \begin{cases} 0 & (p \leq -t), \\ \frac{p+t}{q} & (-t < p \leq \bar{\theta} q - t), \\ \bar{\theta} & (p > \bar{\theta} q - t). \end{cases} \tag{21.1}$$

The first line of (21.1) is a case in which all consumers have a positive net surplus, because the price is relatively low. The second line of (21.1) is a case where only consumers whose θ is larger than θ_1 obtain a positive net surplus. The third line of (21.1) is a case in which no consumers can obtain a positive net surplus, because the price is too high. These differences in consumer surpluses are determined by the difference between the price and the amount of tax. The demand for the product, x, is $\bar{\theta} - \theta_1$.

Next, we consider a case where the monopolist produces two kinds of products. Among consumers whose net surpluses are positives, the consumer θ_1 who has the smallest θ is obtained as follows:

$$\theta_1 = \begin{cases} 0 & (p_1 \leq -t_1), \\ \frac{p_1+t_1}{q_1} & (-t_1 < p_1 \leq \bar{\theta} q_1 - t_1), \\ \bar{\theta} & (p_1 > \bar{\theta} q_1 - t_1). \end{cases} \tag{21.2}$$

Interpretation of the above equation is similar for each line, as in (21.1).

The consumer θ_2 who is indifferent between Product 1 and 2 is obtained as follows:

$$\theta_2 = \begin{cases} 0 & (p_1 - p_2 \leq -t_1 + t_2), \\ \frac{p_1+t_1-p_2-t_2}{q_1-q_2} & (-t_1 + t_2 < p_1 - p_2 \leq \bar{\theta}(q_1 - q_2) - t_1 + t_2), \\ \bar{\theta} & (p_1 - p_2 > \bar{\theta}(q_1 - q_2) - t_1 + t_2). \end{cases} \tag{21.3}$$

The first line of (21.3) is a case in which all consumers have a positive net surplus, because the price is relatively low. The second line of (21.3) is a case where consumers whose θ is larger than θ_2 obtain more net positive surplus from Product 2 than Product 1. The third line of (21.3) is a case in which all consumers obtain more net surplus from Product 1 than Product 2. Demands for the products are as follows: when $\theta_1 < \theta_2$, $x_1 = \theta_2 - \theta_1$, and $x_2 = \bar{\theta} - \theta_2$ and when $\theta_1 > \theta_2$, $x_1 = 0$, and $x_2 = \bar{\theta} - \theta_2$.

Because we assume that production cost consists of variable cost, $q^2 x$, the profit function of the monopolist is defined as follows: when he produces one kind of product,

$$\pi = \left(p + t - cq^2\right) x, \tag{21.4}$$

and when he produces two kinds of products,

$$\pi = \left(p_1 + t_1 - cq_1^2\right) x_1 + \left(p_2 + t_2 - cq_2^2\right) x_2. \tag{21.5}$$

The monopolist determines the quality and price of the products to maximize his profit. Here, to make the description easier to understand, we assume that the monopolist determines the quality and price at two stages: at the first stage, he determines the product quality, and at the second stage, he determines the product price.

In this case, at the second stage, given the product quality, the monopolist determines a product price to maximize his profit. However, because (21.2) and (21.3) are complicated, the profit functions, (21.4) and (21.5), are also complicated in terms of obtaining analytical results. Let us examine this in more detail in the following:

First, let us consider when the monopolist produces one kind of product. Assuming that the condition in which θ_1 does not bind, $0 < \theta_1 < \bar{\theta}$, is satisfied, differentiating (21.4) with respect to the price, and equating the differential to zero, we have the price as follows:

$$p = \frac{q\left(cq_1 + \bar{\theta}\right) - t}{2}. \tag{21.6}$$

If (21.6) satisfies the condition, $0 < \theta_1 < \bar{\theta}$, this price is indeed the equilibrium price. However, if (21.6) does not satisfy the condition, it cannot be the equilibrium price. Thus, it is difficult to obtain an analytical equilibrium price.

Next, let us consider when the monopolist produces two kinds of products. Assuming that the condition in which θ_1 and θ_2 do not bind, $0 < \theta_1 < \theta_2 < \bar{\theta}$, is satisfied, differentiating (21.5) with respect to the prices, and equating them to zero, we have the price as follows:

$$p_1 = \frac{q_1\left(cq_1 + \bar{\theta}\right) - t_1}{2}, p_2 = \frac{q_2\left(cq_2 + \bar{\theta}\right) - t_2}{2}. \tag{21.7}$$

If the equations in (21.7) satisfy the condition, $0 < \theta_1 < \theta_2 < \bar{\theta}$, these prices are definitely equilibrium prices. However, if the equations in (21.7) do not satisfy the condition, they cannot be equilibrium prices. In this case, it is difficult to obtain equilibrium prices analytically. For the above reasons, we obtain equilibrium numerically.

21.3 Social Welfare

Here, we define the SW function represented as the sum of the surpluses of consumers, the monopolist (i.e., his profit), and the government. First, when the monopolist produces one kind of product, the consumer surplus (CS) and SW are given, respectively, as follows:

$$CS = \int_{\theta_1}^{\bar{\theta}} (\theta q - t - p)\, d\theta, \tag{21.8}$$

$$SW = CS + \pi + t\left(\bar{\theta} - \theta_1\right). \tag{21.9}$$

Note that the third term on the right-hand side of (21.9) is the government surplus. In the case of non-taxation, by maximizing the monopolist's profit, (21.4), with respect to the price and quality of the products, we have the following:

$$p = \frac{2\bar{\theta}^2}{9c}, q = \frac{\bar{\theta}}{3c}, \theta_1 = \frac{2\bar{\theta}}{3}, CS = \frac{\bar{\theta}^3}{54c}, PS = \frac{\bar{\theta}^3}{27c}, SW = \frac{\bar{\theta}^3}{18c}. \tag{21.10}$$

To obtain the first best, by maximizing the SW function, (21.9), with respect to the price and quality of the products, we have the following:

$$p = \frac{\bar{\theta}^2}{9c}, q = \frac{\bar{\theta}}{3c}, \theta_1 = \frac{\bar{\theta}}{3}, CS = \frac{2\bar{\theta}^3}{27c}, PS = 0, SW = \frac{2\bar{\theta}^3}{27c}. \tag{21.11}$$

Next, when the monopolist produces two kinds of products, the CS and SW are given, respectively, as follows:

$$CS = \int_{\theta_1}^{\theta_2} (\theta q_1 - t_1 - p_1)\, d\theta + \int_{\theta_2}^{\bar{\theta}} (\theta q_2 - t_2 - p_2)\, d\theta, \tag{21.12}$$

$$SW = CS + \pi + t_1 (\theta_2 - \theta_1) + t_2 \left(\bar{\theta} - \theta_2\right). \tag{21.13}$$

Note that the third and fourth terms on the right-hand side of (21.13) are the government surpluses. In the case of non-taxation, by maximizing the monopolist's profit, (21.5), with respect to the prices and qualities of the products, we have the following:

$$p_1 = \frac{3\bar{\theta}^2}{25c}, p_2 = \frac{7\bar{\theta}^2}{25c}, q_1 = \frac{\bar{\theta}}{5c}, q_2 = \frac{2\bar{\theta}}{5c}, \theta_1 = \frac{3\bar{\theta}}{5}, \theta_2 = \frac{4\bar{\theta}}{5},$$

$$CS = \frac{\bar{\theta}^3}{50c}, PS = \frac{\bar{\theta}^3}{25c}, SW = \frac{3\bar{\theta}^3}{50c}. \tag{21.14}$$

In terms of the first best, by maximizing the SW function, (21.13), with respect to the prices and qualities of the products, we have the following:

$$p_1 = \frac{\bar{\theta}^2}{25c}, p_2 = \frac{4\bar{\theta}^2}{25c}, q_1 = \frac{\bar{\theta}}{5c}, q_2 = \frac{2\bar{\theta}}{5c}, \theta_1 = \frac{\bar{\theta}}{5}, \theta_2 = \frac{3\bar{\theta}}{5},$$

$$CS = \frac{2\bar{\theta}^3}{25c}, PS = 0, SW = \frac{2\bar{\theta}^3}{25c}. \tag{21.15}$$

21.4 Equilibrium

The government determines the threshold and tax amounts for each bracket. Given the government's decisions, the monopolist determines how many different types of products to offer and then decides on the prices and qualities of these products. Here, by considering the response of the monopolist to the taxation in more detail, we analyze the relationship between the monopolist's product strategies and SW. Then, we obtain an optimal taxation level with the threshold and tax amounts of each bracket that maximize SW.

The monopolist determines product prices and qualities to maximize his profit given the threshold and tax amounts of each bracket. The relationship between product qualities and tax brackets can be classified into the following three types: (1) all of the product qualities are located on the low-quality side of the bracket (type L), (2) all of the product qualities are located on the high-quality side of the bracket (type H), and (3) one of the product qualities is located on the low-quality side of the bracket, and the other is on the high-quality side of the bracket (type LH).

To analyze the monopolist's strategy, we consider the following processes in the monopolist's decision. First, we assume that the monopolist wants to maximize profits and locates product qualities according to the three types, i.e., type L, type H, and type LH. We obtain equilibria by assuming that the monopolist chooses the location of each type of product. Then, by choosing maximum profit among the three equilibria, we obtain a conclusive equilibrium.

Given the monopolist's behavior, the government determines the threshold and tax levels for each bracket to maximize SW. To obtain optimal taxation, we consider that the government performs the following process. First, the government determines the tax amounts for each bracket. Next, it sets the tax threshold as zero and calculates the profits and SW for each of the three types of products. After this, it increases the tax threshold and recalculates. When the tax threshold gets to a point when profit and SW do not increase, the process terminates. Then, the government goes back to the beginning of the process, changes the tax amounts for each bracket, and recalculates SW. Finally, optimal taxation is obtained by choosing the threshold and tax amounts for each bracket that give the maximum SW among the results.

Below, we assume that $c = 1.0$ and $\bar{\theta} = 10.0$.[5] In this case, SW is 60 when the government does not levy taxation. Thus, any taxation that gives an SW number greater than 60 is socially preferable.

[5] We find that the results do not change with other parameters.

21.4.1 Type L

The equilibrium in this type can be understood intuitively as follows. When $\bar{q}$ is small, because either the monopolist produces one kind of product and the product quality binds to $\bar{q}$ or he produces two kinds of products and the higher-quality product binds to $\bar{q}$, his profit is less than when no tax is levied. When $\bar{q}$ becomes large, because all product qualities do not bind to $\bar{q}$, profit is maximized, which is the same as the situation with no tax. That is, with this type, the profit is an increasing function of $\bar{q}$. In the following section, let us observe this mechanism in greater detail.

(a) When $t_L < 0$. In this case, two patterns of the monopolist's strategies exist. First, with increasing $\bar{q}$, the monopolist's strategies change from $q_1 = 0$ and $q_2 = \bar{q}$ to $q_1 = 0$ and $q_2 < \bar{q}$, henceforth L(1). Second, with increasing $\bar{q}$, the monopolist's strategies change as $q_1 = 0$ and $q_2 = \bar{q}$, $q_1 > 0$ and $q_2 = \bar{q}$, and $q_1 > 0$ and $q_2 < \bar{q}$, henceforth L(2). In these patterns, when $\bar{q}$ increases from zero, but q_1 remains at zero, q_2 increases with binding to $\bar{q}$. In this case, profit and SW increase. When $\bar{q}$ becomes sufficiently large, depending on t_L, the monopolist's strategies are divided into two patterns, i.e., L(1) and L(2). Numerical analysis shows that the pattern is L(1) when $t_L < -0.5$ and L(2) when $t_L \geq -0.5$.

First, let us consider L(1) with increasing $\bar{q}$. When $t_L < -0.5$, that is, when t_L is small, q_1 remains at zero, while q_2 is a constant value without binding to $\bar{q}$. In this case, profit and SW are also constant values. Because SW is 55.56, which is less than 60, we find that taxation reduces SW.

Next, let us consider L(2) with increasing $\bar{q}$. When $t_L \geq -0.5$, that is, when t_L is not too small, while q_2 remains bound to $\bar{q}$, q_1 increases discontinuously. In this case, SW also increases discontinuously. After that, while q_1 increases further, when $\bar{q}$ exceeds a certain value, q_1 and q_2 remain constant values. In this case, profit and SW are also constant values. Because SW exceeds 60, we find that when the tax threshold is large, SW can be improved when product quality binds to the tax threshold.

(b) When $t_L > 0$. In this case, there is only one pattern of the monopolist's strategies. When $\bar{q}$ is small enough, the monopolist cannot gain positive profit and, hence, does not enter the market. With an increasing $\bar{q}$, the monopolist's strategies change as $q = \bar{q}$, $q_1 > 0$ and $q_2 = \bar{q}$, $q_1 > 0$ and $q_2 < \bar{q}$, henceforth L(3). In this pattern, while when $\bar{q}$ is small the monopolist does not enter the market, when $\bar{q}$ increases and exceeds a certain value, the monopolist produces one kind of product with a quality that binds to the threshold, i.e., $q = \bar{q}$. Profit and SW increase with $\bar{q}$. Further, if $\bar{q}$ exceeds a certain value, q_1 and q_2 do not bind to $\bar{q}$, and profit and SW are constant values. That is, SW is maximized when the product qualities do not bind to the tax threshold. Profit and SW are decreasing functions of t_L.[6] In this case, because SW is less than 60, we find that taxation reduces SW.

[6] Because θ_1 increases with t_L, if the tax amounts increase, the number of consumers who can buy products decreases, and CS also decreases. Thus, if tax amounts increase, SW decreases.

Result 1 In equilibrium with type L, although SW increases with the tax threshold, when the tax threshold exceeds a certain value, SW remains at a certain value. Therefore, SW is maximized when the product qualities do not bind to the tax threshold. That is, the notch is not socially preferable. SW is improved when $t_L \in [-0.5, 0)$, i.e., when the subsidy is small.

21.4.2 Type H

The equilibrium in this type can be understood intuitively as follows. When $\bar{q}$ is small enough, product qualities are the same as or similar to those without taxation, and profit is large. However, when $\bar{q}$ grows, the lower-quality product binds to $\bar{q}$, and profit falls. That is, in this type, the profit function is a decreasing function of $\bar{q}$. In the following section, let us observe this mechanism in more detail.

(a) When $t_H < 0$. In this case, there are three patterns of the monopolist's strategies. First, with increasing $\bar{q}$, the monopolist's strategies change with $q_1 = \bar{q}$ and $q_2 > \bar{q}$, henceforth H(1). Second, with increasing $\bar{q}$, the monopolist's strategies change as $q_1 = \bar{q}$ and $q_2 > \bar{q}$, $q_1 > \bar{q}$ and $q_2 > \bar{q}$, $q_1 = \bar{q}$ and $q_2 > \bar{q}$, henceforth H(2). Third, with increasing $\bar{q}$, the monopolist's strategies change from $q_1 > \bar{q}$ and $q_2 > \bar{q}$ to $q_1 = \bar{q}$ and $q_2 > \bar{q}$, henceforth H(3). In these patterns, numerical analysis shows that the pattern is H(1) when $t_H < -1.60$, H(2) when $t_H \in [-1.6, -0.5)$, and H(3) when $t_H \geq -0.5$.

When $t_H < -0.5$, that is, when the tax amount is small, if $\bar{q}$ is small, the monopolist's strategies are $q_1 = \bar{q}$ and $q_2 > \bar{q}$, that is, the lower-quality product binds to the tax threshold. In this case, with increasing $\bar{q}$, although profit decreases, SW increases. When $\bar{q}$ gets larger, the monopolist's strategy is classified into two patterns at $t_H = -1.6$.

First, when $t_H < -1.6$, the monopolist's strategy is H(1). With increasing $\bar{q}$, the monopolist's strategies are $q_1 = \bar{q}$ and $q_2 > \bar{q}$. In this case, while profit continues to decrease, SW increases until it reaches a peak and then continuously decreases.

Next, when $t_H \geq -1.6$, the monopolist's strategy is H(2). With increasing $\bar{q}$, when $\bar{q}$ reaches a certain value, all product qualities discontinuously increase to $q_1 > \bar{q}$ and $q_2 > \bar{q}$. Until $\bar{q}$ is less than a certain value, all product qualities remains at certain constant values. Afterward, the monopolist's strategies become $q_1 = \bar{q}$ and $q_2 > \bar{q}$ and the lower-quality product binds to the threshold. With increasing $\bar{q}$, while profit continues to decrease, SW increases until it reaches a peak and then continues to decrease afterwards. Therefore, for both H(1) and H(2), SW is maximized when the lower-quality product binds to the threshold. In this case, because SW exceeds 60, SW is improved, compared to the condition without taxation.

Finally, when $t_H \geq -0.5$, the monopolist's strategy is H(3). When $\bar{q}$ is small, the monopolist's strategies are $q_1 > \bar{q}$ and $q_2 > \bar{q}$, that is, all product qualities do not bind to the threshold, and they remain at constant values. In this case, SW exceeds 60. When $\bar{q}$ increases and exceeds a certain value, the lower-quality product binds to the threshold, and the monopolist's strategies are $q_1 = \bar{q}$ and $q_2 > \bar{q}$. With increasing $\bar{q}$, both profit and SW decrease. Thus, SW can be improved when all product qualities do not bind to the threshold.

(b) When $t_H > 0$. In this case, the monopolist's strategy is H(3). The maximum level of SW in this case is, as mentioned above, a certain constant value. However, because both profit and SW are decreasing functions of t_H, the maximum SW is lower than it is without taxation. We find that SW cannot be improved in this case.

Result 2 In equilibrium with type H, when $t_H < 0$, SW increases with the tax threshold. Therefore, the notch can improve SW compared to the condition without taxation.

21.4.3 Type LH

The equilibrium in this type can be classified into the following four cases: (a) $t_L < 0$ and $t_H < 0$, (b) $t_L < 0$ and $t_H > 0$, (c) $t_L > 0$ and $t_H < 0$, and (d) $t_L > 0$ and $t_H > 0$. In the following section, let us analyze SW for each of the four cases.

(a) When $t_L < 0$ *and* $t_H < 0$. In this case, there are four patterns of the monopolist's strategies. First, with increasing $\bar{q}$,the monopolist's strategy changes from producing one kind of product (i.e., the monopolist does not employ the strategies of type LH) to $q_1 = 0$ and $q_2 = \bar{q}$, henceforth LH(1). Second, with increasing $\bar{q}$, the monopolist's strategies change from $q_1 = 0$ and $q_2 > \bar{q}$ to $q_1 = 0$ and $q_2 = \bar{q}$, henceforth LH(2). Third, with increasing $\bar{q}$, the monopolist's strategies change as $q_1 = 0$ and $q_2 > \bar{q}$, $q_1 = 0$ and $q_2 = \bar{q}$, $q_1 < \bar{q}$ and $q_2 = \bar{q}$, henceforth LH(3). Fourth, with increasing $\bar{q}$, the monopolist's strategies change as $q_1 = 0$ and $q_2 > \bar{q}$, $q_1 = \bar{q}$ and $q_2 > \bar{q}$, $q_1 < \bar{q}$ and $q_2 > \bar{q}$, and $q_1 < \bar{q}$ and $q_2 = \bar{q}$, henceforth LH(4).

Numerical analysis shows that the pattern may be LH(1) when $t_L > t_H$with the difference between tax amounts relatively large. In this case, SW is improved compared to that without taxation. SW is maximized when the higher-quality product binds to the threshold. Further, when the absolute values of both tax amounts are not small, or when the difference between the absolute values of both tax amounts is large, SW is improved.

When both t_L and t_H are close to zero, the monopolist's strategy is LH(3). SW is maximized when the higher-quality product binds to the threshold, and it is improved compared to the condition without taxation.

When both t_L and t_H are extremely close to zero, the monopolist's strategy is LH(4). SW is maximized when the higher-quality product binds to the threshold and is improved compared to the situation without taxation.

(b) When $t_L < 0$ *and* $t_H > 0$. In this case, there are two patterns, LH(2) and LH(4). Numerical analysis shows that when the absolute value of $t_L$is not too small relative to t_H, the monopolist's strategy may be LH(2). On the other hand, when

the absolute value of $t_H$is smaller than t_H, the monopolist's strategy may be LH(4). In both cases, when both tax amounts are small, SW is improved compared to the condition without taxation.

(c) When $t_L > 0$ *and* $t_H < 0$. In this case, there are two patterns of the monopolist's strategies. First, with increasing $\bar{q}$, the monopolist's strategy changes from producing one kind of product (i.e., the monopolist does not employ the strategies of type LH) to $q_1 = \bar{q}$ and $q_2 > \bar{q}$, $q_1 < \bar{q}$ and $q_2 > \bar{q}$, and $q_1 < \bar{q}$ and $q_2 = \bar{q}$, henceforth LH(5). Second, with increasing $\bar{q}$, the monopolist's strategy changes from producing one kind of product to $q_1 > 0$ and $q_2 = \bar{q}$, henceforth LH(6).

When both the absolute values of t_L and t_H are small, the monopolist's strategy may be LH(5). Numerical analysis shows that SW may be improved when both the absolute values of tax amounts are small, compared to the condition without taxation.

When both the absolute values of t_L and t_H are not too large, the monopolist's strategy may be LH(6). In this case, SW increases. Numerical analysis shows that when t_L is small, SW is improved compared to the situation without taxation.

When both the absolute values of t_L and t_H are large, there is no equilibrium with type LH, because the monopolist maximizes his profit by producing products with qualities that are higher than the tax threshold.

(d) When $t_L > 0$ *and* $t_H > 0$. In this case, there are two patterns, LH(5) and LH(6). When $t_L > t_H$ and the difference between the tax amounts is small or when $t_L < t_H$, the monopolist's strategy may be LH(5). On the other hand, when $t_L > t_H$ and the difference between the tax amounts is not too large, the monopolist's strategy may be LH(6). When $t_L > t_H$ and the difference between the tax amounts is large, there is no equilibrium with type LH. Numerical analysis shows that in any case SW cannot be improved compared to the situation without taxation.

Result 3 In equilibrium with type LH, when $t_H < 0$ and when $t_L > 0$ and the absolute values of t_L and t_H are not large, SW can be improved if the higher-quality product binds to the threshold.

21.5 Optimal Taxation

Figure 21.1 shows the relationship between the tax amounts and the type of monopolist strategy that maximizes SW. Figure 21.2 shows the relationship between the tax amounts and SW.

From Fig. 21.1, we find that when $t_L < t_H$, basically, equilibrium with type L gives the maximum SW. This is because the monopolist has an incentive to locate all products on the low-quality side of the tax bracket rather than the high-quality side, where the tax amount is large. However, from Fig. 21.2, we find that when t_L is negative with a large absolute value, that is, when the government grants a large subsidy on the low-quality side of the bracket, it cannot give the monopolist an

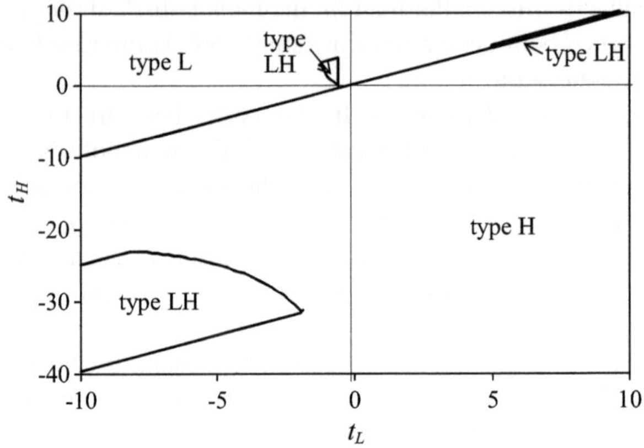

Fig. 21.1 Types of equilibrium with maximum social welfare

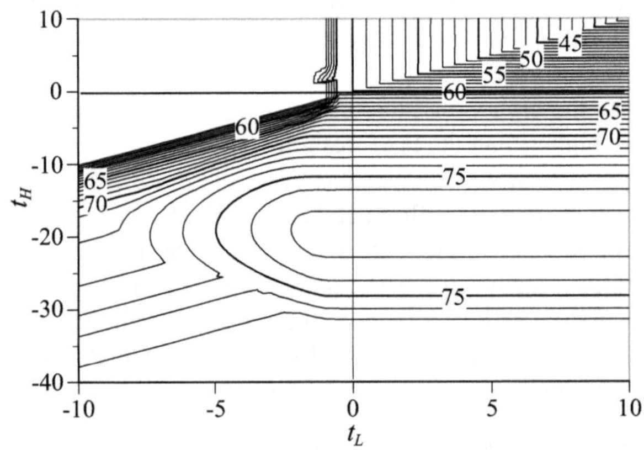

Fig. 21.2 Tax amounts and maximum social welfare

incentive to improve product quality. As a result, the monopolist lowers the quality of all products, and SW decreases compared to the condition without taxation. On the other hand, when t_L is negative and close to zero, we find that SW improves. In this case, because the amount of the subsidy is small, the government can give the monopolist an incentive to improve product quality. Further, when t_L is positive, that is, when the government grants a large subsidy on the low-quality side of the bracket, although all product qualities improve, profit decreases, and SW also decreases compared to the situation without taxation.

When t_L is negative and close to zero and when t_H is close to zero, we find that the equilibrium is type LH. In this case, only when t_H is negative does SW improve. Further, when t_L is larger than 5 and when t_H is close to t_L, the equilibrium is type LH. In this case, SW decreases compared to the condition without taxation.

To summarize the above, when $t_L < t_H$, only when t_L is negative and close to zero do we find that SW is improved.

Figure 21.1 shows that when $t_L > t_H$, basically, the equilibrium is type H, and we have maximum SW. This is because the monopolist has an incentive to locate all of the products on the high-quality side of the tax bracket rather than low-quality side where the tax amount is large. Except in the case of $t_L > 0$ with $t_H > 0$, SW is improved compared to the condition without taxation. Further, in this case, by setting a high threshold, the government can induce the monopolist to improve the quality of all products. That is, by giving a strong incentive to locate all products on the high-quality side of the bracket, setting the threshold to make the lower-quality product bind to the threshold, and increasing the threshold, SW is greatly improved. In other words, by utilizing the notch, SW is improved effectively.

However, when both t_L and t_H are positive and there is equilibrium with type LH, SW cannot be improved. On the other hand, when both t_L and t_H are negative, we find that there may be an equilibrium with type LH that gives maximum SW. In this case, SW is improved compared to the condition without taxation. However, in this case, because the lower-quality product does not bind to the threshold, SW cannot be improved compared to type H, where the government can utilize the notch. Thus, the equilibrium with type LH cannot be expected to have the equivalent socially preferable effect of taxation as with type H.

To summarize the above, when $t_L > t_H$, the notches can greatly improve SW. From Fig. 21.2, numerical analysis shows that the tax amounts and tax threshold that maximize SW, that is, the optimal taxation situation, are as follows:

$$t_L > -1.2,\ t_H = -19.6,\ \bar{q} = 2.68,\ q_1 = 2.68,\ q_2 = 4.23,$$
$$PS = 147.22,\ SW = 77.35. \tag{21.16}$$

Result 4 The optimal taxation program is such that the monopolist positions all products on the high-quality side of bracket (i.e., type H), and the low-quality product binds to the threshold. Therefore, the notches improve SW.

Finally, let us look at the improvements in SW delivered by the notches. If we do not set a tax threshold and set both t_L and t_H as -19.6, the equilibrium quality values are $q_1 = 0$ and $q_2 = 3.33$. SW in this case is 55.56, lower than without taxation. If we set a tax threshold and high tax amount on the low-quality side of the bracket, because all product qualities are increased, SW is improved.

21.6 Conclusion

In this paper, we analyze the optimal commodity taxation with tax brackets for a multiproduct monopoly under vertical differentiation. The results obtained in this paper are as follows: taxation that maximizes SW is such that tax is levied on the low-quality side of the tax bracket, and subsidies are granted on the high-quality side of the tax bracket. The equilibrium under this taxation plan is such that all products are positioned on the high-quality side of the tax bracket. In this case, by granting a large amount of subsidy on the high-quality side of the bracket, the government can give an incentive to the monopolist to improve all product qualities. Further, by levying a large amount of tax on the low-quality side of the tax bracket, the government can induce the monopolist to avoid locating all products on the low-quality side of the bracket. Further, by raising the tax bracket, one of the product qualities is improved by binding it with the threshold, that is, the notches improve SW. In sum, this paper shows that the government can control the tax threshold and improve SW by utilizing notches.

There are a few limitations to these conclusions. In this paper, because we assume a multiproduct monopolist, we cannot consider strategies for product lines under a competitive environment. In the real world, however, firms determine their product lines considering the strategic effects of rivals (see Brander and Eaton 1984). Thus, the remaining problem is to extend this model to a multiproduct oligopoly. Arakawa (2014) considered the endogenous product selection of a duopoly with strategic effect to analyze the optimal level of commodity taxation with a tax bracket and assumed that firms each produced a single differentiated product. He showed that the government can increase SW by forcing out one of the firms by raising or lowering the tax threshold, because this reduces total production costs and exerts pressure, thereby lowering the price of the remaining product with potential entrants as the contestable markets hypothesis. Based on this, we can expect that if we extend this model into a multiproduct duopoly, the government can improve SW by controlling the tax threshold to improve product qualities and lower prices with potential new products. This is a subject for future analysis.

Acknowledgements This research is supported by a Grant-in-Aid for Scientific Research (15K03453) from the Japan Society for the Promotion of Science.

References

Arakawa, K. 2012. The comparison between specific and ad valorem taxation under vertically differentiated oligopoly. *Studied in Applied Economics* 6: 85–104.

Arakawa, K. 2014. An optimal piecewise specific taxation in a vertically differentiated oligopoly. *Studies in Applied Economics* 8: 95–114.

Blinder, A.S., and H.S. Rosen. 1985. Notches. *American Economic Review* 75(4): 736–47.

Brander, J.A., and J. Eaton. 1984. Product line rivalry. *American Economic Review* 74(3): 323–34.

Cremer, H., and J.-F. Thisse. 1994. Commodity taxation in a differentiated oligopoly. *International Economic Review* 35: 613–33.

Dharmapala, D., J. Slemrod, and J.D. Wilson. 2011. Tax policy and the missing middle: Optimal tax remittance with firm-level administrative costs. *Journal of Public Economics* 95(9–10): 1036–1047.

Gillitzer, C., H.J. Kleven, and J. Slemrod. 2015, forthcoming. A characteristics approach to optimal taxation: Line drawing and tax-driven product innovation. *Scandinavian Journal of Economics* 119(2): 240–267.

Kleven, H.J., and M. Waseem. 2013. Using notches to uncover optimization frictions and structural elasticities: Theory and evidence from Pakistan. *Quarterly Journal of Economics* 128(2): 669–723.

Lancaster, K. 1975. Socially optimal product differentiation. *American Economic Review* 65(4): 567–85.

Mussa, M., and S. Rosen. 1978. Monopoly and product quality. *Journal of Economic Theory* 18: 301–317.

Slemrod, J. 2013. Buenas notches: Lines and notches in tax system design. *eJournal of Tax Research* 11(3): 259–283.

Slemrod, J., S. Yitzhaki, J. Mayshar, and M. Lundholm. 1994. The optimal two-bracket linear income tax. *Journal of Public Economics* 53(2): 269–290.

Chapter 22
Role of Public Support in Sports Fan Formation Processes: Approach by Cultural Transmission Model

Hirofumi Fukuyama

22.1 Introduction

The consumption activity of watching sports generates an experience value of "being moved." Through sports, people gain some non-monetary value, such as "being moved" and "being connected" with others, which cannot be replaced by viewing other phenomena. Numerous studies have used the contingent valuation method (CVM) to measure these non-monetary values of "being moved" and "making connections," which cannot be traded in the market. These studies, examining four North American major sports (hockey, basketball, football, and baseball) or European soccer teams as examples (Castellanos et al. 2011), measured the non-monetary values that professional sports teams can generate. For instance, Johnson et al. (2001) measured the annual intangible value that the Pittsburgh Penguins, an American professional ice hockey league, bestowed upon the local community, calculating its value: as much as 5.27 million dollars (on average, 5.57 USD per household). This value is significantly higher among Penguin fans than among those who are not. Fans not only receive experience values through watching their supported team's matches; they are also believed to receive other various benefits such as the existential value of the sports team, including the pride of living in the town that has the team.

Whether or not people become fans of their local sports teams is the result of various influential factors. The first factor is one's parents. If the parents are fans of the local professional sports team and if someone has many opportunities for exposure to the team in question as a child (i.e., watching the matches by visiting the stadium or via media), then the probability that the person would naturally

H. Fukuyama (✉)
Kagoshima University, Kagoshima, Japan
e-mail: fukuyama@leh.kagoshima-u.ac.jp

T. Naito et al. (eds.), *Applied Approaches to Societal Institutions and Economics*,
New Frontiers in Regional Science: Asian Perspectives 18,
DOI 10.1007/978-981-10-5663-5_22

become a fan of that team is high. Fujimoto (2006) interviewed fans of the Osaka Kintetsu Buffaloes, a Japanese professional baseball team, in 2004, asking them what turned them into fans. The interviews revealed that the process of becoming a fan included having parents who were also team fans and the strong influence of their own parents. However, some responses showed that the interview subjects became fans of the sports team through their friendships. In other words, a second factor is an effect from other people met via random matching. The personality, habits, and opinions of people around a person shape a person's personality. If the people one interacts with regularly are fans of a certain sports team, then it is likely that one would also become a fan of that sports team through that influence. This paper presents the use of a cultural transmission model to examine the formation process that turns people into sports fans. Representative literature of the cultural transmission model includes a paper by Bisin and Verdier (2001). For the two culturally characteristic models, they constructed a model that determines which of the two culturally characteristic transmission processes a child will have: effects from within the household (family, direct vertical socialization) and effects from outside the household (i.e., society and peers, oblique socialization). After publication of this paper, the cultural transmission model has been applied in various fields. Such examples include Olivier et al. (2008) who introduced the cultural transmission model into a trade model context and Gradstein and Justman (2005) who applied it to the field of education (for an outline of the cultural transmission model, refer to Bisin and Verdier (2011)). As described herein, the cultural transmission model will be applied to sports. The cultural model is effective when examining a process by which naive (ignorant and undeveloped) children form their preferences based on various influences. Heretofore, no study has analyzed how people become fans of a particular sports team or how the percentage of a team's fans changes.

The role of a local sports team is extremely important during the fan formation process. A local sports team can improve the team quality through actions such as obtaining star players to expand the fan demographic or by creating a new stadium. Improvement of the team's quality provides great benefits to fans. During this time, fans who are parents will harbor strong hopes that their children will form the same preference and become a fan of the same team. Based on these points, the first objective of this study is to apply the cultural transmission model to the context of sports. Thereby, one can elucidate the fan base percentage effects that are produced by sports team investments designed to improve the team quality. In addition, this study examines parental and friend effects on the fan base percentage.

Public support from local municipalities for local sports teams also has an extremely strong effect on the fan base percentage. As described above, the existence of the sports team bestows various benefits to local residents through values derived from the viewing of matches. Particularly regarding intangible benefits (i.e., existential value), the local community does not pay a price through the market, thereby generating a positive externality. The existence of a local sports team having a public financial presence in the community can be regarded as theoretical evidence that the local municipalities provide public support for the sports team. In the USA, public support of sports teams is common, with local municipalities providing support for the construction and management fees of the stadium. According to Leeds and Allmen (2010), of the 11.34 billion dollars used for constructing new stadiums for North American sports during 2000–2011, 6.1 billion dollars were funded through public expenditure. However, as Kobayashi (2015) reported, close scrutiny is given to tax funds that are used for sports in Japan. For that reason, some teams affiliated with Nippon Professional Baseball (NPB) must pay expensive stadium usage fees to the local municipality and are thereby forced to manage their team affairs strictly. For instance, the Yokohama DeNA BayStars pay 25% of their entrance fee revenue to the local municipality as a stadium usage fee. In fact, this fee is the team's major expenditure, followed by the wages paid to the players. If the local municipalities would give public support to the team by reducing the stadium usage fee, then the team might use the money saved to enhance their service to fans or acquire star players to increase the team value. This use of funds will increase the sports fan percentage among the population. In light of that argument, the second point of this paper is to examine effects of public assistance for local sports teams on the sports fan percentage and the sports team value.

The structure of this paper is the following. First, a cultural transmission model will be constructed and applied to the sporting field to assess the educational investment behavior of individuals toward their own children. Next, this study shall assess investment effects on increasing the sports team value and the percentage of its fans. Based on those results, the effects of public support of a sports team on the percentage of sports fans and on the sports team value in a stationary state can be verified. Finally, this paper presents a summary of the study findings and a discussion of future tasks.

22.2 Cultural Transmission Model for Sports Preference

22.2.1 Sports Fan Utility and Imperfect Empathy

As described in this paper, we apply a theoretical study of cultural transmission of sports preferences from parents to children. Bisin and Verdier (2001) constructed a theoretical model of cultural transmission. It has since been applied to various fields. We consider application of the cultural transmission model by which affection for a local sports team is transmitted from parents to children.

We consider an individual who lives during two periods. The first term is assumed as a child period. The second term represents an adult period. An individual has one child. The regional population of a generation is normalized to 1. An individual has either of two preferences (L or N) during the adult period. An individual with preference L loves local professional sports team and obtains value from a team's existence. An individual with preference N has no such preference and derives no value from a local professional sports team. The difference of these two preferences is shown in the utility function. The utility function of an individual with preference L is the following. The model of this paper closely resembles that of Bisin and Verdier (2000), who considered people with preferences of two types: one obtaining benefits from public goods and another not.

$$U_L = u(w - T - f) + v. \tag{22.1}$$

The utility function of an individual with preference N is

$$U_N = u(w - T), \tag{22.2}$$

where w is an individual property and f is the expense for the sport such as the payment of the game watching and the fan club admission fee. T denotes a lump-sum tax. The revenue is used to support the professional sports team in the region. Therefore, $w - T - f$ expresses the amount of consumption of private goods that an individual with preference L can expend aside from sports. u(·) satisfies $u'(\cdot) > 0$, $u''(\cdot) < 0$. v is the benefit derived from the existence of the local professional sports team that only an individual with preference L can obtain, and which includes both an existential value that the existence of the team brings and an experience value such as an impression and a sense of belonging derived through game watching.

The individual in the child period has no preference because the person is naive. The preference prevailing the adult period is determined through parental education and social learning. Then a person has either utility function of (22.1) or (22.2). We assume an altruistic individual who conducts decision-making considering the utility that his child will obtain in the future. Therefore, the utility function during an adult period is a sum of the utility of (22.1) or (22.2) and the utility that the adult's child will obtain in the future.

We assume that an individual with preference L will recognize utility V^{LL} of the child in the future if the child has the same preference L as his own.

$$V^{LL} = u(w - T - f) + v. \tag{22.3}$$

Moreover, we assume that an individual with preference L will recognize the utility V^{LN} of the child in the future if the child has preference N different from his own.

$$V^{LN} = u(w - T). \tag{22.4}$$

We also assume that the individual hopes the child has the same preference as his own in the future, i.e., the following are inferred from (22.3) and (22.4).

Assumption 1

$$V^{LL} = u(w - T - f) + v > V^{LN} = u(w - T). \tag{22.5}$$

However, we assume that an individual with preference N will recognize the utility V^{NN} of the child in the future if the child has the same preference L as his own.

$$V^{NN} = u(w - T). \tag{22.6}$$

Moreover, we assume that an individual with preference N will recognize the utility V^{NL} of the child in the future as follows if the child has preference L different from his own.

$$V^{NL} = u(w - T - f). \tag{22.7}$$

Actually, (22.7) shows that an individual with preference N cannot accurately predict the utility function of the child in the future if the child has preference L different from his own: he has imperfect empathy (Bisin and Verdier 2001). Therefore, an individual with preference N cannot correctly ascertain the benefit v derived through the existence of the professional sports team. For that reason, he might abstract it from the utility function in his child's future, although originally the utility function of an individual with preference L is (22.1). It seems clear from (22.6) and (22.7) that an individual with preference N also hopes his child has the same preference in the future.

22.2.2 Cultural Transmission and Social Learning

An individual educates his child to have the same preference as his own. Therefore, $\tau_i (i = L, N)$ represents the probability that the child will have the same preference as the parent in the future. The child has the same preference as the parent with probability τ_i through education by the parent, but education by the parent does not influence the child with probability $1 - \tau_i$. A child who is not influenced by the parent education is not influenced with probability $1 - \tau_i$ and derives a preference (L or N) through social environment effects, i.e., social learning. When the share of individuals with preference L is denoted as q_t and that with preference N is denoted as $1 - q_t$, the child uninfluenced by the parent education has preference L with probability q_t or preference N with probability $1 - q_t$ by social learning (Fig. 22.1).

Therefore, with probability p_t^{LL}, the child of an individual with preference L has the same preference L at period t. With probability p_t^{LN}, the child of an individual with preference L has a different preference N at period t. With probability p_t^{NN}, the child of an individual with preference N has the same preference N at period t. Also, with probability p_t^{NL} , the child of an individual with preference N has a different preference L at period t. The equations expressing those respective probabilities are shown below.

$$p_t^{LL} = \tau_L + (1 - \tau_L) q_t. \tag{22.8}$$

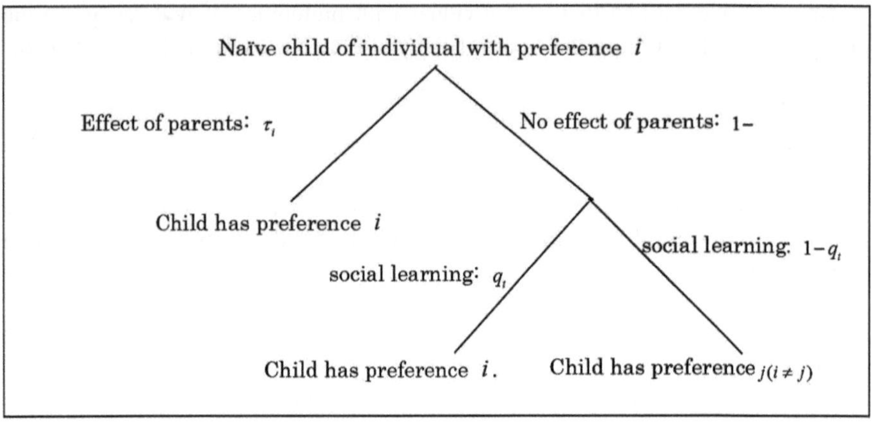

Fig. 22.1 Cultural transmission of an individual with preference i

$$p_t^{LN} = (1 - \tau_L)(1 - q_t). \tag{22.9}$$

$$p_t^{NN} = \tau_N + (1 - \tau_N)(1 - q_t). \tag{22.10}$$

$$p_t^{NL} = (1 - \tau_N)q_t. \tag{22.11}$$

The share of individuals with preference L at period t, i.e., the share of sports team fans is the following, as inferred from (22.8) and (22.11).

$$\begin{aligned} q_{t+1} &= q_t p_t^{LL} + (1 - q_t)p_t^{NL} \\ &= q_t + q_t(1 - q_t)(\tau_L - \tau_N). \end{aligned} \tag{22.12}$$

22.2.3 *Education Effort for a Child By the Parent*

It requires effort for the parent to educate a child to have the same future preferences. For example, an individual with preference L educates a child to love the sports team by increasing the opportunity to be exposed to sports and making his child join a sports club. Let $H(\tau_L)$ $(H'(\cdot) > 0,\ H''(\cdot) > 0)$ represent the education effort cost of individuals with preference L, i.e., it increases as the level τ_L of educational effort by individual with preference L increases. Therefore, the decision problem related to the level of educational effort by an individual with preference L at period t is

$$\max_{\tau_L} u(w - f) + v + \delta[p_t^{LL}V^{LL} + p_t^{LN}V^{LN}] - H(\tau_L).$$

Here, the discount rate is denoted as δ $(0 < \delta < 1)$. Clauses 1 and 2 represent the utility of an individual at this period and the expected utility of the child in the subsequent period. This expected utility signifies that the child of an individual with preference L has preference L with probability p_t^{LL} and obtains utility V^{LL} and he has preference N with probability p_t^{NL} and obtains utility V^{LN}. Clause 3 represents the educational effort cost. An individual decides τ_L to maximize this object function. Therefore, the first-order condition of maximization is the following:

$$\delta(1 - q_t)[u(w - T - f) + v - u(w - T)] = H'(\tau_L). \tag{22.13}$$

Similarly, an individual with preference N educates his child to love anything except sports (e.g., learning, music, and art) by learning lessons other than sports. When the education effort cost of an individual with preference N is denoted as $G(\tau_N)(G'(\cdot) > 0,\ G''(\cdot) > 0)$, then the decision problem related to the level of educational effort by an individual with preference N at period t is the following:

$$\max_{\tau_N}\ u(w) + v + \delta[p_t^{NN}V^{NN} + p_t^{NL}V^{NL}] - G(\tau_N).$$

Solving the maximization problem above, the first-order condition is

$$\delta q_t[u(w - T) - u(w - T - f)] = G'(\tau_N). \tag{22.14}$$

From (22.13) and (22.14), the following Lemma 22.1 holds by using implicit function theorem.

Lemma 22.1 *1. Educational effort of individual with preference L decreases and educational effort of individual with preference N increases as the expense of sports increases.*
2. Educational effort of individual with preference L increases and educational effort of individual with preference N decreases as benefit derived through the sports team existence increases.
3. Educational effort of individual with preference L increases and educational effort of individual with preference N decreases as individual property increases.
4. Educational effort of individual with preference L decreases and educational effort of individual with preference N increases as the share of individuals with preference L increases.
5. Educational effort of individual with preference L decreases and educational effort of individual with preference N increases as the lump-sum tax rate increases.

The growth of expenses for sports decreases the benefit derived from becoming a home team fan. Therefore, 1 of Lemma 22.1 holds. However, because the growth of benefit derived through the sports team existence increases the fan benefit, 2 of Lemma 22.1 holds. Next, because the amount of consumption allocated to non-sports consumption increases as an individual's initial property increases, 3 of Lemma 22.1 holds. 4 of Lemma 22.1 is approved from a substitute relation between learning by education from the parent and social learning. When the share of individuals with preference L increases, an individual with preference L lowers the level of educational effort because the probability that the child has the same preference rises, but an individual with preference N raises the level of educational effort because the probability that the child has a different preference increases through social learning. 5 of Lemma 22.1 is contrary to 3 of Lemma 22.1: because the amount of consumption that can be spent except sports consumption decreases if the rate of lump-sum tax increases, 5 of Lemma 22.1 holds.

22.2.4 Object Function of the Sports Team

A professional sports team exists in a region. The sports team can increase profits by increasing the number of hometown fans and displaying many games to many fans in the stadium, on television, and on the Internet. The professional sports team manager must increase the number of fans in the short term and over the long term. Therefore, the professional sports team manager should devote consideration to profits now and in the future. The professional sports team profit function for t period is

$$\pi_t = q_t R + \delta q^e_{t+1} R - C(v, T). \tag{22.15}$$

Therein, R stands for revenue (sum totals of the ticket income, the goods income, the advertising revenue, the broadcasting right fee, etc.) of the professional sports team per fan in each period. For simplicity, R is the same level in each period. Because q_t is the number of fans in period t, $q_T R$ is the revenue of sports team in period t. q^e_{t+1} is the expected value of the number of fans in period $t+1$. Consequently, $q^e_{t+1}R$ is the future revenue at period $t+1$. $C(v,T)$ represents the investment by the sports team to improve the team quality. To improve the team quality, it is necessary to acquire a star player, to enhance fan service, and to repair the stadium: $C(v,T)$ satisfies $C_v(v,T) > 0$, $C_{vv}(v,T) > 0$. Here, $C_v(v,T) = dC/dv$, $C_{vv}(v,T) = d^2C/dv^2$. Moreover, because the revenue derived from the lump-sum tax (in other words, amount of public support) is used to allay stadium repair costs and stadium maintenance costs etc., i.e., it has the effect of depressing the investment cost of the sports team, $C_T(v,T) < 0$ holds. Here, $C_T(v,T) = dC/dT$. In addition, we assume that $C_{vT}(v,T) < 0$.

22.3 Optimal Investment of a Professional Sports Team

22.3.1 Timeline

Here, we explain the game (Fig. 22.2). In the first stage, a sports team chooses v to maximize (22.15) in period t. At the second stage, an individual with preference $i(= L, N)$ decides level $\tau_i(i = L, N)$ of educational effort for the child after observing v. At the third stage, the child preference is decided depending on the process in Fig. 22.2.

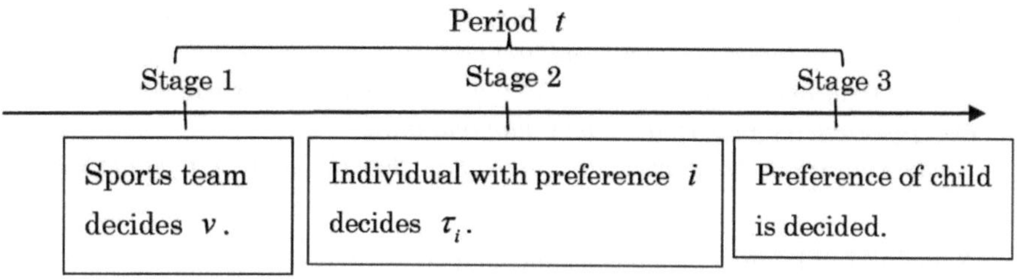

Fig. 22.2 Timeline

22.3.2 Optimal Investment of Professional Sports Team

At the first stage, the sports team chooses the quality v of the team considering the reaction function $\tau_i(v)$ on the educational effort level chosen by an individual with preference $i(= L, N)$ at the second stage. $\tau_i(v)$ influences proportion q_{t+1} of preference L (number of fans) in the next period from (22.12), which influences the sports team profit through q_{t+1}. Substituting $\tau_L(v)$ and τ_N obtained by (22.13) and (22.14) for (22.12), a sports team can predict the number q_{t+1} of fans in period $t + 1$ (here, τ_N is independent of v). Substituting q_{t+1} for (22.15), one can solve the following profit maximization problem.

$$\max_{v} \quad \pi_t = q_t R + \delta[q_t + q_t(1 - q_t)(\tau_L(v) - \tau_N)]R - C(v, T).$$

The following holds from the first-order condition of maximization.

$$\frac{d\pi_t}{dv} = \delta R q_t(1 - q_t)\tau_L'(v) = C_v(v, T). \tag{22.16}$$

We were able to obtain the following by arranging (22.16) from (22.13).

$$\delta^2 R q_t(1-q_t)^2 H'' \circ H'^{-1}(\delta(1-q_t)(u(w-T)+v-u(w)))\tau_L'(v) = C_v(v, T). \tag{22.17}$$

From (22.17), the following Lemma 22.2 holds.

Lemma 22.2 *If it is assumed that the educational effort cost of individual with preference L is $H(\tau_L) = \frac{a}{2}\tau_L^2$, then the following hold.*

1. *The level of the sports team investment increases when the sports team revenue per fan increases.*
2. *The level of sports team investment does not change when individual property increases.*
3. *The level of sports team investment increases when the discount rate increases. The sports team emphasizes future revenues.*

4. *The level of sports team investment decreases when the number of fans increases if the share of individuals with preference L (the number of fans) in period t is greater than one-third. However, the opposite holds if the share of individuals with preference L in period t is less than one-third.*
5. *The level of sports team investment increases when the amount of public support increases.*

Actually, 1 of Lemma 22.2 means that an increase in revenue per fan expands the number of fans; thereby, it promotes investment. Moreover, 2 of Lemma 22.2 means that because an increase in an individual initial property does not influence the marginal educational effort $\tau_L'(v)$, it does not influence the level of investment. Also, 3 of Lemma 22.2 means that if the discount rates rise, i.e., the profit in the future is emphasized. The sports team increases the level of investment to increase the number of fans in the subsequent period. In addition, 4 of Lemma 22.2 shows that if the number of fans is larger, the number of fans increases by virtue of education by individuals with preference L and social learning, i.e., the sports team is not actively making investments. However, if the number of fans is less, then the sports team will actively invest and try to improve future profits as the number of fans increases. Finally, 5 of Lemma 22.2 shows that the investment cost decreases because of an increase in the amount of public support of the sports team. Therefore, the sports team invests actively.

22.4 Preference Dynamics

Here, we assume the educational effort cost function $H(\tau_L)$ of individuals with preference L and the educational effort cost function $G(\tau_N)$ of individuals with preference N for simplicity as follows:

Assumption 2

$$H(\tau) = G(\tau) = \frac{a}{2}\tau^2 \ \textit{for any}\ \tau(= \tau_L = \tau_N). \tag{22.18}$$

Moreover, the investment cost function to improve quality of the sports team is assumed.

Assumption 3

$$C(v, T) = \frac{b(T)}{2}v^2. \tag{22.19}$$

$b(T)$ is a parameter related to the sports team investment amount; $b'(T) < 0$ is assumed. Using (22.18) and (22.19), sports team quality $v(q_t)$ is obtainable depending on q_t, as follows from (22.17).

$$v(q_t) = \frac{\delta^2}{ab(T)} Rq_t(1-q_t)^2. \tag{22.20}$$

Substituting $v(q_t)$ of (22.20) for (22.13), the educational effort $\tau_L(q_t)$ of an individual with preference L obtained using (22.18) depends on q_t as follows:

$$\tau_L(q_t) = \frac{\delta}{a}(1-q_t)[u(w-T-f) + \frac{\delta^2}{ab(T)} Rq_t(1-q_t)^2 - u(w-T)]. \tag{22.21}$$

Moreover, using (22.18), the educational effort $\tau_N(q_t)$ of an individual with preference N obtained from (22.14) is depending on q_t as shown below:

$$\tau_N(q_t) = \frac{\delta}{a} q_t[u(w-T) - u(w-T-f)]. \tag{22.22}$$

Substituting $\tau_L(q_t)$ of (22.21) and $\tau_N(q_t)$ of (22.22) for (22.12), one can rewrite the preference dynamics as shown below.

$$q_{t+1} - q_t = q_t(1-q_t)\frac{\delta}{a}[q_t(1-q_t)^3 \frac{\delta^2}{ab(T)} R - (u(w-T) - u(w-T-f))]. \tag{22.23}$$

A steady state is $q_{t+1} = q_t$. Therefore, the following is satisfied by setting the number of individuals with preference L at steady state as q^*.

$$q^*(1-q^*)[\frac{\delta^2}{ab(T)} Rq^*(1-q^*)^3 - (u(w-T) - u(w-T-f))] = 0. \tag{22.24}$$

From (22.24), the number q^* of individuals with preference L in the steady state is $q^* = 0$ or $q^* = 1$, i.e., all individuals is homogeneous. Alternatively, if $q^* = 0$ and $q^* = 1$ do not hold, then q^* satisfying the following is a stationary solution, i.e., all individuals are heterogeneous.

$$\frac{\delta^2}{ab(T)} Rq^*(1-q^*)^3 = u(w-T) - u(w-T-f). \tag{22.25}$$

Here, when the left side of (22.25) equals A and the right side of (22.25) equals B, it is shown by Fig. 22.3 that q^* satisfying (22.25) exists. The following Theorem 22.3 holds from Fig. 22.3.

Theorem 22.3 *Under Assumptions 2 and 3, if $q^* = 0$ and $q^* = 1$ do not hold, then the number q^* of individual with preference L at steady state satisfies the following.*

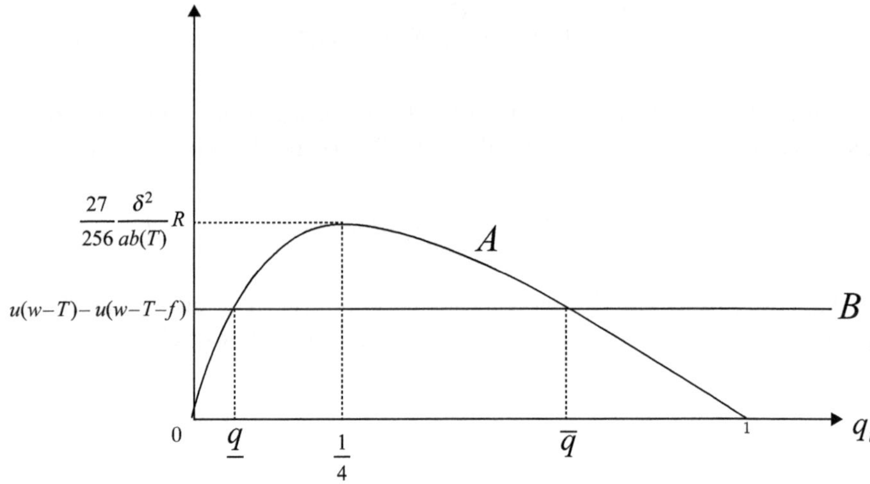

Fig. 22.3 Stationary solutions

1. *If* $\frac{27}{256}\frac{\delta^2}{ab(T)}R > u(w-T) - u(w-T-f)$ *holds, then two stationary solutions* $q^* = \underline{q}, \bar{q}$ *satisfying* $\frac{27}{256}\frac{\delta^2}{ab(T)}R = u(w-T) - u(w-T-f)$ *exist. They satisfy* $0 < \underline{q} < \frac{1}{4}$ *and* $\frac{1}{4} < \bar{q} < 1$.
2. *If* $\frac{27}{256}\frac{\delta^2}{ab(T)}R < u(w-T) - u(w-T-f)$ *holds, then a stationary solution does not exist.*

Theorem 22.3 means that if both discount rate δ and the revenue R per fan are larger and the increment of utility when a child of non-sports fans having the same preference N as his own is less, then two stationary interior solutions exist as $0 < \underline{q}, \bar{q} < 1$, i.e., all individuals are heterogeneous. However, if the reverse case is examined, then no stationary interior solution exists, i.e., all individuals are homogeneous.

Next, we will analyze the stability of stationary solutions. When (22.23) is shown in the figure, it is depicted as in Figs. 22.4 and 22.5. Therefore, the following Theorem 22.4 holds.

Theorem 22.4 *The following hold for the number of fans* q^* *at steady state stability.*

1. *If* $\frac{27}{256}\frac{\delta^2}{ab(T)}R > u(w-T) - u(w-T-f)$ *holds, then four stationary solutions exist for which all individuals are fans of sports team* ($q^* = 1$), *all individuals are non-fans of sports team* ($q^* = 0$), *and fans exist along with non-fans* ($q^* = \underline{q}, \bar{q}$). $q^* = 0, \bar{q}$ *are stable stationary solutions and* $q^* = \underline{q}, 1$ *are unstable stationary solutions (Fig. 22.4).*

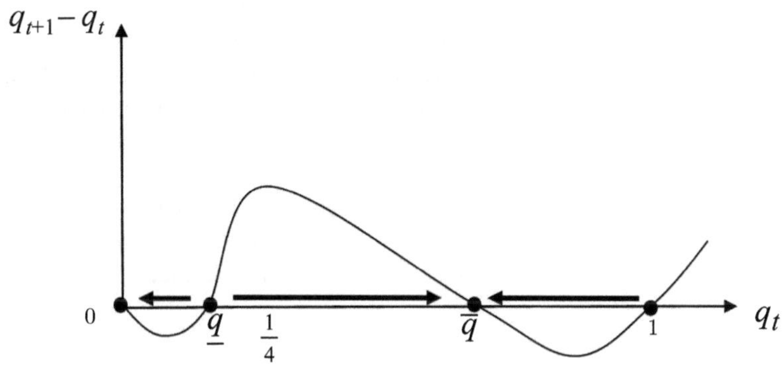

Fig. 22.4 Stability of four stationary solutions

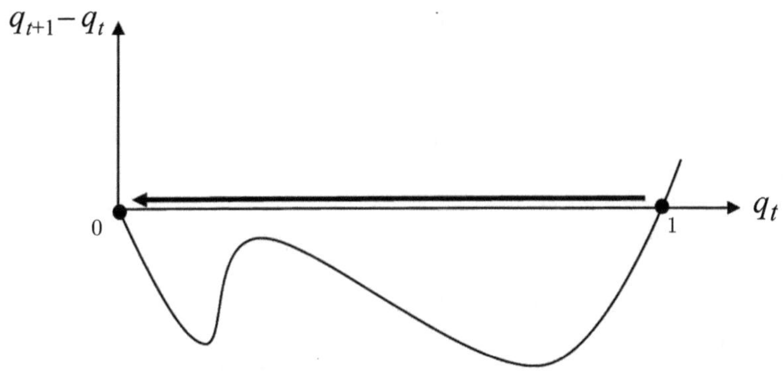

Fig. 22.5 Stability of two stationary solutions

2. *If* $\frac{27}{256}\frac{\delta^2}{ab(T)}R < u(w-T) - u(w-T-f)$ *holds, then two stationary solutions exist for which all individuals are fans of sports team and all individuals are non-fans of sports team* ($q^* = 0, 1$). $q^* = 0$ *is a stable stationary solution and* $q^* = 1$ *is an unstable stationary solution (Fig. 22.5).*

1 of Theorem 22.4 means that if the initial value q_0 of the number of fans is less than $\underline{q} < 1/4$, then the number of fans becomes $q^* = 0$, i.e., all individuals are nonfans. However, if the initial value q_0 is greater than $\underline{q} < 1/4$, then the number of fans becomes $q^* = \bar{q}$, i.e., no fans of the sports team become $1 - \bar{q}$, which indicates that when fans of the sports team are slightly in the minority ($\underline{q} < q_0 < \bar{q}$), an individual with preference L actively undertakes educational investment to make the child have the same preference L. Also, the sports team invests actively to improve future profits. Therefore, the number of fans increases to $\bar{q}$. Additionally, this result suggests that when fans of the sports team are in the majority ($\bar{q} < q_0 < 1$), an individual with preference L does not actively invest to give one's own child the

same preference L; moreover, the sports team does not actively invest to improve future profits. Consequently, the number of fans decreases to $\bar{q}$. However, when fans of the sports team are in the minority ($0 < q_0 < \underline{q}$), the effects of educational investment by an individual with preference L and investment by the sports team are less than the effect of educational investment by an individual with preference N. The number of fans therefore becomes 0.

Actually, 2 of Theorem 22.4 indicates that all individuals become nonfans, irrespective of the initial value. Therefore, the benefit of becoming fans of sports team is less, irrespective of the number of fans. Not all individuals become fans.

22.5 Comparative Statics

Finally, we examine how the number $q^* = \underline{q}, \bar{q}$ of sports team fans in a steady state changes for parameters δ, f, R, w, T. The following Lemma 22.5 holds for the result of comparative statics of stationary solutions $q^* = \underline{q}, \bar{q}$.

Lemma 22.5 *1. $\underline{q}$ decreases and $\bar{q}$ increases, so sports team fans increase when the discount rate increases. The sports team emphasizes future revenues.*

2. *$\underline{q}$ decreases and $\bar{q}$ increases, so sports team fans increase when the sports team revenue per fan increases.*
3. *$\underline{q}$ decreases and $\bar{q}$ increases, so sports team fans increase when individual property increases.*
4. *$\underline{q}$ increases and $\bar{q}$ decreases, so sports team fans decrease when the expense for sports increases.*
5. *Effects of increasing the number of fans by increasing investment in sports teams and enhancing the sports team quality and the effect of decreasing the number of fans by reducing the benefit that a non-fan child derives from becoming a fan occur when public support increases. If the former is larger than the latter, then $\underline{q}$ decreases and $\bar{q}$ increases. Therefore, the sports team fans increase.*

From 5 of Lemma 22.5, we infer that the rise of the amount of public support to sports team can increase the number of fans $\bar{q}$ in a steady state. However, from 4 of Lemma 22.2, when the number of fans $\bar{q}$ is greater than one-third, the rise of $\bar{q}$ decreases the level of investment of the sports team, i.e., the sports team quality. Therefore, the following Theorem 22.6 holds from these two observations.

Theorem 22.6 *Increasing the amount of public support of sports team increases the number of fans, but it might decrease the sports team quality.*

Theorem 22.6 shows that increasing public support of sports teams increases the number of fans and lowers the investment cost of the sports team and consequently improves the level of investment, but increasing the number of fans decreases the sports team quality. That is to say, increasing the number of fans and enhancing the sports team quality share a tradeoff relation. Results show that one should judge whether to carry out public support until after the effects are verified carefully.

22.6 Concluding Remarks

As described in this paper, we used a cultural transmission model to analyze the sports lover formation process. Moreover, we examined how public support of a sports team affects the number of fans and the sports team quality.

Results show the following. First, if both discount rate and the revenue per fan are larger and the increment of utility when a child of a non-sports fan has the same preference as the parent's is less, then two stationary interior solutions $0 < \underline{q}, \bar{q} < 1$ exist, i.e., all individuals are heterogeneous. Second, results demonstrated that if the initial value of the number of fans is less than $\underline{q}(1/4)$, then the number of fans becomes 0. If the initial value is greater than $\bar{q}(1/4)$, then the number of fans becomes $\bar{q}$. Third, results show that increasing public support of sports team increases the number of fans, although it might decrease the sports team quality. The remaining issues in this paper are the following. The first issue is that the sports team revenue has been treated as a constant. A better model might incorporate consideration of how the sports team quality and the educational level of individuals affect the ticket price for watching a game by introducing a sports spectator market. A second issue is that our analysis assumed that only one sports team exists in a region. Introducing a new variable to represent competitive balance among teams can extend the model such that plural sports teams exist in a region. Consequently, one might examine this study by comparison to previous studies that analyzed competitive balance.

References

Bisin, A., and T. Verdier. 2000. A model of cultural transmission, voting and political ideology. *European Journal of Political Economy* 16: 5–29.

Bisin, A., and T. Verdier. 2001. The economics of cultural transmission and the dynamics of preferences. *Journal of Economic Theory* 97: 298–319.

Bisin, A., and T. Verdier. 2011. The economics of cultural transmission and socialization. In *Handbook of social economics, Volume 1A*, eds. J. Benhabib, A. Bisin, and M. Jackson, 339–416. San Diego: Elsevier.

Castellanos, P., J. Garcia, and J.M. Sanchez. 2011. The willingness to pay to keep a football club in a city: How important are the methodological issues? *Journal of Sports Economics* 12(4): 464–486.

Fujimoto, J. 2006. A study of the transfiguration of fans' attitudes toward Osaka Kintetsu Buffaloes: Using longitudinal interview method to examine fans' attitudes toward the team. *Bulletin of Osaka University of Health and Sport Sciences* 37: 57–72.

Gradstein, M., and M. Justman 2005. The melting pot and school choice. *Journal of Public Economics* 89: 871–896.

Johnson, B.K., P.A. Groothuis, and J.C. Whitehead. 2001. The value of public goods generated by a major league sports team. *Journal of Sports Economics* 2(1): 6–21.

Kobayashi, I. 2015. *Economics of sports*. PHP Institute. Tokyo, Japan.

Leeds, M.A., and P.V. Allmen. 2010. *The economics of sports*, Pearson Education. Boston, MA.

Olivier, J., M. Thoening, and T. Verdier. 2008 Globalization and the dynamics of cultural identity. *Journal of International Economics* 76: 356–370.

Chapter 23
A Comparison of National and Local Airport Management

Akio Kawasaki

23.1 Introduction

Airport management, and, specifically, management efficiency, has become a subject of interest worldwide. Generally, there are two types of airports, public and private, and many empirical studies have compared the management efficiencies between them. According to some studies (e.g., Hooper and Hensher 1997; Abbott and Wu 2002; Oum et al. 2006), an airport's efficiency improves when it transitions from government to private ownership.[1]

Some studies adopt the perspective of economic theory to examine how to affect cost efficiency by privatization (Schmidt 1996a,b). In addition, Hart et al. (1997) and Hoppe and Schmitz (2010) investigate how to influence cost reductions and quality improvement investments by privatization. Here, we note that although previous studies compare public and private firms, they do not compare nationally and locally owned public firms. That is, they miss the existence of both types firms in reality, and airports serve as a good example.

For example, almost all airports in the United States are managed locally, though many airports in Canada are nationally managed. In Japan, both types of airport exist. For example, the largest airport in Japan, Haneda Airport, is nationally managed, while Toyama Airport is locally managed. Given this situation,

---

[1]By contrast, Parker (1999) and Domney et al. (2005) argue that airport management efficiency does not always depend on airport privatization. In addition, Oum et al. (2008) argue that a socially preferable airport can be either privately owned or fully nationalized.

A. Kawasaki (✉)
Oita University, 700, Dannoharu, Oita, Japan
e-mail: a-kawasaki@oita-u.ac.jp

T. Naito et al. (eds.), *Applied Approaches to Societal Institutions and Economics*,
New Frontiers in Regional Science: Asian Perspectives 18,
DOI 10.1007/978-981-10-5663-5_23

Akai (2010, p. 12) argues that airports should be managed by a local rather than national government because nationally owned airports face no competition, which engenders inefficient airport management. Furthermore, nationally owned airports have the same airport fee established by the national government. The accounting for all nationally managed airports in Japan is consolidated, so the national government does not realize the revenues and costs for each airport, which explains the single airport fee. Additionally, this single fee is supported by the nature of airports as a universal service.[2] In contrast, the local government can set airport fees in locally owned airports to meet regional characteristics.

Considering this problem, we aim to address the following issues. First, do national or local airports set lower airport fees? Second, which type of airport undertakes more activities to reduce costs? Finally, which management type is socially preferable? To the best of our knowledge, the literature has yet to address these problems. In particular, no paper has compared the management efficiency of nationally owned facilities with that of locally owned ones.[3]

In order to address these problems, this chapter assumes two substitute airports. We then consider national and local management styles. For nationally managed airports, we assume a uniform airport fee.[4] On the other hand, local governments set the fees for locally managed airports.

In this chapter, we address the following vertical relationship: the upstream government that sets the airport fee and cost-reducing activity and the downstream carrier that sets the airfare. We consider the case of two asymmetric regions exist in one country, termed City 1 and City 2. Each city has one airport. The number of passengers in City 1 is different from that in City 2, and we assume that the former has more passengers. Passengers in each city can use both airports. Here, we assume that if a passenger resident in city i uses Airport j located in city j, the passenger incurs an additional traveling cost. In addition, this economy has two carriers, Airline 1 and Airline 2, who compete on airfare. Here, we assume that Airline 1 uses only Airport 1 and Airline 2 uses only Airport 2.

We assume that Airline 1 and Airline 2 compete with each other despite using different airports. With this assumption, we can express indirect competition between Airport 1 and Airport 2. We analyze the scenario with a Dixit (1979) model, which represents price competition with a product differentiation model. Here, when there is a nationally managed airport, there is no indirect competition between airports. Alternatively, the national government sets a uniform airport fee on both

[2]See Anton et al. (1998), Chon et al. (2000), and Valletti et al. (2002) with regard to universal services.

[3]Kawasaki (2012) assumes a cost difference between airports managed at the national and local levels and demonstrates that if the difference is small (large), national (local) management is socially preferable.

[4]Some papers address the problem of uniform pricing considering cost-reducing activities (or R&D investment). DeGraba (1990) shows that the efficiency of a downstream firm is worse under price discrimination than under uniform pricing. Furthermore, Liao (2008) demonstrates that downstream firms invest more in R&D under uniform pricing.

airports by considering the total social welfare while also establishing each airport's cost-reducing activity to maximize total social welfare, which is not uniform. Under local management, each airport sets its own airport fee and cost-reducing activity by considering only its own city, which therefore represents indirect competition.

Considering this set up, this chapter demonstrates the following results. Regarding Airport 1's fee, when City 2 has a small (large) number of passengers, the locally managed airport has a lower (higher) fee than that of the nationally managed airport. However, the nationally managed airport's fee is always lower than that of the locally managed airport. This characteristic influences each airport's cost-reducing activity and leads to the following result: when City 2 has a small (large) number of passengers, Airport 1's cost-reducing activity in the locally managed case is larger (smaller) than that in the nationally managed case. On the other hand, Airport 2's cost-reducing activity in the locally managed case is always smaller than that in the nationally managed case. From these characteristics, we show that if City 2 has a small number of passengers and the additional traveling cost is high, the locally managed airport is socially preferable; otherwise, the nationally managed airport is socially preferable.

The remainder of this chapter is organized as follows. Section 23.2 establishes the basic model for the analysis. Section 23.3 describes the analysis of the airport fee and the cost-reducing activity of the national management case, and Sect. 23.4 does so for the local management case. Based on the results of Sects. 23.3 and 23.4, Sect. 23.5 compares the cost-reducing activities of the nationally and locally owned airports. Section 23.6 compares the social welfare of each case and draws conclusions about the socially superior airport. Section 23.7 concludes and suggests potential future studies.

23.2 The Model

Two cities exist in the economy, City 1 and City 2, each with one airport. There are two carriers, Airline 1 and Airline 2. Airline 1 (2) flies from/to City 1 (2) to/from outside cities. Passengers live in each city. The number of passengers in city i is n_i. We assume that a passenger in city $i(=1,2)$ can use not only city i's airport (Airport i) but also city j's Airport (Airport $j(=1,2,\ i \neq j)$). In other words, each passenger can move between Cities 1 and 2. Passengers incur a cost of t when moving between cities. Since we assume that each carrier faces airfare competition, we use a price competition model with product differentiation.

A passenger using a carrier must pay an airfare. We express Airline i's airfare as p_i, demand for Airline i in city i as q_1^i, and demand for Airline j in city i as q_j^i. Then, following Dixit (1979), we use the following quasi-linear utility function:

$$U_i = a(q_i^i + q_j^i) - \frac{(q_i^i)^2 + 2bq_i^iq_j^i + (q_j^i)^2}{2} + m_i \tag{23.1}$$

Here, parameter $b \in [0, 1)$ expresses the degree of product differentiation between carriers. This parameter would include the difference between the carriers' destinations as an example. That is, if b is nearly equal to 1, both carriers have almost the same destination, and if b is zero, each carrier has an entirely different destination. The budget constraint is as follows:

$$p_i q_i^i + (p_j + t)q_j^i + m_i = I \tag{23.2}$$

Here, p_i and p_j express the airfares of Airline i and Airline j, respectively. As mentioned before, the parameter t expresses the costs to move between Cities 1 and 2. Each passenger decides his/her demand for each carrier to maximize the utility expressed in Eq. (23.1) subject to the budget constraint in Eq. (23.2).

Following Matsumura and Matsushima (2012) and Mantin (2012), this chapter introduces a vertical relationship between the carrier and the airport. That is, the carrier must pay an airport fee of k_i when using the airport facilities. We normalize the number of passengers that each carrier can carry to 1 for simplicity. Therefore, the number of flights equals the carrier's total demand. By contrast, the carrier does not incur any costs except for airport fees. Consequently, each carrier's profit function is

$$\pi_i = (p_i - k_i)(n_i q_i^i + n_j q_i^j). \tag{23.3}$$

Each airport earns revenues from airport fees while also incurring costs. We assume that the initial marginal cost is c. This marginal cost can decrease through a cost-reducing activity e_i. Therefore, the marginal cost after the cost-reducing activity becomes $c - e_i$. The cost-reducing activity requires an investment cost denoted as βe_i^2. Therefore, each airport's profit function is as follows:

$$\Pi_i = (k_i - (c - e_i))(n_i q_i^i + n_j q_i^j) - \beta e_i^2 \tag{23.4}$$

If a national government owns the airport, we assume that it sets a uniform airport fee for both Airport 1 and Airport 2, as is the case in Japan, to maximize total social welfare. At the same time, national government decides the cost-reducing activity for each airport it owns. When local governments own the airport, they set the airport fee considering only their local welfare, while also determining the cost-reducing activity.

This chapter assumes that only City 1 holds shares of Airline 1 and only City 2 holds shares of Airline 2. Therefore, the social welfare of City 1 (2) includes Airline 1 (2)'s profit. Consequently, the social welfare of city i is

$$W_i = n_i U_i + \pi_i + \Pi_i, \tag{23.5}$$

and the total social welfare is

$$SW = W_1 + W_2. \tag{23.6}$$

The timing of this game is as follows. First, the national (or local) government sets the airport fee and the cost-reducing activity simultaneously. Then, each carrier competes with each other by setting the airfare. We derive the subgame perfect equilibrium using backward induction.

23.2.1 Airline Strategy

This subsection analyzes the airfare set by each carrier. First, solving for the passengers' utility maximization problem, we obtain the following demand function per passenger:

$$q_i^i = \frac{a(1-b) - p_i + b(p_j + t)}{1 - b^2} \tag{23.7}$$

$$q_j^i = \frac{a(1-b) - p_j + b(p_i + t)}{1 - b^2} \tag{23.8}$$

Substituting these demand functions into the carrier's profit function in Eq. (23.3) and solving the profit maximization problem, we obtain the following airfare:

$$p_i = \frac{(a(b+2)(b-1) - 2k_i - bk_j)(n_i + n_j) - b(n_i + (-2 + b^2)n_j)t}{(-4 + b^2)(n_i + n_j)} \tag{23.9}$$

23.3 Nationally-Owned Airport

If a national government manages both airports, it sets a single airport fee k for both to maximize the total social welfare SW. The national government decides the cost-reducing activity of each airport e_i simultaneously to maximize the total social welfare.

When solving the total social welfare maximization problem with k, e_i, and e_j, we obtain the following outcomes:

$$\begin{aligned} k^n = &\{(n_1 + n_2)(2a - t) - 2(1 + b)(2a(-1 + b) + 41c + t - b(2c + t))\beta\} \\ &/\{2(n_1 + n_2 - 2(1 + b)\beta)\} \end{aligned} \tag{23.10}$$

$$\begin{aligned} e_i^n = &-\{(n_i^2 - n_j^2)t - 2(-2(-1 + b + b^2)(a - c)(n_i + n_j) \\ &+((-3 + b^2)n_j + (-1 + 2b + b^2)n_i)t)\beta\} \\ &/\{4(-2 + b + b^2)\beta(n_i + n_j - 2(1 + b)\beta)\} \end{aligned} \tag{23.11}$$

By substituting these outcomes into the social welfare function, we can obtain the total social welfare. However, because of a very complex calculation result, we omit the detailed value here. In the following, we express total social welfare as SW^n.

23.4 Locally-Owned Airport

When a local government manages its airport, it chooses an airport fee to maximize its local social welfare. Therefore, airport fees differ among cities. At the same time, each local government determines the cost-reducing activity to maximize its local social welfare.

When solving each local social welfare maximization problem with k_i and e_i, we obtain the following reaction functions:

$$k_i = -\frac{b^2 n_j}{(-4+b^2)n_i + 4(-2+b^2)n_j} k_j + D_i \tag{23.12}$$

$$e_i = \frac{(-2+b^2)(1+n_j)}{2\beta(4-5b^2+b^4)} k_i + \frac{b(n_i+n_j)}{2\beta(4-5b^2+b^4)} k_j + H_i \tag{23.13}$$

Here, due to the complex calculation results, we omit the detailed values for D_i and H_i. Then, we can obtain following Lemma 23.1.

Lemma 23.1 *(1) The fees for Airport 1 and Airport 2 are strategic complements. (2) When Airport i's fee increases, Airport i's cost-reducing activity decreases. (3) When Airport j's fee increases, Airport i's cost-reducing activity increases.*

In this economy, Airport 1 (or City 1) and Airport 2 (or City 2) compete with each other. Therefore, for example, if City 1 decreases Airport 1's fee, City 2 must also decrease Airport 2's fee to avoid losing passengers. In contrast, if City 1 increases Airport 1's fee, City 2 can also increase Airport 2's fee because more passengers use Airport 2. Consequently, the fees for Airport 1 and Airport 2 are strategic complements.

The following mechanism determines cost-reducing investments. When Airport *i* increases its airport fee, the total number of flights that passengers take using Airport 1 decreases, which decreases the marginal benefit of the cost-reducing activity. Therefore, Airport *i*'s cost-reducing activity decreases with Airport *i*'s fee. However, when Airport *j* increases its airport fee, the total number of flights that passengers take using Airport 2 increases, which increases the marginal benefit of the cost-reducing activity. Consequently, Airport *i*'s cost-reducing activity increases with Airport *j*'s fee.

Solving the above reaction functions, we obtain the following outcomes:

$$\begin{aligned} k_i^\ell = & [B^2N^4(aN - n_jt) - 2BN^2\{a(-1+b)(2+b^3)N^2 - (-2+b)(1+b)cBN^2 \\ & + (bBn_i^2 - (3+b)Bn_in_j - Bn_j^2)t\}\beta \end{aligned}$$

$$+4(-1+b)(1+b)(cBN^2\{-4n_iB+(4+(-1+b)b^2n_j)\}$$
$$+4(-1+b^2)(cBN^3 2\{-4Bn_i+(4+-1+b)b^2n_j)\}$$
$$-a(-1+b)N\{-4(1+b)Bn_i^2+(4+(-4+b)b(-1+b+b^2))n_in_j+b^2Bn_j^2\}$$
$$+n_j\{B(-4-4b+b^3)n_i^2+(4-b(-4+b(-3+b+2b^2)))n_in_j-b^2Bn_j^2\}t)\beta^2]$$
$$/\Delta \tag{23.14}$$

$$e_i^\ell = -\{BN^2n_i(bn_i+Bn_j)t+2(bn_i^3B+b(-8+b+7b^2-b^4)n_i^2n_j$$
$$+B(-4+b+2b^2)n_in_j+B^2n_j^3t\beta-(1-a)cA_iBN^2\}/\Delta \tag{23.15}$$

Here,

$$B \equiv -2+b^2 \tag{23.16}$$
$$N \equiv n_i+n_j \tag{23.17}$$
$$A_i \equiv BN^2+2(1+b)(-n_i(4+3b)+Bn_i\beta) \tag{23.18}$$
$$\Delta \equiv B^2N^4-4(6-7b^2+b^4)N^3\beta$$
$$+4(-1+b^2)(4B(n_i^2+n_j)^2-(20-13b^2+b^4))\beta^2 \tag{23.19}$$

By substituting these outcomes into the social welfare function, we obtain total social welfare. However, we omit the detailed value here due to the very complex calculation result. In the following, we express total social welfare as SW^ℓ.

23.5 Comparison of Outcomes

This section compares the airport fees and cost-reducing activities of each type of airport ownership.

23.5.1 Comparison of Airport Fees

First, we compare the airport fees of nationally and locally managed airports. Here, because the calculation result is very complex, we cannot compare these airport fees analytically. Therefore, in the following, we perform a simulation analysis. Hereafter, to satisfy $0 \leq e_i \leq c$, we use the following values: $a = 10$, $c = 1$, and $\beta = 10$. Furthermore, without loss of generality, we normalize $n_1 = 1$. Additionally, we consider the parameter value t as positive demand in all markets.

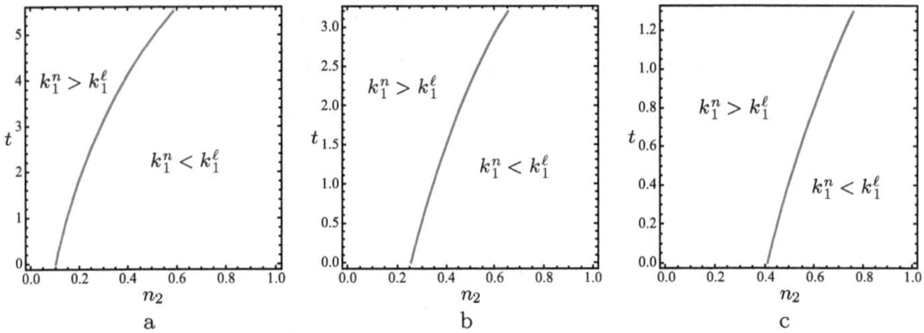

Fig. 23.1 Comparison of Airport 1's fees. (**a**) $b = 0.2$, (**b**) $b = 0.5$, (**c**) $b = 0.8$

First, we consider Airport 1's fees. Figure 23.1 shows the comparison result. Therefore, we can demonstrate the following Lemma 23.2.

Lemma 23.2 *When n_2 is small (large), Airport 1's fee in the nationally managed case is higher (lower) than that in the locally managed case. As t increases, the range of the former is higher than the latter, which widens.*

In the following, we consider Airport 2's fees. Using a simulation analysis, we can immediately obtain the following Lemma 23.3.

Lemma 23.3 *Airport 2's fee in the locally managed case is always higher than that in the nationally managed case.*

First, we discuss the results of Airport 2's fees. In the nationally managed case, the government chooses an airport considering the social welfare of both City 1 and City 2. Therefore, in order to increase not only the consumer surplus of City 2's passengers but also that of City 1's passengers, the national government determines the single airport fee. On the other hand, in the locally managed case, the government in City 2 considers only the consumer surplus of City 2's passengers. In addition, if the profit of Airport 2 increases, the welfare of City 2 increases. Here, it is noteworthy that City 2's welfare does not include City 1's consumer surplus. At the same time, City 2 has fewer passengers than City 1. Therefore, if City 2's local government chooses a high airport fee in order to increase the airport's profit, although the consumer surplus of City 2's passengers decreases, the airport's profits largely increase. In addition, passengers paying the high airport fee are City 1's passengers, whose consumer surplus is not included in City 2's welfare. Therefore, the local government chooses a high airport fee.

In the following, we discuss the results of Airport 1's fees. In contrast to the results of Airport 2's fees, Airport 1's fee depends on n_2 and t.

First, consider the case in which n_2 is small and t is large. In this range, the airport fee in the nationally managed case is higher than that in the locally managed case. In the nationally managed case, because the national government considers not only Airport 1's profit but also Airport 2's profit, there is no competitive relationship between Airports 1 and 2. On the other hand, in the locally managed

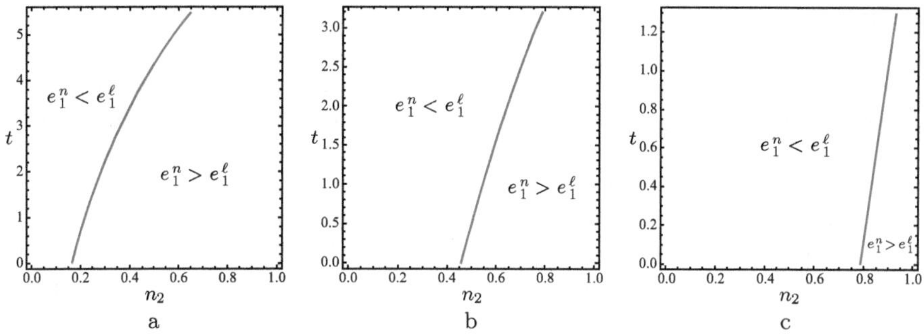

Fig. 23.2 Comparison of Airport 1's cost-reducing activities. (**a**) $b = 0.2$, (**b**) $b = 0.5$, (**c**) $b = 0.8$

case, Airport 1 competes with Airport 2. Furthermore, because City 2 has a small number of passengers, City 1 cannot gain large revenues from City 2's passengers. Furthermore, if passengers in City 1 frequently use Airport 2, Airport 1's profit decreases and passengers in City 1 will have a somewhat small consumer surplus due to the additional traveling cost t. Therefore, to allow City 1's passengers to use City 1's airport, the City 1's local government sets a very low airport fee, and thus the airport fee in the locally managed case is lower than that in the nationally managed case.

In contrast, when n_2 is large and t is small, the local government chooses a high airport fee, as in City 2, to gain larger revenues from City 2's passengers. On the other hand, the national government determines the airport fee considering both cities' welfare. Consequently, the airport fee in the locally managed case becomes higher than that in the nationally managed case.

23.5.2 Comparison of Cost-Reducing Activities

In the following, we compare the cost-reducing activities of the national and local airports. In addition, because the calculation result is very complex, we cannot compare the cost-reducing activity analytically. Therefore, in the following, we perform a simulation analysis. First, we consider Airport 1's cost-reducing activity. Figure 23.2 shows the comparison result.

Therefore, we can demonstrate the following Lemma 23.4.

Lemma 23.4 *When n_2 is small (large), Airport 1's cost-reducing activity in the locally managed case is larger (smaller) than that in the nationally managed case. As t increases, the range of the former is larger than that in the latter, which widens.*

In the following, we consider Airport 2's cost-reducing activity. Using a simulation analysis, we can immediately obtain the following Lemma 23.5.

Lemma 23.5 *Airport 2's cost-reducing activity in the nationally managed case is always larger than that in the locally managed case.*

As is shown in Lemma 23.1, Airport *i*'s cost-reducing activity depends on both Airport *i*'s fee and Airport *j*'s fee. First, we discuss Lemma 23.5. Because Airport 2's fee in the locally managed case is always higher than that in the nationally managed case, Airport 2's cost-reducing activity in the locally managed case tends to be small compared to the nationally managed case. Given this situation, if n_2 is small, Airport 1's fee in the locally managed case is less than that in the nationally managed case. These characteristics leads to less cost-reducing activity at Airport 2 in the locally managed case. Consequently, if n_2 is small, it is apparent that Airport 2's cost-reducing activity in the nationally managed case is larger than that in the locally managed case.

If n_2 is large, although City 2 has an incentive to increase cost-reducing activity at Airport 2 in the locally managed case because Airport 1's fee in the locally managed case is higher than that in the nationally managed case, it has less incentive to increase the cost-reducing activity than it has to decrease Airport 2's cost-reducing activity in the locally managed case. Consequently, even if n_2 is large, Airport 2's cost-reducing activity in the locally managed case is less than that in the nationally managed case.

In the following, we discuss Lemma 23.4. Because Airport 2's fee in the locally managed case is always higher than that in the nationally managed case, City 1 has an incentive to increase Airport 1's cost-reducing activity in the locally managed case compared to the nationally managed case. If n_2 is small, Airport 1's fee in the locally managed case is less than that in the nationally managed case. Therefore, it is apparent that Airport 1's cost-reducing activity in the locally managed case is greater than that in the nationally managed case.

If n_2 is large, Airport 1's fee in the locally managed case increases more than that in the nationally managed case. Therefore, City 1 strengthens the direct incentive for cost-reducing activity in the nationally managed case (and lowers it in the locally managed case). Although City 1 has an indirect incentive to increase the cost-reducing activity in the locally managed case through the Airport 2's fee, its indirect incentive is less than the direct incentive. Consequently, Airport 1's cost-reducing activity in the nationally managed case increases beyond than that in the locally managed case.

23.6 At Which Level Should Airports Be Managed?

Finally, we analyze whether the national or local government should manage airports by comparing the social welfare of each case. Here, due to the heavy, complex calculation, we perform a simulation analysis. Figure 23.3 shows the comparison results.

We thus obtain Theorem 23.6.

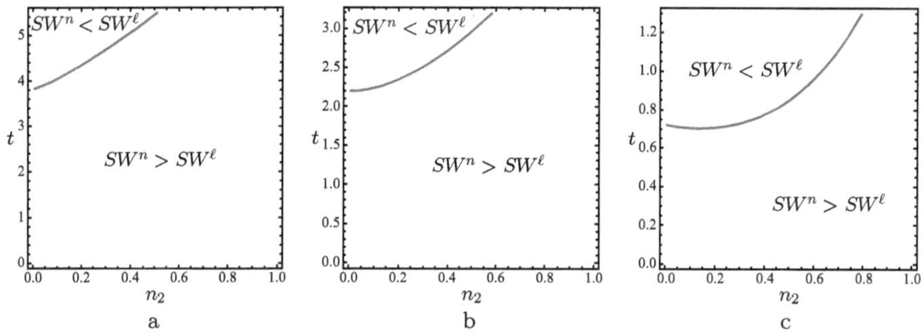

Fig. 23.3 Comparison of social welfare. (**a**) $b = 0.2$, (**b**) $b = 0.5$, (**c**) $b = 0.8$

Theorem 23.6 *When n_2 is small and t is large, the local management is socially preferable to national management. Otherwise, national management is socially preferable.*

When n_2 is small and t is large, the local government in City 1 chooses a very low airport fee so that more of City 1's passengers use Airport 1, which further increases Airport 1's cost-reducing activity. In contrast, the local government in City 2 chooses a "very" high airport fee to increase Airport 2's profit. On the other hand, the national government sets a "somewhat" high single airport fee because the national government considers both cities' welfare, which decreases Airport 1's cost-reducing activity. Therefore, although the national management case is preferable to the local management case in terms of City 2's social welfare, local management is much more preferable to national management in terms of City 1's social welfare. Comparing these trade-offs, the increase in City 1's welfare by adopting local management is larger than that for City 2's welfare from adopting national management. Thus, the local management case becomes socially preferable to the national management case.

When the national management case is socially preferable to the local management case, the range in which Airport 1's fee in the local management case is lower than that in the national management case remains. However, remember that from the viewpoint of City 2's welfare, the national management case is socially preferable to the local management case. Therefore, although City 1's welfare increases by adopting local management, the increase in City 2's welfare by adopting national management is larger than that for City 1. Consequently, the national management case is socially preferable to the local management case.

Finally, when Airport 1's fee in the national management case is lower than that in the local management case, it is apparent that national management is socially preferable to local management.

23.7 Concluding Remarks

This chapter compared national and local airport management. The case considered an economy with two cities, each with one airport. Here, we assumed that passengers in each city can use both airports, but when a passenger living in city i uses the airport in city j, the passenger incurs an additional traveling cost. The (national or local) government determines the airport fee and cost-reducing activity simultaneously. Here, we assumed that in the national management case, airports adopt a uniform airport fee.

Given this scenario, we first examined the airport fee and obtained the following results. Regarding the airport in city i, which has more passengers (hereafter, Airport i), when city j has a small (large) number of passengers, the airport fee in the local management case is lower (higher) than the national management case. For the airport located in city j, which has fewer passengers (hereafter, Airport j), the airport fee in the local management case is always higher than that in the national management case.

We then examined cost-reducing activity and found the following results. For Airport i, when city j has a small (large) number of passengers, the local management case's cost-reducing activity is larger (smaller) than that in the national management case. For Airport j, the local management case's cost-reducing activity is always smaller than that in the national airport management.

Finally, we examined social welfare, with the following results. When city j has a small number of passengers and the additional traveling cost between cities is large, the social welfare in the locally managed case is larger than that in the nationally managed case; otherwise, the social welfare in the national management case is larger than that in the local management case.

We also compared the national and local management cases, though we omitted the private management case. However, airport privatization has recently begun. This leads to the questions of which airport management case results in a lower airport fee, increases cost-reducing activities, and is socially preferable. We should consider this important problem.

This chapter assumed a uniform airport fee in the national management case. However, we could not sufficiently discuss why this assumption is reasonable. If the national government can set individual airport fees for each airport, the first-best situation comes true. However, the national government generally chooses a uniform airport fee. Why? We should consider this reason in the future research.

Third, this chapter does not consider the airport congestion problem, which is also major problem in airport policy. If the airport congestion problem exists, what management arrangement is socially preferable? Although many studies examine this important problem, almost none consider the local management case. Therefore, we want to consider the airport congestion problem by introducing a local airport management case.

Finally, this chapter simply considered a substitute airport instead of omitting the complementary airport. Then, if we introduce a complementary airport into this model, like Matsumura and Matsushima (2012) and Mantin (2012), how do the results change? This problem is also important, and we intend to examine this problem in future research.

References

Abbott, M., and S. Wu. 2002. Total factor productivity and efficiency of Australian airport. *American Economic Review* 35: 244–260.

Akai, N. 2010. Koutuuinfra-to-gabanansu-no-keizaigaku. Yuuhikaku.

Anton, J.J., J. Vander, and N. Vettas. 1998. Strategic pricing and entry under universal service and cross-market pricing constraints. *International Journal of Industrial Organization* 20: 611–629.

Chon, P., L. Flochel, and A. Perrot. 2000. Universal service obligations and competition. *Information Economics and Policy* 12: 249–259.

DeGraba, P. 1990. Input market price discrimination and the choice of technology. *American Economic Review* 80: 1246–1253.

Dixit, A. 1979. A model of Duopoly suggesting a theory of entry barriers. *Bell Journal of Economics* 10: 20–32.

Domney, M.D., H.I.M. Wilson, and E. Chen. 2005. Natural monopoly privatization under different regulatory regimes: A comparison of New Zealand and Australian airports. *International Journal of Public Sector Management* 18: 274–292.

Hart, O., A. Schleifer, and R.W. Vishny. 1997. The proper scope of government: Theory and application to prisons. *Quarterly Journal of Economics* 112: 1127–1161.

Hoppe, E.I., and P.W. Schmitz. 2010. Public versus private ownership: Quantity contracts and the allocation of investments tasks. *Journal of Public Economics* 94: 258–268.

Hooper, O.G., and D.A., Hensher. 1997. Measuring total factor productivity of airports – an index number approach. *Transportation Research Part E* 33: 249–259.

Kawasaki, A. 2012. Who should own component airports? *Bulletin of the Faculty of Education, Kagoshima University Culture and Social Science* 63: 1–26.

Liao, P.C. 2008. Downstream R&D rivalry with spillovers and discriminatory input pricing. *Australian Economic Papers* 47: 376–388.

Mantin, B. 2012. Airport complementarity: Private vs. government ownership and welfare gravitation. *Transportation Research Part B* 46: 381–388.

Matsumura, T., and N. Matsushima. 2012. Airport privatization and international competition. *Japanese Economic Review* 63: 431–450.

Oum, T.H., N. Adler, and C. Yu. 2006. Privatization, corporatization, ownership forms and their effects on the performance of the world's major airports. *Journal of Air Transport Management* 12: 109–121.

Oum, T.H., J. Yan, and C. Yu. 2008. Ownership forms matter for airport efficiency: A stochastic frontier investigation of worldwide airports. *Journal of Urban Economics* 43: 422–435.

Parker, D. 1999. The performance of BAA before and after privatization. *Journal of Transportation Economics and Policy* 33: 113–146.

Schmidt, K.M. 1996a. The costs and benefits of privatization: An incomplete contracts approach. *Journal of Law, Economics, and Organization* 12: 1–24.

Schmidt, K.M. 1996b. Incomplete contracts and privatization. *European Economic Review* 40: 569–579.

Valletti, T.M., S. Hoernig, and P.P. Barros. 2002. Universal service and entry: The role of uniform pricing and coverage constraints. *Journal of Regulatory Economics* 21: 169–190.

Chapter 24
Voting for Secession and Siting Nuisance Facilities in a Federation

Shigeharu Sato

24.1 Introduction

Facilities such as power plants, waste disposal areas, airports, prisons, and military bases are necessary and useful for society, but they can be a nuisance and noxious for neighbors, causing conflicts between governments and residents. These are therefore often called "not in my backyard" (NIMBY) facilities. Governments must construct NIMBY facilities, but their location presents many difficulties.

NIMBY facilities sometimes lie at boundaries with other regions. This phenomenon also occurs in states within federal nations. Monogan et al. (2016) show empirically that state governments and firms with incentives to locate polluting facilities and major air polluters strategically are significantly more likely to be located near a state's downwind border.

In recent years, quite a few subnational regions have held referendums seeking independence from their respective nations. More are expected to do so in the future. Some earlier studies have examined secession and country formation. Friedman (1977) uses a rent-maximizing model to study national borders. Buchanan and Faith (1987) adopted a political economy approach to modeling of the government. Bolton and Roland (1997) argue that democracy raises too many secession demands and relations based on economic integration.

Recent studies of secession by Alesina and Spolaore (1997) analyze the stability of the equilibrium number of countries and optimality. Alesina and Spolaore (2003) have studied numerous topics related to national borders.

S. Sato (✉)
Nagasaki Wesleyan University, Isahaya, Japan
e-mail: s.sato@wesleyan.ac.jp

T. Naito et al. (eds.), *Applied Approaches to Societal Institutions and Economics*, New Frontiers in Regional Science: Asian Perspectives 18,
DOI 10.1007/978-981-10-5663-5_24

This paper presents an examination, from a social perspective, of how NIMBY facilities affect secession and the efficiency of political systems. We model democratic decisions of NIMBY location and compare different political systems: decentralized and centralized.

Our study is related to studies of political economy, such as those of Besley and Coate (2003) and Gradstein (2004). These studies compare decentralized and centralized systems using a citizen candidate model. The citizen candidate model of representative democracy was developed by Osborne and Slivinski (1996) and Besley and Coate (1997). Our model of a federation draws on these frameworks and includes consideration of a strategic voting problem in the context of NIMBY and secession.

The rest of this chapter is organized as follows. Section 24.2 presents the model framework. Section 24.3 derives the social optimum. Section 24.4 defines the political equilibrium and outcomes. Section 24.5 presents the model using a numerical simulation. Section 24.6 concludes the study.

24.2 The Framework

We consider two regions distributed over the interval [0, 1]. Region 1 is the left side regions of the interval. The right side of the interval is region 2. Initially, regions 1 and 2 belong to the same federal country as states. The borders separating region 1 and region 2 are $b \geq 1/2$. Therefore, region sizes are $s_1 = b \geq 1/2$ for region 1 and $s_2 = 1 - b \leq 1/2$ for region 2.[1] The residents are distributed uniformly in [0, 1]. Then, size s_i also means a number of population of region $i \in \{1, 2\}$. We assume that the inhabitants are not allowed to move to another location and refer to each by the point, $X \in [0, 1]$, where they live (Fig. 24.1).

A country needs a single public good, but that good presents a nuisance for local inhabitants. The utility from the public good is $g - C(s_i)$, where g is constant and where $C(s_i)$ represents a congestion effect and is twice differentiable ($C'(s_i) > 0$, $C''(s_i) > 0$). We use quadratic function $C(s_i) = cs_i^2$, later, which indicates that the benefits of the public good are decreasing with the number of users (the region size). We assume that every country's public good cost K is the same for everyone. Every

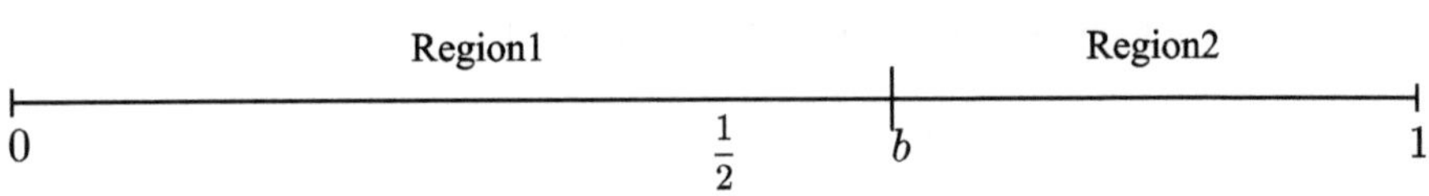

Fig. 24.1 Two regions in a country

[1]This assumption of sizes means the smaller region wants to secede from the larger region. This situation is common in the real world. We can eliminate nonsignificant cases.

individual has the same wage w and must pay tax t to produce the public good. The public good is located at X_i^G, as decided by majority voting. Subscript i denotes that both regions must have the public good if region 2 secedes. Damage d decreases as the distance between the public good location, X_i^G, and the location of individual X increases. This assumption means the public good is NIMBY. Consequently, the utility function of individual X is

$$U(X) = g - cs_i^2 - d\sum_{i=1,2}\left\{1 - \left(X_i^G - X\right)^2\right\} + w - t, \tag{24.1}$$

where we assume that damage d is decreasing with the quadratic function of distance $X^G - X$.

In the initial state, both regions belong to the federal country as stated before. We consider two political systems of the federal country. One is a decentralized system. Under decentralization, the federal government has only weak authority. Regions (states) have the right to secede from the federal country by their own will. The other system is centralized. Under centralization, the federal government has authority to stop secession of the state. We consider only whether region 2 secedes from the country; region 1 does not secede.

The timing of the events is the following:

1. Election of representatives
2. Representatives bargain over compensation to region 2 if possible
3. Region 2 residents vote for secession if the vote is approved
4. Each region government chooses the public good location if region 2 seceded and the central government decides it if region 2 did not secede

24.3 Social Optimum

Now, we consider the first-best optimal conditions for secession. When the country is integrated, the optimal location of public good is $X^G = 0$ or 1 because the damage $d(1 - (X^G - X)^2)$ is minimized. Avoiding multiple equilibria, we assume $X^G = 1$ when there is indifference between $X^G = 0$ and 1. Then, the utility of individual X, when the regions are integrated, is

$$U^I(X) \equiv U\left(X; X^G = 1\right) = g - c - d\left\{1 - (1 - X)^2\right\} + w - K. \tag{24.2}$$

Then, social welfare is defined as

$$W^I \equiv \int_0^1 U^I(X)dX = g - c - \frac{2}{3}d + w - K. \tag{24.3}$$

If region 2 secedes, then utility $U_i^S(X)$ is defined as

$$U_i^S(X) \equiv U\left(X; X_1^G = b, X_2^G = 1\right)$$
$$= g - cs_i^2 - d\left\{1 - (b - X)^2\right\} - d\left\{1 - (1 - X)^2\right\} + w - K, \qquad (24.4)$$

where locations of public goods are $(X_1^G, X_2^G) = (b, 1)$. Then, social welfare is defined as

$$W^S \equiv \int_0^b U_1^S(X)dX + \int_b^1 U_2^S(X)dX$$
$$= g - c(1 - 3b(1 - b)) - d\left\{\frac{4}{3} + b(1 - b)\right\} + w - K. \qquad (24.5)$$

Comparing W^I with W^S, we have

$$W^I - W^S = d\left\{\frac{2}{3} + b(1 - b)\right\} - 3cb(1 - b). \qquad (24.6)$$

Therefore, $W^I \geq W^S$ iff

$$\frac{c}{d} \leq \frac{2 + 3b(1 - b)}{9b(1 - b)}. \qquad (24.7)$$

The following lemma states the optimal secession condition.

Lemma 24.1 *Separation is socially desirable ($W^I < W^S$) if the congestion effect c is large and if the NIMBY effect d is small. Precisely, separation is socially desirable if and only if*

$$\frac{c}{d} > \frac{2 + 3b(1 - b)}{9b(1 - b)}. \qquad (24.8)$$

If not, integration is socially desirable.

24.4 Political Economy

In this section, we derive the equilibrium secession conditions under political procedures. We compare two political systems: decentralized and centralized. Regions have a strong right under the decentralized system; secession is determined by referendum in region 2 only.[2] However, a central government has strong power to suppress secession under a centralized system.[3]

24.4.1 Decentralized System

Under a decentralized system, each regional (state) government has a right to secede. Therefore, region 2 can secede if a vote for secession is a majority in the referendum held in region 2. The central (federal) government chooses the location of the public good if the country is integrated. Each regional government chooses the location if region 2 secedes.

We analyze the model using backward induction. First, we consider locations of public goods. The central government decides the location of a public good if region 2 does not secede. We consider the majority vote to elect a central government representative. The median voter of the whole individual is elected. This individual is $X = 1/2$. The median voter wants to locate the public good as far away as possible. Therefore, $X^G = 1$ is chosen.

If region 2 secedes at time 3 of the time line, each region's government decides the location. The median voter of region 1 is $X = b/2$. She chooses $X_1^G = b$. The median voter of region 2 is $X = (1 + b)/2$. She is indifferent between $X_2^G = b$ and 1. We assume that she chooses $X_2^G = 1$, which is the same as the social optimum in such cases of indifference.

Next, we analyze a referendum for secession of region 2. At time 2, region 1 can compensate for locating a NIMBY facility in region 2. We consider two cases: with compensation and without. If there is no compensation and the country is integrated, then the utility of individual X is $U^I(X)$. If region 2 secedes from the country, then the utility of individual X in region 2 is $U_2^S(X)$. The results of referendum to decide whether or not to secede were determined by the median voter in region 2. Because $X = (1 + b)/2$ is the median voter, her utility when the country integrated is

$$U^I\left(\frac{1+b}{2}\right) = g - c - d\left\{1 - \left(1 - \frac{1+b}{2}\right)^2\right\} + w - K. \tag{24.9}$$

When region 2 secedes, the utility is

---

[2]The case roughly approximates the relation between the EU and the UK. The UK chose secession from the EU by their own referendum, but the EU government cannot stop secession and has no right to do so.

[3]For example, the relation between the Spanish government and Catalonia presents such a case. Catalonia held referendums many times and secessionists won votes many times, but the Spanish government did not approve the referendum outcome: Catalonia cannot secede.

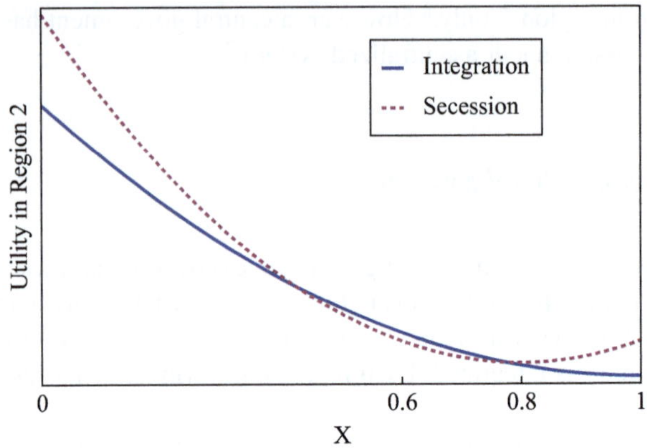

Fig. 24.2 Comparing utilities of region 2 when integration and secession

$$U_2^S\left(\frac{1+b}{2}\right) = g - cs_2^2 - d\left\{1 - \left(b - \frac{1+b}{2}\right)^2\right\}$$
$$- d\left\{1 - \left(1 - \frac{1+b}{2}\right)^2\right\} + w - K \tag{24.10}$$

Comparing these utilities, we have a condition of $U_2^S((1+b)/2) > U^I((1+b)/2)$, as

$$\frac{c}{d} > \frac{3 + b(2-b)}{4b(2-b)}.$$

It is noteworthy that this condition is not coincident with social optimal (24.8). Wittman (2000) explains that secession decided by a referendum achieves social optimum if a distance cost function is quadratic. However, the theorem no longer holds if public goods have a NIMBY effect, as our model does.

Figure 24.2 presents the utility of region 2 in two cases: integration and secession. The horizontal axis displays the location of individuals X. The vertical axis displays their utility. The border is $b = 0.6$. These graphs are valid in interval [0.6, 1]. In this figure's case, the median voter of region 2 is $(1 + b)/2 = 0.8$ as $b = 0.6$. The solid line, the utility of secession, is higher than the dotted line, the utility of integration at the median $X = 0.8$. Therefore, secessionists in region 2 are a majority in this figure.

Subsequently, we examine the effect of compensation.[4] At time 2, state government of region 1 would compensate to region 2 to dissuade secession if possible. The representative is each region's median voter.[5] They bargain over the compensation amount. We assume representative of region 1 has full bargaining power for simplicity. The representative of region 1 decides the minimum amount so that anti-secessionists win the referendum. In another way, the transfer per capita T satisfies the following condition:

$$U^I\left(\frac{1+b}{2}\right) + T = U_2^S\left(\frac{1+b}{2}\right), \tag{24.11}$$

where T is the transfer per capita from region 1 to region 2. Taking the transfer into account, the median voter in region 1 prefers secession if $U_1^S(b/2) > U^I(b/2) - T$. This condition becomes

$$\frac{c}{d} > \frac{1+b(1-b)}{4b(1-b)}.$$

Now, conclude the equilibrium in the decentralized system.

Lemma 24.2 *Under the decentralized system, region 2 secedes if and only if*

$$\frac{c}{d} > \frac{3+b(2-b)}{4b(2-b)}, \tag{24.12}$$

when the compensation transfer is impossible and

$$\frac{c}{d} > \frac{1+b(1-b)}{4b(1-b)}, \tag{24.13}$$

when the compensation transfer is possible.

Comparing (24.12) with (24.13), we show that the latter is larger. Furthermore, we can show that the (24.13) is larger than the social optimum (24.8). In addition, (24.12) can be smaller and larger than the social optimum (24.8). These observations prove that compensation strongly supports integration. However, lack of a compensation scheme can be efficient.

[4]We use simple bargaining to ascertain the amount of compensation; however, many results of studies suggest efficient compensation mechanisms such as auctions for NIMBY. See Kunreuther and Kleindorfer (1986), Kunreuther et al. (1987), and Minehart and Neeman (2002).

[5]In this case, strategic voting might occur. However, region 1 compensates the amount to make the median voter (not the representative) of region 2 indifferent between secession and integration because the referendum by all voters in region 2 decides secession or not. Therefore, strategic voting is invalid.

Proposition 24.3 *Decentralized equilibrium is inefficient. Equilibrium secession can be too much or too little if compensation is impossible. Equilibrium secession tends to arise less if compensation is possible.*

24.4.2 Centralized System: Presidential

Under the centralized system, the federal government has power to halt of invalidate the secession referendum in region 2. In addition to this, the federal government chooses the amount of compensation to region 2.

In the presidential system, because regions have no right to secede, compensation to dissuade secession has no role. Therefore, strategic voting is invalid, the median voter of country $X = 1/2$ is elected president.

First, we consider public good locations. The central government decides the location of public good if integration. President $X = 1/2$ wants to locate the public good as far away as possible $X^G = 1$.

If region 2 secedes at time 3 of the time line, each region's government decides the location. The median voter of region 1 is $X = b/2$. She chooses $X_1^G = b$. The median voter of region 2 is $X = (1+b)/2$. She is indifferent between $X_2^G = b$ and 1. We assume that she chooses $X_2^G = 1$, which is the same as the social optimum assumption.

Next, we will examine the referendum in region 2 at time 3. We restate only the outcome because this analysis is the same as that of the decentralized case. The condition under which secessionists have a majority in region 2 is (24.12)

$$\frac{c}{d} > \frac{3 + b(2-b)}{4b(2-b)}.$$

Then, we derive a condition under which the president approves the referendum before time 2. Comparing the utility $U_1^S(1/2)$ with $U^I(1/2)$, we have

$$U_1^S\left(\frac{1}{2}\right) - U^I\left(\frac{1}{2}\right) = \left\{\frac{3}{4} + b(1-b)\right\} - c(1-b)(1+b). \tag{24.14}$$

The equation above is positive iff

$$\frac{c}{d} > \frac{3 + 4b(1-b)}{4(1-b)(1+b)}. \tag{24.15}$$

The referendum is approved and secessionists have a majority in region 2 if both conditions (24.12) and (24.15) hold however (24.15) includes (24.12). Therefore, the secession condition in the presidential system is (24.15). Now, conclude the equilibrium in the presidential system.

Lemma 24.4 *Under the centralized presidential system, the compensation is invalid. Region 2 secedes if and only if*

$$\frac{c}{d} > \frac{3 + 4b(1-b)}{4(1-b)(1+b)}.$$

Because the LHS of the condition above is larger than that of (24.13) and the social optimal (24.8), the presidential system overly suppresses secession.

Proposition 24.5 *Under a centralized presidential system, the equilibrium is inefficient. The centralized presidential system produces less of a tendency for secession compared to the social optimum.*

24.4.3 Centralized System: Parliamentary

In a parliamentary system, representatives of both regions constitute the federal government. The representatives bargain[6] and decide the federal government policy, the public good location, and the amount of compensation. Therefore, strategic voting occurs. We assume that the federal structure collapses and the equilibrium reverts to a decentralized structure if bargaining breaks down.

Next, let X_i $(i = 1, 2)$ be elected at time 1. They bargain over the location of public good X^G and the amount of compensation transfer T. We assume that the relative size of regions $(s_i/(s_1 + s_2)) = s_i$ is equivalent to bargaining power (probability to offer), which is unlike a decentralized system. A minority region's representative has political power in a parliamentary system. Gradstein (2004) interprets legislative bargaining in a federation similarly.

When region 1's representative X_1 makes an offer, she maximizes her utility while guaranteeing region 2's representative X_2 the utility level under secession $U_2^S(X_2)$.

$$\max_{\{X^G, T\}} \quad U(X_1) = g - c - d\left\{1 - \left(X^G - X_1\right)^2\right\} + w - (K + s_2 T)$$

$$\text{s.t.} \quad U(X_2) = g - c - d\left\{1 - \left(X^G - X_2\right)^2\right\} + w - K + T$$

$$\geq U_2^S(X_2) = g - cs_2^2 - d\left\{1 - (b - X_2)^2\right\}$$

$$-d\left\{1 - (1 - X_2)^2\right\} + w - K$$

[6]We regard bargaining as fundamentally important for the model parliamentary government. Because general bargaining models incorporate the assumption of transferable utilities, we also assume that the compensation transfer is possible.

Region 1's representative minimizes T to satisfy the constraint with equality. Denoting $T_1^*(X_2)$ the minimized transfer, we have

$$T_1^*(X_2) = b^2(d-c) + 2b(c-dX_2) + d\left[X_2^2 + 2X_2(X^G-1) - (X^G)^2\right] \quad (24.16)$$

Substituting $T_1^*(X_2)$ above into the objective function and differentiate with respect to X^G, we have

$$\frac{\partial U(X_1)}{\partial X^G} = d\left[2(X^G - X_1) + 2(1-b)(X^G - X_2)\right], \quad (24.17)$$

where the derivative is positive (negative) iff $X^G > (X_1 + (1-b)X_2)/(2-b)$ ($X^G < (X_1 + (1-b)X_2)/(2-b)$). Therefore, region 1's representative chooses $X^G = 0$ or 1. She chooses $X^G = 1$ iff

$$X_1 \leq 1 - \frac{b}{2} - (1-b)X_2. \quad (24.18)$$

Next, we specifically examine the case in which region 2's representative X_2 makes an offer. The problem is the following:

$$\max_{\{X^G,T\}} \quad U(X_2) = g - c - d\left\{1 - \left(X^G - X_1\right)^2\right\} + w - K + T$$

$$\text{s.t.} \quad U(X_1) = g - c - d\left\{1 - \left(X^G - X_1\right)^2\right\} + w - (K + s_2T)$$

$$\geq U_1^S(X_1) = g - cs_1^2 - d\left\{1 - (b - X_1)^2\right\}$$

$$-d\left\{1 - (1 - X_1)^2\right\} + w - K$$

Region 2's representative maximizes T to satisfy the constraint with equality. Denoting T_2^* the maximized transfer, we have

$$T_2^*(X_1) = \frac{-c(1-b)(1+b) - d\left[(b-X_1)^2 - 2X_1(1-X^G) - (X^G)^2\right]}{1-b}. \quad (24.19)$$

Substituting the above T_2^* into the objective function and differentiating it with respect to X^G, we have

$$\frac{\partial U(X_2)}{\partial X^G} = d\left[2(X^G - X_2) + \frac{2(X^G - X_1)}{1-b}\right], \quad (24.20)$$

where the derivative is positive (negative) iff $X^G > (X_1 + (1-b)X_2)/(2-b)$ ($X^G < (X_1 + (1-b)X_2)/(2-b)$). Therefore, region 2's representative chooses $X^G = 0$ or 1. She chooses $X^G = 1$ iff

$$X_1 \leq 1 - \frac{b}{2} - (1-b)X_2.$$

It is noteworthy that the condition above is the same as (24.18) because a bargaining solution maximizes the sum of utilities.

Next, consider the election of representatives at time 1. We check the case of $X^G = 1$ only if integrated and ignore the condition for $X^G = 1$ is chosen (24.18) for now. We confirm later that it holds. The expected utility of region 1's voter X is

$$EU_1(X; X_1, X_2) = s_1(U^I(X) - s_2 T_1^*(X_2) + s_2(U^I(X) - s_2 T_2^*(X_1)), \qquad (24.21)$$

where $U^I(X)$ is denoted by (24.2). Differentiating this, we have

$$\frac{\partial EU_1(X; X_1, X_2)}{\partial X_1} = -2d(1-b)(b - X_1) < 0 \qquad (24.22)$$

because $X_1 \leq b$. Therefore, all voters in region 1 vote for individual $X_1 = 0$.

A similar argument applies to the case of region 2. The expected utility of region 2's voter X is

$$EU_2(X; X_1, X_2) = s_1(U^I(X) + T_1^*(X_2)) + s_2(U^I(X) + T_2^*(X_1)). \qquad (24.23)$$

Differentiating this, we have

$$\frac{\partial EU_2(X; X_1, X_2)}{\partial X_2} = 2db(X_2 - b) > 0 \qquad (24.24)$$

because $X_2 \geq b$. Consequently, all voters in region 2 vote for individual $X_2 = 1$.

Next, we ascertain whether the condition (24.18) holds in the voting equilibrium, or not. Substituting $X_2 = 1$ to the RHS of (24.18), we have

$$1 - \frac{b}{2} - (1-b) = \frac{b}{2}. \qquad (24.25)$$

Because $X_1 = 0$ is less than $b/2$, we have proved that the condition holds.

Next, we derive the secession condition for a parliamentary system. Region 2 secedes if the representative bargaining fails. This condition is that the sum of representatives' utilities under integration is less than the sum under secession. Subtracting the sum under secession from one under integration, we have $\{1 + 2b(1-b)\}(d-c)$. Therefore, the secession condition is $c > d$.

Lemma 24.6 *Under the centralized parliamentary system, the regions secede if and only if*

$$\frac{c}{d} > 1. \qquad (24.26)$$

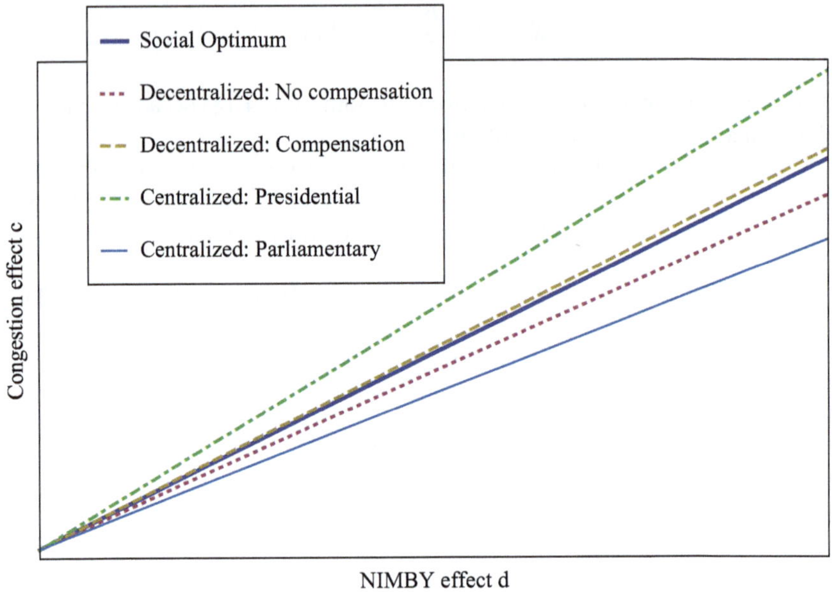

Fig. 24.3 Effects of NIMBY and congestion

The condition explained above can be smaller or larger than the social optimal condition. We summarize the results as described below.

Proposition 24.7 *Under a centralized parliamentary system, the equilibrium is inefficient. The equilibrium secession can be too much or too little. Strategic voting occurs. Voters elect candidates who have extreme positions: The elected representative in region 1 is* $X = 0$*. That in region 2 is* $X = 1$.

24.5 Numerical Simulations

In this section, we use numerical simulations to investigate the model in greater detail. First, compare secession conditions of four political systems and the social optimum. Figure 24.3 presents these secession conditions, the horizontal axis shows the parameter of NIMBY effect d, and the vertical axis shows the parameter of congestion effect d. Regions separate in the area above the line corresponding to each system. The higher NIMBY effect makes integration strengthen, and the higher NIMBY effect promotes secession. The centralized presidential and decentralized with compensation systems produce less of a tendency for secession than the social optimum, as we demonstrated earlier in this report. The decentralized with no compensation and centralized parliamentary system is more likely to lean to secession than the social optimum under parameters we use to illustrate this figure.

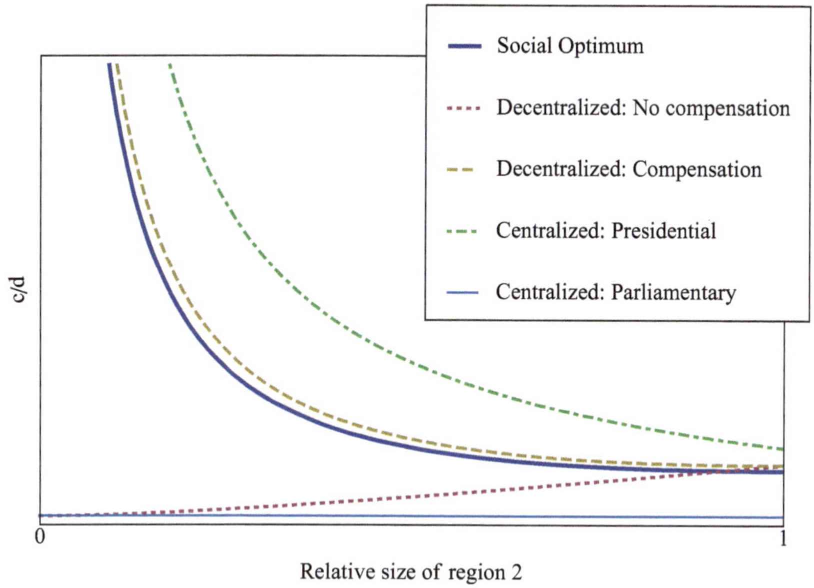

Fig. 24.4 Difference of sizes and secession

Next, we examine the secession condition from another perspective. Figure 24.4 shows how the difference of a region's size affects secession. We use a relative size of region 2 as the following:

$$\text{Relative size of region 2} = \frac{s_2}{s_1} = \frac{1-b}{b}. \tag{24.27}$$

Therefore, if the relative size approaches 0, the difference of region's sizes is large, and if the relative size closes to 1, then the region size differences are small. The vertical axis shows c/d, which congestion effect is compared to the NIMBY effect. As the figure shows, outcomes under decentralized with no compensation and centralized parliamentary engender too much separation compared to the social optimum if the size difference is large.

Next, we examine fairness. Figure 24.5 presents utilities in an integrated country. First, check the utility for secession. $b = 0.6$ is the border of regions. The utility increases at $b = 0.6$ because of a congestion effect. The congestion effect raises utility when secession as country size becomes smaller. Under cases of decentralization with no compensation and centralized presidential, the same utility exists except for when region 2 secedes. The utility of region 2 under decentralization with compensation is lower than in the case of no compensation. This result derives from the congestion effect and bargaining power allocation. This outcome contrasts starkly against that from the case under the centralized

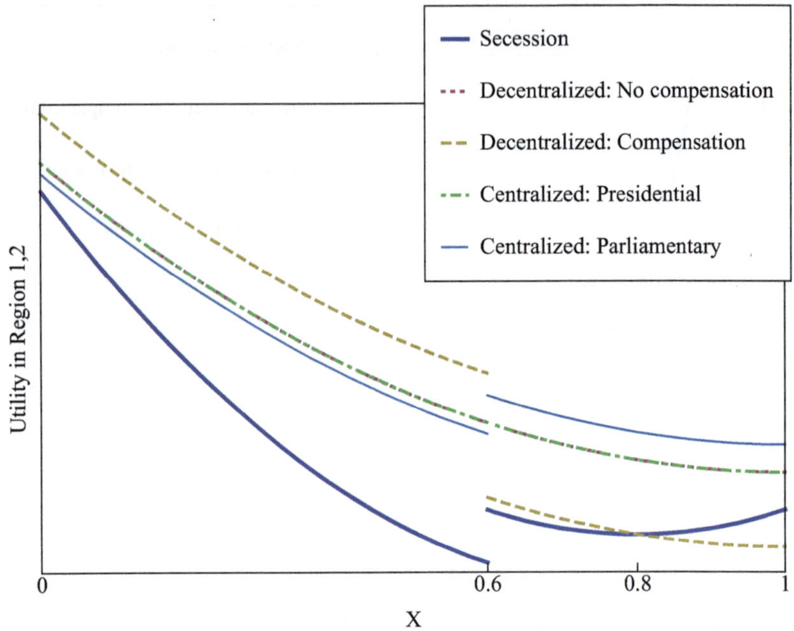

Fig. 24.5 Utilities in both of regions

parliamentary system. Under the system, region 2 has a certain degree of bargaining power and has higher utility. Therefore, the parliamentary system has a virtue of fairness.

24.6 Concluding Remarks

This study investigates a political decision of NIMBY facilities in a federation. Our model has the following main features. First, public goods have a NIMBY effect. Second, the public good location is decided endogenously. Third, we compare a citizen candidate model and a direct voting model for secession.

The main outcomes are the following: (1) a decentralized system tends to produce less secession than the social optimum and a centralized presidential system (Proposition 24.3). (2) A centralized parliamentary system tends to produce too much or little secession compared to the social optimum. Voters elect extreme representatives strategically to draw better bargaining outcomes (Proposition 24.5). (3) Numerical simulation shows a difference of region sizes is not always the cause of failure in a centralized system. The centralized decision can be more efficient than a decentralized one even for a great size difference (Proposition 24.7). Furthermore, we suggest that a centralized parliamentary system has the virtue of fairness over other systems.

Acknowledgements I am grateful to Moriki Hosoe, whose enormous support and insightful comments were invaluable.

References

Alesina, A., and E. Spolaore. 1997. On the number and size of nations. *Quarterly Journal of Economics* 112(4): 1027–1056.

Alesina, A., and E. Spolaore. 2003. *The size of nations*. Cambridge: MIT Press.

Besley, T., and S. Coate. 1997. An economic model of representative democracy. *Quarterly Journal of Economics* 112(1): 85–114.

Besley, T., and S. Coate. 2003. Centralized versus decentralized provision of local public goods: A political economy approach. *Journal of Public Economics* 87(12): 2611–2637.

Bolton, P., and G. Roland. 1997. The breakup of nations: A political economy analysis. *Quarterly Journal of Economics* 112(4): 1057–1090.

Buchanan, J.M., and R.L. Faith. 1987. Secession and the limits of taxation: Toward a theory of internal exit. *American Economic Review* 77(5): 1023–1031.

Friedman, D. 1977. A theory of the size and shape of nations. *Journal of Political Economy* 85(1): 59–77.

Gradstein, M. 2004. Political bargaining in a federation: Buchanan meets Coase. *European Economic Review* 48(5): 983–999.

Kunreuther, H., and P.R. Kleindorfer. 1986. A sealed-bid auction mechanism for siting noxious facilities. *American Economic Review* 76(2): 295–299.

Kunreuther, H., P. Kleindorfer, P.J. Knez, and R. Yaksick. 1987. A compensation mechanism for siting noxious facilities: Theory and experimental design. *Journal of Environmental Economics and Management* 14(4): 371–383.

Minehart, D., and Z. Neeman. 2002. Effective siting of waste treatment facilities. *Journal of Environmental Economics and Management* 43(2): 302–324.

Monogan, J.E., D.M. Konisky, and N.D. Woods. 2017. Gone with the wind: Federalism and the strategic location of air polluters. *American Journal of Political Science*, 61(2): 257–270.

Osborne, M., and A. Slivinski. 1996. A model of political competition with citizen-candidates. *Quarterly Journal of Economics* 111(1): 65–96.

Wittman, D. 2000. The wealth and size of nations. *Journal of Conflict Resolution* 44(6): 868–884.

Chapter 25
Labor Standards and Export-Platform FDI in Unionized Oligopoly

Ki-Dong Lee

25.1 Introduction

Reflecting the growing importance of domestic labor market institution on FDI flow, many theoretical attempts have been conducted on the role of domestic labor market institution such as labor union's bargaining power and unions' relative preferences toward wages, as potential influences on the direction of FDI flow (Smith 1987; Horstmann and Markusen 1987; Mezzetti and Dinopoulos 1991; Bughin and Vannini 1995; Straume 2002; Naylor and Santoni 2003; Lommerud et al. 2003; Hur and Zhao 2009; Lee and Lee 2016). It should be noted that since the above studies on strategic FDI incorporating domestic labor market institution, which normally uses international unionized oligopoly model, were limited to a simple two-country model, they could not appropriately capture more complexed FDI mode of these days. A prominent example of such complex FDI is the export-platform FDI.[1] Export-platform FDI refers to a situation where a multinational firm (MNF) sets up a plant in a host country to supply its products to third-country markets, not the parent country or host-country markets. And the rise of trade blocs such as free trade agreements (FTAs), which have low trade barriers among member countries but have high external barriers to nonmember countries, may contribute to this trend.[2]

[1]The increasing importance of export-platform type FDI is documented in many studies. See for instance, Ekholm et al. (2007), Hanson et al. (2001), and Ito (2013).

[2]That is, MNFs are establishing production subsidiaries within a trade bloc in order to serve the entire market as in horizontal investments, but a specific location within the region is chosen from

K.-D. Lee (✉)
Keimyung University, Daegu, South Korea
e-mail: kdlee@kmu.ac.kr

T. Naito et al. (eds.), *Applied Approaches to Societal Institutions and Economics*,
New Frontiers in Regional Science: Asian Perspectives 18,
DOI 10.1007/978-981-10-5663-5_25

More importantly, the literature on international unionized oligopoly normally does not take into account the possibility of the government's strategic use of union legislation. However, as can be seen in the arguments between developed and developing countries over trade-linked labor standards, the labor standard of a country is closely related to the labor policy of that country. The industrialized countries have concerns that most developing countries, by making use of cheap labor and relaxing their labor market regulations, may be able to enjoy unfair advantages not only in international trade but also in their ability to attract and/or retain investment. Most industrialized countries warn the dangers of race to the bottom in labor standards as governments may be tempted to intentionally relax their standards in order to compete for jobs. In this context, advocates, mostly industrialized countries, argue that labor standards provisions should be included in trade agreements in order to eliminate a source of unfair economic advantage (so-called trade-linked labor standards). On the other hand, developing countries blame the developed countries from the recognition that international pressures for the establishment of monitoring labor practices and to meet an acceptable level of labor condition are a typical method of hidden protectionism.

The current paper tries to fill this gap. In this paper, we construct a locational model of unionized oligopoly, where export and export-platform FDI are alternative modes for serving a third-country market, and examine welfare effects of outward FDI induced by union activities. More specifically, by assuming that the government has the power to affect the bargaining power of the union through the legislation, we derive the optimal level of labor standard from the viewpoint of FDI source country. Here, we link weak labor standards to weak bargaining power of unions.

From the analysis, we first show that when there is only one domestic firm in the market to begin with, increasing the bargaining power of labor union is always welfare decreasing irrespective of whether the monopolist is a national firm (i.e., firm with no foreign operation) or multinational firm. Therefore, the government of the home country has an incentive to restrict union's bargaining power at the lowest level when there is only one domestic firm. Given this result, one would like to predict that restricting unions' bargaining power is generally welfare improving even in the case of oligopoly. As it turns out, however, this conclusion does not necessarily hold true with the addition of another rival firm in the market. One key finding is that, when it comes to oligopoly, there are two conflicting effects with regard to welfare effects of unions' bargaining power: the increase in the firms' profit due to the strategic interaction between firms, which are not derived in the monopoly model, and the workers' loss due to the weakened market competitiveness. And when the level of union bargaining power is sufficiently low, the former overweighs the latter, implying that an increase in the union bargaining

the perspective of cost minimization, as in vertical investments. For example, FDI from the USA and other countries into Ireland belongs to this type; plants are established to serve the EU market, but Ireland is chosen as a location site for the production cost reasons.

power may increase social welfare. Therefore, the optimal level of labor standards in terms of union bargaining power might be positive level in an international unionized oligopolistic market.

The key differences of this paper to the existing literature on international unionized oligopoly model are twofold. First, while the welfare analysis of outward FDI offers critical policy implications, studies on the effect of outward FDI incorporating labor market institution are relatively scarce, both theoretically and empirically. In general, the literature on the welfare effects of FDI has mainly focused on the effect of inward FDI on the host country. In our model, we explore the welfare effects and policy implications of outward FDI with detailed consideration for the domestic labor market institution. This theoretical framework enables us to derive policy implication with respect to labor market institution especially when employment matters in the home country.

Second, unlike the literature on labor standards and international trade which does not normally treat labor standards as policy variables, this study treats labor standards in terms of union's bargaining power as a policy variable. In this context, this paper examines the endogenous choice of labor standard in the home country using the three-country unionized oligopoly model. It is somewhat surprising that only a few studies examine the endogenous choice of labor standards as a policy variable in the oligopoly. Among them are Hur and Zhao (2009) and Leahy and Montagna (2005). However, in these studies, either export-platform type FDI is ignored due to the adoption of two-country model (Hur and Zhao 2009) or the analysis is focused on welfare effects of labor standard from the viewpoint of FDI host country, not source country (Leahy and Montagna 2005).

The rest of this paper is organized as follows. In Sect. 25.2, we develop a monopoly model, which is a benchmark case to be compared. In Sect. 25.3, we extend the benchmark model to a duopoly setting in which one national firm and one multinational firm (MNF), both unionized in the home country, engage in Cournot competition in the world market and examine the location decision of MNF. In Sect. 25.4, we investigate the welfare effects of the MNF's location decision and solve for optimal labor standard policy of FDI source country. Section 25.5 provides concluding remarks.

25.2 Model: Monopoly Case

25.2.1 The Basic Model

Consider an economy composed of three countries: home, foreign, and a third country (world market). There is an industry in which a monopolist,[3] firm M produces a product, which is sold in a third-country market only. The monopolist

[3]In the next section, we deal with the duopoly case.

locates headquarters at home, but it can choose the production location either at home or in foreign country. If the monopolist decides to locate its plant in the foreign country, then it faces a plant-specific fixed cost k. The decision of production location depends on many factors, such as production costs, trade cost, and government policies. Here, we focus on the difference in production costs due to wage differentials. To look at this matter, we model a situation where workers are organized into unions only in the home country.

Labor is the only production factor in our model. By the appropriate choice of units, we assume that just one unit of labor is required for each unit of the final good. Consumers' preferences in the third country are quasi-linear, and the demand for the good X is represented by a linear demand function, $p = a - X$ $(a > 0)$, where p and X refer to the market price and the output level of the firm. Given the wage level in each country, the profit function of the monopolist is given by

$$\pi_M = \begin{cases} \Pi_M = (p - w_M - t)x_M & \text{if the monopolist produces in the home country} \\ \Pi_M - k = (p - \bar{w} - t)x_M - k & \text{if the monopolist produces in the foreign country} \end{cases} \tag{25.1}$$

where Π_M, w_M, and t represent variable profits, the wages at home country, and a transport costs to ship one unit of output from home or foreign country to the world market, respectively. Note that there is a once-off, fixed, and sunk cost associated with FDI, k. Here, we interpret trade liberalization as a reverse process of protectionism.

The wages in the home country is determined through a cooperative generalized Nash bargaining process between the union and the firm, whereas the wage in the foreign country, where workers are nonunionized, is given exogenously at the competitive level, $\bar{w}$. We assume the competitive wages in the two countries are equal and the union in the home market sees this wage level as their reservation wage. In this paper, we adopt a modified Stone-Geary-type utility function to represent the union's preference, $u = (w - \bar{w})^{\beta} \times x$, where $\beta(> 0)$is the weight that the union attaches to wage level and x, the output level of the monopolist, equals to its labor input. The union is referred to as wage oriented if $\beta > 1$, employment oriented if $\beta < 1$, and neutral if $\beta = 1$.

Following the definition used in Mezzetti and Dinopoulos (1991), Bughin and Vannini (1995), and Ishida and Matsushima (2009), social welfare of home country, W, can be defined as the sum of firm's profits and the union rents. That is,

$$W = \pi_M + r_M = (p - w_M - t)x + (w_M - \bar{w})x_M, \tag{25.2}$$

where $r_M(\equiv (w_M - \bar{w})x_M)$ is the union rents. The following sequential game is considered. In stage 1 of the game, the government decides the labor standard level. Stage 2 is about the firm's location decision. There are two possible location mode of the monopolist: it produces in the home country (we term this as "export entry mode"), and it produces in the foreign country ("FDI entry mode"). In stage 3, wage level in the home country is determined as a consequence of Nash bargaining between firm and union. Finally, in stage 4, the monopolist chooses its profit-maximizing output level (i.e., employment level).

25.2.2 Market Equilibrium

We can solve the profit maximization problem backward. For each production location, the profit maximization problem of the monopolist is $\max\limits_{x_M} \pi_M(x_M; w_M, t)$ in the export entry mode, while that is $\max\limits_{x_M} \pi_M(x_M\ ; \bar{w}, t, k)$ in the FDI entry mode. Then, we have $\pi_M = \Pi_M = \left(\frac{a-w_M-t}{2}\right)^2$ for export mode while $\pi_M = \Pi_M - k = \left(\frac{a-\bar{w}-t}{2}\right)^2 - k$ for FDI mode. Clearly, variable profits under export mode are strictly smaller than those under FDI mode if the following condition, $w_M > \bar{w}$, is met. We assume that this condition is met so that the monopolist could choose to produce at foreign.

In stage 3, for wage determination in the home country, we have the following Nash maximand[4]: $V_M(w_M\ ; \beta, \theta, t) = u_M^{\theta}\pi_M^{1-\theta} = [(w_M - \bar{w})^{\beta} x_M]^{\theta}[x_M^2]^{1-\theta}$, where $\theta \in [0, 1]$ denotes the exogenous bargaining power of the union. For reasons discussed in the introduction, we use θ to represent the labor standard in the home country and assume that it is determined endogenously by the government in the first stage of the game. As the monopolist and the union bargain over wages simultaneously, the equilibrium wage in the home country is obtained by solving the following problem:

$$w_M^*(\theta, \beta, t) = \arg\max_{w_M} V_M(w_M; \beta, \theta, t) := \bar{w} + \frac{\beta\theta(a - \bar{w} - t)}{2 - \theta + \beta\theta}, \tag{25.3}$$

$$\text{where } \frac{\partial w_M^*}{\partial \theta} = \frac{2\beta(a - \bar{w} - t)}{(2 - \theta + \beta\theta)^2} > 0, \quad \frac{\partial w_M^*}{\partial(-t)} = \frac{2\beta\theta}{(2 - \theta + \beta\theta)^2} > 0.$$

In Eq. (25.3), superscript "*" denotes the equilibrium in the export entry mode. The difference between the equilibrium wage and the reservation wage might be interpreted as the union wage markup. By substituting w_M^* from Eq. (25.3) into the variables such as firm's output, profits, union rents, and social welfare, we get

$$x_M^*(\theta, \beta, t) = \frac{(2 - \theta)(a - \bar{w} - t)}{2(2 - \theta + \beta\theta)}, \quad \pi_M^*(\theta, \beta, t) = \Pi_M^*(\theta, \beta, t) = (x_M^*)^2, \tag{25.4.1}$$

[4]For simplicity we assume that the country-specific conflict payoffs to the firm (more correctly, the plant) and to the union are exogenous and set equal to zero.

$$r_M^*(\theta,\beta,t)=(w_M^*-\bar{w})x_M^*=\frac{2\beta\theta}{2-\theta}(x_M^*)^2,\quad W^*(\theta,\beta,t)=\pi_M^*+r_M^*=\frac{2-\theta+2\beta\theta}{2-\theta}(x_M^*)^2, \tag{25.4.2}$$

On the other hand, the equilibrium output, profits, union rents, and social welfare in the FDI mode are obtained as follows. Superscript "**" denotes FDI entry mode.

$$x_M^{**}(t)=\frac{a-\bar{w}-t}{2},\qquad \pi_M^{**}(t,k)=W^{**}(t,k)=\Pi_M^{**}(t)-k=(x_M^{**})^2-k. \tag{25.5}$$

From the market equilibriums given by Eqs. (25.4.1), (25.4.2), and (25.5), it follows that

$$\frac{\partial x_M^*}{\partial\theta}=\frac{-\beta(a-\bar{w}-t)}{(2-\theta+\beta\theta)^2}<0,\quad \frac{\partial\pi_M^*}{\partial\theta}=2x_M^*\frac{\partial x_M^*}{\partial\theta}<0,\quad \frac{\partial x_M^{**}}{\partial\theta}=\frac{\partial\pi_M^{**}}{\partial\theta}=0, \tag{25.6.1}$$

$$\frac{\partial x_M^*}{\partial(-t)}=\frac{\beta\theta}{2(2-\theta+\beta\theta)}>0,\quad \frac{\partial\pi_M^*}{\partial(-t)}=2x_M^*\frac{\partial x_M^*}{\partial(-t)}>0,\quad \frac{\partial x_M^{**}}{\partial(-t)}=\frac{1}{2}>0,$$
$$\frac{\partial\pi_M^{**}}{\partial(-t)}=2x_M^{**}\frac{\partial x_M^{**}}{\partial(-t)}>0, \tag{25.6.2}$$

The impact of union bargaining power on domestic social welfare is obtained from Eq. (25.2). Using the envelope theorem, we differentiate W^* with respect to θ to get x

$$\frac{\partial W^*}{\partial\theta}=-\frac{\partial w_M^*}{\partial\theta}x_M^*+\frac{\partial(w_M^*-\bar{w})}{\partial\theta}x_M^*+(w_M^*-\bar{w})\frac{\partial x_M^*}{\partial\theta}=(w_M^*-\bar{w})\frac{\partial x_M^*}{\partial\theta}<0, \tag{25.7}$$

As can be seen in the second expression of Eq. (25.7), an increase in union bargaining power affects home country's welfare through three channels: a decrease in producer surplus due to the wage increase (the first term), an increase in the union rents via the change in rents per employee (the second term), and a decrease in the union rents due to the loss of market competitiveness (the last term). However, because the first and second terms offset each other, an increase in union's bargaining power leads to a fall in the social welfare through the loss of union rent, which comes from the loss of market competitiveness of the monopolist.

Lemma 25.1 *Suppose that the monopolist takes the export entry mode and is unionized. An increase in union bargaining power obviously decreases the social welfare of the FDI source country (i.e.,* $\frac{\partial W^*}{\partial\theta}<0$*).*

We can draw one policy implication from Lemma 25.1. When there is only one national firm (i.e., firm with no foreign operations) that is unionized and all the products are sold into the world market, then the government's optimal labor policy toward the union is to take away the bargaining power as much as possible from the labor union, that is, $\theta^{\text{opt}}=0$, where superscript "opt" denotes the optimal level of relevant variable.

25.2.3 Location Decision and Welfare Analysis

Then, let us examine whether the above Lemma 25.1 holds when we allow the overseas operation (i.e., undertaking FDI). This relates to the second stage of the game. The monopolist undertakes FDI (resp. produces in the home country), if the increase in the variable profits by undertaking FDI, $\Delta\Pi_M$, is greater (resp. less) than the fixed costs incurred in the FDI, k. Using the market equilibrium given by Eqs. (25.4.1), (25.4.2), and (25.5), we can obtain the value of $\Delta\Pi_M$ as a function of θ and other parameters as follows:

$$\Delta\Pi_M(\theta;\beta,t) = \Pi_M^{**}(t) - \Pi_M^{*}(\theta;\beta,t) = \frac{\beta\theta(4-2\theta+\beta\theta)(a-\bar{w}-t)^2}{4(2-\theta+\beta\theta)^2}. \quad (25.8)$$

Figure 25.1 depicts $\Delta\Pi_M(\theta,\beta,t)$ by curve OM in θ, k space.[5] Curve OM divides the (θ, k) space into two regions. And the monopolist produces in the home (resp. foreign) country when k is relatively high (resp. low) and θ is relatively low (resp. high), that is, the combination (θ, k) is above (resp. below) the curve OM. Suppose that the fixed costs are given at level $k_1 \in [0, k_M^{\max}]$, that is, OF in Fig. 25.1. There exists critical value θ^P(i.e., point N) that satisfies $k_1 = \Delta\Pi_M(\theta^P;\beta,t)$. Obviously, the monopolist is indifferent between home production (i.e., export entry mode) and overseas production (i.e., FDI entry mode) at $\theta = \theta^P(k;\beta,t)$.

Fig. 25.1 The determination of location pattern

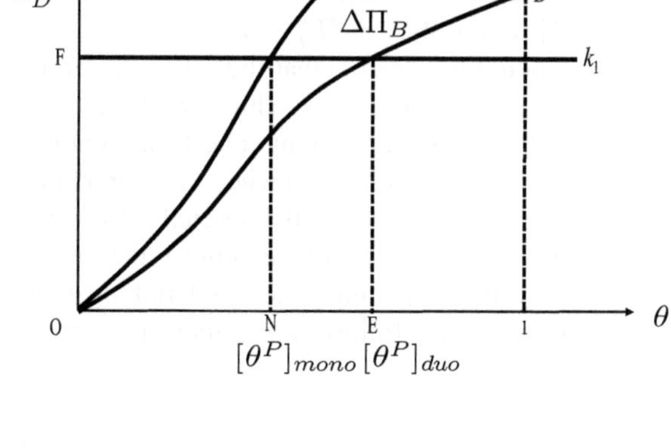

[5]We obtain $\frac{\partial\Delta\Pi_M}{\partial\theta} = \frac{\beta(2-\theta)(a-\bar{w}-t)^2}{(2-\theta+\beta\theta)^3} > 0$ and $\frac{\partial\Delta\Pi_M}{\partial(-t)} = \frac{\beta\theta(4-2\theta+\beta\theta)(a-\bar{w}-t)}{2(2-\theta+\beta\theta)^2} > 0$ from Eq. (25.8).

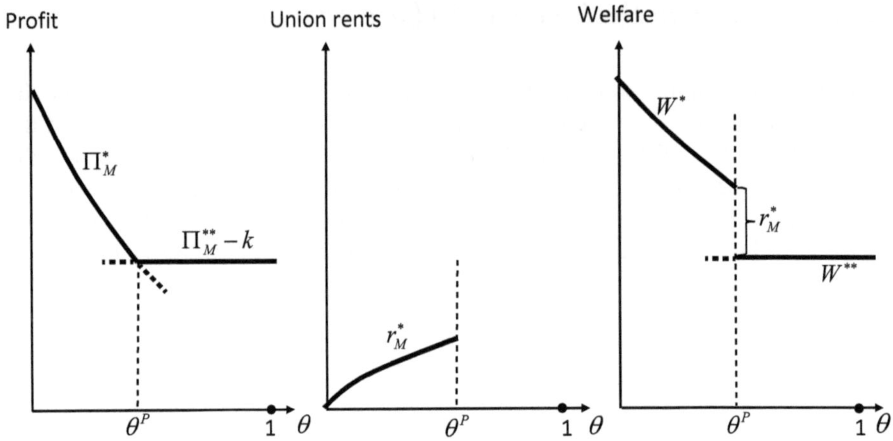

Fig. 25.2 The effects of entry mode shift: monopoly case

Proposition 25.1 *Suppose that the monopolist can choose its production location either at home or in foreign country and that it is always unionized if it is located in the home country. There exists critical value $\theta^P(k; \beta, t)$, where the monopolist is indifferent between home and overseas production. If $\theta < \theta^P$ (resp. $\theta > \theta^P$), then it is profitable for the monopolist to remain in the home country (resp. undertake FDI).*

We now turn to the welfare analysis. Figure 25.2 shows the monopolist's profits, the union's rents, and the social welfare of the home country with respect to θ. The intersection of schedules $\Pi^*_M(\theta, \beta, t)$ and $\Pi^{**}_M(t) - k$ gives a critical value of θ^P, and if $\theta < \theta^P$ (resp. $\theta > \theta^P$), then the monopolist chooses domestic production (resp. overseas production). Union rents increase in $\theta \in [0, \theta^P]$ if $\beta < 1$ or $\theta^P < \frac{2}{1+\beta}$[6] but equals to zero over $\theta \in [\theta^P, 1]$ due to the extinction of the labor union. Social welfare W^*decreases in $\theta \in [0, \theta^P]$ from Eq. (25.7), but is independent of $\theta \in [\theta^P, 1]$, where $W^{**} = \Pi^{**}_M - k$.

What should be noted is that there is a discontinuous drop in social welfare of FDI source country at $\theta = \theta^P$. This is because undertaking FDI by the monopolist results in the loss of union rents due to the extinction of the labor union, which are not taken into consideration when the monopolist moves its production location to the foreign country. Since $W^*$is strictly decreasing in θ and $W^{**} < [W^*]_{\theta=\theta^P}$, social welfare of the FDI source country has maximum at $\theta = 0$ even when we allow the overseas operation (i.e., undertaking FDI) of the monopolist. From the above discussion, the following lemma is immediate.

[6]From Eq. (25.4.2), we have $\frac{\partial r^*_M}{\partial \theta} = \frac{2-\theta-\beta\theta}{2-\theta} x^*_M \frac{\partial w^*_M}{\partial \theta}$. Since $\frac{\partial w^*_M}{\partial \theta} > 0$ from Eq. (25.3), $\frac{\partial r^*_M}{\partial \theta} > 0$ if $\beta < 1$ or $\theta < \frac{2}{1+\beta}$.

Lemma 25.2 *Suppose that the monopolist can choose its production location either at home or in the foreign country. The monopolist undertakes FDI by private incentive at $\theta = \theta^P$, where the union rents and social welfare show a discontinuous plunge. And the social welfare of the FDI source country is maximized at $\theta = 0$.*

In addition, combining Lemma 25.2 with Lemma 25.1, we obtain the following proposition with regard to government policy on labor standard toward monopolist of FDI source country.

Proposition 25.2 *Suppose that the monopolist, if located in the home country, is always unionized. Government's optimal choice of labor standard is $\theta^{opt} = 0$ irrespective of whether the monopolist is national firm (i.e., firm with no foreign operation) or multinational firm.*

Next, let's examine the effects of trade liberalization on government policy. Since $\frac{\partial \Delta \Pi_M}{\partial(-t)} > 0$ as in Footnote 5, the curve OM in Fig. 25.1 shifts upward with trade liberalization, and hence the critical value θ^P will move from point N to a point that lies on the left side of N (i.e., $\frac{\partial \theta^P}{\partial(-t)} < 0$). That is, if trade liberalization proceeds, then the monopolist undertakes FDI at a lower level of union bargaining power than would otherwise be the case. However, since welfare-maximizing labor standard is determined at $\theta = 0$ as a corner solution, trade liberalization cannot affect government optimal policy on labor standard.

Proposition 25.3 *Suppose that the monopolist located at a home country is always unionized. If trade liberalization proceeds, then the monopolist undertakes FDI at a lower level of bargaining power of the union than would otherwise be the case. However, trade liberalization cannot affect government optimal policy on labor standard.*

25.3 Strategic Location Decision

25.3.1 Market Equilibrium Under Each Entry Mode

Now let us extend the previous model to a setting with two home firms: firm A and firm B. Both firms produce identical product that is sold in a third- country market only. However, here, we introduce heterogeneity between firms in terms of firm's mobility between countries. In our model, we assume that firm A is national firm (i.e., firm with no foreign operations) while firm B is multinational firm. And both firms face labor unionization when they produce in the home country. Since firm A is national firm, there are two possible outcomes with respect to locational pattern of MNEs: export mode and FDI mode, where export (resp. FDI) mode represents the case where firm B chooses home (resp. foreign) country as its plant location. We use these terms in the duopoly by the analogy of the monopoly case.

The variable profits of firm i is given by $\Pi_i(x_i, x_{-i}, w_i, t) = (p - w_i - t)x_i, i = A, B$, where $p = a - (x_A + x_B)$ and '$-i$' denotes the other firm. Note that $w_B = \bar{w}$ under

FDI mode because only firm B produces in the foreign country under this entry mode. The profit maximization problem of firm i in the fourth stage of the game is $\max_{x_i} \Pi_i(x_i, x_{-i}; w, t)$, which yields reaction function $R_i(x_{-i}, w_i, t) = \frac{1-x_{-i}-(w_i+t)}{2}$. By solving the system of the two reaction functions, we get the equilibrium output under each entry mode and variable profits as a function of w_i, w_{-i}, and t:

$$x_i(w_i, w_{-i}; t) = \frac{1 - 2(w_i + t) + (w_{-i} + t)}{3} \quad \text{for Export entry mode} \qquad (25.9.1)$$

$$\begin{cases} x_A(w_A, \bar{w}; t) = \frac{1-2(w_A+t)+(\bar{w}+t)}{3} \\ x_B(w_A, \bar{w}; t) = \frac{1-2(\bar{w}+t)+(w_A+t)}{3} \end{cases} \quad \text{for FDI entry mode} \qquad (25.9.2)$$

Now we examine the wage determination under each entry mode. In stage three of the game, the wage determination stage, each union/firm pair solves the following problem given that the wage set by other firm as fixed:

$$\max_{w_i} V_i(w_i, w_{-i}, t) = \{(w_i - \bar{w})^{\beta} x_i\}^{\theta} (x_i^2)^{1-\theta} \quad \textit{for Export entry mode} \qquad (25.10.1)$$

$$\max_{w_A} V_A(w_A; t) = \{(w_A - \bar{w})^{\beta} x_A\}^{\theta} (x_A^2)^{1-\theta} \textit{for FDI entry mode} \qquad (25.10.2)$$

where x_i for the export entry mode and x_A for the FDI entry mode are given by Eqs. (25.9.1)and (25.9.2). The first order condition of above maximization problem is as follows:

$$\frac{\partial V_i}{\partial w_i} = (x_i)^{2-\theta} (w_i - \bar{w})^{\beta\theta} \left\{ \frac{\beta\theta}{w_i - \bar{w}} - \frac{2(2-\theta)}{3x_i} \right\} = 0$$

$$\Leftrightarrow \quad w_i - \bar{w} = \frac{3\beta\theta}{2(2-\theta)} x_i, \qquad (25.11)$$

where $i = A, B$ under export entry mode and $i = A$ under FDI entry mode. Basically, Eq. (25.11) suggests that the economic rent per employee, $w_i - \bar{w}$, is positively related to rent for firm, x_i.[7] Furthermore, considering that firm i's output x_i is positively related with rival's wage w_{-i} from Eq. (25.9.1), above Eq. (25.11) implies that w_i is positively related with rival firm's wage level w_{-i}. There exist positive wage externalities between firms in the unionized oligopolies. That is, labor union i competes indirectly against rival firm's union via final good market.

Given identical firms and unions under export entry mode, the solution to the bargaining process implies the symmetric wage, i.e., $w_i = w_{-i} = w_i^*$. And firm A's equilibrium wage w_A^{**} under FDI entry mode is obtained from Eq. (25.11) by considering that rival firm B's effective marginal cost is $\bar{w} + t$. Therefore, we have

[7]From the first order condition of final good market, we have $p - (w_i + t) = x_i$.

Table 25.1 Market equilibrium under each entry mode

	Export entry mode	FDI entry mode
Wage level	$w_i^* = \bar{w} + \frac{\beta\theta(a-\bar{w}-t)}{4-2\theta+\beta\theta}$	$w_A^{**} = \bar{w} + \frac{\beta\theta(a-\bar{w}-t)}{2(2-\theta+\beta\theta)}, \quad w_B^{**} = \bar{w}.$
Output level	$x_i^* = \frac{2(2-\theta)(a-\bar{w}-t)}{3(4-2\theta+\beta\theta)}$	$x_A^{**} = \frac{(2-\theta)(a-\bar{w}-t)}{3(2-\theta+\beta\theta)}$, $x_B^{**} = \frac{(4-2\theta+3\beta\theta)(a-\bar{w}-t)}{6(2-\theta+\beta\theta)}$
Total output and price	$X^* = \frac{4(2-\theta)(a-\bar{w}-t)}{3(4-2\theta+\beta\theta)}$ $p^* = \frac{a(4-2\theta+3\beta\theta)+4(2-\theta)(\bar{w}+t)}{3(4-2\theta+\beta\theta)}$	$X^{**} = \frac{(8-4\theta+3\beta\theta)(a-\bar{w}-t)}{6(2-\theta+\beta\theta)}$ $p^{**} = \frac{a(4-2\theta+3\beta\theta)+(8-4\theta+3\beta\theta)(\bar{w}+t)}{6(2-\theta+\beta\theta)}$
Profits	$\pi_i^* = \Pi_i^* = (x_i^*)^2$	$\pi_A^{**} = \Pi_A^{**} = (x_A^{**})^2$, $\pi_B^{**} = \Pi_B^{**} - k = (x_B^{**})^2 - k$
Union rents	$r_i^* = (w_i^* - \bar{w})x_i^* = \frac{3\beta\theta}{2(2-\theta)}(x_i^*)^2$	$r_A^{**} = (w_A^{**} - \bar{w})x_A^{**} = \frac{3\beta\theta}{2(2-\theta)}(x_A^{**})^2$
Social welfare	$W^* = 2\left[(x_i^*)^2 + \frac{3\beta\theta}{2(2-\theta)}(x_i^*)^2\right]$ $= \frac{4-2\theta+3\beta\theta}{2-\theta}(x_i^*)^2$	$W^{**} = (x_A^{**})^2 + (x_B^{**})^2 - k + \frac{3\beta\theta}{2(2-\theta)}(x_A^{**})^2$ $= \frac{4-2\theta+3\beta\theta}{2(2-\theta)}(x_A^{**})^2 + (x_B^{**})^2 - k$

$$w_i^*(\theta;\beta,t) = \bar{w} + \frac{\beta\theta(a-\bar{w}-t)}{4-2\theta+\beta\theta}, \quad i = A, B,$$

$$w_A^{**}(\theta;\beta,t) = \bar{w} + \frac{\beta\theta(a-\bar{w}-t)}{2(2-\theta+\beta\theta)}. \tag{25.12}$$

Equation (25.12) implies that the union wage is equal to the reservation wage plus a union markup over product market rents accruing to the unionized domestic firms.[8] These rents depend on the firms' location decision, thus potentially on the labor market institutions of countries where the firms are located. In this sense, $w_i^* > w_A^{**}$ holds. Substituting w_i^* and w_A^{**} into the output market variables gives the equilibrium output level, profits, and union rents for each firm under each regime. Table 25.1 summarizes the market equilibria at this stage.

From the equilibrium values given in Table 25.1, the following comparative statics with respect to firm's output and profits can be obtained.

$$\frac{\partial x_i^*}{\partial \theta} = \frac{-4\beta(a-\bar{w}-t)}{3(4-2\theta+\beta\theta)^2} < 0, \; \frac{\partial x_A^{**}}{\partial \theta} = \frac{-2\beta(a-\bar{w}-t)}{3(2-\theta+\beta\theta)^2} < 0,$$
$$\frac{\partial x_B^{**}}{\partial \theta} = \frac{\beta(a-\bar{w}-t)}{3(2-\theta+\beta\theta)^2} > 0, \tag{25.13.1}$$

[8]From Eq. (25.12), we have $\frac{\partial w_i^*}{\partial \theta} = \frac{4\beta(a-\bar{w}-t)}{(4-2\theta+\beta\theta)^2} > 0$, $\frac{\partial w_A^{**}}{\partial \theta} = \frac{\beta(a-\bar{w}-t)}{(2-\theta+\beta\theta)^2} > 0$, $\frac{\partial w_i^*}{\partial(-t)} = \frac{\beta\theta}{4-2\theta+\beta\theta} > 0$, and $\frac{\partial w_A^{**}}{\partial(-t)} = \frac{\beta\theta}{2(2-\theta+\beta\theta)} > 0$.

$$\frac{\partial \pi_i^*}{\partial \theta} = 2x_i^* \frac{\partial x_i^*}{\partial \theta} < 0, \quad \frac{\partial \pi_A^{**}}{\partial \theta} = 2x_A^{**} \frac{\partial x_A^{**}}{\partial \theta} < 0, \quad \frac{\partial \pi_B^{**}}{\partial \theta} = 2x_B^{**} \frac{\partial x_B^{**}}{\partial \theta} > 0, \tag{25.13.2}$$

When both firms produce in home country (i.e., export mode), wage increase caused by union's strengthened bargaining power raises the "effective" marginal costs of firms and, hence, reduces their outputs in the market ($\frac{\partial x_i^*}{\partial \theta} < 0$). On the other hand, under FDI mode, wage increases in the home country raise the effective marginal costs of unionized firm A and hence reduce its output in the market ($\frac{\partial x_A^{**}}{\partial \theta} < 0$) but increase the output of the rival nonunionized firm ($\frac{\partial x_B^{**}}{\partial \theta} > 0$). In addition, equilibrium profits rise (resp. fall), if and only if the equilibrium output rises (resp. falls).

Next, let us examine the effects of θ on union rents. Since $r_i = (w_i - \bar{w})x_i$, we get

$$\frac{\partial r_i^*}{\partial \theta} = \underbrace{\frac{\partial w_i^*}{\partial \theta} x_i^*}_{(+)} + \underbrace{(w_i^* - \bar{w})\frac{\partial x_i^*}{\partial \theta}}_{(-)} = \frac{4\beta(4 - 2\theta - \beta\theta)(a - \bar{w} - t)^2}{3(4 - 2\theta + \beta\theta)^3}, \tag{25.14.1}$$

$$\frac{\partial r_A^{**}}{\partial \theta} = \underbrace{\frac{\partial w_A^{**}}{\partial \theta} x_A^{**}}_{(+)} + \underbrace{(w_A^{**} - \bar{w})\frac{\partial x_A^{**}}{\partial \theta}}_{(-)} = \frac{\beta(2 - \theta - \beta\theta)(a - \bar{w} - t)^2}{3(2 - \theta + \beta\theta)^3}. \tag{25.14.2}$$

An increase in union's bargaining power generates two conflicting effects on the union rents: the positive effects due to the increase in the rents per employee (the first term of the second expression) and the negative effects due to the market competitiveness loss associated with wage increase (the second term). Because the market equilibria are functions of θ, the net effects could potentially be either positive or negative depending on the values of θ. The greater θ, the less the former (first term) and the greater the latter (second term). In the above equations, $\frac{\partial r_i^*}{\partial \theta} > 0$ (resp. $\frac{\partial r_A^{**}}{\partial \theta} > 0$) for all $\theta \in [0, 1]$ if $\beta < 2$ (resp. $\beta < 1$). However, if $\beta > 2$ (resp. $\beta > 1$), then r_i^* (resp. r_A^{**}) has its maximum at $\theta = \theta^{R*}$ (resp. $\theta = \theta^{R**}$), where $\theta^{R*} = \frac{4}{2+\beta}$ and $\theta^{R**} = \frac{2}{1+\beta}$. This implies that there exists critical value θ^R, which maximize the union rents under each entry mode. And if $\theta < \theta^R$, then the former effect (increase in rents per employee) is greater than the latter (loss in market competitiveness associated with wage increase), inducing union rent increases as θ increases and vice versa. From the above discussion, the following Lemma is immediate.

Lemma 25.3 *Suppose that firms are always unionized in the home country. If $\beta < 2$ (resp. $\beta < 1$) under export mode (resp. FDI mode), then a rise in θ increases union rents. However, if $\beta > 2$ (resp. $\beta > 1$), there exists critical value of θ that maximizes the union rents under each entry mode, that is, $\theta^{R*} = \frac{4}{2+\beta}$ for export mode while $\theta^{R**} = \frac{2}{1+\beta}$ for FDI mode.*

We now turn to the effects of union's bargaining power on the social welfare of FDI source country. In case of export entry mode, differentiating social welfare function with respect to θ and applying the envelope theorem yields

$$\frac{\partial W^*}{\partial \theta} = 2\left\{\underbrace{p'\left(\frac{\partial x_{-i}}{\partial w_i}+\frac{\partial x_{-i}}{\partial w_{-i}}\right)\frac{\partial w_i^*}{\partial \theta}x_i^*}_{(+)}+\underbrace{(w_i^*-\bar{w})\left(\frac{\partial x_i}{\partial w_i}+\frac{\partial x_i}{\partial w_{-i}}\right)\frac{\partial w_i^*}{\partial \theta}}_{(-)}\right\}$$
$$= \frac{(4-2\theta-3\beta\theta)}{3(2-\theta)}\frac{\partial w_i^*}{\partial \theta}x_i^*, \tag{25.15}$$

The second term in the square bracket of the second expression in Eq. (25.15) represents a decrease in the union rents due to the loss in the market competitiveness, which also appears in the monopoly case (see Eq. (25.7)). However, in the duopoly case, there is an additional effect. The first term in the square bracket captures the standard rent shift effects from the rival firm to firm i, which is caused by an increase in the equilibrium wage and has positive effects on social welfare. This is an external effect and does not exist in the monopoly model, where there is no strategic interaction between firms. Therefore, this result appears only in the duopoly model. And the greater θ, the lesser the rent shift effects and the greater the market competitiveness effects. Therefore, the net effects of θ on social welfare depend on the relative magnitude of above two mentioned effects. Since $\left(\frac{\partial W^*}{\partial \theta}\right)_{\theta=0} > 0$ and $\left(\frac{\partial W^*}{\partial \theta}\right)_{\theta=1} < 0$ when $\beta < \frac{2}{3}$, Eq. (25.15) implies that W^* has maximum at $\theta = \theta^{V*}(\equiv \frac{4}{2+3\beta})$ if $\beta < \frac{2}{3}$.

Lemma 25.4 *Suppose that firms A and B both take the export strategy (i.e., export entry mode). If $\beta < \frac{2}{3}$, then $\frac{\partial W^*}{\partial \theta} > 0$ for the domain of $\theta \in [0, 1]$. However, if $\beta > \frac{2}{3}$, then W^* has maximum at $\theta = \theta^{V*}(\equiv \frac{4}{2+3\beta} < 1)$.*

Next, let us look at the case of FDI entry mode, where only one firm, firm B, undertakes FDI. Differentiating Eq. (25.2) with respect to θ and applying the envelope theorem yield

$$\frac{\partial W^{**}}{\partial \theta} = \underbrace{\sum_{i=A,B}\frac{\partial x_i}{\partial w_A}\frac{\partial w_A^{**}}{\partial \theta}x_i^{**}}_{(+)} + \underbrace{(w_A^{**}-\bar{w})\frac{\partial x_A}{\partial w_A}\frac{\partial w_A^{**}}{\partial \theta}}_{(-)} = \frac{(2-\theta)(a-\bar{w}-t)}{9(2-\theta+\beta\theta)}\frac{\partial w_A^{**}}{\partial \theta} > 0, \tag{25.16}$$

As in export mode, there are two conflicting effects with regard to welfare effects of unions' bargaining power: usual strategic effect arising in the imperfect competition market, which has positive impact on social welfare, and changes in the union rents by market competitiveness loss, which has negative impact on social welfare. However, since the former overweighs the latter, the net effects are positive (i.e., $\frac{\partial W^{**}}{\partial \theta} > 0$).

Lemma 25.5 *Suppose that firm A produces in the home country while firm B produces in the foreign country (i.e., FDI entry mode). An increase in union bargaining power increases the social welfare of FDI source country (i.e.,* $\frac{\partial W^{**}}{\partial \theta} > 0$*). W^{**} has maximum at $\theta = 1$.*

25.3.2 Determination of Plant Location

We introduce the following notation: $\Delta\Pi_B[\theta;\beta,t] = \Pi_B^{**}[\theta;\beta,t] - \Pi_B^{*}[\theta;\beta,t]$. Using the market equilibrium in Table 25.1, we can obtain the values of $\Delta\Pi_B$ as follows:

$$\begin{aligned}\Delta\Pi_B(\theta;\beta,t) &= (x_B^{**} + x_B^{*})(x_B^{**} - x_B^{*})\\ &= \frac{\beta\theta(8-4\theta+3\beta\theta)\{32(1-\theta)+24\beta\theta+(8-12\beta+3\beta^2)\theta^2\}(a-\bar{w}-t)^2}{36(4-2\theta+\beta\theta)^2(2-\theta+\beta\theta)^2} > 0,\end{aligned} \tag{25.17}$$

$\Delta\Pi_B$ is given by curve OD in Fig. 25.1. Here, we can easily find that $\Delta\Pi_B(0,\beta,t) = 0$ and $\frac{\partial \Delta\Pi_B}{\partial \theta} > 0$. For the same reason in the monopoly case, both firms produce in the home country when the combination (θ, k) is in the region above the curve OD, whereas firm A produces in the home country and firm B produces in the foreign country when (θ, k) is in the region below the OD. For a given fixed cost level, for instance, k_1 in Fig. 25.1, there exists critical value θ^P that satisfies $k = \Delta\Pi_B(\theta^P;\beta,t)$, that is, point E. Given the fixed costs of FDI and other parameter values, if the negotiation power of the union is high (resp. low) enough, that is, θ is in the right (resp. left) segment of point E, then it is profitable for firm B to undertake FDI (resp. remain in the home country), and thus export (resp. FDI) entry mode would be realized.

Note that $\Delta\Pi_M > \Delta\Pi_B$ except for $\theta = 0$. And hence, critical value θ^P under duopoly is higher than that under monopoly, that is, $[\theta^P]_{\text{duo}} > [\theta^P]_{\text{mono}}$ in Fig. 25.1. The intuition of this is straightforward. Labor union competes indirectly against rival firm's union via final good market under oligopolistic competition. Therefore, when market is under oligopoly, each union/firm pair has some incentive to cut wages to keep competitiveness in the product market, inducing lower equilibrium wage compared to that under the monopoly case, i.e., $w_M^{*} = \bar{w} + \frac{\beta\theta(a-\bar{w}-t)}{2-\theta+\beta\theta} > \bar{w} + \frac{\beta\theta(a-\bar{w}-t)}{4-2\theta+\beta\theta} = w_i^{*}$. The following Lemma can be obtained.

Lemma 25.6 *If other things being equal, compared to monopoly case, the duopolist undertakes FDI at a higher level of bargaining strength of the union. That is, $[\theta^P]_{duo} > [\theta^P]_{mono}$.*

Next, there are examinations on the role of either the trade liberalization (a reduction in t) or domestic labor institutions. With respect to labor institutions, we are particularly interested in whether the conventional wisdom holds, that is, a strong union (an increase in β) tends to make a country less attractive place for the firms' location. Using the comparative statics, the following lemma is obtained.

Lemma 25.7 *Multinational firm (MNF) tends to undertake FDI at a lower level of union bargaining power, with higher wage-oriented behavior by the union, deeper trade liberalization, and lower fixed costs of FDI. That is,* $\frac{\partial \theta^P}{\partial \beta} < 0$, $\frac{\partial \theta^P}{\partial(-t)} < 0$, *and* $\frac{\partial \theta^P}{\partial k} > 0$.

Proof In Fig. 25.1, θ^P is determined at the intersecting point between the two schedules $\Delta\Pi_B$ and k, implying that $\Delta\Pi_B[\theta^P(\beta,k,t),\beta,t] \equiv k$ holds identically. By differentiating the above identical equation with respect to β, k, and t, we obtain $\frac{\partial \theta^P}{\partial \beta} = -\frac{\partial \Delta\Pi_B}{\partial \beta}\Big/\frac{\partial \Delta\Pi_B}{\partial \theta}$, $\frac{\partial \theta^P}{\partial(-t)} = -\frac{\partial \Delta\Pi_B}{\partial(-t)}\Big/\frac{\partial \Delta\Pi_B}{\partial \theta}$, and $\frac{\partial \theta^P}{\partial k} = -1\Big/\frac{\partial \Delta\Pi_B}{\partial \theta}$, where $\frac{\partial \Delta\Pi_B}{\partial \theta} > 0$. Since $\frac{\partial \Delta\Pi_B}{\partial \beta} > 0$ and $\frac{\partial \Delta\Pi_B}{\partial(-t)} > 0$, we have $\frac{\partial \theta^P}{\partial \beta} < 0$, $\frac{\partial \theta^P}{\partial(-t)} < 0$, and $\frac{\partial \theta^P}{\partial k} > 0$. Here, $\frac{\partial \Delta\Pi_B}{\partial \beta} > 0$ (resp. $\frac{\partial \Delta\Pi_B}{\partial(-t)} > 0$) implies that an increase in β (resp. a decrease in t) shifts the schedule OD upward, inducing the critical value θ^P, which is determined at the intersection between k and OD, to move from point E to a point that is located on the left side of E. That is, if a labor union becomes more wage oriented or if trade liberalization progresses, then firm B tends to undertake FDI at a lower level of union bargaining power than would otherwise be the case. Above lemma confirms conventional wisdom that a stronger labor union will tend to make a country a less attractive location for MNFs, because of a concern that the rent-extracting activities of labor unions will tend to restrict the profitability of those firms.

25.4 Welfare Analysis and Policy Implications

In this section, we solve for optimal policies of home country in terms of labor standard by maximizing home country's social welfare consisting of firms' profit and labor union rent. We denote optimal level of union bargaining power, which maximizes social welfare, by θ^{opt}. In the previous section, we have derived critical values of union bargaining power that maximize the social welfare as well as union rents under each entry mode. Those are $\theta^{R*}(=\frac{4}{2+\beta})$, $\theta^{V*}(=\frac{4}{2+3\beta})$, $\theta^{R**}(=\frac{2}{1+\beta})$, and θ^{V**}, where $\theta^{V*} < \theta^{R**} < \theta^{R*}$ and $\theta^{V**} = 1$ hold. Note that these values are independent of the fixed cost (k) incurred to FDI. Depending on the relative magnitude of θ^P, which determines firm B's location shift by private incentive, in connection with above critical values, different labor standard policy might be obtained. Since there are three critical values that are functions of β, i.e., θ^{R*}, θ^{V*}, and θ^{R**}, we set up the following three cases with respect to the range of β; case I: $1 < \theta^{V*}$ (i.e., $\beta < \frac{2}{3}$), case II: $\theta^{V*} < 1 < \theta^{R*}$(i.e., $\frac{2}{3} < \beta < 2$), and case III: $\theta^{R*} < 1$ (i.e., $2 < \beta$).

Figure 25.3 represents case I (i.e., $\beta < \frac{2}{3}$). The bold lines in each panel show the change in each variable as θ increases. Since $1 < \theta^{V*}(\theta^{R**} < \theta^{R*})$, we find that $\frac{\partial \Pi_i^*}{\partial \theta} < 0, \frac{\partial r_i^*}{\partial \theta} > 0$, and $\frac{\partial w^*}{\partial \theta} > 0$ while $\frac{\partial \Pi_A^{**}}{\partial \theta} < 0$, $\frac{\partial \Pi_B^{**}}{\partial \theta} > 0$, $\frac{\partial r_A^{**}}{\partial \theta} > 0$,

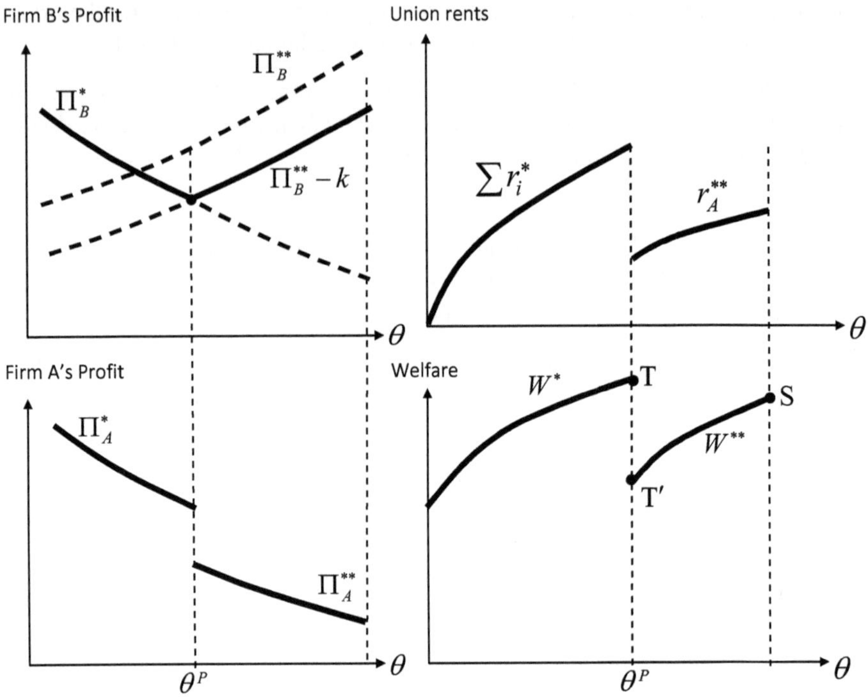

Fig. 25.3 The effects of entry mode shift : $\beta < \frac{2}{3}$

and $\frac{\partial W^{**}}{\partial \theta} > 0$. The intersection of schedules Π_B^* and $\Pi_B^{**} - k$ gives a critical value θ^P, where firm B is indifferent between domestic and foreign location. It is noteworthy that social welfare plunges from point T to T' at $\theta = \theta^P$,[9] where the entry mode shifts from export to FDI. Therefore, if θ lies in the right neighborhood of θ^P, firm B undertakes FDI even if domestic production is socially desirable. Since both $W^*$and W^{**} are increasing in θ, the social welfare of FDI source country is maximized either at $\theta = \theta^P$(point T in the Figure) or at $\theta = 1$(point S). The following proposition is obtained.

Proposition 25.4 *Suppose that $\beta < \frac{2}{3}$. Firm B undertakes FDI by private incentive at $\theta = \theta^P(k, \beta, t)$. There exists a critical value $\bar{k}$ that satisfies $W^*[\theta^P(\bar{k}, \beta, t), \beta, t] = W^{**}[1, \beta, t; \bar{k}]$. And it follows that*

$$\begin{cases} \theta^{opt} = \theta^P \; if \;\; k > \bar{k} \\ \theta^{opt} = 1 \;\; if \;\; k < \bar{k} \end{cases}.$$

[9]This is because FDI of firm B results in the reduction of rival firm A's profits and the loss of union rents, due to both a decrease in firm A's profits and the extinction of firm B's labor union, which are not taken into consideration when firm B chooses its production location.

Proof. Skipped due to the space limitation.[10]

The intuition of the above proposition is as follows. When labor union is relatively employment oriented (i.e., $\beta < \frac{2}{3}$), the greater bargaining power union has, the higher the social welfare (i.e., $\frac{\partial W^*}{\partial \theta} > 0$). In this case, if fixed costs of FDI are large enough (i.e., $k > \bar{k}$), then firm B undertakes FDI at a high level of union bargaining power, causing a massive drop in social welfare reflecting a decrease in firm A's profits, the extinction of firm B's union, and high fixed costs incurred to FDI. And since θ^P has large values, the welfare increase under FDI mode $[W^{**}]_{\theta=1} - [W^{**}]_{\theta=\theta^P}$ is not sufficient to recover the social welfare plunge from point T to T' at $\theta = \theta^P$. As a result, $[W^*]_{\theta=\theta^P} > [W^{**}]_{\theta=1}$ holds when $k > \bar{k}$, implying that preventing firm from moving overseas is socially desirable for the FDI source country, i.e., $[W^*]_{\theta=\theta^P} > [W^{**}]_{\theta=1}$. Therefore, the optimal policy of the FDI source country is offering the union the strongest bargaining power providing that the firm remains within home country. We call this type of labor policy with respect to labor standard as "exit-deterring strategy." However, if fixed costs of FDI are small enough (i.e., $k < \bar{k}$), then firm B undertakes FDI even at a low level of union bargaining power, causing only a slight drop in social welfare at $\theta^{\rm opt} = \theta^P$. In this case, the optimal policy of the FDI source country is offering the union the full bargaining power, i.e., $\theta^{\rm opt} = 1$, and induces outward FDI by firm B, because the profit loss of firm A would be more than compensated by gains not only in firm B's profits but also in union rents of firm A.

Figure 25.4 examines the case where $\frac{2}{3} < \beta < 2$ (case II). In this case, W^* is no longer monotonically increasing in θ and has maximum at $\theta = \theta^{V*}(= \frac{4}{2+3\beta} > \frac{1}{2})$ (see Table 25.1). Depending on whether θ^P is greater than θ^{V*} or not, the optimal labor standard policy differs. Panel (a) in Fig. 25.4 illustrates the changes in union rents and social welfare in θ when $\theta^P < \theta^{V*}$, while Panel (b) shows the case when $\theta^P > \theta^{V*}$.

If $\theta^P < \theta^{V*}$ as in Fig. 25.4(a),[11] W^* and W^{**} are monotonic increasing function in θ within its domain, respectively. And Proposition 25.4 still holds. On the other hand, if $\theta^P > \theta^{V*}$ as in Fig. 25.4(b), $W^*$is not monotonically increasing function within the range of $\theta \in [0, \theta^P]$ and has maximum value at $\theta = \theta^{V*}(= \frac{4}{2+3\beta})$. The following proposition is immediate.[12]

Proposition 25.5 *Suppose that $\beta \in [\frac{2}{3}, 2]$. (1) If $\theta^P < \frac{4}{2+3\beta}$, then Proposition 25.4 still holds. That is, there exists a critical value $\bar{k}$ which satisfies $W^*[\theta^P(\bar{k}, \beta, t), \beta, t] = W^{**}[1, \beta, t; \bar{k}]$, and if $k < \bar{k}$ (resp. $k > \bar{k}$), then the welfare-maximizing labor standard are $\theta^{opt} = 1$ (resp. $\theta^{opt} = \theta^P$).*

---

[10]The proof is available upon request from the author.

[11]Here, we have suppressed the graphs on firms' profit change in θ not only to economize the use of figures but also because it shows similar shape with that in Fig. 25.3.

[12]When $\beta \in (1, 2)$, r_A^{**} in Fig. 25.4 might has maximum value at $\theta^{R**}(= \frac{2}{1+\beta})$ that lies between $\theta^P$and $\theta = 1$. However, this does not affect the effectiveness of Proposition 25.4.

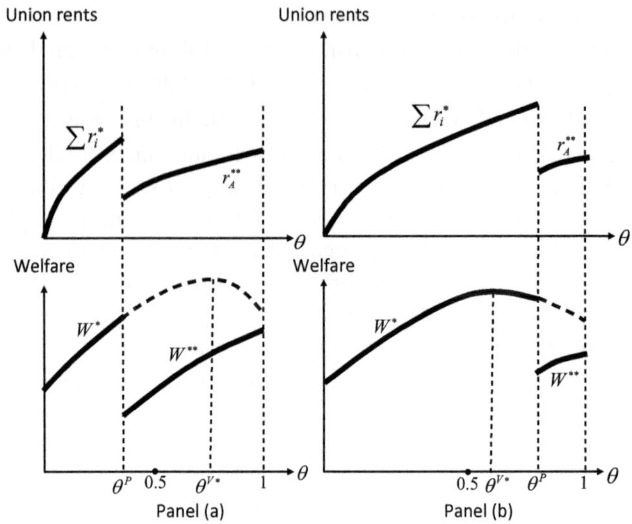

Fig. 25.4 The effects of entry mode shift: $\frac{2}{3} < \beta < 2$

(2) If $\theta^P > \theta^{V*}(=\frac{4}{2+3\beta})$, social welfare of home country is maximized at $\theta = \theta^{V*}$ as an interior solution, i.e., $\theta^{opt} = \theta^{V*}(=\frac{4}{2+3\beta} > \frac{1}{2})$. Union rents are maximized at $\theta = \theta^P$.

Proof Skipped due to the space limitation.[13]

Proposition 25.5 (2) implies that if union's preference for wage is intermediate level and if firm B undertakes FDI at a relatively high level of union bargaining power (i.e., $\theta^P > \theta^{V*}$) due to the high fixed costs to FDI, then government's optimal policy in terms of labor standard is obtained as interior solution at $\theta^{V*}(=\frac{4}{2+3\beta} > \frac{1}{2})$, which is less than θ^P. And it is noteworthy that the optimal level θ^{V*} is negatively related to β and independent of t.

Next, we examine the case where $\beta > 2$ (case III). In this case, the critical values $\theta^{V*}$and $\theta^{R*}$are less than unity, and hence both the social welfare and union rents show different shape over $\theta \in [0, 1]$ depending on the relative magnitude of θ^P. There are three possible subcases with respect to firm B's location shifting timing: Sub-case (a), $\theta^P < \theta^{V*}(=\frac{4}{2+3\beta} < \frac{1}{2})$; Sub-case (b), $\theta^{V*} < \theta^P < \theta^{R*}$; and Sub-case (c), $\theta^{V*} < \theta^{R*} < \theta^P < 1$. Figure 25.5 shows the change in union rents and social welfare in θ for each three possible cases when $\beta > 2$.

(i) Sub-case (a): $\theta^P < \theta^{V*}(=\frac{4}{2+3\beta} < \frac{1}{2})$ In this case, firm B undertakes FDI even at a low level of union bargaining strength, $\theta^P < \theta^{V*}(=\frac{4}{2+3\beta} < \frac{1}{2})$, due to the low fixed cost of FDI. Since both $W^*$and W^{**} are increasing in θ,

[13]The proof is available upon request from the author.

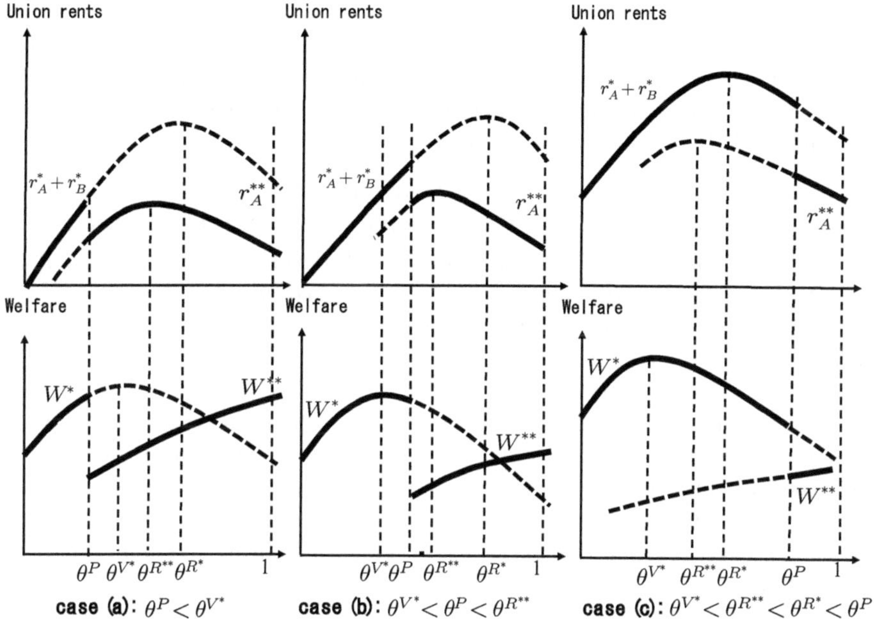

Fig. 25.5 The effects of entry mode shift:$\beta > 2$

Proposition 25.4 holds. That is, social welfare is maximized either at θ^P or unity. With respect to union rents, since $\sum r_i^*$ is increasing over $\theta \in [0, \theta^P]$ and r_A^{**} has its maximum at θ^{R**} as an interior solution, union rents have its maximum at either $\theta = \theta^P$ or $\theta = \theta^{R**}$.

(ii) Sub-case (b) : $\theta^{V*} < \theta^P < \theta^{R*}$[14] In Sub-case (b), W^* has maximum at $\theta^{V*}(= \frac{4}{2+3\beta})$as an interior solution, and $[W^*]_{\theta=\theta^{V*}} > [W^{**}]_{\theta=1}$. With respect to union rents, since $\sum r_i^*$ is increasing over $\theta \in [0, \theta^P]$, it has maximum value at θ^P, while r_A^{**} over $\theta \in (\theta^P, 1]$ is less than $[r_A^{**}]_{\theta=\theta^{R**}}$. However, since $[r_A^{**}]_{\theta=\theta^{R**}}<[\sum r_i^*]_{\theta=\theta^{V*}}$ holds,[15] Union rents has maximum value at maximum value at $\theta = \theta^P$ under export entry mode.

(iii) Sub-case (c): $\theta^{V*} < \theta^{R**} < \theta^{R*} < \theta^P < 1$ In this case, firm B undertakes FDI at a high level of union bargaining strength due to the high entry cost of FDI. As in Fig. 25.5, both W^* and $\sum r_i^*$ show inverted U-curve over $\theta \in [0, \theta^P]$, implying that W^* has maximum at $\theta^{V*}(< \theta^P)$ and $\sum r_i^*$ has at θ^{R*}. Over the range of $\theta \in [\theta^P, 1]$, since $W^{**}$is increasing in $\theta \in [\theta^P, 1]$, it has maximum

[14]Here, we represent only the case $\theta^{V*} < \theta^{R**} < \theta^P < \theta^{R*}$. However, the main results obtained in the above case are still effective even when we assume that $\theta^{V*} < \theta^P < \theta^{R**} < \theta^{R*}$.

[15]Since $\sum r_i^*$is increasing in θ, $[\sum r_i^*]_{\theta=\theta^{R**}}<[\sum r_i^*]_{\theta=\theta^P}$ holds. And we obtain from Table 25.1 that $[\sum r_i^*]_{\theta=\theta^{R**}} - [r_A^{**}]_{\theta=\theta^{R**}} = \frac{4}{27}(a-\bar{w}-t)^2 - \frac{1}{12}(a-\bar{w}-t)^2 > 0$. That is, $[r_A^{**}]_{\theta=\theta^{R**}} < [\sum r_i^*]_{\theta=\theta^{R**}}$. Therefore, we have $[r_A^{**}]_{\theta=\theta^{R**}} < [\sum r_i^*]_{\theta=\theta^P}$.

value at $\theta = 1$ while r_A^{**}, which is a decreasing function in the same range of θ, has maximum at$\theta = \theta^P$. However, since $[W^{**}]_{\theta=1} < [W^*]_{\theta=\theta^{V*}}$ and $[r_A^{**}]_{\theta=\theta^P} < [\sum r_i^*]_{\theta=\theta^P} < [\sum r_i^*]_{\theta=\theta^{R*}}$, domestic social welfare is maximized at $\theta = \theta^{V*}$ over the full domain of $\theta \in [0, 1]$ while union rents are maximized at $\theta = \theta^{R*}$ within the same domain.

Proposition 25.6 *Suppose that $\beta > 2$. Therefore, $\theta^{V*} < \theta^{R**} < \theta^{R*} < \theta^P < 1$ holds. (1) If $\theta^P < \theta^{V*}(= \frac{4}{2+3\beta})$, then Proposition 25.4 still holds. That is, $\theta^{opt} = \theta^P$ for $k > \bar{k}$ while $\theta^{opt} = 1$ for $k < \bar{k}$, where $\bar{k}$ satisfies $W^*[\theta^P(\bar{k}, \beta, t), \beta, t] = W^{**}[1, \beta, t; \bar{k}]$. In this case, union rents are maximized at either $\theta = \theta^P$ or $\theta = \theta^{R**}$. (2) If $\theta^{V*} < \theta^P < \theta^{R*}$, then $\theta^{opt} = \theta^{V*}$. However, union rents has maximum value at $\theta = \theta^P$ under export entry mode. (3) If $\theta^{R*} < \theta^P < 1$, then $\theta^{opt} = \theta^{V*}$. And union rents are maximized at $\theta = \theta^{R*}$.*

Next, we turn to the effects of trade liberalization (a reduction in t) on government policy toward labor standard. Considering that the sharp increase in the export-platform FDI in the 1990s is attributed to the rise in the regional trade bloc (ex. FTA) aiming at removing internal trade barriers among member countries, examining the effects of trade liberalization on the government labor policy in terms of labor standard is very meaningful. The following proposition is obtained.

Proposition 25.7 *Suppose that the government can affect the level of labor standard. If the government of FDI source country takes the exit-deterring strategy toward its MNF (i.e., $\theta^{opt} = \theta^P$), then trade liberalization reduces union bargaining power, that is, $\frac{\partial \theta^{opt}}{\partial(-t)} < 0$. However, if government policy on labor standard is determined at $\theta^{opt} = \theta^{V*}(= \frac{4}{2+3\beta})$ as an interior solution or at $\theta^{opt} = 1$ as a corner solution, then trade liberalization cannot affect union bargaining power.*

The above proposition is very straightforward. In Lemma 25.7, we have shown that as trade liberalization progresses, MNF (i.e., firm B) tends to undertake FDI at a lower level of union bargaining power, i.e., $\frac{\partial \theta^P}{\partial(-t)} < 0$. A decrease in t makes foreign country more attractive via the two channels: first, since it increases the negotiated wage in the home country, it expands the wage gap between home and foreign country, and second, if other things being equal, trade liberalization reduces firm's effective marginal costs and magnifies its export size, causing an increase in the profitability of FDI. As a result, if the government of FDI source country adopts exit-deterring strategy toward its MNFs (i.e., $\theta^{\text{opt}} = \theta^P$), then it tries to reduce the union bargaining power to deter firms from engaging in outward FDI when faced with trade liberalization. But if government policy on labor standard is determined at $\theta^{\text{opt}} = \theta^{V*}(= \frac{4}{2+3\beta})$ or at $\theta^{\text{opt}} = 1$, the trade liberalization cannot affect these levels because those are independent of transport costs (t).

25.5 Concluding Remarks

In this paper, using a theoretical framework of export-platform FDI, where two firms engage in Cournot competition in the world market, we investigated the government incentive to restrict union's bargaining power to maximize social welfare. We have shown that, in case of monopoly, government has an incentive to restrict union's bargaining power at the lowest level irrespective of whether the monopolist is a national firm (i.e., firm with no foreign operation) or multinational firm (MNF). But, it is different when it comes to oligopoly. In the oligopolistic competition market, there are two conflicting effects with regard to welfare effects of unions' bargaining power: the increase in the firms' profit due to the strategic interaction between firms, which are not derived in the monopoly model, and the decrease in the union rents by market competitiveness loss. And when the level of union bargaining power is sufficiently low, the former overweighs the latter, implying that an increase in the union bargaining power may increase social welfare. However, undertaking FDI results in the plunge in social welfare because firms do not take into account the negative impacts (i.e., decrease in the rival firm's profit and the extinction of labor union) overseas production has on social welfare. And the greater the fixed costs, the greater plunge in the social welfare.

The above argument implies that the firms in the oligopoly undertake overseas production at a critical level of union bargaining power even though domestic production is socially desirable from the viewpoint of home. And if fixed costs of FDI are large enough, "exit-deterring strategy" toward domestic firms might be optimal labor policy, that is, social welfare can be maximized by offering the union the strongest bargaining power providing that the firm remains within home country.

On the other hand, if labor union's preference for wage is relatively high and if the MNF undertakes FDI at a high level of union bargaining power due to great fixed costs incurred to FDI, then the government's optimal policy in terms of labor standard is obtained either at exit-deterring level or at the specific level, which is negatively related to union's wage preference and independent of transport costs, as interior solution. Furthermore, we have shown that trade liberalization affects government optimal policy in terms of labor standard to reduce union bargaining power only when it takes the exit-deterring strategy toward its MNF.

The above discussion provides rationales for government intervention in the labor standard setting. We have shown that in the monopoly model, since the government of FDI source country can raise its social welfare by reducing union bargaining power, the optimal labor standard policy toward the union is to take away the bargaining power from the union. However, in the oligopoly model, the government policy of labor standard is influenced by the fixed costs of FDI, the union's preference for wage, and the transport costs. The FDI source country, in the unionized oligopoly model, can obtain socially desirable equilibrium by adopting one of the following strategies: FDI-deterring strategy in terms of union bargaining power (i.e., offers the highest bargaining power to the union providing that the firms remain in the home country), offering the union the full bargaining power, and setting at a specific level which is endogenously determined by union's preference for wage.

This study has some limitations. We do not address the issue of reverse imports because the model rules out the FDI source country's domestic market. Empirical evidences suggest that firms in developed countries move their production facilities to developing countries to utilize the cheap labor and export the output produced there to their home countries as well as other developed countries. In addition, we do not consider the interdependence of labor standard policies between the FDI source and host countries. In this regard, further research should include these factors to provide better understanding of firms' locational decision behavior and its welfare effects of labor standard policy.

Acknowledgements This research was supported by the National Research Foundation of Korea Grant funded by the Korean government (NRF-2014S1A3A2044643).

References

Bughin, J., and S. Vannini. 1995. Strategic direct investment under unionized oligopoly. *International Journal of Industrial Organization* 13: 127–145.

Ekholm, K., R. Forslid, and J.R. Markusen. 2007. Export-platform foreign direct investment. *Journal of the European Economic Association* 5: 776–795.

Hanson, G.H., R.J. Mataloni, and M.J. Slaughter. 2001. Expansion strategies of U.S. multinational firms. In Susan M. Collins and D. Rodrick (eds), *Brookings Trade Forum 2001*, Washington, DC: Brookings Institution, pp. 245–282.

Horstmann, I.J., and J.R. Markusen. 1987. Strategic investments and the development of multinationals. *International Economic Review* 28: 109–121.

Hur, J., and L. Zhao. 2009. Labor standards, labor-management bargaining and international rivalry. *Journal of Economic Behavior & Organization* 71: 259–272.

Ishida, J., and N. Matsushima. 2009. Should civil servants be restricted in wage bargaining? A mixed-duopoly approach. *Journal of Public Economics* 93: 634–646.

Ito, T. 2013. Export platform foreign direct investment: Theory and evidence. *The World Economy* 36: 563–581.

Leahy, D., and C. Montagna. 2005. Union legislation and export platform FDI. *Journal of International Trade & Economic Development* 14: 437–452.

Lee, K.-D., and W. Lee. 2016. Export vs export-platform FDI with endogenous wage determination. *Economic Modelling* 54: 479–489.

Lommerud, K.E., F. Meland, and L. Sørgard. 2003. Unionized oligopoly, trade liberalization and location choice. *Economic Journal* 113: 782–800.

Mezzetti, C., and E. Dinopoulos. 1991. Domestic unionization and import competition. *Journal of International Economics* 31: 79–100.

Naylor, R., and M. Santoni. 2003. Foreign direct investment and wage bargaining. *Journal of International Trade and Economic Development* 12: 1–18.

Smith, A. 1987. Strategic investment, multinational corporations and trade policy. *European Economic Review* 31: 89–96.

Straume, O.R. 2002. Union collusion and intra-industry trade. *International Journal of Industrial Organization* 20: 631–652.

MIX
Papier aus verantwortungsvollen Quellen
Paper from responsible sources
FSC® C105338

If you have any concerns about our products,
you can contact us on
ProductSafety@springernature.com

In case Publisher is established outside the EU,
the EU authorized representative is:
Springer Nature Customer Service Center GmbH
Europaplatz 3, 69115 Heidelberg, Germany

Printed by Libri Plureos GmbH
in Hamburg, Germany